AutoCAD® 2008 For Dummies®

Cheat Sheet

AutoCAD Drawing Setup Roadmap

See Chapter 4 for details of each step.

Menu	Command	Description
Model space:		
1. File⇨New	NEW (Ctrl+N)	Specifies a template drawing (DWT file)
2. Format⇨Units	UNITS	Specifies linear and angular units
3. Format⇨Drawing Limits	LIMITS	Specifies working area
4. View⇨Zoom⇨All	ZOOM, All	Zooms to limits
5. Tools⇨Drafting Settings	DSETTINGS	Specifies snap and grid spacings
6. —	LTSCALE	Sets linetype scale
7. Format⇨Dimension Style	DIMSTYLE	Sets dimension scale (on the Fit tab)
8. File⇨Drawing Properties	DWGPROPS	Enters drawing informational properties
Paper space:		
9. Tools⇨Wizards⇨Create Layout	LAYOUTWIZARD	Creates a paper space layout
10. File⇨Save	QSAVE (Ctrl+S)	Saves the drawing

Ten Top AutoCAD Keyboard Shortcuts

Keyboard Shortcut	Command	Purpose
Ctrl+S	QSAVE	Saves the drawing
Ctrl+O	OPEN	Displays the Select File dialog box
Ctrl+P	PLOT	Displays the Plot dialog box
Ctrl+Tab	—	Switches to the next open drawing
Ctrl+PgUp/Ctrl+PgDn	—	Switches to the previous/next tab in the current drawing
F2	TEXTSCR	Toggles the AutoCAD Text Window on and off
F3	OSNAP	Toggles running object snap mode on and off
F8	ORTHO	Toggles ortho mode on and off
F9	SNAP	Toggles snap mode on and off
F10	POLAR	Toggles polar mode on and off

For Dummies: Bestselling Book Series for Beginners

AutoCAD® 2008 For Dummies®

Cheat Sheet

Drawing Scale and Limits Charts: Feet and Inches

Drawing Scale	8-1/2" x 11"	11" x 17"	24" x 36"	30" x 42"	36" x 48"
1/16" = 1'–0"	136' x 176'	176' x 272'	384' x 576'	480' x 672'	576' x 768'
1/8" = 1'–0"	68' x 88'	88' x 136'	192' x 288'	240' x 336'	288' x 384'
1/4" = 1'–0"	34' x 44'	44' x 68'	96' x 144'	120' x 168'	144' x 192'
1/2" = 1'–0"	17' x 22'	22' x 34'	48' x 72'	60' x 84'	72' x 96'
3/4" = 1'–0"	11'–4" x 14'–8"	14'–8" x 22'–8"	32' x 48'	40' x 56'	48' x 64'
1" = 1'–0"	8'–6" x 11'	11' x 17'	24' x 36'	30' x 42'	36' x 48'
1-1/2" = 1'–0"	5'–8" x 7'–4"	7'–4" x 11'–4"	16' x 24'	20' x 28'	24' x 32'
3" = 1'–0"	2'–10" x 3'–8"	3'–8" x 5'–8"	8' x 12'	10' x 14'	12' x 16'

Drawing Scale and Limits Charts: Millimeters

Drawing Scale	210 x 297 mm	297 x 420 mm	420 x 594 mm	594 x 841 mm	841x 1,189 mm
1:200	42,000 x 59,400 mm	59,400 x 84,000 mm	84,000 x 118,800 mm	118,800 x 168,200 mm	168,200 x 237,800 mm
1:100	21,000 x 29,700 mm	29,700 x 42,000 mm	42,000 x 59,400 mm	59,400 x 84,100 mm	84,100 x 118,900 mm
1:50	10,500 x 14,850 mm	14,850 x 21,000 mm	21,000 x 29,700 mm	29,700 x 42,050 mm	42,050 x 59,450 mm
1:20	4,200 x 5,940 mm	5,940 x 8,400 mm	8,400 x 11,880 mm	11,880 x 16,820 mm	16,820 x 23,780 mm
1:10	2,100 x 2,970 mm	2,970 x 4,200 mm	4,200 x 5,940 mm	5,940 x 8,410 mm	8,410 x 11,890 mm
1:5	1,050 x 1,485 mm	1,485 x 2,100 mm	2,100 x 2,970 mm	2,970 x 4,205 mm	4,205 x 5,945 mm

Drawing Scale and Text Height Chart: Feet and Inches

Drawing Scale	Drawing Scale Factor	1/8" Text Height	3/32" Text Height
1/16" = 1'–0"	192	24"	18"
1/8" = 1'–0"	96	12"	9"
1/4" = 1'–0"	48	6"	4-1/2"
1/2" = 1'–0"	24	3"	2-1/4"
3/4" = 1'–0"	16	2"	1-1/2"
1" = 1'–0"	12	1-1/2"	1-1/8"
1-1/2" = 1'–0"	8	1"	3/4"
3" = 1'–0"	4	1/2"	3/8"

Drawing Scale and Text Height Chart: Millimeters

Drawing Scale	Drawing Scale Factor	3 mm Text Height	2.5 mm Text Height
1:200	200	600 mm	500 mm
1:100	100	300 mm	250 mm
1:50	50	150 mm	125 mm
1:20	20	60 mm	50 mm
1:10	10	30 mm	25 mm
1:5	5	15 mm	12.5 mm

For Dummies: Bestselling Book Series for Beginners

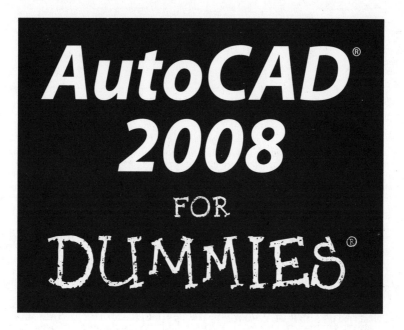

AutoCAD® 2008

FOR

DUMMIES®

by David Byrnes

Wiley Publishing, Inc.

AutoCAD® 2008 For Dummies®

Published by
Wiley Publishing, Inc.
111 River Street
Hoboken, NJ 07030-5774
www.wiley.com

WILEY

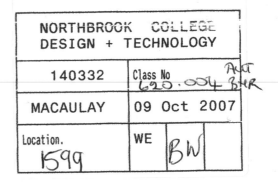

About the Author

David Byrnes is one of those grizzled old-timers you'll find mentioned every so often in *AutoCAD 2008 For Dummies*. He began his drafting career on the boards in 1979 and discovered computer-assisted doodling (you always wondered what CAD stood for, didn't you?) shortly thereafter. He first learned AutoCAD with version 1.4, around the time when personal computers switched from steam to diesel power. Dave is based in Vancouver, British Columbia, and has been an AutoCAD consultant and trainer for 15 years, in which time he has been a contributing author to ten books on AutoCAD. He teaches AutoCAD and other computer graphics applications at Emily Carr Institute of Art + Design and British Columbia Institute of Technology in Vancouver. Dave was the technical editor for four *AutoCAD For Dummies* and two *AutoCAD LT For Dummies* titles.

Dedication

To Annie and Delia, the two women in my life, who remind me there are other things besides keyboards and mice (and sometimes they have to try *really* hard).

Author's Acknowledgments

Thanks, first of all, to Mark Middlebrook for bringing me into the *AutoCAD For Dummies* world. Mark asked me to tech edit both *AutoCAD 2000 For Dummies* and *AutoCAD LT 2000 For Dummies* and their following four editions, then to join him as coauthor, and finally to take over the title altogether. I hope my torch bearing comes close to the high standards that Mark set, and I wish him well in his new career in the world of fine wine (what, *me* jealous?).

Thanks, too, to colleagues and friends at Autodesk: Shaan Hurley and Bud Schroeder, who never seem to mind being asked even the dumbest questions, and Denis Cadu and Jim Quanci, who always come through with software and technical support almost before I ask for it.

My thanks also to the good people at Wiley. Acquisitions Editor Kyle Looper was a consistently reliable source of calm but firm direction. It was a great pleasure to work with project editor Jean Rogers and copy editor Andy Hollandbeck. And by no means least (but someone has to bring up the rear), thanks to Lee Ambrosius for once again taking on the tech-editing job. Lee's expertise is well known and respected in the AutoCAD community, and I'm delighted to have him along as technical overseer.

Publisher's Acknowledgments

We're proud of this book; please send us your comments through our online registration form located at www.dummies.com/register/.

Some of the people who helped bring this book to market include the following:

Acquisitions, Editorial, and Media Development

Associate Project Editor: Jean Rogers

Acquisitions Editor: Kyle Looper

Copy Editor: Andy Hollandbeck

Technical Editor: Lee Ambrosius

Editorial Manager: Kevin Kirschner

Media Development and Quality Assurance: Angela Denny, Kate Jenkins, Steven Kudirka, Kit Malone

Media Development Coordinator: Jenny Swisher

Media Project Supervisor: Laura Moss-Hollister

Editorial Assistant: Amanda Foxworth

Sr. Editorial Assistant: Cherie Case

Cartoons: Rich Tennant (www.the5thwave.com)

Composition Services

Project Coordinator: Erin Smith

Layout and Graphics: Carl Byers, Denny Hager, Joyce Haughey, Stephanie D. Jumper, Barbara Moore

Proofreaders: ConText, John Greenough, Christy Pingleton

Indexer: Aptara

Anniversary Logo Design: Richard Pacifico

Publishing and Editorial for Technology Dummies

Richard Swadley, Vice President and Executive Group Publisher

Andy Cummings, Vice President and Publisher

Mary Bednarek, Executive Acquisitions Director

Mary C. Corder, Editorial Director

Publishing for Consumer Dummies

Diane Graves Steele, Vice President and Publisher

Joyce Pepple, Acquisitions Director

Composition Services

Gerry Fahey, Vice President of Production Services

Debbie Stailey, Director of Composition Services

Contents at a Glance

Table of Contents

Introduction

• •

*I*t's amazing to think that AutoCAD came into being a quarter of a *century* ago, at a time when most people thought that personal computers weren't capable of industrial-strength tasks like CAD. (The acronym stands for Computer-Aided Drafting, Computer-Aided Design, or both, depending on whom you talk to.) What's equally amazing to the grizzled old-timer writing these words is the fact that many of today's hotshot AutoCAD users weren't even born when the program first hit the street! It's almost as amazing that, 25 years after its birth, AutoCAD remains the king of the microcomputer CAD hill by a tall margin. It's conceivable that the long-term future of CAD may belong to special-purpose, 3D-based software such as the Autodesk Inventor and Revit programs, but for the present and the near future anyway, AutoCAD is where the CAD action is.

AutoCAD has grown more complex over the years, in part to keep up with the increasing complexity of the design and drafting processes that AutoCAD is intended to serve. It's not enough just to draw nice-looking lines anymore. If you want to play CAD with the big boys and girls, you need to appropriately organize the objects you draw, their properties, and the files in which they reside. You need to coordinate your CAD work with other people in your office who will be working on or making use of the same drawings. You need to be savvy about shipping drawings around via the Internet.

AutoCAD 2008 provides the tools for doing all these things, but it's not always easy to figure out which hammer to pick up or which nail to bang on first. With this book, you have an excellent chance of creating a presentable, usable, printable, and sharable drawing on your first or second try without putting a T square through your computer screen in frustration.

What's Not in This Book

Unlike many other *For Dummies* books, this one *does* sometimes tell you to consult the official software documentation — such as it is. AutoCAD is just too big and complicated for a single book to attempt to describe it completely.

AutoCAD is also too big and complicated for me to cover every feature. I don't address advanced topics like database connectivity, customization, 3D object creation, and programming in the interest of bringing you a book of a reasonable size — one that you'll read rather than stick on your shelf with those other thousand-page tomes!

Autodesk likes to keep its users (and us authors!) guessing about new features in future versions of the software. The surprises this time were pleasant, and it was fun revising this edition of the book. I didn't need to make any major structural changes like last time, when I replaced a chapter on sheet sets with one on navigating and viewing 3D models. Instead, I was able to spread AutoCAD 2008's best new feature — annotative objects — over several chapters, without cutting anything substantial.

This book focuses on AutoCAD 2008 and addresses its slightly less-capable but much lower-priced sibling, AutoCAD LT 2008. I do occasionally mention differences with previous versions, sometimes going back as far as the highly popular AutoCAD Release 14, so that everyone has some context, and upgraders can more readily understand the differences. I also mention the important differences between full AutoCAD and AutoCAD LT so that you'll know what you — or your LT-using colleagues — are missing. This book does *not* cover the discipline-specific features in AutoCAD-based products such as Autodesk AutoCAD Architecture 2008, except for some general discussion in Chapter 1, but most of the information in this book applies to the general-purpose AutoCAD features in the AutoCAD 2008–based versions of those programs as well.

Who Do I Think You Are?

AutoCAD has a large, loyal, dedicated group of long-time users. This book is not for the sort of people who have been using AutoCAD for a decade, who plan their vacation time around Autodesk University, or who consider 1,000-page-plus technical tomes about AutoCAD to be pleasure reading. This book *is* for people who want to get going quickly with AutoCAD, but who also know the importance of developing proper CAD techniques from the beginning.

However, you do need to have some idea of how to use your computer system before tackling AutoCAD — and this book. You need to have a computer system with AutoCAD or AutoCAD LT (preferably the 2008 version). A printer or plotter and a connection to the Internet will be big helps, too.

You also need to know how to use your version of Windows to copy and delete files, create a folder, and find a file. You need to know how to use a mouse to select (highlight) or to choose (activate) commands, how to close a window, and how to minimize and maximize windows. Make sure that you're familiar with the basics of your operating system before you start with AutoCAD.

How This Book Is Organized

Appearances can be deceptive. For example, had you wandered into my office and seen the apparently random piles of stuff that covered my desk while I was writing this book, you might wonder how I could possibly organize a sentence, let alone an entire book. But, given a suitable degree of concerted thought, I know *exactly* where to put my hands on that list of new dimension variables, my bag of ½" binder clips, or the rest of that bagel and cream cheese I started at coffee break.

I hope you'll find that the book also reflects some concerted thought about how to present AutoCAD in a way that's both easy-to-dip-into and smoothly-flowing-from-beginning-to-end.

The organization of this book into parts — collections of related chapters — is one of the most important, uh, *parts* of this book. You really can get to know AutoCAD one piece at a time, and each part represents a group of closely related topics. The order of parts also says something about priority; yes, you have my permission to ignore the stuff in later parts until you've mastered most of the stuff in the early ones. This kind of building-block approach can be especially valuable in a program as powerful as AutoCAD.

The following sections describe the parts that the book breaks down into.

Part 1: AutoCAD 101

Need to know your way around the AutoCAD screen? Why does AutoCAD even exist, anyway? What are all the different AutoCAD-based products that Autodesk sells, and should you be using one of them — for example, AutoCAD LT — instead of AutoCAD? Is everything so slooow because it's supposed to be slow, or do you have too wimpy a machine to use this wonder of modern-day computing? And why do you have to do this stuff in the first place?

Part I answers all these questions and more. This part also includes what may seem like a great deal of excruciating detail about setting up a new drawing in AutoCAD. But what's even more excruciating is doing your setup work incorrectly and then feeling as if AutoCAD is fighting you every step of the way. With a little drawing setup work done in advance, it won't.

Part II: Let There Be Lines

In this part, you discover some essential concepts, including object properties and CAD precision techniques. I know that you're raring to make some drawings, but if you don't get a handle on this stuff early on, you'll be terminally confused when you try to draw and edit objects. If you want to make drawings that look good, plot good, and *are* good, read this stuff!

After the concepts preamble, the bulk of this part covers the trio of activities that you'll probably spend most of your time in AutoCAD doing: drawing objects, editing them, and zooming and panning to see them better on the screen. These are the things that you do in order to create the *geometry* — that is, the CAD representations of the objects in the real world that you're designing. This part of the book ends by explaining how to navigate around in an AutoCAD 3D model and how to change its appearance on-screen. By the end of Part II, you should be pretty good at geometry, even if your ninth-grade math teacher told you otherwise.

Part III: If Drawings Could Talk

CAD drawings do not live on lines alone — most of them require quite a bit of text, dimensioning, and hatching in order to make the design intent clear to the poor chump who has to build your amazing creation. (Whoever said "a picture is worth a thousand words" must not have counted up the number of words on the average architectural drawing!) This part shows you how to add these essential features to your drawings.

After you've gussied up your drawing with text, dimensions, and hatching, you'll probably want to create a snapshot of it to show off to your client, contractor, or grandma. Normal people call this process *printing,* but CAD people call it *plotting.* Whatever you decide to call it, I show you how to do it.

Part IV: Share and Share Alike

A good CAD user, like a good kindergartner, plays well with others. AutoCAD encourages this behavior with a host of drawing- and data-sharing features. Blocks, external reference files, and raster images encourage reuse of parts of drawings, entire drawings, and bitmap image files. CAD standards serve as the table manners of the CAD production process — they define and regulate how people create drawings so that sharing can be more productive and predictable. AutoCAD's Internet features enable sharing of drawings well beyond your hard disk and local network.

The drawing- and data-sharing features in AutoCAD take you way beyond old-style, pencil-and-paper design and drafting. After you've discovered how to apply the techniques in this part, you'll be well on your way to full CAD nerd-hood (you may want to warn your family beforehand).

Part V: The Part of Tens

This part contains guidelines that minimize your chances of really messing up drawings (your own or others') and techniques for swapping drawings with other people and accessing them from other computer programs. There's a lot of meat packed into these two chapters — juicy tidbits from years of drafting, experimentation, and fist-shaking at things that don't work right — not to mention years of compulsive list-making. I hope that these lists help you get on the right track quickly and stay there.

Icons Used in This Book

Throughout this book, I point out certain morsels of particularly important or useful information by placing handy little icons in the margin. Naturally, different icons indicate different types of information:

This icon tells you that herein lies a pointed insight that can save you time and trouble as you use AutoCAD. In many cases, Tip paragraphs act as a funnel on AutoCAD's impressive but sometimes overwhelming flexibility: After telling you all the ways that you *can* do something, I tell you the way that you *should* do it in most cases.

The Technical Stuff icon points out places where I delve a little more deeply into AutoCAD's inner workings or point out something that most people don't need to know most of the time. These paragraphs definitely are not required reading the first time through, so if you come to one of them at a time when you've reached your techie detail threshold, feel free to skip over it.

This icon points out text that tells you how to stay out of trouble when living close to the edge. Failure to heed its message may have unpleasant consequences for you or your drawing — or both.

There's a lot to remember when you're using AutoCAD, so I've remembered to remind you not to forget about some of those things that you should remember. These paragraphs usually refer to a crucial point earlier in the chapter or in a previous chapter. So if you're reading sequentially, a Remember paragraph serves as a friendly reminder. If you're not reading sequentially, this kind of paragraph may help you realize that you need to review a central concept or technique before proceeding.

This icon points to new stuff in AutoCAD 2008 (and sometimes AutoCAD LT 2008). It's mostly designed for those of you who are somewhat familiar with a previous version of AutoCAD and want to be alerted to what's new in this version. New AutoCAD users starting out their CAD working lives with AutoCAD 2008 will find this stuff interesting, too — especially when they can show off their new book learnin' to the grizzled AutoCAD veterans in the office who don't yet know about all the cool, new features.

This icon highlights text that shows the differences between AutoCAD LT and AutoCAD. If you're using AutoCAD LT, you'll find out what you're missing compared to "full" AutoCAD. If your friend is using LT, you'll know where to look to find stuff in AutoCAD to brag about.

A Few Conventions — Just in Case

You can probably figure out for yourself all the information in this section, but here are the details just in case.

Text you type into the program at the command line, in a dialog box, in a text box, and so on appears in **boldface type**. Examples of AutoCAD prompts appear in a `special typeface`, as does any other text in the book that echoes a message, a word, or one or more lines of text that actually appear on-screen. Sequences of prompts that appear in the AutoCAD command line area have a shaded background, like so:

```
Specify lower left corner or [ON/OFF] <0.0000,0.0000>:
```

(Many of the figures — especially in Chapters 6 and 7 — also show AutoCAD command line sequences that demonstrate AutoCAD's prompts and example responses.)

Often in this book, you see phrases such as "choose File⇨Save As from the menu bar." The funny little arrow (⇨) separates the main menu name from the specific command on that menu. In this example, you open the File menu and choose the Save As command. If you know another way to start the same command (in this example, type **SAVEAS** and press Enter), you're welcome to do it that way instead.

Many AutoCAD commands have *aliases* — shortcut (fewer-letter) versions for the benefit of those who like to type commands at the AutoCAD command line. In this book, I show command names in uppercase letters. Chapters 6 and 7 include tables listing, respectively, the most commonly used drawing and editing commands, and in these tables I list both the full command name and its alias in parentheses; for example, LINE (L), ARRAY (AR), and so forth. If you're using the keyboard to enter commands, this means you can type either **LINE** or simply **L** and then press the Enter key to execute the command. You can view a list of all the command aliases by choosing Tools⇨ Customize⇨Edit Program Parameters in either AutoCAD or AutoCAD LT — *but just look, and be careful not to change anything!*

Where to Go from Here

If you read this Introduction, you're like me — you like to read. (The cut-to-the-chase people tend to flip to the index right away and look up what they need to know at that instant.) If you're a total AutoCAD newbie, you can read this book in order, from front to back; it follows a straightforward road through setting up your drawing environment, to outputting your masterworks to hard copy, to sharing your work with others. If you're an experienced user, you'll probably be one of those index flippers looking for the missing information you need to complete a specific task. You can probably find the index on your own, but I encourage you to browse through the book anyway, with highlighter or sticky notes in hand, so you can find those particularly important places when you need them again. If you're competent in most areas of AutoCAD and pretty familiar with the previous version, look for the New In 2008 icons in the margins to find out the latest features you never knew you couldn't live without. Whichever route you choose, I hope you enjoy your time with *AutoCAD 2008 For Dummies*. And . . . *you're off!*

Part I
AutoCAD 101

In this part . . .

AutoCAD 2008 is more than just another drawing program; it's a complete environment for drafting and design. So if you're new to AutoCAD, you need to know several things to get off to a good start — especially how to use the command line area and how to set up your drawing properly. These key techniques are described in this part of the book.

If you've used earlier versions of AutoCAD, you'll be most interested in the high points of the new release, including some newer interface components. The lowdown on what's new is here, too.

Chapter 1

Introducing AutoCAD
and AutoCAD LT

*M*aybe you're one of the few remaining holdouts who continue to practice the ancient art of manual drafting with pencil and vellum. Or maybe you're completely new to drafting and yearn for the wealth and fame (would I lead you on?) of the drafter's life. Maybe you're an engineer or architect who needs to catch up with the young CAD hotshots in your office. Or maybe you're a full-time drafter whose fingers haven't yet been pried away from your beloved drafting board. Maybe you tried to use AutoCAD a long time ago, but gave up in frustration or just got rusty. Or maybe you currently use an older version, such as AutoCAD 2004 or even (if you're into antiques) AutoCAD 2000.

Whatever your current situation or motivation, I hope that you enjoy the process of becoming proficient with AutoCAD. Drawing with AutoCAD is challenging at first, but it's a challenge worth meeting. CAD rewards those who think creatively about their work and look for ways to do it better. You can always find out more, discover a new trick, or improve the efficiency and quality of your drawing production.

AutoCAD first hit the bricks in the early 1980s, around the same time as the first IBM PCs. It was offered for a bewildering variety of operating systems, including CP/M (ask your granddad about that one!), various flavors of UNIX, and even Apple's Macintosh. By far, the most popular of those early versions was for MS-DOS (your dad can tell you about that one). Eventually, Autodesk settled on Microsoft Windows as the sole operating system for AutoCAD. AutoCAD 2008 works with Windows Vista, Windows XP — Professional, Home, and Tablet PC editions — and Windows 2000.

Because of AutoCAD's MS-DOS heritage and its emphasis on efficiency for production drafters, it's not the easiest program to master, but it has gotten easier and more consistent. AutoCAD is pretty well integrated into the Windows environment now, but you still bump into some vestiges of its MS-DOS legacy — especially the command line (that text area lurking at the bottom of the AutoCAD screen — see Chapter 2 for details). But even the command line — oops! command *window* — is kinder and gentler in AutoCAD 2008. This book guides you around the bumps and minimizes the bruises.

Why AutoCAD?

AutoCAD has been around a long time — since 1982. AutoCAD ushered in the transition from *really expensive* mainframe and minicomputer CAD systems costing tens of thousands of dollars to *merely expensive* microcomputer CAD programs costing a few thousand dollars.

AutoCAD is, first and foremost, a program for creating *technical drawings:* drawings in which measurements and precision are important because these kinds of drawings often get used to build something. The drawings you create with AutoCAD must adhere to standards established long ago for hand-drafted drawings. The up-front investment to use AutoCAD is certainly more expensive than the investment needed to use pencil and paper, and the learning curve is much steeper, too. Why bother? The key reasons for using AutoCAD rather than pencil and paper are

- **Precision:** Creating lines, circles, and other shapes of the exact dimensions is easier with AutoCAD than with pencils.

- **Modifiability:** Drawings are much easier to modify on the computer screen than on paper. CAD modifications are a lot cleaner, too.

- **Efficiency:** Creating many kinds of drawings is faster with a CAD program — especially drawings that involve repetition, such as floor plans in a multistory building. But that efficiency takes skill and practice. If you're an accomplished pencil-and-paper drafter, don't expect CAD to be faster at first!

Figure 1-1 shows several kinds of drawings in AutoCAD 2008.

Figure 1-1:
Cities, houses, little toy trains — what do you want to draw today?

Why choose AutoCAD? AutoCAD is just the starting point of a whole industry of software products designed to work with AutoCAD. Autodesk has helped this process along immensely by designing a series of programming interfaces to AutoCAD that other companies — and Autodesk itself — have used to extend the application. Some of the add-on products have become such winners that Autodesk acquired them and incorporated them into its own products. When you compare all the resources — including the add-ons, extensions, training courses, books, and so on — AutoCAD doesn't have much PC CAD competition.

The Importance of Being DWG

To take full advantage of AutoCAD in your work environment, you need to be aware of the DWG file format, the format in which AutoCAD saves drawings.

✔ In some cases, an older version of AutoCAD can't open a DWG file that's been saved by a newer version of AutoCAD.

✔ A newer version of AutoCAD can *always* open files saved by older versions.

✔ *Some* previous versions of AutoCAD can open files saved by the subsequent one or two versions. For example, AutoCAD 2007 can open DWG files saved by AutoCAD 2008. That's because Autodesk didn't change the DWG file format between the two versions. Similarly, the file format didn't change between AutoCAD 2004 and 2006, so the older program (AutoCAD 2004) can open drawings created in AutoCAD 2005 and AutoCAD 2006.

✔ If you're working in AutoCAD 2007 or AutoCAD 2008, you can use the Save As option to save the file to some older DWG formats. In fact, AutoCAD 2008 will save as far back as AutoCAD Release 14, which was released in 1997!

Table 1-1 shows which versions (described later in this chapter) use which DWG file formats.

Table 1-1	AutoCAD Versions and DWG File Formats		
AutoCAD Version	**AutoCAD LT Version**	**Release Year**	**DWG File Format**
AutoCAD 2008	AutoCAD LT 2008	2007	Acad 2007
AutoCAD 2007	AutoCAD LT 2007	2006	Acad 2007
AutoCAD 2006	AutoCAD LT 2006	2005	Acad 2004
AutoCAD 2005	AutoCAD LT 2005	2004	Acad 2004
AutoCAD 2004	AutoCAD LT 2004	2003	Acad 2004
AutoCAD 2002	AutoCAD LT 2002	2001	Acad 2000
AutoCAD 2000i	AutoCAD LT 2000i	2000	Acad 2000
AutoCAD 2000	AutoCAD LT 2000	1999	Acad 2000
AutoCAD Release 14	AutoCAD LT 98 & 97	1997	Acad R14
AutoCAD Release 13	AutoCAD LT 95	1994	Acad R13
AutoCAD Release 12	AutoCAD LT Release 2	1992	Acad R12

Working with AutoCAD is easier when your coworkers and colleagues in other companies all use the same version of AutoCAD and AutoCAD-related tools. That way, your DWG files, add-on tools, and even the details of your CAD knowledge can be mixed and matched among your workgroup and partners. In the real world, you may work with people, probably from other companies, who use AutoCAD versions as old as Release 14.

Many programs claim to be *DWG compatible* — that is, capable of converting data to and from AutoCAD's DWG format. But achieving this compatibility is a difficult thing to do well. Even a small error in file conversion can have results ranging in severity from annoying to appalling. If you exchange DWG files with people who use other CAD programs, be prepared to spend time finding and fixing translation problems.

Seeing the LT

AutoCAD LT is one of the best deals around, a shining example of the old 80/20 rule: roughly 80 percent of the capabilities of AutoCAD for roughly 20 percent of the money. (Actually, with recent price creep, it's now more like a 75/25 rule!) Like AutoCAD, AutoCAD LT runs on mainstream Windows computers and doesn't require any additional hardware devices. With AutoCAD LT, you can be a player in the world of AutoCAD, the world's leading CAD program, for a comparatively low starting cost.

AutoCAD LT is a very close cousin to AutoCAD. Autodesk creates AutoCAD LT by starting with the AutoCAD program, taking out a few features to justify charging a lower price, adding a couple of features to enhance ease of use versus full AutoCAD, and testing the result. As a result, AutoCAD LT looks and works much like AutoCAD. The opening screen and menus of the two programs are nearly identical. (LT is missing a few commands from the AutoCAD menus.)

In fact, the major difference between the programs has nothing to do with the programs themselves. The major difference is that AutoCAD LT lacks support for several customization and programming languages that are used to develop AutoCAD add-ons. So almost none of the add-on programs or utilities offered by Autodesk and others are available to LT users.

AutoCAD LT also has only limited 3D support. You can view and edit 3D objects in AutoCAD LT, so you can work with drawings created in AutoCAD that contain 3D objects. However, you cannot create true 3D objects in LT.

The lack of 3D object creation in LT is not as big a drawback for many users as you may think. Despite a lot of hype from the computer press and CAD vendors (including Autodesk), 3D CAD remains a relatively specialized activity. The majority of people use CAD programs to create 2D drawings.

Although you may hear claims that AutoCAD LT is easier to master and use than AutoCAD, the truth is that they're about equally difficult (or easy, depending on your NQ [nerd quotient]). The LT learning curve doesn't differ significantly from that of AutoCAD. AutoCAD was originally designed for maximum power and then modified somewhat to improve ease of use. AutoCAD LT shares this same heritage.

Fortunately, the minimal differences between LT and AutoCAD mean that after you have climbed that learning curve, you'll have the same great view. You'll have almost the full range of AutoCAD's 2D drafting tools, and you'll be able to exchange DWG files with AutoCAD users without data loss.

This book covers AutoCAD 2008, but almost all the information in it applies to AutoCAD LT 2008 as well. The icon that you see to the left of this paragraph highlights significant differences.

Step Up to the Plate with 2008

If you're upgrading from AutoCAD 2007 or another recent version and you work mostly or entirely in 2D, you're probably already current with system requirements. If you want to use AutoCAD's 3D features *productively,* however, it may be time for some new wheels, as I describe next.

You should know the following before you upgrade from any older AutoCAD release:

- ✔ **Wash those old Windows:** AutoCAD 2008 does *not* support older versions of Windows, such as Windows NT, 98, and Me. You must use Windows Vista (in any of its five flavors), Windows XP (Professional, Home, or Tablet PC), or Windows 2000, all patched with the latest service packs. AutoCAD 2008 also comes in 64-bit versions for users of 64-bit XP or Vista.

- ✔ **DWG file compatibility:** AutoCAD's DWG file format changed with AutoCAD 2007. Users of that version can open drawings created in AutoCAD 2008, but you have to use File⇨Save As to create DWG files for users of AutoCAD 2006 and earlier versions. You can save as far back as Release 14, and if you need to go even further back, you can save to the Release 12 DXF format — see Chapter 17 for instructions.

- ✔ **Application compatibility:** If you use third-party applications with a previous version of AutoCAD, they may not work with AutoCAD 2008. AutoCAD 2007 applications developed with the ARX (AutoCAD Runtime eXtension) will work, but earlier ARX applications will need to be recompiled. VBA (Visual Basic for Applications) applications may or may not work with AutoCAD 2008, but AutoLISP files should work without change.

  Many LSP (AutoLISP) programs written for the last several versions of AutoCAD work with AutoCAD 2008.

- ✔ **Computer system requirements:** For AutoCAD 2008, Autodesk recommends an 800 MHz Pentium III or better processor, at least 512MB of RAM, 1024 x 768 or higher display resolution with True Color graphics, 750MB of available hard disk space, an Internet connection, and Microsoft Internet Explorer 6.0 with Service Pack 1 or later.

✔ **Additional requirements for working in 3D:** AutoCAD recommends a 3 GHz or better processor, 2GB or more of RAM, a workstation-class, OpenGL-capable graphics card with at least 128MB of memory, and an additional 2GB of hard disk space beyond the 750MB required for installation.

I find even the recommended system requirements on the minimal side. For example, my desktop computer runs at a screen resolution of 1280 x 1024, and my notebook runs at 1600 x 1200. The figures in this book were shot at a resolution of 1024 x 768, and as you can see, things can get pretty crowded at that resolution. I also think 512MB of RAM is on the low side for productive work — get at least a gigabyte.

Although AutoCAD 2008 comes out a mere year after AutoCAD 2007, it sports some substantial and impressive new features. Last time around, in AutoCAD 2007, the focus was almost entirely on 3D modeling. AutoCAD 2008, however, is the drafter's release. There are some outstanding new features for drawing in 2D, one of which — annotative objects — is going to drastically reduce, if not eliminate, the need for most of those drawing scale factor calculations I describe in Chapter 4. Among the worthy new or improved features are

✔ **Annotative objects:** This is the biggie in AutoCAD 2008. A large part of drafting is annotating your drawings, and one of the more onerous tasks is figuring out your drawing's scale factor (as I demonstrate in Chapter 4) and then multiplying that value by things like text height and hatch scale. With annotative objects — which include text, dimensions, hatches, blocks, and the new multileaders (see below), you set the *paper size* (that is, the desired plotted size), and then assign one or more annotation scales. Then, when you change the annotation scale through a drop-down list on the status bar, all the annotative objects automatically update to the appropriate size. Chapter 10 introduces annotative objects. To my mind, this is not only the best new feature in AutoCAD 2008, it's the best new feature in AutoCAD for years.

✔ **2D Drafting & Annotation Workspace:** Workspaces have been part of AutoCAD and AutoCAD LT for several releases now, but the Dashboard (new in AutoCAD 2007, missing in AutoCAD LT 2007) made workspaces really noticeable. The 2D Drafting & Annotation workspace joins 3D Modeling (in the full version of AutoCAD) and AutoCAD Classic — the traditional, Dashboard-less environment — and includes a set of 2D control panels for drawing and editing objects, working with layers, adding text and dimensions, and so forth.

✔ **External references enhancements:** In AutoCAD 2008, you can attach MicroStation v8 DGN files as underlays to the current drawing through the External References palette, the same way you attach DWGs, image files, and DWF underlays. In addition, the new version introduces layer visibility control to DWF underlays. See Chapter 14 for the lowdown on external references.

No Express service?

If your menu bar doesn't include the Express menu (it's at the far right in Figure 1-1), you should consider installing the Express Tools from your AutoCAD CD (AutoCAD LT does not include or support the Express Tools).

When you first install AutoCAD 2008, you choose between a Typical and a Custom installation. If you choose Typical, the next screen asks if you want to install the Express Tools. If you choose a Custom installation, in the next screen, make sure to check the Express Tools item in the list of components. If you do not install the Express Tools during initial setup, you'll have to rerun AutoCAD 2008's installation routine. If you haven't installed AutoCAD yet, I strongly recommend that you choose the Typical installation option — or, at least, make sure the Express Tools box is checked during a Custom installation.

✔ **New dimension commands:** There are four brand-new commands, at least two of which will be of use to just about every drafter. With DIMSPACE, you select a bunch of existing angular or parallel linear dimensions and align them or set a uniform separation. The effect is similar to Baseline dimensions, but you have to set those up before the fact. DIMBREAK applies an opaque mask over dimension or extension lines or leaders that cross one another, making for much clearer dimensions. For more on those and the other new dimension commands, refer to Chapter 11.

✔ **Multileaders:** Multileaders (or multiple leaders) are a completely new annotation object that replaces the old-style leaders and the slightly less old quick leaders. AutoCAD 2008's multileaders are single objects, not separate objects as the older types. Multileaders are formatted according to multileader styles, and supporting commands let you add multiple leader lines to a single note or line up a group of leaders. And, like text and dimensions, multileaders can be annotative objects. Find out more about multileaders in Chapter 11.

✔ **But Wait — There's More:** AutoCAD 2008 has many more new 2D features than I can list here. Among the others are control of layer properties by layout viewports (Chapter 4), a SETBYLAYER command that lets you change explicitly set object properties to their ByLayer status (Chapter 5), column and paragraph controls in multiline text (Chapter 10), multiline block attributes and an inverted mode for clipping xrefs (Chapter 14), and a 64-bit version of AutoCAD 2008 (but not AutoCAD LT 2008) for XP and Vista 64-bit versions.

As I said before, AutoCAD 2008 is really the drafter's release. Some parts are more successful than others — for example, I think the Dashboard needs more work — but overall it's a must-have release. Especially if you skipped AutoCAD 2007 because you don't do 3D!

Chapter 2

Le Tour de AutoCAD 2008

*A*utoCAD 2008 is a full-fledged citizen of the Windows world, with toolbars, dialog boxes, right-click menus, a multiple-document interface, and all the other trappings of a real Windows program. And it's becoming more and more Windows-like with each release. One of the last weird but essential holdovers from the DOS days is the AutoCAD command line. The command line area is still there (and wouldn't you know it, officially it's now known as the command *window*), but in AutoCAD 2008, you'll be less reliant on this "look down here — now look up here" method of interacting with the program.

AutoCAD 2008, like the fanciest Detroit iron, bristles with heads-up display features. The *dynamic input system* puts much of the command line information right under your nose (or at least in your crosshairs). And recently entered data is just a right-click away.

Like the rest of the book, this chapter is written for someone who has used other Windows programs but has little or no experience with AutoCAD. If you *are* experienced with recent versions of AutoCAD, some of this chapter will be old hat for you. But don't stray too far — there are some subtle (and not so subtle) changes lurking under the familiar skin.

AutoCAD 2007, the previous release, focused on 3D modeling and visualization. You don't do any actual 3D modeling in this book, but in Chapter 9, I introduce you to AutoCAD's 3D viewing and navigation tools. AutoCAD 2008 focuses on new and enhanced 2D drafting tools, and luckily, *AutoCAD 2008 For Dummies* is mainly a 2D book. In this book, I focus on 2D drafting which, after all, is still what the great majority of AutoCAD users do with the software.

AutoCAD Does Windows

Like all good Windows programs, AutoCAD's latest version is designed to run in the latest version of Windows, and to prove it, all the figures in this chapter show AutoCAD 2008 running in Windows Vista. However, as I write this chapter, Vista has not been officially released, and there's only so much thin ice I'm willing to skate across — so the figures in all the other chapters are done in good old Windows XP.

Whether you're a total newcomer or an experienced user from a few versions back, finding your way around AutoCAD 2008 can be an odd experience. You recognize from other Windows applications much of the appearance and workings of the program, such as its toolbars and pull-down menus, which you use for entering commands or changing system settings. But other aspects of the program's appearance — and some of the ways in which you work with it — are quite different from other Windows programs. You can, in many cases, tell the program what to do in at least five ways — pick a toolbar button, pick from a pull-down menu, pick a tool button from a Dashboard panel, type at the keyboard, or pick from a right-click menu — none of which is necessarily the best method to use for every task.

Profiling your display

The illustrations and descriptions in this chapter and throughout the book show the *default* configuration of AutoCAD — that is, the way the screen looks if you use the standard version of AutoCAD 2008 (not a flavored version, such as AutoCAD Architecture 2008) and haven't changed the display settings. You can change the appearance of the screen with settings on the Display tab of the Options dialog box (choose Tools⇨Options⇨Display) and by dragging toolbars and other screen components.

The main change I've made for this book is to configure the drawing area background to be white instead of black because the figures show up better that way. You may want to set a white background on your own system or stay with the default black background — it's your choice, and there's no right or wrong. Some of AutoCAD's colors show up better on a white background, and some are better on a black one.

As with other Windows programs, the menus at the top of the AutoCAD screen enable you to access most of the program's functions and are the easiest-to-remember method of issuing commands. When you want to get real work done, you need to combine the pull-down menus with other methods — especially entering options at the keyboard or choosing them from the right-click menus. I show you how throughout this book.

And They're Off: AutoCAD's Opening Screen

The first time you start AutoCAD 2008, the program opens by default in a workspace named 2D Drafting & Annotation. After that, AutoCAD remembers which workspace you last used and opens in that one. There are three standard workspaces installed with AutoCAD 2008 (and two with AutoCAD LT):

- ✔ **AutoCAD Classic:** Opens a new drawing configured for a 2D drafting environment, with toolbars and tool palette arrangements similar to those in AutoCAD 2007 and earlier. In case you forget which program you're using, in AutoCAD LT this workspace is called *AutoCAD LT Classic.*

- ✔ **2D Drafting & Annotation:** Opens a new drawing configured for a 2D drafting environment, with toolbars and Dashboard panels optimized for technical drawing in two dimensions.

- ✔ **3D Modeling:** Opens a new drawing file configured for a 3D modeling environment, with navigation, visualization, and modeling tools suitable for working in 3D. Since AutoCAD LT doesn't do 3D, this workspace is not included in that version.

Both AutoCAD 2008 and AutoCAD LT 2008 display an Autodesk Impression toolbar in all workspaces. Autodesk Impression is not part of AutoCAD; it's a separate program in which you can dress up 2D drawings with presentation-style graphics. I won't be mentioning Autodesk Impression again and so I suggest you close the toolbar — but if you'd like more information, visit http://labs.autodesk.com.

A *workspace* is a collection of menus, palettes, toolbars, and Dashboard panels tailored for specific tasks, such as 3D modeling or 2D drafting. AutoCAD 2008 includes two task-specific workspaces for just those purposes, called *3D Modeling* and *2D Drafting & Annotation.* A third workspace, *AutoCAD Classic,* replicates the interface of earlier versions of AutoCAD, and you can easily create additional workspaces to suit your requirements. For more information, look up *workspace* in the online help system.

In this chapter (and for most of the book), I focus on 2D drafting rather than modeling — I discuss visualizing and navigating in 3D space in Chapter 9.

I stay primarily in the AutoCAD Classic workspace — I'm not convinced that the Dashboard panels and absent toolbars in the new 2D Drafting & Annotation workspace provide a very efficient work environment. Nevertheless, I do suggest you give it a try, and in the next chapter, I show you how to construct a simple architectural detail using the new workspace.

If you want to work with a file in the AutoCAD Classic interface, follow these steps:

1. **Choose Tools⇨Workspaces⇨AutoCAD Classic.**

   Assuming either the 3D Modeling workspace or the 2D Drafting & Annotation workspace is current, a bunch of toolbars and palettes open and close. You end up with the superfluous Autodesk Impressions toolbar floating in the graphics area and the Tool Palettes displayed on the right side of the screen. (Don't worry about what those are for right now — I get to them in later chapters.)

2. **Choose File⇨New to start a new file, or choose File⇨Open to open an existing 2D AutoCAD drawing file.**

   If you choose to start a new file, the Select Template dialog box opens.

3. **If you started a new file, choose acad.dwt if you want to work in imperial units, or choose acadiso.dwt if you want to work in metric units, and then click Open (in LT, the respective file names are acadlt.dwt and acadltiso.dwt).**

To switch to 3D modeling from the AutoCAD Classic environment, proceed as follows:

1. **Choose Tools⇨Workspaces⇨3D Modeling.**

   After more whizzing and whirring, AutoCAD closes Sheet Set Manager and opens the Modeling tab of the Tool Palettes and several 3D panels in the Dashboard (I discuss these features in Chapter 9).

2. **Choose File⇨New to start a new file, or choose File⇨Open to open an existing 3D AutoCAD model file.**

   If you choose to start a new file, the Select Template dialog box opens.

3. **If you started a new file, choose acad3d.dwt if you want to work in imperial units, or choose acadiso3d.dwt if you want to work in metric, and then click Open.**

LT doesn't have a 3D workspace or 3D templates, so choose 2D Drafting & Annotation (your only other workspace) and the available templates.

There's a quicker way of changing workspaces than going through the menus. In the Workspaces toolbar (by default, it's docked at the top of the screen, right below the menu bar), open the drop-down list and choose from the available workspaces. After still more whizzing and whirring, several toolbars close and the Dashboard opens.

If you want to start a new file, repeat Step 2 in the preceding list.

For the remainder of this chapter (and nearly all the rest of the book), I focus on 2D drafting, by far the easier way of getting your feet wet with AutoCAD. And I suggest you switch back to the AutoCAD Classic workspace — just choose Tools⇨Workspaces⇨AutoCAD Classic to get there.

After you switch to the AutoCAD Classic workspace, AutoCAD displays its old familiar 2D interface, as shown in Figure 2-1. You can close the Sheet Set Manager and Tool Palettes for now — I describe how to turn them back on and how to use them later in this chapter.

Title bar   Menu bar   Info center

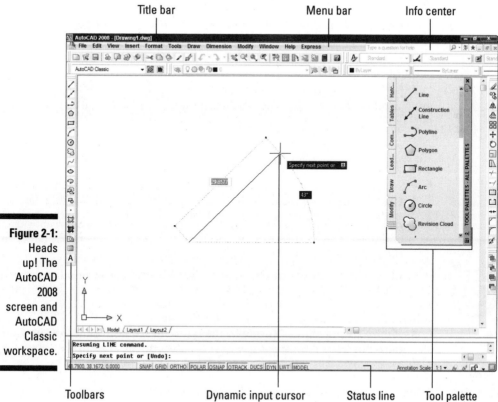

Figure 2-1:
Heads
up! The
AutoCAD
2008
screen and
AutoCAD
Classic
workspace.

Toolbars   Dynamic input cursor   Status line   Tool palette

If you have a previous version of AutoCAD on your computer, AutoCAD 2008 displays a Migrate Settings dialog box the first time you run the program. Unless you're a competent AutoCAD user who is reading this book to find out about the new features, I recommend that you click Cancel and start fresh. If you later decide you want to migrate your custom settings, you can do so by choosing Start⇨All Programs⇨Autodesk⇨AutoCAD 2008⇨Migrate Custom Settings⇨Migrate From a Previous Release and then choosing the installed version from which you want to migrate settings. Be warned, however, that doing so will overwrite any new customization you've added to AutoCAD 2008.

As I noted previously, migrating custom settings from a previous release will overwrite any new customization in AutoCAD 2008. But in this version, you can export your 2008 settings to an XML file, and then import them should you ever need to reinstall AutoCAD.

Those well-washed Windows

As shown in Figure 2-1, whether you're running in XP or Vista, much of the AutoCAD screen is standard Windows fare — title bars, a menu bar, toolbars, and a status bar.

A hierarchy of title bars

Like most Windows programs, AutoCAD has a *title bar* at the top of its program window that reminds you which program you're in (not that you'd ever mistake the AutoCAD window for, say, Microsoft Word!).

- ✔ At the right side of the title bar is the standard set of three Windows control buttons: Minimize, Maximize/Restore, and Close.

- ✔ Each drawing window within the AutoCAD program window has its own title bar. You use the control buttons on a drawing window's title bar to minimize, maximize/restore, or close that drawing instead of the entire AutoCAD program.

As in other Windows programs, if you maximize a drawing's window, it expands to fill the entire drawing area. (AutoCAD 2008 starts with the drawing maximized in this way.) As shown in Figure 2-1, the drawing's control buttons move onto the menu bar, below the control buttons for the AutoCAD program window; the drawing's name appears in the AutoCAD title bar. To unmaximize (restore) the drawing so that you can see any other drawings that you have open, click the lower Restore button. The result is as shown in Figure 2-2: a separate title bar for each drawing with the name and controls for that drawing.

Figure 2-2:
The
AutoCAD
screen with
the drawing
window
restored.

Making choices from the menu bar

The *menu bar* contains the names of all the primary menus in your version of AutoCAD. As with any program that's new to you, it's worth spending a few minutes perusing the menus in order to familiarize yourself with the commands and their arrangement. (If your menu bar doesn't include the Express menu — and note that AutoCAD LT does not include the Express menu — see the end of Chapter 1 for installation instructions.)

AutoCAD 2008 has a new way of asking for help. At the right end of the menu bar, between the last menu item and the control buttons, is AutoCAD 2008's InfoCenter, where you can ask for help by typing a question or use the Communication Center button to look for tips and program updates. The new menu bar InfoCenter replaces AutoCAD 2007's Info Palette.

Cruising the toolbars

As in other Windows programs, the toolbars in AutoCAD provide rapid access to the most commonly used AutoCAD commands. AutoCAD 2008 ships with toolbars in this default arrangement (as shown in Figure 2-3):

✓ **Standard toolbar:** Located just below the menu bar. You find file management and other common Windows functions here, plus some specialized AutoCAD stuff such as zooming and panning.

✔ **Styles toolbar:** To the right of the Standard toolbar. Used for selecting and formatting AutoCAD's text, dimension, and table styles. Chapters 10 and 11 cover these features.

✔ **Workspaces toolbar:** Below the Standard toolbar. Used to switch between or manage workspaces.

✔ **Layers toolbar:** To the right of the Workspaces toolbar. Includes commands and a drop-down list for manipulating *layers,* which are AutoCAD's fundamental tools for organizing and formatting objects. Chapter 5 contains the layer lowdown.

✔ **Properties toolbar:** To the right of the Layers toolbar. Used for formatting AutoCAD object properties, such as colors, linetypes, and lineweights. See Chapter 5 when you're ready to play with AutoCAD's object properties.

✔ **Draw toolbar:** Vertically down the left edge of the screen. Includes the most commonly used commands from the Draw menu. Chapter 6 covers most of the items on this toolbar.

✔ **Modify toolbar:** Vertically down the right edge of the screen. Includes the most commonly used commands from the Modify menu. Chapter 7 shows you how to use almost everything on this toolbar.

✔ **Draw Order toolbar:** Vertically below the Modify toolbar. Offers commands for controlling which objects appear on top of which other objects. If you need this kind of flexibility, look up "DRAWORDER command" in the AutoCAD online help system.

If you like toolbars, you won't like the new 2D Drafting & Annotation workspace. Switching to it closes five of the six toolbars in the AutoCAD Classic workspace. It also replaces the Standard toolbar with a truncated "Standard Annotation" version that's missing the Windows Clipboard and the Pan and Zoom tool buttons. Tool buttons for many — but not all — of these functions are found in the Dashboard.

You can rearrange, open, and close toolbars as in other Windows programs:

✔ To move a toolbar, point to its border (the double-line control handle at the leading edge of the toolbar is the easiest part to grab), click, and drag.

✔ To open or close toolbars, right-click any toolbar button and choose from the list of available toolbars, as shown in Figure 2-3.

The AutoCAD screen in Figure 2-3 shows the default toolbar arrangement, which works fine for most people. Feel free to close the Draw Order toolbar; you aren't likely to use its features frequently. You may want to turn on a couple of additional toolbars, such as Object Snap and Dimension, as you discover and make use of additional features. Throughout this book, I point out when a particular toolbar may be useful.

Standard toolbar

Workspaces toolbar   Layers toolbar   Styles toolbar   Properties toolbar   Modify toolbar

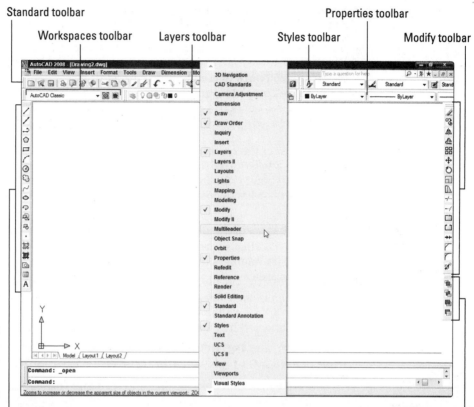

Figure 2-3:
A toolbar
tasting.

Draw toolbar   Draw Order toolbar

If you're not satisfied with just rearranging the stock AutoCAD toolbars, you can customize their contents or even create new ones. The procedures are beyond the scope of this book; they involve bouncing among the Interfaces, Commands, Toolbars, and Properties areas in the Customize User Interface dialog box in not entirely intuitive ways. Resist slicing and dicing the stock AutoCAD toolbars until you're at least somewhat familiar with them. If you want to get creative thereafter, check out *AutoCAD and AutoCAD LT All-In-One Desk Reference For Dummies,* by Lee Ambrosius and David Byrnes (Wiley). Although the *All-In-One* was produced using AutoCAD 2007, many of the techniques and tips you'll find there still apply to AutoCAD 2008.

AutoCAD tool buttons provide *tooltips,* those short descriptions that appear in little text boxes when you pause the crosshairs over a button. A longer description of the icon's function appears in the status bar at the bottom of the screen.

Looking for Mr. Status Bar

The *status bar* (see Figure 2-4) appears at the bottom of the AutoCAD screen. The status bar displays and allows you to change several important settings that affect how you draw and edit in the current drawing. Some of these settings won't make complete sense until you've used the AutoCAD commands that they influence, but here's a brief description, with pointers to detailed descriptions elsewhere in this book of how to use each setting:

✔ **Coordinates of the crosshairs:** The coordinates readout displays the current *X,Y,Z* location of the crosshairs in the drawing area, with respect to the origin point (whose coordinates are 0,0,0). Chapter 5 describes AutoCAD's coordinate conventions and how to use this area of the status bar.

   If the coordinates in the lower-left corner of the screen are grayed out, coordinate tracking is turned off. Click the coordinates so that they appear in dark numbers that change when you move the crosshairs in the drawing area.

   If dynamic input is enabled, the tooltip at the crosshairs also displays the current X,Y,Z location of the crosshairs. This constantly active display is not affected by changes to coordinate tracking in the status bar.

✔ **SNAP, GRID, and ORTHO mode buttons:** These three buttons control three of AutoCAD's tools for ensuring precision drawing and editing:

   • *SNAP* constrains the crosshairs to regularly spaced hot spots, enabling you to draw objects a fixed distance apart more easily.

   • *GRID* displays a series of regularly spaced dots, which serve as a distance reference.

   • *ORTHO* constrains the crosshairs to horizontal and vertical movement, which makes drawing orthogonal (straight horizontal and vertical) lines easy.

   See Chapter 4 for instructions on how to configure these modes and Chapter 5 for information about why, when, and how to use them in actual drawing operations.

✔ **POLAR tracking mode button:** Polar tracking causes the crosshairs to prefer certain angles when you draw and edit objects. By default, the preferred angles are multiples of 90 degrees, but you can specify other angle increments, such as 45 or 30 degrees. See Chapter 5 for instructions on specifying the polar tracking angles that you prefer. Clicking the POLAR button toggles polar tracking on and off. Ortho and polar tracking are mutually exclusive — turning on one mode disables the other.

Figure 2-4:
Status (bar)
check.

✔ **Object Snap (OSNAP) and Object Snap Tracking (OTRACK) buttons:**
Object snap is another AutoCAD tool for ensuring precision drawing and
editing. You use object snaps to grab points on existing objects — for
example, the endpoint of a line or the center of a circle.

- When you turn on *running object snap,* AutoCAD continues to hunt
  for object snap points. Chapter 5 contains detailed instructions on
  how to use this feature.

- When you turn on *object snap tracking,* AutoCAD hunts in a more
  sophisticated way for points that are derived from object snap
  points. Chapter 5 briefly describes this advanced feature.

✔ **Dynamic User Coordinate System (DUCS) button:** This one's for 3D
object creation (and so is not included in AutoCAD LT). I don't cover
3D modeling in this book. All you need know for now is that when it's
enabled, you can align your current construction plane with the face of
a 3D solid. (See — wouldn't you rather have waited 'til Chapter 9?)

✔ **Dynamic Input (DYN) button:** *Dynamic input* displays commands, options,
prompts, and user input in a tooltip adjacent to the crosshairs and
enables you to keep focused on what you're drawing. In addition, the
dynamic input tooltip displays what you type in response to prompts.

✔ **Lineweight (LWT) display mode button:** One of the properties that you
can assign to objects in AutoCAD is *lineweight* — the thickness that lines
appear when you plot the drawing. This button controls whether you
see the lineweights on the screen. (This button doesn't control whether
lineweights appear on plots; that's a separate setting in the Plot dialog
box.) Chapter 5 gives you the skinny (and the wide) on lineweights.

✔ **MODEL/PAPER space button:** As I describe in the section, "Down the
main stretch: The drawing area," later in this chapter, the drawing area
is composed of overlapping tabbed areas labeled Model, Layout1,

and Layout2 by default. The Model tab displays a part of the drawing called *model space,* where you create most of your drawing. Each of the remaining tabs displays a *paper space layout,* where you can compose a plottable view with a drawing title block. A completed layout will include one or more *viewports,* which reveal some or all the objects in model space at a particular scale.

The MODEL/PAPER status bar button (not to be confused with the Model *tab*) comes into play after you click one of the paper space layout tabs. The MODEL/PAPER button provides a means for moving the crosshairs between model and paper space while remaining in the particular layout.

- When the MODEL/PAPER button says *MODEL,* drawing and editing operations take place in model space, inside a viewport.

- When the button says *PAPER,* drawing and editing operations take place in paper space on the current layout.

Don't worry if you find model space and paper space a little disorienting at first. The paper space layout setup information in Chapter 4 and plotting instructions in Chapter 13 will help you get your bearings and navigate with confidence.

✔ **Maximize/Minimize Viewport button** (appears on paper space layouts only): When you're looking at one of the Layout tabs instead of the Model tab, the status bar displays an additional Maximize Viewport button. Click this button to expand the current paper space viewport so that it fills the entire drawing area. Click the button — now called Minimize Viewport — again to restore the viewport to its normal size. (Chapter 4 describes viewports.)

✔ **Annotation Scale controls:** These three buttons control the size and appearance of AutoCAD 2008's new annotative objects. Because "annotative objects" refers to text more than anything else, I explain this new feature in Chapter 10:

- The Annotation Scales drop-down list contains a list of preset annotation scales; changing a scale here causes all annotative objects to update to the new scale if the AUTOANNOUPDATE button is toggled on.

- The Annotation Visibility button toggles the visibility of annotative objects. When the light bulb is off (gray), only annotative objects of the current annotation scale are visible; when the light bulb is on (yellow), all annotative objects in the drawing, regardless of scale, are visible.

- The Automatically Add Scales button toggles the AUTOANNOUPDATE system variable, which controls automatic updating of annotative object scales when the scale is changed.

- ✔ **Lock/Unlock Toolbar Palette Positions:** "Now, where did I leave that Properties palette?" You'll never have to ask yourself again — AutoCAD 2008 lets you lock toolbars or palettes (which for some reason it's started calling *windows*) in position, so you'll always know where they are.

- ✔ **Trusted Autodesk DWG:** You see this button when AutoCAD opens a drawing that was created by AutoCAD or AutoCAD LT. In recent years, more and more programs have been able to save in DWG format, but in Autodesk's eyes, these files are not to be trusted.

- ✔ **Associated Standards File:** You see this button if you've enabled CAD standards checking and configured a drawing standards (DWS) file. Clicking this button displays the Check Standards dialog box. I don't cover standards checking in this book.

- ✔ **Manage Xrefs:** You won't see this combination button and notification symbol until you open a drawing that contains xrefs (external DWG files that are incorporated into the current drawing). Chapter 14 tells you how to use xrefs and what the Manage Xrefs button does.

- ✔ **Status Bar Menu:** When you click the easy-to-miss, downward-pointing arrow near the right end of the status bar, you open a menu with options for toggling off or on each status bar button. Now you can decorate your status bar to your taste.

- ✔ **Clean Screen:** No, it doesn't squeegee your monitor. Clicking this button frees up a bit more screen space by first maximizing the AutoCAD window and then turning off the title bar, toolbars and palettes, and the Windows task bar. Click the button again to restore those elements.

You can open dialog boxes for configuring many of the status bar button functions by right-clicking the status bar button and choosing Settings. Chapters 4 and 5 give you specific guidance about when and how to change these settings.

A button's appearance shows whether the setting is turned on or off. Depressed, or down, doesn't mean sad, it means on; raised, or up, means off. If you're unclear whether your buttons are depressed or not, click one; its mood . . . er, mode changes, and the new setting is reflected on the command line — <Osnap off>, for example. Click again to restore the previous setting.

The Dashboard: An instrument panel too far?

The *Dashboard* is a relatively new interface feature introduced in the full version of AutoCAD 2007 and in AutoCAD LT 2008. The Dashboard is intimately connected with workspaces, and each of the two task-specific workspaces in

AutoCAD 2008 (those being *3D Modeling* and *2D Drafting & Annotation*) has its own configuration of Dashboard elements, called *control panels.* The third workspace that's included in AutoCAD 2008 is called *AutoCAD Classic,* and it doesn't use the Dashboard at all. Instead, it displays a half-dozen toolbars docked at the top, left, and right sides of the almost full-screen drawing area, with one floating palette to the right of the drawing area itself.

My opinion — you wanted my opinion, didn't you? — is that the Dashboard is not quite ready for prime time. Apart from taking up a big whack of screen space, and having no easy way of accessing frequently used commands, a major shortcoming is the lack of a scrolling feature. Open many panels, and they simply disappear off the bottom of your screen; you'll have to close some open ones to see the rest. On the positive side, you can customize the Dashboard to make it behave more to your liking. For more information, check out Help⇨Customization Guide⇨Customize the User Interface⇨ Customize Dashboard Panels.

So I'm suggesting you stick with the AutoCAD Classic workspace while you're working in 2D. I do that for most of the book, although I do introduce you to the Dashboard in Chapter 3, where I show you how to draw a simple architec-tural detail.

A smoother ride: Dynamic input

One of the tasks faced by every AutoCAD instructor is the frequent need to badger students to "Watch the command line!" because the command line can be confusing for people who are new to CAD and computers. To anyone familiar with any other Windows graphic program, the command line is really tough to take — a throwback to an earlier time, when the knuckles of computer-aided drafters dragged on the ground. The challenge for experi-enced AutoCAD users now is going to be "Stop watching the command line!"

When dynamic input is enabled, the crosshairs take on some extra features:

✔ The coordinates of the current pointer location are always visible at the crosshairs.

✔ Typed commands appear in the tooltip adjacent to the crosshairs.

✔ When a command is started, you can display options by pressing the down-arrow key on the keyboard.

✔ Values that you type appear in the tooltip, and the dynamic input system displays dimensions when you're drawing things or moving them around. (Refer to Figure 2-1.)

Dynamic input is enabled by default, so it's going to be one of the first things you notice when you get behind the wheel.

If there's not enough room at the crosshairs to show all command options, the dynamic input tooltip shows a tiny down-arrow icon. Press the down-arrow key on your keyboard to see more options (see Figure 2-5).

Figure 2-5:
Dynamic
crosshairs
with all the
options.

The DYN status bar button controls AutoCAD 2008's dynamic input system. You can toggle off dynamic input by clicking this button, but I recommend you use it — you won't have to keep looking down at the command line nearly so often!

Let your fingers do the talking: The command window

If the title bars, menu bar, status bar, and dynamic input tooltips are the Windows equivalent of comfort food — familiar, nourishing, and unthreatening — then the command window, shown in Figure 2-6, must be the steak tartare or blood sausage of the AutoCAD screen feast. It looks weird, turns the stomachs of newcomers, and delights AutoCAD aficionados. Despite the promise of AutoCAD 2008's heads-up dynamic input, for now at least, the hard truth is that you have to come to like — or at least tolerate — the command line if you want to become at all comfortable using AutoCAD.

Figure 2-6:
Obey the
command
line.

```
Command: LINE
Specify first point:
Specify next point or [Undo]:
```

You should cotton on and cozy up to the command line because the command line is still AutoCAD's primary communications conduit with you. AutoCAD sometimes displays prompts, warnings, and error messages in the command window that dynamic input doesn't show — there simply isn't room in the dynamic input tooltip to show as much information as you get at the command line. True, when using dynamic input, you can press the down-arrow key to see more options. But then which is less efficient: moving your eyes down the screen to glance at the command line or taking your eyes right off the screen to find the down-arrow key on your keyboard?

The key (board) to AutoCAD success

Despite (or is it because of?) AutoCAD's long heritage as the most successful microcomputer CAD software, newcomers are still astonished at the amount of typing they have to do. Some more modern programs may have much less dependency on the keyboard than AutoCAD, but as you get used to it, you'll find that no other input method gives you as much flexibility as pounding the ivories . . . oops, wrong keyboard!

Typing at your *computer's* keyboard is an efficient way to run some commands and the *only* way to run a few others. Instead of clicking a toolbar button or a menu choice, you can start a command by typing its command name and then pressing Enter. Even better, for most common commands, you can type the keyboard shortcut for a command name and press Enter. Most of the keyboard shortcuts (called *aliases*) for command names are just one or two letters — for example, L for the LINE command and CP for the COPY command. Most people who discover how to use the shortcuts for the commands that they run most frequently find that their AutoCAD productivity improves noticeably. Even if you're not worried about increasing your productivity with this technique, there are some commands that aren't on the toolbars or pull-down menus. If you want to run those commands, you have to type them!

Not all command aliases are as obvious as L for LINE (for example, CP for COPY or — believe it or not — T for MTEXT). To see a complete list of command aliases, look in the AutoCAD (or the AutoCAD LT) Program Parameters (PGP) file by choosing Tools⇨Customize⇨Edit Program Parameters (acad.pgp) or (acadlt.pgp) and scroll about halfway down the file.

After you've started a command — whether from a toolbar, from a menu, or by typing — the dynamic input tooltip and the command line are where AutoCAD prompts you with options for that command. You activate one of these options by typing the uppercase letter(s) in the option and pressing Enter.

In many cases, you can activate a command's options by right-clicking in the drawing area and choosing the desired option from the menu that appears, instead of by typing the letter(s) for the option and pressing Enter.

I like dynamic input. Really, I do. But sometimes it fights with normal command input, and that can make things really confusing. In the following chapters I tell you when to be wary.

The following sequence demonstrates how you use the keyboard to run commands and view and select options. If you have dynamic input toggled on, your results are going to be different from what I say, so I suggest you click the DYN button to turn it off, temporarily at least. In the following steps, watch the command line, and pay attention to messages from AutoCAD:

1. **Type L and press Enter.**

   AutoCAD starts the LINE command and displays the following prompt in the command window:

   ```
   LINE Specify first point:
   ```

2. **Click a point anywhere in the drawing area.**

   The command line prompt changes to

   ```
   Specify next point or [Undo]:
   ```

3. **Click another point anywhere in the drawing area.**

   AutoCAD draws the first line segment.

4. **Click a third point anywhere in the drawing area.**

   AutoCAD draws the second line segment and prompts:

   ```
   Specify next point or [Close/Undo]:
   ```

   The command line now displays two options, Close and Undo, separated by a slash.

   In this case, the Close and Undo options appear in brackets. AutoCAD's command line always displays command options in square brackets. To activate an option, type the letter(s) shown in uppercase and press Enter. (You can type the option letter(s) in lowercase or uppercase.)

5. **Type U and press Enter.**

   AutoCAD undoes the second line segment.

6. **Type 3,2 (without any spaces) and press Enter.**

   AutoCAD draws a new line segment to the point whose X coordinate is 3 and Y coordinate is 2.

7. **Click several more points anywhere in the drawing area.**

   AutoCAD draws additional line segments.

8. Type X **and press Enter.**

X isn't a valid option of the LINE command, so AutoCAD displays an error message and prompts you again for another point:

```
Point or option keyword required.
Specify next point or [Close/Undo]:
```

Option keyword is programmer jargon for the letter(s) shown in upper-case that you type to activate a command option. This error message is AutoCAD's way of saying "I don't understand what you mean by typing **X**. Either specify a point or type a letter that I do understand."

9. Type C **and press Enter.**

AutoCAD draws a final line segment, which creates a closed figure and ends the LINE command. A blank command line returns, indicating that AutoCAD is ready for the next command:

```
Command:
```

10. Press the F2 key.

AutoCAD displays the AutoCAD Text Window, which is simply an enlarged, scrollable version of the command window, as shown in Figure 2-7.

The normal three-line command window usually shows you what you need to see, but occasionally you'll want to review a larger chunk of com-mand line history. ("What was AutoCAD trying to tell me a minute ago?!")

Figure 2-7:
My how
you've
grown: F2
expands the
command
line to a
command
text
window.

```
AutoCAD Text Window - Drawing2.dwg
Edit
Command: L
LINE Specify first point:
Specify next point or [Undo]:   <Ortho off>
Specify next point or [Undo]:
Specify next point or [Close/Undo]: U

Specify next point or [Undo]: 3,2

Specify next point or [Close/Undo]:
Specify next point or [Close/Undo]:
Specify next point or [Close/Undo]:
Specify next point or [Close/Undo]: X

Point or option keyword required.

Specify next point or [Close/Undo]: C

Command:
```

11. Press the F2 key again.

AutoCAD closes the AutoCAD Text Window.

Here are a few other tips and tricks for effective keyboarding:

✔ **Use the Esc key to bail out of the current operation.** There will be times when you get confused about what you're doing in AutoCAD and/or what you're seeing in the command window or the dynamic input tooltip. If you need to bail out of the current operation, just press the Esc key one or more times until you see a blank command line — Command: at the bottom of the command window, with nothing after it. As in most other Windows programs, Esc is the cancel key. Unlike many other Windows programs, AutoCAD keeps you well informed of whether an operation is in progress. The blank command line indicates that AutoCAD is resting, waiting for your next command.

✔ **Press Enter to accept the default action.** Some command prompts include a default action in angled brackets. For example, the first prompt of the POLYGON command is

```
Enter number of sides <4>:
```

The default here is four sides, and you can accept it simply by pressing Enter. (That is, you don't have to type **4** first.)

AutoCAD uses two kinds of brackets when it prompts.

• *Command options appear in regular square brackets:* [Close/Undo].

To activate a command option, type the letter(s) that appear in uppercase and then press Enter. The dynamic input tooltip does not display options in brackets; instead, you press the down-arrow key to display additional command options in rows next to the crosshairs (refer to Figure 2-5).

• *A default value or option appears in angled brackets:* <4>.

To choose the default value or option, simply press Enter. Default values in angled brackets appear in both the dynamic input tooltip and the command line prompts.

You don't always have to press the Enter key to forward your input to AutoCAD. Depending on what you're doing, you can often right-click and pick Enter from the top of the shortcut menu. And most efficient of all, even for the most inept typists, you can use the Spacebar as an Enter key — as long as you're not entering text.

✔ **Watch the command line.** You'll discover a lot about how to use the command line simply by watching it after each action that you take. When you click a toolbar button or menu choice, AutoCAD types the name of the command automatically and displays it in the dynamic input tooltip and at the command line. If you're watching the command line, you'll absorb the command names more or less naturally.

When AutoCAD types commands automatically in response to your tool-bar and menu clicks, it usually adds one or two extra characters to the front of the command name.

- AutoCAD usually puts an underscore in front of the command name (for example, _LINE instead of LINE). The underscore is an Autodesk programmers' trick that enables non-English versions of AutoCAD to understand the English command names that are embedded in the menus.

- AutoCAD sometimes puts an apostrophe in front of the command name and any underscore (for example, '_ZOOM instead of ZOOM). The apostrophe indicates a *transparent* command; you can run the command in the middle of another command without canceling the first command. For example, you can start the LINE command, run the ZOOM command transparently, and then pick up where you left off with the LINE command.

✔ **Leave the command line in the default configuration initially.** The command window, like most other parts of the AutoCAD screen, is resizable and movable. The default location (docked at the bottom of the AutoCAD screen) and size (three lines deep) work well for most people. Resist the temptation to mess with the command window's appearance — at least until you're comfortable with how to use the command line.

✔ **Right-click in the command window for options.** If you right-click in the command window, you'll see a menu with some useful choices, including Recent Commands — the last six commands that you ran.

✔ **Press the up- and down-arrow keys to cycle through the stack of commands that you've used recently.** This is another handy way to recall and rerun a command. Press the left- and right-arrow keys to edit the command line text that you've typed or recalled.

Down the main stretch: The drawing area

After all these warm-up laps, you're probably getting ready for the main event — the AutoCAD drawing area. This is where you do your drawing, of course. In the course of creating drawings, you click points to specify locations and distances, click objects to select them for editing, and zoom and pan to get a better view of what you're working on.

Most of this book shows you how to interact with the drawing area, but you should know a few things up front.

The Model and Layout tabs (Model and paper space)

One of the initially disorienting things about AutoCAD is that finished drawings can be composed of objects drawn in different *spaces,* which AutoCAD indicates with the tabs along the bottom of the drawing area (Model, Layout1, and Layout2 by default).

- *Model space* is where you create and modify the objects that represent things in the real world — walls, widgets, waterways, or whatever.

- *Paper space* is where you create particular views of these objects for plotting, usually with a title block around them. Paper space comprises one or more *layouts,* each of which can contain a different arrangement of model space views and different title block information.

You can gain a tiny bit more screen space by hiding the model space and layout tabs. Right-click one of the tabs and choose Hide Layout and Model Tabs. Icons for the model and layout tabs appear on the status bar, replacing the MODEL button. To restore the default configuration, right-click either of the status bar icons and choose Display Layout and Model Tabs.

When you click the Model tab in the drawing area, you see pure, unadulterated model space, as shown in Figure 2-8. When you click one of the paper space layout tabs (Layout1 or Layout2, unless someone has renamed or added to them), you see a paper space layout, as shown in Figure 2-9. A completed layout usually includes one or more *viewports,* which are windows that display all or part of model space at a particular scale. A layout also usually includes a title block or other objects that exist only in the layout and don't appear when you click the Model tab. (Think of the viewport as a window looking into model space and the title block as a frame around the window.) Thus, a layout displays model space and paper space objects together, and AutoCAD lets you draw and edit objects in either space. See Chapter 4 for information about creating paper space layouts and Chapter 13 for the lowdown on plotting them.

As I describe in the "Looking for Mr. Status Bar" section, earlier in this chapter, after you've clicked one of the layout tabs, the status bar's MODEL/PAPER button moves the crosshairs between model and paper space while remaining in the particular layout. (As shown in Figures 2-8 and 2-9, the orientation icon in the lower-left corner of the AutoCAD drawing area changes between an X-Y axis for model space and a drafting triangle for paper space as an additional reminder of which space the crosshairs currently reside in.) Chapter 4 describes the consequences of changing the MODEL/PAPER setting and advises you on how to use it.

This back-and-forth with the MODEL/PAPER button or by double-clicking is necessary only when you're drawing things while viewing one of the paper space layouts or adjusting the view of the drawing objects within the viewport. In practice, you probably won't draw very much using this method. Instead, you'll do most of your drawing on the Model tab and, after you've set up a paper space layout, click its layout tab only when you want to plot.

Drawing on the drawing area

Here are a few other things to know about the AutoCAD drawing area:

✔ Efficient, confident use of AutoCAD requires that you continually glance from the drawing area to the command window (to see those all-important prompts!) and then back up to the drawing area. This sequence is not a natural reflex for most people, and that's why the dynamic input tooltip at the crosshairs was introduced. But you still get information from the command line that you don't get anywhere else. Get in the habit of looking at the command line after each action that you take, whether picking something on a toolbar, on a menu, or in the drawing area.

✔ Clicking at random in the drawing area is not quite as harmless in AutoCAD as it is in many other Windows programs. When you click in the AutoCAD drawing area, you're almost always performing some action — usually specifying a point or selecting objects for editing. Feel free to experiment, but look at the command line after each click. If you get confused, press the Esc key a couple of times to clear the current operation and return to the naked command prompt.

✔ In most cases, you can right-click in the drawing area to display a menu with some options for the current situation.

Keeping Tabs on Palettes

Palettes, or *modeless dialog boxes* as the geekier types prefer to call them, made their debut in AutoCAD 2004 and were enhanced and expanded in AutoCAD 2006. (*Modeless* is just a fancy way of saying that these dialog boxes don't take over AutoCAD in the way that *modal* dialog boxes do. While a modal dialog box is open, you can't do anything else in AutoCAD. A modeless dialog box, on the other hand, can remain open while you execute other commands that have nothing to do with the dialog box. You return to the modeless dialog box when or if you need its features.)

AutoCAD 2008 contains more than a dozen palettes (more than a half-dozen in AutoCAD LT), plus one new *super-palette* called the Dashboard. I've already had my say about the Dashboard, but I do show you how to use it in the next chapter for 2D drafting and in Chapter 9 for 3D visualization. The more commonly used palettes are

- **Properties** and **DesignCenter:** Used to control object properties and named objects (layers, blocks, and so on), respectively. Chapter 5 shows you how.

- **Tool Palettes:** Unlike a splodgy painter's palette, each tool palette holds *content* (drawing symbols and hatch patterns) and/or *commands* (not regular AutoCAD commands — what would be the point? — but macros that make commands do specific things) instead of paints. Chapters 12 and 14 help you unlock your inner Tool Palette artistry.

- **Sheet Set Manager:** Provides tools for managing all of a project's drawings as a *sheet set.* Chapter 13 gives you some brief theory on why you might want to use sheet sets and how to do so. (AutoCAD LT does not support sheet sets.)

- **External References:** Used to attach external files to the current drawing; file types include raster images, Drawing Web Format (DWF) files, MicroStation DGN files, and other drawing files. I discuss attaching external reference files in Chapter 14.

AutoCAD 2008 adds support for MicroStation DGN files. The External References palette lets you attach DGN files as underlays in much the same way as you can underlay DWF files. You can also import DGN data directly by choosing File⇨Import.

- **Markup Set Manager:** Displays design and drafting review comments from users of Autodesk Design Review. For more information on markup sets, see the online help.

- **QuickCalc:** A handy pushbutton scientific calculator. You'll know if you need this.

There are several additional palettes whose functionality is beyond the scope of this book; the dbConnect palette lets you link drawings with external databases, and there are four rendering and visualization palettes. For more information on these tools, check the online help.

You toggle palettes on and off by clicking their respective buttons near the right end of the Standard toolbar. Alternatively, several palettes have Ctrl-key shortcuts. You can toggle these by pressing Ctrl+1 (Properties), Ctrl+2 (DesignCenter), Ctrl+3 (Tool Palettes), Ctrl+4 (Sheet Set Manager), Ctrl+7 (Markup Set Manager), or Ctrl+8 (QuickCalc). Figure 2-10 shows some of these palettes toggled on.

Properties palette   DesignCenter palette   Tool palettes   Sheet Set Manager

Figure 2-10:
A modeless
menagerie.
Now
where's that
drawing?

Driving Miss AutoCAD

Knowing how to read the command line, as described in the section, "Let
your fingers do the talking: The command window," earlier in this chapter, is
one of the secrets of becoming a competent AutoCAD user. In reading about
and using AutoCAD, you encounter two additional topics frequently: *system
variables,* which are AutoCAD's basic control levers, and *dialog boxes,* many
of which put a friendlier face on the system variables.

Under the hood: System variables

System variables are settings that AutoCAD checks before it decides how to
do something. If you set the system variable SAVETIME to 10, AutoCAD automatically saves your drawing file every ten minutes; if you set SAVETIME to
60, the time between automatic saves is one hour. Hundreds of system variables control AutoCAD's operations.

To change the value of a system variable, just type its name at the AutoCAD command prompt and press Enter. AutoCAD displays the current value of the system variable setting and prompts you for a new value. Press Enter alone to keep the existing setting, or type a value and press Enter to change the setting.

Being able to change system variables by typing their names is a boon to power users and occasionally a necessity for everybody else. The only problem is finding or remembering what the names are. In most cases, you'll be told what system variable name you need to type — by me in this book or by the local AutoCAD guru in your office.

To see a listing of all the system variables in AutoCAD and their current settings, use the following steps:

1. **Type** SETVAR **and press Enter.**

   AutoCAD prompts you to type the name of a system variable (if you want to view or change just one) or a question mark (if you want to see the names and current settings of more than one).

   ```
   Enter variable name or [?]
   ```

2. **Type ? (question mark) and press Enter.**

   AutoCAD asks which system variables to list:

   ```
   Enter variable(s) to list <*>:
   ```

3. **Press Enter to accept the default asterisk (which means "list all system variables").**

   AutoCAD opens a text window and displays the first group of system variables and their settings:

   ```
   3DCONVERSIONMODE    1
   3DDWFPREC           2
   3DSELECTIONMODE     1
   ACADLSPASDOC        0
   ACADPREFIX          "C:\Documents and..."  (read only)
   ACADVER             "17.1s (LMS Tech)"     (read only)
   ACISOUTVER          70
   AFLAGS              16
   ANGBASE             0.0000
   ANGDIR              0
   ANNOALLVISIBLE      0
   ANNOAUTOSCALE       -1
   ANNOTATIVEDWG       0
   APBOX               0
   APERTURE            10
   AREA                0.000                  (read only)
   Press ENTER to continue:
   ```

Not all versions of AutoCAD are going to list the identical system variables or corresponding values. For example, AutoCAD LT lacks several of the variables previously listed. Even in the full version of AutoCAD, you may see a different value for ACADVER if your copy of the program has had a service release applied.

4. Press Enter repeatedly to scroll through the entire list or press Esc to bail out.

AutoCAD returns to the command prompt:

```
Command:
```

If you want to find out more about what a particular system variable controls, see the System Variables section in the Command Reference in the AutoCAD online help.

The three kinds of system variables are

- **Those saved in the Windows Registry.** If you change this kind of system variable, it affects all drawings when you open them with AutoCAD on your system.

- **Those saved in the drawing.** If you change this kind, the change affects only the current drawing.

- **Those that aren't saved anywhere.** If you change this kind, the change lasts only for the current drawing session.

The System Variables section of the online Command Reference tells you which kind of system variable each one is.

Chrome and gloss: Dialog boxes

Fortunately, you don't usually have to remember the system variable names. AutoCAD exposes most of the system variable settings in dialog boxes so that you can change their values simply by clicking check boxes or typing values in edit boxes. This approach is a lot more user friendly than remembering an obscure name like *ACADLSPASDOC*.

For example, many of the settings on the tabs in the Options dialog box, shown in Figure 2-11, are in fact system variables. If you use the dialog box What's This? help (click the question mark in the Options dialog box's title bar and then click an option in the dialog box), the pop-up description not only describes the setting, but also tells which system variable it corresponds to.

Figure 2-11:
Options — a
handy way
to change
some
system
variable
settings.

Fun with F1

The AutoCAD 2008 Help menu, shown in Figure 2-12, offers a slew of online help options (easily accessed with the F1 key). I describe most of them here:

- ✔ **Help:** The main AutoCAD 2008 online help system, shown in Figure 2-13, uses the same help engine as the Microsoft Office programs, Internet Explorer, and other modern Windows applications. As with these other programs, AutoCAD's help is context-sensitive; for example, if you start the LINE command and just don't know what to do next, Help will . . . er, help. Click the Contents tab to browse through the various online reference manuals, click the Index tab to look up commands and concepts, and click the Search tab to look for specific words. In this book, I sometimes direct you to the AutoCAD online help system for information about advanced topics.

- ✔ **New Features Workshop:** This describes the new and enhanced features in AutoCAD 2008. It's especially useful for people who are upgrading from a previous AutoCAD version.

- ✔ **Additional Online Resources:** Most of the choices in the Online Resources submenu connect you to various parts of Autodesk's Web site. The most useful is Product Support. From the support Web page, you can search the Autodesk Knowledge Base, download software updates, and get help from Web- and newsgroup-based discussion groups.

Figure 2-12:
Lots of
AutoCAD
help.

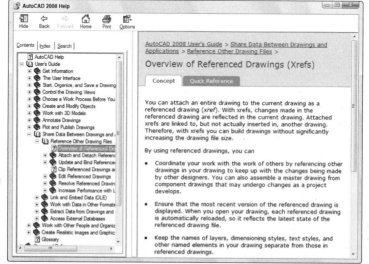

Figure 2-13:
Help is at
your F1
fingertip.

AutoCAD is one program with which you really need to take advantage of the online help resources. AutoCAD contains many commands, options, and quirks, and everyone from the greenest beginner to the most seasoned expert can find out something by using the AutoCAD online help. Take a moment to peruse the Contents tab of the main help system so that you know what's available. Throughout this book, I direct you to pages in the help system that I think are particularly useful, but don't be afraid to explore on your own when you get stuck or feel curious.

Chapter 3

A Lap around the CAD Track

In This Chapter

▶ Setting up a simple drawing

▶ Drawing some objects

▶ Zooming and panning in your drawing

▶ Editing some objects

▶ Plotting your drawing

*T*he previous two chapters introduce you to the AutoCAD world and the AutoCAD interface. Chapters 4 and 5 present the properties and techniques that underlie good drafting practice. By now, you're probably eager to start moving the crosshairs around and draw something! This chapter takes you on a gentle tour of the most common CAD drafting functions:

✔ **Setting up a new drawing**

✔ **Drawing some objects**

✔ **Editing those objects**

✔ **Zooming and panning so that you can view those objects better**

✔ **Plotting (printing) the drawing**

Most of the stuff in this chapter will be mysterious to you. Don't worry — I tell you where to look for more information on specific topics. In this chapter, you're simply taking AutoCAD out for a test drive to get a feel for what it can do. Go ahead and kick the tires — and don't worry about putting a dent in the fender!

In this chapter, you create a drawing of an architectural detail — a base plate and column, shown in Figure 3-1. Even if you don't work in architecture or building construction, this exercise gives you some simple shapes to work with and demonstrates commands you can use. And who knows — if the CAD thing doesn't work out, at the very least you'll know how to put your best footing forward.

The figures in this chapter show AutoCAD running in the 2D Drafting & Annotation workspace that's present in both the full version of AutoCAD and AutoCAD LT. In the remainder of the book, the figures show the AutoCAD Classic workspace and the more common toolbars (because that's still my preferred way of working in AutoCAD, and I'm the decider). In the exercise steps in this chapter, I point out several ways of executing commands, usually starting with the Dashboard controls, but also pointing out toolbar buttons in the AutoCAD Classic workspace and menu choices that are the same in both workspaces. I suggest that you try the different input methods described in this chapter. Then, as I explain in Chapter 2, you should feel free to choose whichever interface seems more useful to you.

Although the drafting example in this chapter is simple, the procedures that it demonstrates are real, honest-to-CADness, proper drafting practice. I emphasize from the beginning the importance of proper drawing setup, putting objects on appropriate layers, and drawing and editing with due concern for precision. Some of the steps in this chapter may seem a bit complicated at first, but they reflect the way that experienced AutoCAD users work. My goal is to help you develop good CAD habits and do things the right way from the very start.

Figure 3-1:
How base is
my plate.

The step-by-step procedures in this chapter, unlike those in most chapters of this book, form a sequence. You must do the steps in order. It's like learning to drive, except that here you're free to stop in the middle of the trip and take a break.

If you find that object selection or editing functions work differently from how I describe them in this chapter, you or someone else probably changed the configuration settings on the Option dialog box's Selection tab. Chapter 7 describes these settings and how to restore the AutoCAD defaults.

A Simple Setup

During the remainder of this chapter, I walk you through creating, editing, viewing, and plotting a new drawing — refer to Figure 3-1 if you want to get an idea of what the finished product looks like. You can do follow these steps using either imperial or metric units; I show metric values in brackets after the imperial ones, like this: Type **1.5 [38]** and press Enter.

As Chapter 2 advises, make sure that you pay attention to AutoCAD's feed-back. Glance at the messages AutoCAD sends after each step via the dynamic input tooltip, and especially the command window, so that you begin to get familiar with the names of commands and their options. (If you don't see any messages next to the crosshairs, click the DYN button on the status bar.)

In this first set of steps, you create a new drawing from a template, change some settings to establish a 1:10 (1 to 10) scale, and save the drawing. As I describe in Chapter 4, drawing setup is not a simple task in AutoCAD. Nonetheless, drawing setup is an important part of the job, and if you don't get in the habit of doing it right, you run into endless problems later on — especially when you try to plot. (See Chapter 13 for the lowdown on plotting your drawings.)

1. **Start AutoCAD by double-clicking its shortcut on the Windows desktop.**

   If you don't have an AutoCAD shortcut on your desktop, choose Start⇨ All Programs (Programs in Windows 2000)⇨Autodesk⇨AutoCAD 2008⇨ AutoCAD 2008 (the last two will be AutoCAD LT 2008, if that's your version).

   If your screen layout doesn't look like Figure 3-1, with the gray panel full of tool buttons at the right of the screen, choose Tools⇨Workspaces⇨ 2D Drafting & Annotation to reset the workspace.

2. **Choose File⇨New.**

Don't click the New button — use the menu. I explain why in Chapter 4, but just humor me for now. The Select Template dialog box appears with a list of drawing templates (DWT files), which you can use as the starting point for new drawings. Chapter 4 describes how to create and use drawing templates.

3. **Select the `acad.dwt` [`acadiso.dwt`] template, as shown in Figure 3-2, and click Open. (For AutoCAD LT, select `acadlt.dwt` [`acadltiso.dwt`].)**

   AutoCAD creates a new, blank drawing with the settings in `acad.dwt` or `acadiso.dwt`. `acad.dwt` is AutoCAD's default, plain-Jane drawing template for drawings in *imperial units* (that is, units expressed in inches and/ or feet). `acadiso.dwt` (`acadltiso.dwt` in AutoCAD LT) is the corresponding drawing template for drawings created in metric units. Chapter 4 contains additional information about these and other templates.

Figure 3-2: Starting a new drawing from a template.

4. **Click all status bar buttons except DYN and MODEL until they look like they're pressed out.**

   Some of these settings can make selecting points difficult. It's best to start with them all turned off, and then toggle them on and off as needed. I tell you which ones to use in the steps that follow. I start you off with Dynamic Input enabled, but you're going to turn it off before you actually draw anything.

If you accidentally did press MODEL, you find yourself in a paper space layout, and pressing the same button (now labeled PAPER) won't get you back to where you were. To return to full screen model space, click the Model *tab*, right above the command window.

5. Choose Format⇨Drawing Limits or type LIMITS **and press Enter.**

Drawing limits define your working area. AutoCAD prompts you to reset the Model space limits. For now, ignore the dynamic input tooltip next to the crosshairs and look at the command window. The command line reads:

```
Specify lower left corner or [ON/OFF] <0.0000,0.0000>:
```

6. Press Enter to keep 0,0 as the lower-left corner value.

AutoCAD prompts for the upper-right corner. The command line reads:

```
Specify upper right corner <12.0000,9.0000>
        [<420.0000,297.0000>]:
```

7. Type 100,75 [2750,1850] **(no spaces) and press Enter.**

AutoCAD echoes the values you enter at the command line.

100 x 75 corresponds to 10 inches by 7.5 inches (a little smaller than an 8.5-x-11-inch piece of paper turned on its long side) times a drawing scale factor of 10 (because you're eventually going to plot at 1:10 scale). For you metric types, 2750 x 1850 corresponds to 275 mm by 185mm (slightly smaller than an ISO A4 sheet turned lengthways) times a drawing scale factor of 10 (because you, too, are eventually going to plot at 1:10 scale). See Chapter 4 for more information about drawing scales.

8. Right-click the SNAP button on the AutoCAD status bar and choose Settings.

The Snap and Grid tab of the Drafting Settings dialog box appears, as shown in Figure 3-3. (In AutoCAD LT, the dialog box might look slightly different.)

Figure 3-3:
Snap and
Grid
settings.

9. **Change the values in the dialog box, as shown in Figure 3-3:**

   • *Snap On:* Checked

   • *Grid On:* Checked

   • *Snap X Spacing:* 0.5 [10]

   • *Snap Y Spacing:* 0.5 [10]

   Snap constrains your crosshairs to moving in an invisible grid of
   equally spaced points (0.5 [10] units apart in this case).

   When Equal X and Y Spacing is checked, changing the X spacing
   value causes the Y spacing to automatically update to the same
   number, thereby saving you typing.

   • *Grid X Spacing:* 5 [100]

   • *Grid Y Spacing:* 5 [100]

   Grid displays a visible grid of little dots on the screen (5 [100]
   units apart in this case), which you can use as reference points.
   The grid doesn't appear on printed drawings.

10. **Click OK.**

    You see some grid dots, 5 [100] units apart, in the drawing area. If you
    move your mouse around and watch the coordinate display area on the
    status bar, you notice that it moves in 0.5-unit [100-unit] increments.

11. **Choose View⇨Zoom⇨All.**

    AutoCAD zooms out so that the entire area defined by the limits — as
    indicated by the grid dots — is visible.

12. **Click the Save button on the Standard toolbar or press Ctrl+S.**

    Because you haven't saved the drawing yet, AutoCAD opens the Save
    Drawing As dialog box.

13. **Navigate to a suitable folder by choosing from the Save In drop-down
    list and/or double-clicking folders in the list of folders below it.**

    Remember where you save the file so you can go back to it later.

14. **Type a name in the File Name box and click Save.**

    For example, type **Detail** or **My Plate is Base**.

    Depending on your Windows Explorer settings, you may or may not see
    the .dwg extension in the File Name edit box. In any case, you don't
    need to type it. AutoCAD adds it for you.

    AutoCAD saves the new DWG file to the folder you specified.

Whew — that was more work than digging a post hole — and all just to set up
a simple drawing! Chapter 4 goes into more detail about drawing setup and
describes why all these gyrations are necessary.

Drawing a (Base) Plate

With a properly set up drawing, you're ready to draw some objects. In this example, you use the RECTANG command to draw a steel base plate and column, the CIRCLE command to draw an anchor bolt, and the POLYGON command to draw a hexagonal nut. (Both the RECTANG and POLYGON commands create *polylines* — objects that contain a series of straight-line segments and/or arc segments.)

AutoCAD, like most CAD programs, uses *layers* as an organizing principle for all the objects that you draw. Chapter 5 describes layers and other object properties in detail. In this example, you create separate layers for the base plate, column, anchor bolts, and nuts. This might seem like layer madness, but when you're doing complex drawings, you need to use a lot of layers just to keep things organized.

Rectangles on the right layers

The following steps demonstrate how to create and use layers, as well as how to draw rectangles. You also see how to apply fillets to objects and offset them. (Chapter 5 describes layers in detail, and Chapter 6 covers the RECTANG command. Chapter 7 explains the FILLET and OFFSET commands.) Start by creating a Column layer and a Plate layer and then drawing a column on the Column layer and drawing a square base plate on the Plate layer:

1. **Make sure that you complete the drawing setup in the previous section of this chapter and have the drawing open in AutoCAD.**

2. **In the top Dashboard panel, choose Layer Properties Manager.**

   In the AutoCAD Classic workspace, the Layer Properties Manager button is at the left end of the Layers toolbar. Or you can choose Format↬ Layers. The LAYER command starts, and AutoCAD displays the Layer Properties Manager dialog box.

3. **Click the New Layer button.**

   AutoCAD adds a new layer to the list and gives it the default name Layer1 (see Figure 3-4).

4. **Type a more suitable name for the layer on which you'll draw the column and press Enter.**

   For this example, type **Column**.

5. **Click the color swatch or name (white) in the Column layer row.**

   The Select Color dialog box appears (see Figure 3-5). If you're using AutoCAD LT, you only get the first tab labeled Index Color.

Figure 3-4:
Creating a
new layer.

Figure 3-5:
Blue is the
color —
select it
from the
standard
color tiles.

6. **Click color 5 (blue) in the single, separate row to the left of the ByLayer and ByBlock buttons and click OK.**

   The Select Color dialog box closes, and AutoCAD changes the color of the Column layer to blue.

7. **Repeat Steps 3 through 6 to create a new layer named Plate, and set its color to 4 (cyan).**

8. **With layer Plate still highlighted, click the Set Current button (the green check mark).**

   Plate becomes the current layer, and everything you draw is placed on that layer until you set a different layer current.

9. **Click OK to close the Layer Properties Manager dialog box.**

   The Layer drop-down list on the Dashboard or the Layers toolbar displays Plate as the current layer. Now you can draw a rectangular plate on the Plate layer.

10. **Click the Rectangle button on the second panel from the top of the Dashboard (2D Drafting & Annotation workspace) or the Draw toolbar (AutoCAD Classic workspace).**

    The RECTANG command starts, and AutoCAD prompts you to specify the first corner point. The command line shows:

    ```
    Specify first corner point or [Chamfer/Elevation/
            Fillet/Thickness/Width]:
    ```

11. **Click in the drawing area at the point 20,20 [500,500].**

    By watching the coordinate display on the dynamic input tooltip, you can see the coordinates of the current crosshairs location. Because snap is set to 0.5 [10] units, you can land right on the point 20,20 [500,500]. Picking the first corner in this location gives you enough room to work.

    AutoCAD prompts:

    ```
    Specify other corner point or [Area/Dimensions/
            Rotation]:
    ```

12. **Type @36,36 [@900,900] (without any spaces) and press Enter.**

    The @ sign indicates that you're using a *relative* coordinate — that is, 36 [900] units to the right and 36 [900] units above the point that you picked in the previous step. See Chapter 5 for more information about typing absolute and relative coordinates.

    Make sure that the DYN button is off for this step; Dynamic Input mode treats relative coordinate input in its own unique — and confusing — way.

    AutoCAD draws the 36 x 36 [900 x 900] rectangle, as shown in Figure 3-6. It's on the Plate layer and inherits that layer's cyan color.

    You draw the column next, but first you have to change layers.

13. **Click the Layer drop-down list on the Dashboard or the Layers toolbar to display the list of layers. Click Column to set it as the current layer.**

    Using the Layer drop-down list saves you having to open the dialog box, select the layer, click the Set Current button, and click OK. Becoming an AutoCAD master is *all* about efficiency!

14. **Press Enter to repeat the RECTANG command.**

    You can repeat the last command at any time by pressing Enter.

    In the next steps, you create a hollow steel column.

Figure 3-6:
Your (base)
plate is
empty.

15. **At the** `Specify first corner point` **prompt, type** 32,29 [800,725] **and press Enter.**

16. **At the** `Specify other corner point` **prompt, type** @12,18 [@300,450] **and press Enter.**

    A second rectangle is drawn in the middle of the base plate.

    Next, you round the corners of the column with the FILLET command and then use OFFSET to give it some thickness. But first, some interface tweaking.

    If your Dashboard looks like mine does in Figure 3-5, FILLET is going to be hiding in a flyout toolbar. You have two options. You can click the little black down-arrow (officially known as an overflow control — see Figure 3-6) at the right end of the second row of buttons, drag your mouse pointer down to the Fillet button, and then let go of the mouse button. Or, you can grab the edge of the Dashboard with your mouse pointer and drag it farther into the drawing area.

There's no denying that the Dashboard takes a whack of screen space compared with the AutoCAD Classic workspace and no Dashboard. You can get the best of both worlds by *anchoring* the Dashboard. An anchored Dashboard combines docking and auto-hiding. Click the Dock button at the top-left corner of the docked Dashboard (see Figure 3-6) to anchor it to the right side of the screen. When you move the mouse pointer over the title bar, the Dashboard expands to full width, and then rolls up again when you move back to the drawing.

Okay — back to drafting!

17. Click Fillet on the Dashboard (2D Drafting & Annotation) or the Modify toolbar (AutoCAD Classic).

The FILLET command starts, and AutoCAD prompts you to select the first object. Look at the command line to see the options for this command. Apply a 2-inch [50 mm] radius fillet to all four corners as follows.

18. Type R and press Enter to set a new fillet radius. Type 2 [50] and press Enter.

AutoCAD again prompts you to select the first object. You could pick each of the eight lines that need to be filleted, but because the column is a continuous polyline, a more efficient method, in this case, is to use the FILLET command's Polyline option to fillet all four corners in one fell swoop.

19. Type P to choose the Polyline option, and then press Enter.

AutoCAD prompts you to select a 2D polyline.

20. Select the rectangle you drew in Steps 14 to 16.

All four corners of the column are rounded with a 2-inch [50 mm] radius fillet.

Next, offset the polyline to create a ¾-inch [19 mm] thick steel column.

21. Click the Offset button on the Modify toolbar or the Dashboard.

22. At the `Specify offset distance` prompt, type .75 [19] and press Enter.

23. At the `Select object to offset` prompt, click the rounded rectangle. At the `Specify point on side to offset` prompt, click anywhere *inside* the rounded rectangle. Press Enter to complete the command.

AutoCAD offsets the selected object toward the inside of the rounded rectangle (see Figure 3-7).

24. Press Ctrl+S to save the drawing.

AutoCAD saves the drawing and renames the previously saved version *drawingname*.bak — for example, My Plate is Base.bak. .bak is AutoCAD's extension for a backup file; Chapter 16 describes BAK files and how to use them.

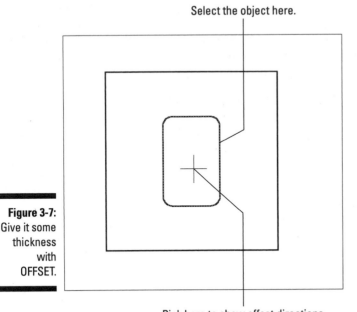

Select the object here.

Pick here to show offset directions.

Circling your plate

You can use the CIRCLE command to draw a 1½-inch diameter anchor bolt on an Anchor Bolts layer by following these steps:

1. **Repeat Steps 2 through 6 in the previous section to create a new layer for the anchor bolts. Give the layer the name Anchor Bolts, assign it the color 3 (green), and set it as the current layer.**

   The Layer drop-down list on the Layers toolbar and in the Dashboard displays Anchor Bolts as the current layer.

2. **Click the Circle button on the Dashboard or the Draw toolbar.**

   The CIRCLE command starts, and AutoCAD prompts you to specify the center point. The command line shows:

   ```
   Specify center point for circle or [3P/2P/Ttr (tan tan
   radius)]:
   ```

3. **Click in the drawing area at point 26,26 [650,650].**

   AutoCAD asks you to specify the size of the circle. The command line shows:

   ```
   Specify radius of circle or [Diameter]:
   ```

You decide that you want 1½-inch [38 mm] diameter anchor bolts. AutoCAD is asking for a radius. Although you probably can figure out the radius of a 1½-inch [38 mm] diameter circle, specify the Diameter option and let AutoCAD do the hard work.

4. Type D and press Enter to select the Diameter option.

AutoCAD prompts you at the command line:

```
Specify diameter of circle:
```

5. Type 1.5 [38] and press Enter.

AutoCAD draws the 1½-inch [38 mm] diameter circle. It's on the Anchor Bolts layer and inherits that layer's green color (see Figure 3-8).

6. Press Ctrl+S to save the drawing.

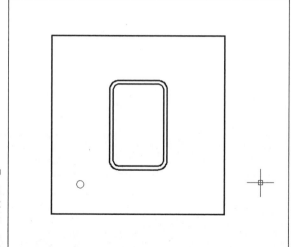

Figure 3-8:
Anchor it
with
CIRCLE.

Place your polygon

Every good bolt deserves a nut. Use the POLYGON command to draw a hexagonal shape on a Nuts layer (well, what else would you call it?). Besides showing you how to draw polygons, these steps introduce you to a couple of AutoCAD's more useful precision techniques: object snaps and ortho.

1. Repeat Steps 2 through 6 in the "Rectangles on the right layers" section to create a new layer for the nuts and set it as the current layer. Give the layer the name Nuts and assign it the color 1 (red).

The Layer drop-down list on the Layers toolbar displays Nuts as the current layer.

You don't have to create a separate layer for every type of object that you draw. For example, you can draw both the anchor bolts and nuts on a layer called Hardware. Layer names and usage depend on industry and office practices in addition to a certain amount of individual judgment. Having too many layers is better than having too few because lumping two or more layers together is much easier than dividing the objects on one layer into two or more layers.

2. **Click the Polygon button — the one that looks like a plan of the Pentagon — on the Dashboard or the Draw toolbar.**

   The POLYGON command starts, and AutoCAD prompts you to:

   ```
   Enter number of sides <4>:
   ```

   Peek ahead to Figure 3-9 in order to get an idea of how the nut will look after you draw it. Four-sided nuts can be a little difficult to adjust in the real world, so I stick with the conventional hexagonal sort.

3. **Type 6 and press Enter.**

   AutoCAD next prompts you for the center of the polygon:

   ```
   Specify center of polygon or [Edge]:
   ```

   As you move the crosshairs around near the anchor bolt, notice that AutoCAD tends to grab certain points briefly, especially on existing objects. This behavior is the result of running object snaps and tracking, which I discuss in Chapter 5. (If AutoCAD does not seem grabby, click the OSNAP button on the status bar until the command line shows <Osnap on>.)

4. **Move the crosshairs over the anchor bolt you just drew.**

   A tooltip should show Center and pull the crosshairs to the center of the anchor bolt circle. You may also see tracking vectors across the screen from this point — you can ignore those.

5. **Click when the tooltip reads Center — not Center-Intersection or something similar — just Center.**

   The POLYGON command draws regular closed polygons based on an imaginary circle; the center of this circle is the point you just picked.

   AutoCAD prompts:

   ```
   Enter an option [Inscribed in circle/Circumscribed
   about circle] <I>:
   ```

6. **Press Enter to accept the default Inscribed in Circle option.**

   The *Inscribed* option draws a polygon whose corners touch the circumference of the imaginary circle. The *Circumscribed* option draws a polygon whose sides are tangent to the circumference of the circle.

AutoCAD then asks you to:

```
Specify radius of circle:
```

7. **Turn on ortho mode by clicking the ORTHO button on the status bar until it looks popped in and you see <Ortho on> on the command line.**

8. **Click and drag the mouse to the right so the top and bottom sides of the polygon are horizontal,** *but don't click yet.*

9. **Type** 1.5 [38] **and press Enter.**

   AutoCAD draws the nut, as shown in Figure 3-9. It's on the Nuts layer and inherits that layer's red color.

   Occasionally, ortho and running object snaps interfere with drafting in AutoCAD. You can disable both features by clicking their status bar buttons.

Figure 3-9:
Bolts and
nuts . . .
ready to
anchor.

10. **Turn off ortho mode and running object snaps by clicking the ORTHO and OSNAP buttons on the status bar until they look popped out and you see <Ortho off> and <Osnap off> on the command line.**

11. **Press Ctrl+S to save the drawing.**

Not much of a base plate yet, is it? But don't worry — I cover creating more nuts and bolts with editing commands later in this chapter. If your brain is feeling full, now is a good time to take a break and go look out the window. If you exit AutoCAD, just restart the program and reopen your drawing when you're ready to continue.

Get a Closer Look with Zoom and Pan

The example drawing in this chapter is pretty uncluttered and small, but most real CAD drawings are neither of those. Technical drawings are usually jam-packed with lines, text, and dimensions. CAD drawings often get plotted on sheets of paper that measure two to three feet on a side — that's in the hundreds of millimeters, for you metric mavens. Anyone who owns a monitor that large probably can afford to hire a whole room of drafters and, therefore, isn't reading this book. The rest of us need to zoom and pan in our drawings — a lot. I cover zooming and panning in detail in Chapter 8. Quick definitions should suffice for now:

- ✔ **Zoom** means changing the magnification of the display. When you zoom in, you move closer to the drawing objects so you can see detail, and when you zoom out, you move farther away so you can see more of the drawing area.

- ✔ **Pan** means moving from one area to another without changing the magnification. If you've used the scroll bars in any application, you've panned the display.

Zooming and panning frequently lets you see the details better, draw more confidently (because you can see what you're doing), and edit more quickly (because object selection is easier when a zillion objects aren't on the screen).

Fortunately, zooming and panning in AutoCAD is as simple as it is necessary. The following steps describe how to use AutoCAD's Zoom and Pan Realtime feature, which is pretty easy to operate and provides a lot of flexibility. Chapter 8 covers additional zoom and pan options.

To zoom and pan in your drawing, follow these steps:

1. **Click the Zoom Realtime button (the one that looks like a magnifying glass with a plus/minus sign next to it).**

   Look on the Standard toolbar in the AutoCAD Classic workspace, or in the bottom row of buttons in the Dashboard if you're working in the 2D Drafting & Annotation workspace.

   The Realtime option of the ZOOM command starts. The crosshairs change to a magnifying glass, and AutoCAD prompts you at the command line:

   ```
   Press ESC or ENTER to exit, or right-click to display
   shortcut menu.
   ```

2. **Move the crosshairs near the middle of the screen, press and hold the left mouse button, and drag the crosshairs up and down until the plate almost fills the screen.**

   As you can see, dragging up increases the zoom magnification, and dragging down decreases it.

3. **Right-click in the drawing area to display the Zoom/Pan Realtime menu, shown in Figure 3-10, and choose Pan from the menu.**

Figure 3-10:
The Zoom/
Pan
Realtime
shortcut
menu.

The magnifying glass cursor changes to a hand.

4. **Click and drag to pan the drawing until the plate is more or less cen-tered in the drawing area.**

You can use the right-click menu to toggle back and forth between Zoom and Pan as many times as you like. If you get lost, choose Zoom Original or Zoom Extents to return to a recognizable view.

5. **Right-click in the drawing area and choose Exit from the Zoom/Pan Realtime menu.**

The hand cursor returns to the normal AutoCAD crosshairs.

Modify to Make It Merrier

When you have a better view of your base plate, you can edit the objects on it more easily. In the following sections, you use the ARRAY command to add more anchor bolts, the STRETCH command to change the shape of the plate, and the HATCH command to add crosshatching to the column.

Hooray for array

Using the ARRAY command is a great way to generate a bunch of new objects from existing objects at regular angles or spacings. The array pattern can be either rectangular (that is, columns and rows of objects) or polar (in a circle around a center point, like the spokes of a wheel around its hub). In this example, you use a rectangular array to create three additional anchor bolts:

1. **Click the Array button — the one with four squares — on the Modify toolbar or the second panel from the top of the Dashboard.**

The ARRAY command starts, and AutoCAD displays the Array dialog box.

2. **Select Rectangular Array.**

3. **Click the Select Objects button.**

   The standard AutoCAD object selection and editing sequence — start a command and then select objects — may seem backward to you until you get used to it. See Chapter 7 for more information.

   The Array dialog box temporarily disappears, and AutoCAD prompts you to select objects.

4. **Turn off Snap mode by clicking the SNAP button on the status bar until it looks popped out and you see <Snap off> on the command line.**

   Turning off Snap mode temporarily makes selecting objects easier.

5. **Click the anchor bolt and then click the nut.**

   If you encounter any problems while trying to select objects, press the Esc key a couple of times to cancel the command and then restart the ARRAY command. Chapter 7 describes AutoCAD object selection techniques.

   AutoCAD continues to prompt you at the command line:

   ```
   Select objects: 1 found, 2 total
   ```

6. **Press Enter to end object selection.**

   The Array dialog box reappears.

7. **Click inside the Rows text box and set the value to 2. Press Tab to move to the Columns Text box and set the value to 2.**

   The source object is included in AutoCAD arrays. The preview shows that you've set up a rectangular array of four evenly spaced objects (see Figure 3-11).

Figure 3-11:
The Array dialog box, ready to bolt your base plate.

8. **In the Row Offset text box, type** 24 [600]. **Click inside the Column Offset text box and type** 24 [600].

   ARRAY creates regularly spaced rows and columns. The Row Offset is the vertical distance separating the rows; Column Offset is the horizontal distance separating columns.

9. **Click the Preview button.**

   AutoCAD shows you what the array will look like if you accept the current settings and displays a small dialog box with Accept, Modify, and Cancel buttons.

10. **If anything looks wrong, click the Modify button, make changes, and preview again. When everything looks right, click the Accept button.**

    AutoCAD adds the additional objects to the drawing, as shown in Figure 3-12.

11. **Press Ctrl+S to save the drawing.**

Perfect! Except that nutbar engineer has decided the column needs to be 18 x 18 inches [450 x 450 mm] instead of 12 x 18 inches [300 x 450mm — unfortunately, there are just as many metric nutbars as imperial ones]. And that means the base plate is too small, and the anchor bolts are in the wrong place, too. If you were working on the drawing board, you'd be getting out an eraser and rubbing out all your efforts. AutoCAD to the rescue!

Figure 3-12:
Buttoned-down base plate.

Stretch out

The STRETCH command is powerful but a little complicated — it can stretch or move objects, depending on how you select them. The key to using Stretch is specifying a *crossing selection box* properly. (Chapter 7 gives you more details about crossing boxes and how to use them with the STRETCH command.)

Follow these steps to stretch the column and base plate:

 1. **Click the Stretch button — the one with the corner of the rectangle being stretched — on the Dashboard or the Modify toolbar.**

    If you're using the default Dashboard configuration, you have to do the click-and-drag thing with the little arrow at the right end of the second row of Modify tool buttons — that's the row with the pencil eraser at the left end.

    The STRETCH command starts, and AutoCAD prompts you to select objects. This is one of those times (and one of those commands) that really does require you to look at the command line:

    ```
    Select objects to stretch by crossing-window or
            crossing-polygon...
    Select objects:
    ```

 2. **Click a point above and to the right of the upper-right corner of the plate (Point 1 in Figure 3-13).**

 3. **Move the crosshairs to the left.**

    The pointer changes to a dashed rectangle enclosing a rectangular green area, which indicates that you're specifying a crossing box. AutoCAD prompts you at the command line:

    ```
    Select objects: Specify opposite corner:
    ```

 4. **Click a point below the plate, roughly under the center of the column (Point 2 in Figure 3-13).**

    The crossing box must cut through the plate and column in order for the STRETCH command to work (refer to Figure 3-13).

    AutoCAD prompts you at the command line:

    ```
    Select objects: Specify opposite corner: 7 found
    Select objects:
    ```

 5. **Press Enter to end object selection.**

    AutoCAD prompts you to specify the base point.

Point 1

Figure 3-13:
Specifying a
crossing
box for the
STRETCH
command.

Point 2

6. **Turn on Snap mode, ortho mode, and running object snap mode by clicking the SNAP, ORTHO, and OSNAP buttons on the status bar until they appear pushed in.**

7. **Click the lower-right corner of the plate.**

   This point serves as the base point for the stretch operation. Chapter 7 describes base points and displacements in greater detail.

   AutoCAD prompts you at the command line:

   ```
   Specify second point or <use first point as
   displacement>:
   ```

8. **Move the crosshairs to the right until the dynamic input tooltip shows a displacement of 6 [150] units to the right and then click in the drawing space (see Figure 3-14).**

   AutoCAD *stretches* the column and plate by the distance that you indicate and *moves* the anchor bolts that were completely inside the crossing window rectangle, as shown in Figure 3-14.

Figure 3-14:
Stretching
the base
plate.

If your first stretch didn't work right, click the Undo button on the Standard toolbar and try again. Stretch is an immensely useful command — one that makes you wonder how drafters used to do it all with erasers and pencils — but it does take some practice to get the hang of those crossing boxes.

9. **Press Ctrl+S to save the drawing.**

Cross your hatches

Your final editing task is to add some crosshatching to the space between the inside and outside edges of the column to indicate that the drawing shows a section of the column. To do so, follow these steps:

1. **Turn off Snap, Ortho, and running object snaps by clicking the SNAP, ORTHO, and OSNAP buttons on the status bar until they look popped out.**

2. **Repeat Steps 2 through 6 from the "Rectangles on the right layer" section to create a new layer named Hatch. Set its color to 2 (yellow) and make it the current layer.**

3. **Click the Hatch button — the one that shows a diagonal line pattern inside four lines — on the Dashboard or the Draw toolbar.**

   Once again, on the Dashboard you need to press the little down-arrow at the right end of the upper row of buttons in the second panel from the top and drag down to get to this tool.

   The Hatch and Gradient dialog box appears. (If you're using AutoCAD LT, you'll notice that the box is simply called Hatch.) For more information on this dialog box, and hatching in general, refer to Chapter 12.

4. **In the Hatch tab's Hatch and Pattern area, click the Pattern drop-down list and select ANSI31.**

   The ANSI31 pattern fills the selected area with an arrangement of parallel angled lines.

5. **On the right side of the dialog box, click Add: Pick Points.**

   The dialog box temporarily closes.

6. **At the `Pick internal point` prompt, pick a point between the inside and outside edges of the column. Zoom in if you need to get closer.**

   AutoCAD selects the two filleted polylines.

7. **Press Enter to end object selection.**

   The Hatch and Gradient dialog box reappears. To check if the hatch parameters are correct, click the Preview button. It looks like the hatch pattern is too fine.

8. **Press Esc to return to the Hatch and Gradient dialog box.**

9. **In the Scale box, set the value to 5 and click Preview again. If it looks okay, right-click to accept the hatch pattern.**

   Your finished column and base plate should look like Figure 3-15.

10. **Choose View⇨Zoom⇨All.**

    AutoCAD zooms out so that the entire area defined by the limits is visible.

11. **Press Ctrl+S to save the drawing.**

After some drawing and editing, you may wonder how you're supposed to know when to turn off or on the various status bar modes (Snap, Grid, Ortho, Osnap, and so on). You will start to get an instinctive sense of when each mode is useful and when it gets in the way. In subsequent chapters of this book, I give you some more specific guidelines.

Figure 3-15:
Your column
is hatched.

Follow the Plot

Looking at drawings on a computer screen and exchanging them with others
via e-mail or Web sites is all well and good. But sooner or later, someone —
maybe you! — will want to see a printed version. Printing drawings — or *plotting,* as CAD geeks like to call it — is much more complicated than printing
a word processing document or a spreadsheet. That's because you have to
worry about things such as drawing scale, lineweights, title blocks, and weird
paper sizes. I get into plotting in Chapter 13, but here's an abbreviated procedure that helps you generate a recognizable printed drawing.

The following steps show you how to plot the model space portion of the
drawing. As Chapter 4 describes, AutoCAD includes a sophisticated feature
called *paper space layouts* for creating arrangements of your drawing that you
plot. These arrangements usually include a title block. Because I promised
you a gentle tour of AutoCAD drafting functions, I left the paper space layout
and title block issues for the next chapter. When you're ready for the whole
plotting enchilada, turn to Chapter 4 for information about how to set up
paper space layouts and Chapter 13 for full plotting instructions.

Follow these steps to plot a drawing:

1. **Click the Plot button on the Standard Annotation toolbar (2D Drafting & Annotation) or the Standard toolbar (AutoCAD Classic).**

   AutoCAD opens the Plot dialog box.

2. **Click the More Options button (in the bottom-right corner of the dialog box, next to the Help button).**

   The Plot dialog box reveals additional settings, as shown in Figure 3-16.

Figure 3-16: The Plot dialog box with the More Options area visible.

3. **In the Printer/Plotter area, select a printer from the Name list.**

4. **In the Paper Size area, select a paper size that's loaded in your printer or plotter.**

   Anything Letter size (8½ x 11 inches) [A4 (210 x 297 mm)] or larger works for this example.

5. **In the Plot Area, choose Limits.**

   This is the entire drawing area, which you specified when you set up the drawing earlier in this chapter.

6. **In the Plot Offset area, select the Center the Plot option.**

   Alternatively, you can specify offsets of 0 or other amounts in order to position the plot at a specific location on the paper.

7. **In the Plot Scale area, deselect the Fit to Paper check box and choose 1:10 from the Scale drop-down list.**

   1:10 is the scale used to set up the drawing (in the earlier section, "A Simple Setup"). No prizes for guessing the metric equivalent of 1:10!

8. **In the Plot Style Table area, click the Name drop-down list and choose `monochrome.ctb`.**

   The `monochrome.ctb` plot style table ensures that all your lines appear solid black, rather than as weird shades of gray. See Chapter 13 for information about plot style tables and monochrome and color plotting.

9. **Click Yes when a question dialog box appears, asking Assign This Plotstyle Table to All Layouts?**

   You can leave the remaining settings at their default values (refer to Figure 3-16).

   Some printers let you print closer to the edges of the sheet than others. To find out the actual printable area of your own printer, move the mouse pointer to the postage stamp–sized partial preview in the middle of the Plot dialog box and pause. A tooltip appears, listing the Paper Size and Printable Area for the printer and paper size that you selected.

   AutoCAD 2008's annotative scaling feature adds a new wrinkle to plotting. Annotative scaling controls the printed size of text, dimensions, hatching, and other types of annotation object at plot time — as long as the drawing's annotation scale matches the plot scale. I explain annotative objects in Chapters 10, 11, 12, and 14.

10. **Click the Preview button.**

    If the plot scale you entered in the Plot dialog box is out of sync with the drawing's annotation scale, a Plot Scale Confirm dialog box appears, advising you that the annotation scale is not equal to the plot scale. This drawing doesn't contain any text or dimensions, and I didn't bother making the hatch annotative, so it's fine to click OK and continue with the plot.

    The Plot dialog box disappears temporarily, and AutoCAD shows how the plot will look on paper. In addition, AutoCAD prompts you on the status bar:

    ```
    Press pick button and drag vertically to zoom, ESC or
    ENTER to exit, or right-click to display shortcut
    menu.
    ```

11. **Right-click in the preview area and choose Exit.**

12. **If the preview doesn't look right, adjust the settings in the Plot dialog box and look at the preview again until it looks right.**

13. **Click OK.**

    The Plot Scale Confirm dialog box pops up again. You may be tempted to click Don't Show Me This Again, but I recommend against that until you've gained a little familiarity with annotative objects, starting with Chapter 10.

    The Plot dialog box closes. AutoCAD generates the plot and sends it to the printer. After generating the plot, AutoCAD displays a Plot and Publish Job Complete balloon notification from the right end of the status bar. (A Click to View Plot and Publish Details link displays more information about the plot job.)

14. **Click the X (close) button in the Plot and Publish Job Complete balloon notification.**

    The balloon notification disappears.

    If you're not happy with the lineweights of the lines on your plot at this point, fear not. You can use the lineweights feature (Chapter 5) or plot styles (Chapter 13) to control plotted lineweights.

15. **Press Ctrl+S to save the drawing.**

    When you change the plot settings, AutoCAD saves them with the tab of the drawing that you plotted (the Model tab or one of the paper space layout tabs). Save the drawing after you plot if you want the modified plot settings to become the default plot settings the next time you open the drawing.

Congratulations! You successfully executed your first plot in AutoCAD. Chapter 13 tells you more — much more — about AutoCAD's highly flexible but occasionally perplexing plotting system.

Chapter 4

Setup for Success

● ●

In This Chapter

▶ Developing a setup strategy

▶ Starting a new drawing

▶ Setting up model space

▶ Setting up paper space layouts

▶ Creating and using drawing templates

● ●

*S*urprisingly, drawing setup is one of the trickier aspects of using AutoCAD. It's an easy thing to do incompletely or incorrectly, and AutoCAD 2008 doesn't provide a dialog box or other simple, all-in-one-fell-swoop tool to help you do all of it right. And yet, drawing setup is a crucial thing to get right. Setup steps that you omit or don't do right will come back to bite you — or at least gnaw on your leg — later.

Sloppy setup really becomes apparent when you try to plot (print) your drawing. Things that seemed more or less okay as you zoomed around on the screen are suddenly the wrong size or scale on paper. And nothing brands someone as a naive AutoCAD wannabe as quickly as the inability to plot a drawing at the right size and scale. Chapter 13 covers plotting procedures, but the information in this chapter is a necessary prerequisite to successful plotting. If you don't get this stuff right, there's a good chance you'll find that . . . the plot sickens.

This chapter describes the decisions you need to make before you set up a new drawing, shows the steps for doing a complete and correct setup, and demonstrates how to save setup settings for reuse.

Don't assume that you can just create a new blank DWG file and start drawing things. *Do* read this chapter before you get too deep into the later chapters in this book. Many AutoCAD drawing commands and concepts depend on proper drawing setup, so you'll have a much easier time of drawing and editing things if you've done your setup homework. A few minutes invested in setting up a drawing well can save hours of thrashing around later on.

After you've digested the detailed drawing setup procedures described in this chapter, use the AutoCAD Drawing Setup Roadmap on the Cheat Sheet at the front of this book as a quick reference to guide you through the process.

A Setup Roadmap

You have to set up AutoCAD correctly, partly because AutoCAD is so flexible and partly because, well, you're doing *CAD* — computer-aided drafting (or design). The computer can't aid your drafting (or design) if you don't clue it in on things like system of measure, drawing scale, paper size, and units. In this context, the following reasons help explain why AutoCAD drawing setup is important:

- **Electronic paper:** The most important thing you can do to make using AutoCAD fun is to work on a correctly set up drawing so that your screen acts like paper, only smarter. When drawing on real paper, you constantly have to translate between units on the paper and the real-life units of the object you're drawing. But when drawing in AutoCAD, you draw directly in real-life units — feet and inches, millimeters, or whatever you typically use on your projects. AutoCAD can then calculate distances and dimensions for you and add them to the drawing. You can make the mouse pointer jump directly to hot spots on-screen, and a visible, resizable grid gives you a better sense of the scale of your drawing. However, this smart paper function works well only if you tell AutoCAD some crucial parameters for your specific drawing. AutoCAD can't really do its job until you tell it how to work.

- **Dead-trees paper:** Creating a great drawing on-screen that doesn't fit well on paper is all too easy. After you finish creating your drawing on the smart paper AutoCAD provides on-screen, you then usually have to plot it on the good, old-fashioned paper that people have used for thousands of years. At that point, you must deal with the fact that people like to use certain standard paper sizes and drawing scales. (Most people also like everything to fit neatly on one sheet of paper.) If you set up AutoCAD correctly, good plotting results automatically; if not, plotting time can become one colossal hassle.

- **It ain't easy:** AutoCAD provides templates and Setup Wizards for you, but the templates don't work well unless you understand them, and some of the wizards don't work well even if you do understand them. This deficiency is one of the major weaknesses in AutoCAD. You must figure out on your own (with the help of this book, of course) how to make the program work right. If you just plunge in without carefully setting up, your drawing and printing efforts are likely to wind up a real mess.

Fortunately, setting up AutoCAD correctly is a bit like following a roadmap to a new destination. Although the directions for performing your setup are complex, you can master them with attention and practice. Even more fortunately, this chapter provides a detailed and field-tested route. And soon, you'll know the route like the back of your hand.

While you're working in AutoCAD, always keep in mind what your final output should look like on real paper. Even your first printed drawings should look just like hand-drawn ones — only without all those eraser smudges.

Before you start the drawing setup process, you need to make decisions about your new drawing. The following three questions are absolutely critical; if you don't answer them or your answer is wrong, you'll probably need to rework the drawing later:

✔ **What drawing units will you use?**

✔ **At what scale — or scales — will you plot it?**

✔ **On what size paper does it need to fit?**

In some cases, you can defer answering one additional question, but it's usually better to deal with it up front: What kind of border or title block does your drawing require?

If you're in a hurry, it's tempting to find an existing drawing that was set up for the drawing scale and paper size that you want to use, make a copy of that DWG file, erase the objects, and start drawing. Use this approach with care, though. When you start from another drawing, you inherit any setup mistakes in that drawing. Also, drawings that were created in much older versions of AutoCAD may not take advantage of current program features and CAD practices. If you can find a suitable drawing that was set up in a recent version of AutoCAD by an experienced person who is conscientious about doing setup right, consider using it. Otherwise, you're better off setting up a new drawing from scratch.

Choosing your units

AutoCAD is extremely flexible about drawing units; it lets you have them *your* way. Usually, you choose the type of units that you normally use to talk about whatever you're drawing: feet and inches for a building in the United States, millimeters for a metric screw, and so on.

Speaking of millimeters, there's another choice you have to make even before you choose your *units* of measure, and that's your *system* of measure.

Most of the world abandoned local systems of measure generations ago. Even widely adopted ones like the imperial system have mostly fallen by the way-side, just like their driving force, the British Empire. Except, of course, in the United States, where feet, inches, pounds, gallons, and degrees Fahrenheit still rule.

Enter the metric system

. . . or, "Let's forget everything we learned about measuring stuff and start over again!" All (well, nearly all) the world is metric. Instead of a system of linear measure based on twelves, of volume measure based on sixteens, and of temperature measure based on who knows *what*, metric bases all types of measure on tens. (Of course, *For Dummies* books are in the metric vanguard because every single *For Dummies* title includes a Part of *Tens*.)

The metric system first gained a toe-hold (ten toes, of course) in France during the Revolution. Over time, it became apparent that some standardization was called for, and a mere century-and-a-half later, SI Metric became that standard. SI is short for *Systeme International d'Unites*. (That's International System of Units in English. Isn't it great to speak more than one language?)

The United States may be late coming to the party, but the U.S. federal government *has* made a commitment to adopt SI Metric. For more information, point your browser to the National Institute of Standards and Technology's Special Publication 814 (`http://ts.nist.gov/WeightsAndMeasures/Metric/pub814.cfm`).

During drawing setup, you choose two unit characteristics: a *type* of unit — Scientific, Decimal, Engineering, Architectural, or Fractional — and a *precision* of measurement in the Drawing Units dialog box, shown in Figure 4-1. (I show you how later in this chapter.) The unit types are as follows:

- ✔ **Engineering** units are in feet and inches and use *decimals* to represent partial units.

- ✔ **Architectural** units are in feet and inches and use *fractions* to represent partial units.

- ✔ **Decimal, Fractional,** and **Scientific** are *unitless* because AutoCAD doesn't know or care what the base unit is.

   If you configure a drawing to use Decimal units, for example, each drawing unit could represent a micron, millimeter, inch, foot, meter, kilometer, mile, parsec, the length of the king's forearm, or any other unit of measurement that you deem convenient. It's up to you to decide.

After you specify a type of unit, you draw things on-screen at full size in those units just as though you were laying them out on the construction site or in the machine shop. You draw an 8-foot-high line, for example, to indicate the height of a wall, and an 8-inch-high line to indicate the cutout for a doggie door (for a Dachshund, naturally). The on-screen line may actually be only 2 inches long at a particular zoom resolution, but AutoCAD stores the length as 8 feet. This way of working is easy and natural for most people for whom CAD is their first drafting experience, but it seems weird to people who've done a lot of manual drafting. If you're in the latter category, don't worry; you'll soon get the hang of it.

Figure 4-1:
The
Drawing
Units dialog
box.

When you use dash-dot linetypes (Chapter 5) and hatching (Chapter 12) in a drawing, it matters to AutoCAD whether the drawing uses an imperial (inches, feet, miles, and so on) or metric (millimeters, meters, kilometers, and so on) system of measure. The MEASUREMENT system variable controls whether the linetype and hatch patterns that AutoCAD lists for you to choose from are scaled with inches or millimeters in mind as the plotting units. MEASUREMENT=0 means inches (that is, an imperial units drawing), whereas MEASUREMENT=1 means millimeters (that is, a metric units drawing). If you start from an appropriate template drawing, as described later in this chapter, the MEASUREMENT system variable will be set correctly, and you won't ever have to think about it.

Weighing up your scales

The next decision you should make before setting up a new drawing is choosing the scale at which you'll eventually plot the drawing. This decision gives you the *drawing scale* and *drawing scale factor* — two ways of expressing the same relationship between the objects in the real world and the objects plotted on paper.

You shouldn't just invent some arbitrary scale based on your CD-ROM speed or camera's zoom lens resolution. Most industries work with a fairly small set of approved drawing scales that are related to one another by factors of 2 or 10. If you use other scales, you'll at best be branded a clueless newbie — and, at worst, have to redo all your drawings at an accepted scale.

Drawing scale versus the drawing scale factor

CAD users employ two different ways of talking about a drawing's intended plot scale: drawing scale and drawing scale factor.

Drawing scale is the traditional way of describing a scale — traditional in that it existed long before CAD came to be. Drawing scales are expressed with an equal sign or colon; for example ⅛" = 1'–0", 1:20, or 2:1. Translate the equal sign or colon as "corresponds to." In all cases, the measurement to the left of the equal sign or colon indicates a paper measurement, and the number to the right indicates a CAD drawing and real-world measurement. In other words, the imperial drawing scale ⅛" = 1'–0" means that ⅛" on the plotted drawing corresponds to 1'–0" in the CAD drawing and in the real world, assuming that the plot was made at the proper scale. A metric drawing scale is usually expressed without units, as a simple ratio. Thus, a scale of 1:20 means one unit on the plotted drawing corresponds to 20 units in the real world (or the CAD drawing, since you're drawing everything full size, right?). In architectural and engineering drawings, the numbers usually refer to millimeters.

Drawing scale factor is a single number that represents a multiplier, such as 96, 20, or 0.5. The drawing scale factor for a drawing is the conversion factor between a measurement on the plot and a measurement in a CAD drawing and the real world.

Those of you who did your math homework in junior high will realize that drawing scale and drawing scale factor are two interchangeable ways of describing the same relationship. The drawing scale factor is the multiplier that converts the first number in the drawing scale into the second number.

Table 4-1 lists some common architectural drawing scales, using both imperial and metric units. The table also lists the drawing scale factor corresponding to each drawing scale and the common uses for each scale. If you work in industries other than those listed here, ask drafters or coworkers what the common drawing scales are and for what kinds of drawings they're used.

Table 4-1	Common Architectural Drawing Scales	
Drawing Scale	*Drawing Scale Factor*	*Common Uses*
¹⁄₁₆" = 1'–0"	192	Large building plans
⅛" = 1'–0"	96	Building plans
¼" = 1'–0"	48	House plans
½" = 1'–0"	24	Plan details
1" = 1'–0"	12	Details
1:200	200	Large building plans
1:100	100	Building plans

Drawing Scale	Drawing Scale Factor	Common Uses
1:50	50	House plans
1:20	20	Plan details
1:10	10	Details

After you choose a drawing scale, engrave the corresponding drawing scale factor on your desk, write it on your hand (don't mix those two up, okay?), and put it on a sticky note on your monitor. You need to know the drawing scale factor for many drawing tasks, as well as for some plotting. You should be able to recite the drawing scale factor of any drawing you're working on in AutoCAD without even thinking about it.

Even if you're going to use the Plot dialog box's Fit to Paper option, rather than a specific scale factor, to plot the drawing, you still need to choose a scale to make text, dimensions, and other annotations appear at a useful size. Choose a scale that's in the neighborhood of the Fit to Paper plotting factor, which AutoCAD displays in the Plot Scale area of the Plot dialog box. For example, if you determine that you need to squeeze your drawing down about 90 times to fit on the desired sheet size, choose a drawing scale of ⅛ inch = 1'–0" (drawing scale factor = 96) if you're using architectural units or 1:100 (drawing scale factor = 100) for other kinds of units.

Most of the time, for most people, there are way too many scales in the lists you see in the Viewports toolbar and the Plot dialog box. AutoCAD has a handy dandy Edit Scale List dialog box that lets you remove those imperial scales if you never work in feet and inches. And vice versa, for the metrically challenged. To run through your scales, choose Format⇨Scale List. If you make a mistake, the Reset button will restore all the default scales.

Thinking about paper

With knowledge of your industry's common drawing scales, you can choose a provisional scale based on what you're depicting. But you won't know for sure whether that scale works until you compare it with the size of the paper that you want to use for plotting your drawing. Here again, most industries use a small range of standard sheet sizes. Three common sets of sizes exist, as shown in Figure 4-2 and Table 4-2:

- ✔ ANSI (American National Standards Institute)
- ✔ Architectural
- ✔ ISO (International Organization for Standardization)

Figure 4-2:
Relation-
ships
among
standard
paper sizes.

Table 4-2	**Common Plot Sheet Sizes**	
Sheet Size	*Dimensions*	*Comment*
ANSI *E*	34 x 44"	
ANSI *D*	22 x 34"	*E* sheet folded in half
ANSI *C*	17 x 22"	*D* sheet folded in half
ANSI *B*	11 x 17"	*C* sheet folded in half
ANSI *A*	8½ x 11"	*B* sheet folded in half
Architectural Large *E*	36 x 48"	
Architectural *E*	30 x 42"	
Architectural *D*	24 x 36"	Large *E* sheet folded in half
Architectural *C*	18 x 24"	*D* sheet folded in half
Architectural *B*	12 x 18"	*C* sheet folded in half
Architectural *A*	9 x 12"	*B* sheet folded in half
ISO *A0*	841 x 1189 mm	
ISO *A1*	594 x 841 mm	*A0* sheet folded in half
ISO *A2*	420 x 594 mm	*A1* sheet folded in half
ISO *A3*	297 x 420 mm	*A2* sheet folded in half
ISO A4	210 x 297 mm	A3 sheet folded in half

You select a particular set of sheet sizes based on the common practices in your industry. You then narrow down your choice based on the area required by what you're going to draw. For example, most imperial-units architectural plans are plotted on Architectural D- or E-size sheets, and most metric architectural plans go on ISO A1 or A0 sheets.

If you know the desired sheet size and drawing scale factor, you can calculate the available drawing area easily. Simply multiply each of the sheet's dimensions by the drawing scale factor. For example, if you choose an 11-x-17-inch sheet and a drawing scale factor of 96 (corresponding to a plot scale of ⅛" = 1'–0"), you multiply 17 times 96 and 11 times 96 to get an available drawing area of 1,632 inches x 1,056 inches (or 136 feet x 88 feet). If your sheet size is in inches but your drawing scale is in millimeters, you need to multiply by an additional 25.4 to convert from inches to millimeters. For example, with an 11-x-17-inch sheet and a scale of 1:200 (drawing scale factor = 200), you multiply 17 times 200 times 25.4 and 11 times 200 times 25.4 to get 86,360 x 55,880 mm or 86.36 x 55.88 m — not quite big enough for a football field (American *or* European football).

Conversely, if you know the sheet size that you're going to use and the real-world size of what you're going to draw, and you want to find out the largest plot scale you can use, you have to divide, not multiply. Divide the needed real-world drawing area's length and width by the sheet's dimensions. Take the larger number — either the length result or the width result — and round up to the nearest real drawing scale factor (that is, one that's commonly used in your industry). For example, suppose you want to draw a 60-x-40-foot (or 720-x-480-inch) floor plan and print it on 11-x-17-inch paper. You divide 720 by 17 and 480 by 11 to get 42.35 and 43.64, respectively. The larger number, 43.64, corresponds in this example to the short dimension of the house and the paper. The nearest larger common architectural drawing scale factor is 48 (corresponding to ¼" = 1'–0"), which leaves a little room for the plotting margin and title block.

The Cheat Sheet at the front of this book includes two tables that list the available drawing areas for a range of sheet sizes and drawing scales. Use those tables to help you decide on an appropriate paper size and drawing scale; revert to the calculation method for situations that the tables don't cover. If you don't keep a favorite old calculator on your physical desktop, don't despair — AutoCAD 2008 has one lurking on the Standard toolbar — look for the QuickCalc button. (Hint: It looks like a calculator!)

If you're using the 2D Drafting & Annotation workspace, you may think you're using the *Standard* toolbar, but you're actually using a truncated version called *Standard Annotation*. The Standard Annotation toolbar is missing tool buttons for the Windows Clipboard commands as well as nearly all the Zoom options. If you prefer the "standard" Standard toolbar over the new abbreviated version, right-click any tool button and uncheck Standard Annotation to remove it; then repeat and check Standard.

When you select a sheet size and drawing scale, always leave some extra room for the following two reasons:

✔ Most plotters and printers can't print all the way to the edge of the sheet — they require a small margin. For example, my trusty old Hewlett-Packard LaserJet 4050 has a printable area of about 8.0 x 10.7 inches on an 8.5-x-11-inch ANSI A-size (letter-size) sheet. (You'll find this information in the Plot dialog box, as described in Chapter 13.) If you're a stickler for precision, you can use the printable area instead of the physical sheet area in the calculations described earlier in this section.

✔ Most drawings require some annotations — text, grid bubbles, and so on — outside the objects you're drawing, plus a title block surrounding the objects and annotations. If you don't leave some room for the annotations and title block, you'll end up having to cram things together too much or change to a different sheet size. Either way, you'll be slowed down later in the project, when you can least afford it. Figure 4-3 shows an extreme example of selecting a sheet size that's too small or, conversely, a drawing scale that's too large. In this example, the building is too long for the sheet, and it overlaps the title block on both the right and left sides.

Some industries deal with the "sheet-is-too-small/drawing-scale-is-too-large" problem by breaking drawings up onto multiple plotted sheets. You might consider doing the same.

Figure 4-3:
"This sheet size is too small," said Goldilocks.

Don't be afraid to *start* with paper. Experienced drafters often make a quick, throwaway, pencil-and-paper sketch called a *cartoon*. A drawing cartoon usually includes a rectangle indicating the sheet of paper you intend to plot on, a sketch of the title block, and a very rough, schematic sketch of the thing you're going to draw. It helps to scribble down the dimensions of the sheet, the main title block areas, and the major objects to be drawn. By sketching out a cartoon, you'll often catch scale or paper size problems before you set up a drawing, when repairs take only a few minutes — not after you've created the drawing, when fixing the problem can take hours.

Defending your border

The next decision to make is what kind of border your drawing deserves. The options include a full-blown title block, a simple rectangle, or nothing at all around your drawing. If you need a title block, do you have one, can you borrow an existing one, or will you need to draw one from scratch? Although you can draw title block geometry in an individual drawing, you'll save time by reusing the same title block for multiple drawings. Your company may already have a standard title block drawing ready to use, or someone else who's working on your project may have created one for the project.

The right way to draw a title block is in a separate DWG file at its normal plotted size (for example, 36 inches long by 24 inches high for an architectural D-size title block, or 841 mm long by 594 mm high for an ISO A1-size version). You then insert or xref the title block drawing into each sheet drawing. Chapter 14 describes how to insert and xref separate DWG files.

All system variables go

As Chapter 2 describes, AutoCAD includes a slew of *system variables* that control the way your drawing and the AutoCAD program work. Much of the drawing setup process involves setting system variables based on the drawing scale, sheet size, and other desired properties of the drawing. You can set some system variables in AutoCAD dialog boxes, but a few must be entered at the keyboard. Table 4-3 shows the settings that you most commonly need to change — or at least check — during drawing setup, along with the names of the corresponding system variables. Later in the chapter, in the "Making the Most of Model Space" section, I show you the procedure for changing these settings.

Table 4-3	System Variables for Drawing Setup	
Setting	*Dialog Box*	*System Variables*
Linear units and precision	Drawing Units	LUNITS, LUPREC
Angular units and precision	Drawing Units	AUNITS, AUPREC
Grid spacing and visibility	Drafting Settings	GRIDUNIT, GRIDMODE, GRIDDISPLAY, GRIDMAJOR
Snap spacing and on/off	Drafting Settings	SNAPUNIT, SNAPMODE
Drawing limits	None (use keyboard input)	LIMMIN, LIMMAX
Linetype scale	Linetype Manager	LTSCALE, PSLTSCALE, MSLTSCALE, CELTSCALE
Dimension scale	Dimension Style Manager	DIMSCALE
Annotation Scaling	Various	ANNOAUTOSCALE, ANNOTATIVEDWG, SELECTIONANNODISPLAY

A Template for Success

When you start in the AutoCAD Classic workspace, AutoCAD creates a new, blank drawing configured for 2D drafting. Depending on where you live (your country, not your street address!) and the dominant system of measure used there, AutoCAD will base this new drawing on one of two default template drawings: acad.dwt (imperial system of measure, as used in the United States) or acadiso.dwt (metric system, used throughout the rest of the galaxy). (In AutoCAD LT, the two default templates are named acadlt.dwt and acadltiso.dwt.) When you explicitly create a new drawing from within AutoCAD, the Select Template dialog box, shown in Figure 4-4, appears by default so that you can choose a template on which to base your new drawing.

You may be familiar with the Microsoft Word or Excel template documents, and AutoCAD template drawings work pretty much the same way — because Autodesk stole the idea from them (encouraged, of course, by Microsoft).

A *template* is simply a drawing whose name ends in the letters DWT, which you use as the starting point for another drawing. When you create a new drawing from a template, AutoCAD makes a copy of the template file and opens the copy in a new drawing editor window. The first time you save the file, you're prompted for a new filename to save to; the original template file stays unchanged.

Figure 4-4:
A toolbox
of tem-
plates to
contem-
plate.

Using a suitable template can save you time and worry because many of the setup options are already set correctly for you. You know the drawing will print correctly; you just have to worry about getting the geometry and text right. Of course, all this optimism assumes that the person who set up the template knew what he or she was doing.

The stock templates that come with AutoCAD are okay as a starting point, but you'll need to modify them to suit your purposes or create your own from scratch. In particular, the stock AutoCAD templates aren't set up for the scales that you'll want to use. The instructions in the rest of this chapter tell you how to specify scale-dependent setup information.

So the only problems with templates are creating good ones and then later finding the right one to use when you need it. Later in this chapter, in the "Making Templates Your Own" section, I show you how to create templates from your own setup drawings. Here I show you how to use an already created template, such as one of the templates that comes with AutoCAD 2008 or from one of your CAD-savvy colleagues. If you're lucky, someone in your office will have created suitable templates that you can use to get going quickly.

Follow these steps to create a new drawing from a template drawing:

1. **Run the NEW command by pressing Ctrl+N or choosing File⇨New.**

   The Select Template dialog box appears.

   The first button on the Standard toolbar runs the QNEW (Quick NEW) command instead of the ordinary NEW command. Unless you or some-one else has changed the Default Template File Name for QNEW in the Options dialog box, QNEW does the same thing as NEW. See the "Making Templates Your Own" section, later in this chapter, for information about how to take advantage of QNEW.

2. **Click the name of the template that you want to use as the starting point for your new drawing and click the Open button.**

   A new drawing window with a temporary name, such as `Drawing2.dwg`, appears. (The template you opened remains unchanged on your hard disk.)

   Depending on which template you choose, your new drawing may open with a paper space layout tab, not the Model tab, selected. If that's the case, click the Model tab (in the lower-left corner of the drawing area) before changing the settings described in the "Making the Most of Model Space" section. (If your model and layout tabs are not visible, click the Model button immediately to the right of the LWT button in the status bar.) The "Plotting a Layout in Paper Space" section, later in this chapter, describes how to set up and take advantage of paper space layouts.

3. **Press Ctrl+S and save the file under a new name.**

   Take the time to save the drawing to the appropriate name and location now.

4. **Make needed changes.**

   With most of the templates that come with AutoCAD, you need to consider changing the units, limits, grid and snap settings, linetype scale, and dimension scale. See the "Making the Most of Model Space" section for instructions.

5. **Save the drawing again.**

   If you'll need other drawings in the future similar to the current one, consider saving your modified template as a template in its own right. See the "Making Templates Your Own" section, later in this chapter.

The simplest, no-frills templates are `acad.dwt` (for people who customarily work in imperial units) and `acadiso.dwt` (for people who customarily work in metric). (The corresponding templates in AutoCAD LT are named `acadlt.dwt` and `acadltiso.dwt`, respectively.) Most of the remaining templates that come with AutoCAD include title blocks for various sizes of sheets. In addition, most templates come in two versions — one for people who use color-dependent plot styles and one for people who use named plot styles. You probably want the color-dependent versions. (Chapter 13 describes the two kinds of plot styles and why you probably want the color-dependent variety.) I warned you that this drawing setup stuff would be complicated!

Making the Most of Model Space

Most drawings require a two-part setup:

1. Set up the Model tab, where you'll create most of your drawing.

2. Create one or more paper space layout tabs for plotting.

After you've decided on drawing scale and sheet size, you can perform model space setup as described in this section.

Setting your units

First, you should set the linear and angular units that you want to use in your new drawing. The following procedure describes how:

1. **Choose Format⇨Units from the menu bar.**

   The Drawing Units dialog box appears, as shown in Figure 4-5.

Figure 4-5:
The default unitless units.

2. **Choose a linear unit type from the Length Type drop-down list.**

   Choose the type of unit representation that's appropriate for your work. Engineering and Architectural units are displayed in feet and inches; the other types of units aren't tied to any particular unit of measurement. You decide whether each unit represents a millimeter, centimeter, meter, inch, foot, or something else. Your choice is much simpler if you're working in metric: Choose Decimal units.

   AutoCAD can think in inches! If you're using Engineering or Architectural units (feet and inches), AutoCAD understands any coordinate you enter as a number of inches. You use the ' (apostrophe) character on your keyboard to indicate a number in feet instead of inches.

3. **From the Length Precision drop-down list, choose the level of precision you want when AutoCAD displays coordinates and linear measurements.**

   The precision setting controls how precisely AutoCAD displays coordinates, distances, and prompts in some dialog boxes. In particular, the Coordinates box on the status bar displays the current coordinates of the crosshairs using the current precision. A *grosser* — that is, less precise — precision setting makes the numbers displayed in the status bar more readable and less jumpy. So be gross for now; you can always act a little less gross later.

   The linear and angular precision settings affect AutoCAD's *display* of coordinates, distances, and angles on the status bar, in dialog boxes, and in the command line and dynamic input tooltip areas. For drawings stored as DWG files, AutoCAD always uses maximum precision to store the locations and sizes of all objects that you draw. In addition, AutoCAD provides separate settings for controlling the precision of dimension text — see Chapter 11 for details.

4. **Choose an angular unit type from the Angle Type drop-down list.**

   Decimal Degrees and Deg/Min/Sec are the most common choices.

   The Clockwise check box and the Direction button provide additional angle measurement options, but you'll rarely need to change the default settings: Measure angles counterclockwise and use east as the 0 degree direction.

5. **From the Angle Precision drop-down list, choose the degree of precision you want when AutoCAD displays angular measurements.**

6. **In the Insertion Scale area, choose the units of measurement for this drawing.**

   Choose your base unit for this drawing — that is, the real-world distance represented by one AutoCAD unit.

7. **Click OK to exit the dialog box and save your settings.**

AutoCAD 2008's Drawing Units dialog box includes a Lighting area where you specify the units type to be used to measure the intensity of photometric lights. That's a fairly advanced 3D feature that I don't cover in this book. If you want more information, visit the online help.

Telling your drawing its limits

The next model space setup task is to set your drawing's *limits*. You wouldn't want it staying out all night and hanging out with just anybody, would you? The limits represent the rectangular working area that you'll draw on, which usually corresponds to the paper size. Setting limits correctly gives you the following advantages:

✔ If you use default settings, when you turn on the grid (described in the following section), the grid appears in the rectangular limits area. With the grid on, the grid settings at their defaults, and the limits set correctly, you see the working area that corresponds to what you'll eventually be plotting, so you won't accidentally sail off the edge of your paper.

✔ The ZOOM command's All option zooms to the greater of the limits or the drawing extents. (The extents of a drawing consist of a rectangular area just large enough to include all the objects in the drawing.) When you set limits properly and color within the lines, ZOOM All gives you a quick way to zoom to your working area.

✔ If you plot from model space, you can choose to plot the area defined by the drawing limits. This option gives you a quick, reliable way to plot your drawing, but only if you've set limits correctly!

Many CAD drafters don't set limits properly in their drawings. After you read this section, you can tell them — in a nice way, of course — why they should and how.

You can start the LIMITS command from a menu choice, but all subsequent action takes place on the command line or the dynamic input tooltip; despite the importance of the topic, AutoCAD has no dialog box for setting limits.

The following procedure shows you how to set your drawing limits:

1. **Choose Format⬄Drawing Limits from the menu bar to start the LIMITS command.**

   AutoCAD prompts you, both with a dynamic input tooltip and at the command line at the bottom of the screen, to reset the model space limits:

   ```
   Command: LIMITS
   Reset Model space limits:
   Specify lower left corner or [ON/OFF] <0.0000,0.0000>:
   ```

   The value at the end of the last line of the command line prompt is the default value for the lower-left corner of the drawing limits. It appears according to the units and precision that you selected in the Drawing Units dialog box — for example, 0'-0" if you selected Architectural units with precision to the nearest inch.

2. **Type the lower-left corner of the limits you want to use and press Enter.**

   The usual value to enter at this point is **0,0**. (Type a zero, a comma, and then another zero, with no spaces.) You can just press Enter to accept the default value.

   Regardless of what you see in the dynamic input tooltip, when you press Enter to accept a default value, the value that will be accepted is the one that shows in the command line.

AutoCAD now prompts you for the upper-right corner of the limits:

```
Specify upper right corner <12.0000,9.0000>:
```

The initial units offered by AutoCAD correspond to an Architectural A- size sheet of paper in landscape orientation. (Almost no one uses Architectural A-size paper; here's a classic example of a programmer choosing a silly default that no one has bothered to change in 22 years!)

If you live in a metric-dominant location, the second prompt will read:

```
Specify upper right corner <420.0000,297.0000>:
```

These numbers correspond to an ISO A3-size sheet (much more up-to-date than those silly, old-fashioned imperial settings!).

3. **Type the upper-right corner of the limits you want to use and press Enter.**

   You calculate the usual setting for the limit's upper-right corner by multiplying the paper dimensions by the drawing scale factor. For example, if you're setting up a ⅛" = 1'–0" drawing (drawing scale factor = 96) to be plotted on a 24-x-36-inch sheet in landscape orientation, the upper-right corner of the limits should be 36 inches times 96, 24 inches times 96. Okay, pencils down. The correct answer is 3456,2304 (or 288 feet, 192 feet).

   Alternatively, you can cheat when specifying limits and read the limits from the tables on the Cheat Sheet in the front of this book.

   If you have the grid turned on, AutoCAD by default redisplays it in the new limits area after you press Enter.

   If you're using Architectural or Engineering units and you want to enter measurements in feet and not inches, you must add the foot designator after the number, such as **6'**; otherwise, AutoCAD assumes that you mean inches.

4. **Choose View⇨Zoom⇨All.**

   AutoCAD zooms to the new limits.

Making the drawing area snap-py (and grid-dy)

AutoCAD's *grid* is a set of evenly spaced dots that serve as a visual distance reference. (As I describe in the preceding section, "Telling your drawing its limits," the grid [by default] also indicates how far the drawing limits extend.) AutoCAD's *snap* feature creates a set of evenly spaced, invisible *hot spots,* which make the crosshairs move in nice, even increments. Both grid and snap are like the intersection points of the lines on a piece of grid paper, but the grid is simply a visual reference, whereas snap constrains the points that you can pick with the mouse. You can — and usually will — set the grid and snap spacing to different distances.

Making snap (and grid) decisions

You can set your grid spacing to work in one of two ways: to help with your drawing or to help you remain aware of how objects will relate to your plot. For *a grid that helps with your drawing,* set the grid points a logical number of measurement units apart. For example, you might set the grid to 30 feet (10 yards) on a drawing of a (U.S.) football field. This kind of setting makes your work easier as you draw.

Another approach is to choose *a grid spacing that represents a specific distance,* such as 1 inch or 25 millimeters, on your final plot. If you want the grid to represent 1 inch on the plot and your drawing units are inches, enter the drawing scale factor. For example, in a ¼" = 1'–0" drawing, you'd enter the drawing scale factor of 48. A 48-inch grid interval in your drawing corresponds to a 1-inch interval on the plot when you plot to scale. If your drawing units are millimeters and you want the grid to represent 25 millimeters on the plot, enter the drawing

scale factor times 25. For example, in a 1:50 drawing, you'd enter 25 x 50, or 1250.

In most cases, you'll want to set the snap interval considerably smaller than the grid spacing. A good rule is to start with a snap spacing in the range of the size of the smallest objects that you'll be drawing — 6 inches or 100 millimeters for a building plan, ½ inch or 5 millimeters for an architectural detail, ¹⁄₁₆ inch or 1 millimeter for a small mechanical component, and so on.

To use snap effectively, you need to make the snap setting smaller as you zoom in and work on more detailed areas, and larger as you zoom back out. You will likely change the snap setting fairly frequently. The grid setting, on the other hand, can usually remain constant even as you work at different zoom settings; that keeps you oriented as to how far zoomed-in you are in the drawing.

Set the grid and the snap intervals in the Drafting Settings dialog box by following these steps:

1. **Right-click the Snap or Grid button in the status bar and choose Settings.**

   The Drafting Settings dialog box appears with the Snap and Grid tab selected, as shown in Figure 4-6.

   The Snap and Grid tab has five parts, but the Snap and Grid sections within that tab are all you need to worry about for most 2D drafting work.

2. **Select the Snap On check box to turn on snap.**

   This action creates default snaps half a unit apart.

   You can also click the SNAP button on the status bar to toggle snap on and off; the same goes for the GRID button and the grid setting.

3. **Enter the snap interval you want in the Snap X Spacing box.**

   Use the information in the sections preceding this procedure to decide on a reasonable snap spacing.

Figure 4-6:
Get your
drafting
settings
here!

> If Equal X and Y Spacing is checked, the Y spacing automatically changes to equal the X spacing, which is almost always what you want.

4. **Select the Grid On check box to turn on the grid.**

5. **Enter the desired grid spacing in the Grid X Spacing box.**

   Use the information in the sections preceding this procedure to decide on a reasonable grid spacing.

   Just like with snap spacing, if the Equal X and Y Spacing box is checked, the Y spacing automatically changes to equal the X spacing. Again, you usually want to leave it that way.

   X measures horizontal distance; Y measures vertical distance. The AutoCAD drawing area normally shows an X and Y icon in case you forget.

6. **Specify additional grid display options in the Grid behavior area.**

   If you check Allow Adaptive Grid, AutoCAD changes the density or spacing of the grid dots as you zoom in and out. If you also check Allow Subdivision Below Grid Spacing, the spacing can go lower than what you've set, and it may go higher if you're zoomed a long way out of your drawing. (If it didn't, you couldn't see your drawing for the grid dots!)

   Selecting Display Grid Beyond Limits allows the grid to display over the entire graphics area, no matter how far you're zoomed out. Clearing this check box makes AutoCAD behave the way it's always behaved — that is, the grid is displayed only in the area defined by the drawing limits.

> I recommend you leave this box unchecked as an effective way to tell whether you're drawing beyond your drawing limits. What's the point of setting limits if you don't know where they are?

The Follow Dynamic UCS option (not available in AutoCAD LT) is a 3D-specific feature that changes your drawing plane as you mouse over 3D objects. I don't cover Dynamic UCS or 3D modeling in this book.

7. Click OK to close the Drafting Settings dialog box.

Setting linetype and dimension scales

Even though you've engraved the drawing scale factor on your desk and written it on your hand — not vice versa — AutoCAD doesn't know the drawing scale until you enter it. Keeping AutoCAD in the dark is fine as long as you're just drawing continuous lines and curves representing real-world geometry, because you draw these objects at their real-world size, without worrying about plot scale.

As soon as you start adding dimensions (measurements that show the size of the things you're drawing) and using dash-dot linetypes (line patterns that contain gaps in them), you need to tell AutoCAD how to scale the parts of the dimensions and the gaps in the linetypes based on the plot scale. If you forget this, the dimension text and arrowheads can come out very tiny or very large when you plot the drawing, and dash-dot linetype patterns can look waaaay too big or too small. Figure 4-7 shows what I mean.

Figure 4-7: The dimension and linetype scales need to be just right.

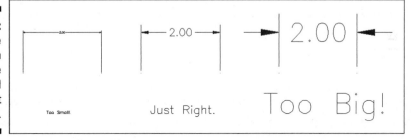

Too Small.   Just Right.   Too Big!

I vote for *annotative objects* as the most significant new feature in AutoCAD 2008. Annotative objects are created with a special property (or modified after the fact) so that when you change the annotation scale of a layout viewport or of the model tab, all of the annotative objects — including text, dimensions, dash-dot linetypes, hatch patterns, and symbol blocks — change automatically to their correct size for the chosen scale. I give you a closer look at annotative objects in Chapter 10, but in the meantime, it's still worthwhile getting familiar with the standard way of controlling these annotation features.

The scale factor that controls dash-dot linetypes is found in a system variable called *LTSCALE* (as in LineType SCALE). The scaling factor that controls dimensions is found in a system variable called *DIMSCALE*. You can change either of these settings at any time, but it's best to set them correctly when you're setting up the drawing.

AutoCAD 2008's annotative objects feature introduces a number of new system variables to help keep things running smoothly. The MSLTSCALE variable changes the linetype scaling of dash-dot linework in the model tab according to the annotation scale you select.

The following sequence includes directions for typing system variable and command names. To set the linetype scale at the keyboard, follow these steps:

1. **Type** LTSCALE **(or** LTS**) and press Enter.**

   AutoCAD responds with a prompt, asking you for the scale factor. The value at the end of the prompt is the current linetype scale setting, as shown in the following command line example:

   ```
   Enter new linetype scale factor <1.0000>:
   ```

2. **Type the value you want for the linetype scale and press Enter.**

   The easiest choice is to set the linetype scale to the drawing scale factor. Some people, however, find that the dashes and gaps in dash-dot linetypes get a bit too long when they use the drawing scale factor. If you're one of those people, set LTSCALE to one-half of the drawing scale factor. (Feel free to experiment with this value; some people prefer a linetype scale of three-quarters the scale factor. If you're working in metric, try 0.75 times the scale factor instead — just ask your calculator if you don't believe me.)

Alternatively, you can specify linetype scale in the Linetype Manager dialog box: Choose Format➪Linetype, click the Show Details button, and type your desired linetype scale in the Global Scale Factor text box.

To change the dimension scale, the quick and dirty method — that is, using the keyboard — is most efficient. I describe dimensions in detail in Chapter 11, but you should get in the habit of setting the dimension scale during drawing setup. To do so, follow these steps:

1. **Type** DIMSCALE **and press Enter.**

   Once again, AutoCAD displays the current dimension scale at the command line and prompts you to enter a new value:

   ```
   Enter new value for DIMSCALE <1.0000>:
   ```

2. Type the desired dimension scale value and press Enter.

While *linetype* scale can fall within a range of values as just described, the *dimension* scale must be set to precisely the same value as the drawing scale factor in order for dimension components to print at exactly the right size.

Now when you draw dimensions, AutoCAD scales the dimension text and arrowheads correctly.

The procedure described here for setting both linetype scale and dimension scale assumes that you're starting a new drawing from one of the plain-jane templates (acad.dwt or acadiso.dwt in the full version, acadlt.dwt or acadltiso.dwt in AutoCAD LT) and using the default dimension style (I cover dimension styles in Chapter 11). Don't change LTSCALE or — especially — DIMSCALE in existing drawings without knowing exactly why you're doing it and what values to set them to, in case someone before you set their values for good reasons.

Entering drawing properties

You should do one last bit of bookkeeping before you're finished with model space drawing setup: Enter summary information in the Drawing Properties dialog box, as shown in Figure 4-8. Choose File⇨Drawing Properties to open the Drawing Properties dialog box; then click the Summary tab. Enter the drawing scale and the drawing scale factor you're using, plus any other information you think useful.

Figure 4-8:
Surveying your drawing's properties.

Setting Up a Layout in Paper Space

As I describe in Chapter 2, *paper space* is a separate space in each drawing for composing a printed version of that drawing. You create the drawing itself, called the *model,* in *model space.* You then can create one or more plottable views, complete with title block. Each of these plottable views is called a *layout.* AutoCAD saves separate plot settings with each layout — and with the Model tab — so that you can plot each tab differently. In practice, you'll probably need to use only one of the paper space layout tabs, especially when you're getting started with AutoCAD.

A screen image is worth a thousand paper space explanations. If you haven't yet seen an example out in the wild, refer to Chapter 2. You may also want to open a few of the AutoCAD 2008 sample drawings and click the Model and Layout tabs to witness the variety of ways in which paper space is used. A good place to start is `Program Files\AutoCAD 2008\Sample\Sheet Sets\Civil\Existing Conditions Plan.dwg`. AutoCAD LT users can scope out `Program Files\AutoCAD 2008\Sample\Bygginga Plan.dwg` (you can practice your Icelandic at the same time with this one).

After you complete model space setup, you should create a layout for plotting. You don't need to create the plotting layout right after you create the drawing and do model space setup; you can wait until after you've drawn some geometry. You should set up a layout sooner, not later, however. If any scale or sheet size problems exist, it's better to discover them early.

In AutoCAD 2008, it's still possible to ignore paper space layouts entirely and do all your drawing *and* plotting in model space. But you owe it to yourself to give layouts a try. You'll probably find that they make plotting more consistent and predictable. They'll give you more plotting flexibility when you need it. And you'll certainly encounter drawings from other people that make extensive use of paper space, so you need to understand it if you plan to exchange drawings with anyone else.

Creating a layout

Creating a simple paper space layout is straightforward, thanks to the AutoCAD 2008 Create Layout Wizard, shown in Figure 4-9. (Yes! Finally, a useful AutoCAD wizard.) The command name is LAYOUTWIZARD, which is not to be confused with the WAYOUTLIZARD command for drawing guitar-playing iguanas! In any event, you can avoid a lot of typing by choosing Tools⇨Wizards⇨Create Layout.

Although the Create Layout Wizard guides you step by step through the process of creating a paper space layout from scratch, it doesn't eliminate the necessity of coming up with a sensible set of layout parameters. The sheet size and plot scale that you choose provide a certain amount of space for showing your model (see the information earlier in this chapter), and wizards aren't allowed to bend the laws of arithmetic to escape that fact. For example, a map of Australia at a scale of 1 inch = 1 foot won't fit on an 8½-x-11-inch sheet, no way, no how. In other words, garbage in, garbage (lay)out. Fortunately, the Create Layout Wizard lends itself to experimentation, and you can easily delete layouts that don't work.

Figure 4-9:
The Create
Layout
Wizard.

Follow these steps to create a layout:

1. **Choose Tools⇨Wizards⇨Create Layout, or type** LAYOUTWIZARD **and press Enter.**

2. **Give the new layout a name and click Next.**

   In place of the default name, Layout3, I recommend something more descriptive — for example, *D-Size Sheet.* Or you can call it *A1-Size Sheet* if you're of the metric persuasion.

3. **Choose a printer or plotter to use when plotting this layout and click Next.**

   Think of your choice as the *default* plotter for this layout. You can change to a different plotter later or create page setups that plot the same layout on different plotters.

   Many of the names in the configured plotter list should look familiar because they're your Windows printers (*system printers* in AutoCAD lingo). Names with a .pc3 extension represent non-system printer drivers. See Chapter 13 for details.

4. **Choose a paper size, specify whether to use inches or millimeters to represent paper units, and click Next.**

   The available paper sizes depend on the printer or plotter that you selected in Step 3.

5. **Specify the orientation of the drawing on the paper and click Next.**

   The icon showing the letter *A* on the piece of paper shows you which orientation is which.

6. **On the Create Layout – Title Block page, click Next.**

   AutoCAD 2007 and earlier included a handy set of pre-drawn title blocks for a range of both imperial and metric paper sizes. Alas, Autodesk removed those drawing files from AutoCAD 2008. However, you can always draw, insert, or xref a title block later. See Chapter 14 for information about inserting or xrefing a title block.

   You can add custom title block drawings to your AutoCAD Template folder. If you want to know where to put them, see the "Making Templates Your Own" section, later in this chapter.

7. **Define the arrangement of viewports that AutoCAD should create and the plot scale for all viewports. Then click Next.**

   A layout viewport is a window from paper space into model space. You must create at least one viewport to display the model in your new layout. For most 2D drawings, a single viewport is all you need. 3D models often benefit from multiple viewports, each showing the 3D model from a different perspective.

   The default Viewport scale, Scaled to Fit, ensures that all of your model drawing appears in the viewport, but it results in an arbitrary scale factor. Most technical drawings require a specific scale, such as 1:100 or ⅛" = 1'–0".

8. **Click Select Location to specify the location of the viewport(s) on the paper; then pick the viewport's corners. When the Wizard returns, click Next.**

   After you click the Select Location button, the Create Layout Wizard displays the preliminary layout with any title block that you've chosen. Pick two points to define a rectangle that falls within the drawing area of your title block (or within the plottable area of the sheet, if you chose no title block in Step 6).

   AutoCAD represents the plottable area of the sheet with a dashed rectangle near the edge of the sheet. If you don't select a location for the viewport(s), the Create Layout Wizard creates a viewport that fills the plottable area of the sheet.

9. **Click Finish.**

   AutoCAD creates the new layout.

Copying and changing layouts

After you create a layout, you can delete, copy, rename, and otherwise manipulate it by right-clicking its tab or simply dragging it to a new position. Figure 4-10 shows the right-click menu options.

The From Template option refers to layout templates. After you create layouts in a template (DWT) or drawing (DWG) file, you can use the From Template option to import these layouts into the current drawing. For details, see the LAYOUT command's Template option in the Command Reference section of online help.

Many drawings require only one paper space layout. If you always plot the same view of the model and always plot to the same device and on the same size paper, a single paper space layout should suffice. If you want to plot your model in different ways (for example, at different scales, with different layers visible, with different areas visible, or with different plotted line characteristics), you may want to create additional paper space layouts.

Figure 4-10: The right-click menu for a layout tab.

Layouts have become a little easier to manage in AutoCAD and AutoCAD LT 2008. You don't have to open the right-click menu to copy or move a layout — just drag it to the new location. Hold down Ctrl while you drag if you want a copy. And you can rename a layout with the standard slow-double-click Windows mouse action.

Some different ways of plotting the same model can be handled in a single paper space layout with different page setups. See Chapter 13 for more details. If your projects require lots of drawings, you can parlay layouts into *sheet sets* — a feature that makes for more sophisticated creation, management, plotting, and electronic transfer of multisheet drawing sets. (Sorry, LT users — AutoCAD LT doesn't support sheet sets.) Again, see Chapter 13 for more information.

If you want to add another viewport to an existing layout, you need to become familiar with the MVIEW command. (See the MVIEW command in the Command Reference section of AutoCAD online help.) After you have the concepts down, using the Viewports dialog box (choose View➪Viewports➪ View Viewports) and Viewports toolbar can help you create, scale, and manage viewports more efficiently.

Lost in paper space

After you create a paper space layout, you suddenly have two views of the same drawing geometry: the view on your original Model tab and the new layout tab view (perhaps decorated with a handsome title block and other accoutrements of plotting nobility). It's important to realize that both views are of the *same* geometry. If you change the model geometry on one tab, you're changing it on all tabs because all tabs display the same model space objects.

When you make a paper space layout current by clicking its tab, you can switch the active space between paper space (that is, drawing and zooming on the sheet of paper) and model space (drawing and zooming on the model, inside the viewport) in several ways, including the following:

- ✔ Clicking the PAPER/MODEL button on the status bar.

- ✔ In the drawing area, double-clicking over a viewport to move the crosshairs into model space in that viewport or double-clicking outside all viewports (for example, in the gray area outside the sheet) to move the crosshairs into paper space.

- ✔ Clicking the Maximize/Minimize Viewport button on the status bar (for more information, see Chapter 2).

- ✔ Entering **MSPACE** (the command alias is **MS**) or **PSPACE** (**PS**) at the keyboard.

When the crosshairs are in model space, anything you draw or edit changes the model (and thus appears on the Model tab and on all paper space layout tabs). When the crosshairs are in paper space, anything you draw appears only on that one paper space layout. It's as though you were drawing on an acetate sheet over the top of that sheet of plotter paper — the model beneath remains unaffected.

This distinction can be disorienting at first. To avoid confusion, stick with the following approach (at least until you're more familiar with paper space):

✔ If you want to edit the model, switch to the Model tab first. (Don't try to edit the model in a paper space viewport — in the first place, it's a very inefficient use of your screen space.)

✔ If you want to edit a particular plot layout without affecting the model, switch to that layout's tab and make sure that the crosshairs are in paper space.

Making Templates Your Own

You can create a template from any DWG file by using the Save As dialog box. Follow these steps to save your drawing as a template:

1. **Choose File⇨Save As from the menu bar.**

   The Save Drawing As dialog box appears, as shown in Figure 4-11.

Figure 4-11: Saving a drawing as a template and applying options.

2. **From the Files of Type drop-down list, choose AutoCAD Drawing Template (*.dwt) or AutoCAD LT Drawing Template (*.dwt).**

3. **Navigate to the folder where you want to store the drawing.**

AutoCAD 2008's default folder for template drawings is called Template and is buried deep in the bowels of your Windows user profile. Save your templates there if you want them to appear in AutoCAD's Select Template list. You can save your templates in another folder, but if you want to use them later, you have to navigate to that folder each time to use them. See the Technical Stuff paragraph that follows this procedure for additional suggestions.

4. **Enter a name for the drawing template in the File Name text box and click Save.**

   A dialog box for the template description and units appears.

5. **Specify the template's measurement units (English or Metric) in the drop-down list.**

   Enter the key info now — you can't do it later unless you save the template to a different name. Don't bother filling in the Description field; AutoCAD doesn't display it in the Select Template dialog box.

6. **Click OK to save the file.**

7. **To save your drawing as a regular drawing, choose File⇨Save As from the menu bar.**

   The Save Drawing As dialog box appears again.

8. **From the Files of Type drop-down list, choose AutoCAD 2007 Drawing (*.dwg).**

   AutoCAD 2008 uses the AutoCAD 2007 DWG file format. Choose the AutoCAD LT equivalent, if that's your version. Choose an earlier version if you want to be able to open your drawing in AutoCAD 2006 or previous.

9. **Navigate to the folder where you want to store the drawing.**

   Use a different folder from the one with your template drawings.

10. **Enter the name of the drawing in the File Name text box and click Save.**

    The file is saved. Now, when you save it in the future, the regular file, not the template file, gets updated.

AutoCAD 2008 can notify you if you or someone else adds layers that are not *reconciled* — that is, not already stored by name in the drawing database. This can be useful for maintaining standards in a large office where many different people work on drawings. You can tell AutoCAD to notify you if unreconciled layers are added to the drawing when you save a drawing as a template file. Clicking Save in the Save Drawing As dialog box displays the new Template Options dialog box (see Figure 4-11). Choosing to save layers as reconciled will generate a balloon message on the status bar if new, unreconciled layers are added to a drawing started from this template. You can also specify the template file's system of measure in the Template Options dialog box.

AutoCAD 2008 includes a command called QNEW (Quick NEW), which, when properly configured, can bypass the Select Template dialog box and create a new drawing from your favorite template. The first button on the Standard toolbar — the one with the plain white sheet of paper — runs the newer QNEW command instead of the older NEW command.

To put the Quick into QNEW, though, you have to tell AutoCAD which default template to use: Choose Tools⇨Options⇨Files⇨Template Settings⇨Default Template File Name for QNEW. AutoCAD 2008's QNEW default setting for Default Template File Name is None, which causes QNEW to act just like NEW (that is, QNEW opens the Select Template dialog box).

AutoCAD 2008 stores template drawings and many other support files under your Windows user folder. To discover where your template folder is hiding, go to AutoCAD's menu bar and choose Tools⇨Options⇨Files⇨Template Settings⇨Drawing Template File Location, as shown in Figure 4-12.

Figure 4-12: Seek and you shall find your template folder.

You don't have to keep your template files where that nice Mister Gates tells you. Create a folder that you can find easily (for example, `C:\Acad-templates` or `F:\Acad-custom\templates` on a network drive), put the templates that you actually use there, and change the Drawing Template File Location setting so that it points to your new template folder.

As this chapter demonstrates, you have to do quite a bit to set up a drawing in AutoCAD. As with any other initially forbidding task, take it step by step, and soon the sequence will seem natural. The Drawing Setup Roadmap on the Cheat Sheet will help you stay on the road and avoid taking the wrong turnoff.

Part II
Let There Be Lines

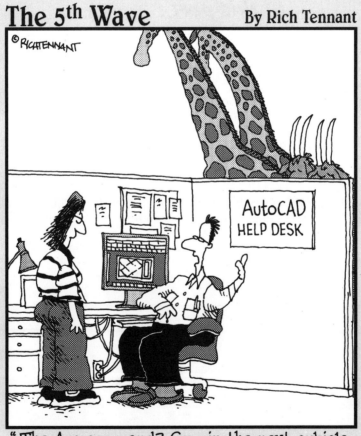

The 5th Wave   By Rich Tennant

© RICHTENNANT

AutoCAD
HELP DESK

"The Arc command? Guy in the next cubicle
seems to know a lot about that."

In this part . . .

*L*ines, circles, and other elements of geometry make up the heart of your drawing. AutoCAD offers many different drawing commands, many ways to use them to draw objects precisely, and many properties for controlling the on-screen and plotted appearance of objects. After you draw your geometry, you'll probably spend at least as much time editing it as your design and drawings evolve. And in the process, you need to zoom in and out and pan all around to see how the entire drawing is coming together.

Drawing geometry, editing it, and changing the displayed view are the foundation of the drawing process; this part shows you how to make that foundation solid. And for those who want to build a little higher, this section ends with an introduction to AutoCAD 2008's newly enhanced 3D visualization and presentation features.

Chapter 5

Get Ready to Draw

CAD programs are different from other drawing programs. You need to pay attention to little details like object properties and the precision of the points that you specify when you draw and edit objects. If you just start drawing objects without heeding these details, you'll end up with an unruly mess of imprecise geometry that's hard to edit, view, and plot.

This chapter introduces you to the AutoCAD tools and techniques that help you prevent CAD messes. This information is essential before you start drawing and editing objects, procedures that I describe in Chapters 6 and 7.

When you first start using AutoCAD, its most daunting requirement is the number of property settings and precision controls that you need to pay attention to — even when you draw a simple line. Unlike many other programs, it's not enough to draw a line in a more-or-less adequate location and then slap some color on it. But all those settings and controls can inspire the feeling that you have to find out how to drive a Formula 1 car to make a trip down the street. (The advantage is that, after you *are* comfortable in the driver's seat, AutoCAD will take you on the long-haul trips and get you there faster.)

Following are the three keys to good CAD drawing practice:

- ✔ Pay attention to and manage the *properties* of every object that you draw — especially the layer that each object is on.

- ✔ Pay attention to and utilize the *named objects* in every drawing — the layers, text styles, block definitions, and other non-graphical objects that serve to define the look of all the graphical objects in the drawing.

- ✔ Pay attention to and control the *precision* of every point and distance that you use to draw and edit each object.

These can seem like daunting tasks at first, but the following three sections help you cut them down to size.

Managing Your Properties

All the objects that you draw in AutoCAD are like good Monopoly players: They own *properties.* In AutoCAD, these properties aren't physical things; they're an object's characteristics, such as layer, color, linetype, lineweight, and plot style. You use properties to communicate information about the characteristics of the objects you draw, such as the kinds of real-world objects they represent, their materials, their relative location in space, or their relative importance. In CAD, you also use properties to organize objects for editing and plotting purposes.

You can view — and change — all of an object's properties in the Properties palette. In Figure 5-1, the Properties palette shows properties for a line object.

To toggle the Properties palette on and off, click the Properties button on the Standard toolbar or use the Ctrl+1 key combination. Before you select an object, the Properties palette displays the *current properties* — properties that AutoCAD applies to new objects when you draw them. After you select an object, AutoCAD displays the properties for that object. If you select more than one object, AutoCAD displays the properties that they have in common.

Putting it on a layer

Every object has a *layer* as one of its properties. You may be familiar with layers — independent drawing spaces that stack on top of each other to create an overall image — from using drawing programs. AutoCAD, like most

CAD programs, uses layers as the primary organizing principle for all the objects that you draw. You use layers to organize objects into logical groups of things that belong together; for example, walls, furniture, and text notes usually belong on three separate layers, for a couple of reasons:

- ✔ Layers give you a way to turn groups of objects on and off — both on the screen and on the plot.

- ✔ Layers provide the most efficient way of controlling object color, linetype, lineweight, and plot style.

So, to work efficiently in AutoCAD, you first create layers, assigning them names and properties such as color and linetype. Then you draw objects on those layers. When you draw an object, AutoCAD automatically puts it on the *current* layer — the layer that you see in the Layers toolbar drop-down list when no objects are selected.

Figure 5-1:
A line rich in properties.

Before you draw any object in AutoCAD, you should set an appropriate layer current — creating it first, if necessary, by using the procedure described later in this section. If the layer already exists in your drawing, you can make it the current layer by choosing it in the Layers toolbar, as shown in Figure 5-2.

Figure 5-2:
Set a
current
layer before
you draw.

Make sure that no objects are selected before you use the Layer drop-down list to change the current layer. (Press the Esc key twice to be sure.) If objects are selected, the Layer drop-down list displays (and lets you change) those objects' layers. When no objects are selected, the Layer drop-down list displays (and lets you change) the current layer.

Stacking up your layers

How do you decide what to call your layers and which objects to put on them? Some industries have developed layer guidelines, and many offices have created documented layer standards. Some projects even impose specific layer requirements. (But be careful; if someone says, "You need a brick layer for this project," that can mean a couple of different things.) Ask experienced CAD drafters in your office or industry how they use layers in AutoCAD. If you can't find any definitive answer, create a chart of layers for yourself. Each row in the chart should list the layer name, default color, default linetype, default lineweight, and what kinds of objects belong on that layer. If you use named plot styles to control your plotted output, add default plot style to the list — that's not necessary for traditional color-based plotting.

If you forget to set an appropriate layer before you draw an object, you can select the object and then change its layer by using either the Properties palette or the Layer drop-down list.

Accumulating properties

Besides layers, the remaining object properties that you're likely to want to use often are color, linetype, lineweight, and possibly plot style. Table 5-1 summarizes these four properties.

Table 5-1	Useful Object Properties
Property	*Controls*
Color	Displayed color and plotted color or line width
Linetype	Displayed and plotted dash-dot line pattern
Lineweight	Displayed and plotted line width
Plot style	Plotted characteristics (see Chapter 13)

Long before AutoCAD was able to display lineweights on the screen and print those same lineweights on paper, object *colors* controlled the printed lineweight of objects. AutoCAD 2000 introduced a more logical system, where you could assign an actual plotted thickness to *objects*. As logical as that method seems, the older method, in which the color of objects determines their plotted lineweight, continues to dominate. You may find yourself working this way even in AutoCAD 2008, for compatibility with drawings (and coworkers) that use the old way, as described in the "About colors and lineweights" sidebar.

AutoCAD gives you two different ways of controlling object properties:

- ✔ **By Layer:** Each layer has a default color, linetype, lineweight, and plot style property. Unless you tell AutoCAD otherwise, objects inherit the properties of the layers on which they're created. AutoCAD calls this approach controlling properties *By Layer*.

- ✔ **By Object:** AutoCAD also enables you to override an object's layer's property setting and give the object a specific color, linetype, lineweight, or plot style that differs from the layer's. AutoCAD calls this approach controlling properties *By Object*.

About colors and lineweights

AutoCAD drafters have traditionally achieved different printed lineweights by mapping various on-screen display colors of drawing objects to different plotted lineweights. A company may decide that red lines are to be plotted thin, green lines are to be plotted thicker, and so on. Not many people plotted in color until recently, so few folks minded the fact that color was used for a different purpose.

More recent versions of AutoCAD have lineweight as an inherent property of objects and the layers that they live on. Lineweights are handy, but they have quirks. Watch for these problems as you work with them:

✔ Although lineweights may have been assigned to objects in a drawing that you open, you won't necessarily see them on the screen. You must turn on the Show/Hide Lineweight button on the AutoCAD status bar (the button labeled LWT).

✔ On a slow computer or in a complex drawing, showing lineweights may cause AutoCAD to redraw the screen more slowly when you zoom and pan.

✔ You may need to zoom in on a portion of the drawing before the differing lineweights become apparent.

If you've worked with other graphics programs, you may be used to assigning properties such as color to specific objects. If so, you'll be tempted to use the By Object approach to assigning properties in AutoCAD. Resist the temptation. Did you catch that? One more time: *Resist the temptation*.

In almost all cases, it's better to create layers, assign properties to each layer, and let the objects on each layer inherit that layer's properties. Here are some benefits of using the By Layer approach:

✔ You can easily change the properties of a group of related objects that you put on one layer. You simply change the property for the layer, not for a bunch of separate objects.

✔ Experienced drafters use the By Layer approach, so if you work with drawings from other people, you'll be much more compatible with them if you do it the same way. You'll also avoid getting yelled at by irate CAD managers, whose job duties include haranguing any hapless newbie who assigns properties By Object.

If you take my advice and assign properties By Layer, all you have to do is set layer properties in the Layer Properties Manager dialog box (I tell you how in this section), as shown in Figure 5-3. Before you draw any objects, make sure the Color Control, Linetype Control, and Lineweight Control drop-down lists on the Properties toolbar are set to ByLayer, as shown in Figure 5-4. If the drawing is set to use color-based plot styles instead of named plot styles (see Chapter 13), the Plot Style Control drop-down list will be inactive and will display ByColor.

Figure 5-3:
Use layer
properties
to control
object
properties.

Figure 5-4:
ByLayer all
the way.

If the drawing is set to use named plot styles instead of color-based plot styles (see Chapter 13), the Plot Style Control drop-down list should also display ByLayer.

If you want to avoid doing things the wrong way and getting yelled at by CAD managers, don't assign properties to objects in either of these ways:

✔ Don't choose a specific color, linetype, lineweight, or plot style from the appropriate drop-down list on the Properties toolbar or from the Properties palette and then draw the objects.

✔ Don't draw the objects, select them, and then choose a property from the same drop-down lists.

If you prefer to do things the right way, assign these properties By Layer, as I describe in this section.

AutoCAD 2008's new SETBYLAYER command lets you correct those non-ByLayer properties — choose Modify➪Change to ByLayer and answer the prompts at the command line. The new SETBYLAYERMODE system variable controls which specific properties get reset. For more information, refer to SETBYLAYER and SETBYLAYERMODE in the online help.

Creating new layers

If a suitable layer doesn't exist, you need to create one by using the Layer Properties Manager dialog box. Follow these steps:

1. **Click the Layer button on the Layers toolbar; or type** LAYER **(or** LA**) at the command line and press Enter.**

Don't forget the 2D Drafting & Annotation workspace and Dashboard in both AutoCAD and AutoCAD LT. I show how to use them in Chapter 3, but as I mention there, I'm going to be using the tried-and-true AutoCAD Classic workspace for most of the book. If you *are* a convert to the Dashboard, just mouse over the panels and read the tooltips to find out where things are.

   The Layer Properties Manager dialog box appears. A new drawing has only one layer: Layer 0. You need to add the layers necessary for your drawing.

2. **Click the New Layer button (the little yellow explosion just above the Status column) to create a new layer.**

   A new layer appears. AutoCAD names it Layer1 but highlights the name in an edit box so you can type a new name to replace it easily, as shown in Figure 5-5.

Figure 5-5:
Adding a new layer in the Layer Properties Manager dialog box.

3. **Type a name for the new layer.**

Type the layer name with *initial caps* (only the first letter of words in uppercase). Layer names written completely in uppercase are much wider, which means that they often get truncated in the Layers toolbar's Layer drop-down list.

4. On the same line as the new layer, click the color block or color name (White by default) of the new layer.

The Select Color dialog box appears, as shown in Figure 5-6.

Figure 5-6:
The Select
Color dialog
box.
Magenta is
selected
from the
Standard
Colors list.

The normal AutoCAD color scheme — AutoCAD Color Index (ACI) — provides 255 colors. So many choices are overkill for ordinary drafting.

For now, stick with the first nine colors — the ones that appear in a single, separate row to the left of the ByLayer and ByBlock buttons on the Index Color tab of the Select Color dialog box — for the following reasons:

- These colors are easy to distinguish from one another.

- Using a small number of colors makes configuring your plot parameters easier. (I describe the procedure in Chapter 13.)

AutoCAD (but not AutoCAD LT) provides an even more extravagant set of color choices than the 255 shown on the Index Color tab. In the Select Color dialog box, the True Color tab offers a choice of more than 16 million colors, which you can specify by using HSL (Hue Saturation Luminance) or RGB (Red Green Blue) numbers. The Color Books tab enables you to use PANTONE and RAL color schemes, which are popular in publishing. If your work requires tons of colors or close color matching between the computer screen and printed output, you're probably familiar with the relevant color palette and how to use it. If you're using AutoCAD for ordinary drafting or design, stick with the AutoCAD Color Index palette.

5. Click a color to select it as the color for this layer and click OK.

The Layer Properties Manager dialog box reappears. In the Color column, the new layer color changes to either the name or the number of the color that you selected.

AutoCAD's first seven colors have both numbers and standard names: 1 = red, 2 = yellow, 3 = green, 4 = cyan, 5 = blue, 6 = magenta, and 7 = white (which appears black when displayed on a white background). The remaining 248 colors have numbers only.

6. **On the same line as the new layer, click the Linetype name of the new layer.**

   The default AutoCAD linetype is Continuous, which means no gaps in the line.

   The Select Linetype dialog box appears, as shown in Figure 5-7.

Figure 5-7:
The Select
Linetype
dialog box.

If you already loaded the linetypes you need for your drawing, or if the template file you started from has some linetypes loaded, the Select Linetype dialog box displays them in the Loaded Linetypes list. If not, click the Load button to open the Load or Reload Linetypes dialog box. By default, AutoCAD displays linetypes from the standard AutoCAD or AutoCAD LT linetype definition file — `acad.lin` for imperial units drawings or `acadiso.lin` for metric units drawings (`acadlt.lin` and `acadltiso.lin` in AutoCAD LT). Load the desired linetype by selecting its name and clicking the OK button.

Unless you have a really good reason (for example, your boss tells you so), avoid loading or using any linetypes labeled ACAD_ISO. These linetypes are normally used only in metric drawings and rarely even then. They overrule everything I'm trying to show you about printed lineweight in what follows, so if at all possible, just say NO to ACAD_ISO. I promise you'll find it easier to use the linetypes with the more descriptive names: CENTER, DASHED, and so on.

7. **Click the desired linetype in the Loaded Linetypes list to select it as the linetype for the layer; say that really fast five times and then click OK.**

   The Select Linetype dialog box disappears, returning you to the Layer Properties Manager dialog box. In the Name list, the linetype for the selected layer changes to the linetype you just chose.

8. **On the same line as the new layer, click the new layer's lineweight.**

   The Lineweight dialog box appears, as shown in Figure 5-8.

Figure 5-8:
The
Lineweight
dialog box.

9. **Select the lineweight you want from the scrolling list and click OK.**

   The lineweight 0.00 mm tells AutoCAD to use the thinnest possible lineweight on the screen and on the plot. I recommend that, for now, you leave lineweight set to Default and instead map screen color to plotted lineweight, as described briefly in the "About colors and lineweights" sidebar, earlier in this chapter, and in greater detail in Chapter 13.

   The default lineweight for the current drawing is defined in the Lineweight Settings dialog box. After you close the Layer Properties Manager dialog box, choose Format⇨Lineweight or enter **LWEIGHT** (or **LW**) at the command line to change the default lineweight.

   You use the plot style property to assign a named plot style to the layer, but only if you're using named plot styles in the drawing. (Chapter 13 explains why you might not want to.) The Plot property controls whether the layer's objects appear on plots. Toggle this setting off for any layer whose objects you want to see on the screen but hide on plots.

10. **If you want to add a description to the layer, scroll the layer list to the right to see the Description column, click in the Description box corresponding to your new layer, and type a description.**

    If you choose to use layer descriptions, stretch the Layer Properties Manager dialog box to the right so that you can see the descriptions without having to scroll the layer list.

11. **Repeat Steps 2 through 10 to create any other layers that you want.**

12. **Select the new layer that you want to make current and click the Set Current button (the green check mark).**

The current layer is the one on which AutoCAD places new objects that you draw.

13. **Click OK to accept the new layer settings.**

The Layer Control drop-down on the Layers toolbar now displays your new layer as the current layer.

After you create layers, you can set any one of them to be the current layer. Make sure that no objects are selected and then choose the layer name from the Layer drop-down list on the Layers toolbar.

A load of linetypes

This chapter's layer-creation procedure shows how to load a single linetype. But AutoCAD comes with a whole lot of linetypes, and there are other ways of working with them. You don't have to go through the Layer Properties Manager dialog box to load linetypes. You can perform the full range of linetype management tasks by choosing Format⇨Linetype, which displays the Linetype Manager dialog box. This dialog box is similar to the Select Linetype dialog box described in the layer-creation procedure, but it includes some additional options.

In the Linetype Manager dialog box, click the Load button to display the Load or Reload Linetypes dialog box; you can load multiple linetypes in one fell swoop by holding down the Shift or Ctrl key while you click linetype names. As in most Windows dialog boxes, Shift-clicking lets you select all objects between the first and second clicks, and Ctrl-clicking lets you select multiple objects even if they aren't next to each other.

When you load a linetype, AutoCAD copies its *linetype definition* — a formula for how to create the dashes, dots, and gaps in that particular linetype — from the acad.lin (imperial units) or acadiso.lin (metric units) file into the drawing. (The files are acadlt. lin and acadltiso.lin, respectively, in

AutoCAD LT.) The definition doesn't automatically appear in other drawings; you have to load each linetype that you want to use into each drawing in which you want to use it. If you find yourself loading the same linetypes repeatedly into different drawings, consider adding them to your template drawings instead. (See Chapter 4 for information about templates and how to create them.) After you add linetypes to a template drawing, all new drawings that you create from that template will start with those linetypes loaded automatically.

Don't go overboard on loading linetypes. For example, you don't need to load *all* the linetypes in the acad.lin file on the off chance that you might use them all someday. The resulting linetype list would be long and unwieldy. Most drawings require only a few linetypes, and most industries and companies settle on a half dozen or so linetypes for common use. Your industry, office, or project may have guidelines about which linetypes to use for which purposes.

If you're the techno-dweeb type and don't mind editing a text file that contains linetype definitions, you can define your own linetypes. Choose Contents⇨Customization Guide⇨Custom Linetypes in the AutoCAD 2008 online help system.

Manipulating layers

After you create layers and draw objects on them, you can turn a layer off or on to hide or show the objects on that layer. In the Layer Properties Manager dialog box, the first three icons to the right of the layer name control AutoCAD's layer visibility modes:

- ✔ **Off/On:** Click the light bulb icon to toggle visibility of all objects on the selected layer. AutoCAD does not regenerate the drawing when you turn layers back on. (I give you the lowdown on regenerations in Chapter 8.)

- ✔ **Freeze/Thaw:** Click the sun icon to toggle off visibility of all objects on the selected layer. Click the snowflake icon to toggle visibility on. AutoCAD regenerates the drawing when you thaw layers.

- ✔ **Lock/Unlock:** Click the padlock icon to lock and unlock layers. When a layer is locked, you can see but not edit objects on that layer.

You can rearrange column order by simply dragging and dropping the column label to a new place. And you can right-click any column label to display a menu from which you can turn columns off and on.

Off/On and Freeze/Thaw do almost the same thing — both settings let you make objects visible or invisible by layer. In the old days, turning layers off and on was often a faster process than thawing frozen layers because thawing layers always required regenerating the drawing. But modern computers, modern operating systems, and recent AutoCAD versions make regenerations much less of an issue on all but the largest drawings. You'll probably find it makes no appreciable difference whether you freeze and thaw layers or turn them off and on.

You can turn layers off and on, freeze and thaw them, and lock and unlock them by clicking the appropriate icons in the Layer drop-down list on the Layers toolbar.

Say you have a floor plan of a house that includes a layer showing the framing and another layer showing the wiring. You'd practically never show both of those elements on the same drawing, so you'd need to do some layer management when you showed your drawing to the framers or the electricians. Rather than turning a dozen layers off and a different dozen layers on when you want a different view into your drawing, you can save groups of layer settings as a named *layer state*. You can manage your layer states in the appropriately named Layer States Manager dialog box by clicking the Layer States Manager button in the Layer Properties Manager.

In AutoCAD 2008, you can access the Layer States Manager without going through the Layer Properties Manager. Choose Format⇨Layer States Manager or enter LAYERSTATES at the command line.

AutoCAD 2008 now fades locked layers, giving you a really effective visual reference without confusing you about which layers might be locked or not. You can control the amount of fading by setting a non-zero value for the system variable LAYLOCKFADECTL. Turn off the fading altogether by setting this value to 0.

If you find yourself using lots of layers, you can create *layer filters* to make viewing and managing the layer list easier. A *group filter* is simply a subset of layers that you choose (by dragging layer names into the group filter name or by selecting objects in the drawing). A *property filter* is a subset of layers that AutoCAD creates and updates automatically based on layer property criteria that you define (for example, all layers whose names contain the word *Wall* or whose color is green). To find out more, click the Help button on the Layer Properties Manager dialog box and read about the New Property Filter and New Group Filter buttons.

Both AutoCAD and AutoCAD LT include a set of layer tools that, in previous releases, were part of the Express Tools that I mention in Chapter 1 (and therefore not available in LT). You can access these Layer Tools through the Format menu (see Figure 5-9) and a subset of them by opening the Layers II toolbar. Layer Isolate and Layer Off are especially useful — you simply click an object to specify the layer to isolate (that is, fade all layers except the chosen one) or turn off altogether. For more information, open the online help system and choose User's Guide⇨Create and Modify Objects⇨Control the Properties of Objects⇨Work with Layers⇨Use Layers to Manage Complexity.

Prior to AutoCAD 2008, Layer Isolate turned off the visibility of all layers except those on which the objects you picked reside. AutoCAD 2008's LAYISO command (Format⇨Layer Tools⇨Layer Isolate) incorporates the same layer fading feature described previously for locked layers — and it locks the layers as well. Set it up the way you want by typing **S** (for Settings) and pressing Enter and then typing the option letter for the specific settings you want. Look up LAYISO in the online help Index for more information. This may seem like a small change, but it's one of my favorite new features!

Using Named Objects

Every drawing includes a set of *symbol tables,* which contain *named objects.* For example, the *layer table* contains a list of the layers in the current drawing, along with the settings for each layer (color, linetype, on/off setting, and so on). Each of these table objects, be it a layer or some other type, has a name, so Autodesk decided to call them *named objects* (duh!).

Figure 5-9:
Tooling
through the
Layer Tools.

Neither the symbol tables nor the named objects appear as graphical objects in your drawing. They're like the hard-working pit crew that keeps the cars running smoothly behind the scenes. The named objects include

- Layers (covered in this chapter)
- Linetypes (covered in this chapter)
- Text styles (see Chapter 10)
- Table styles (see Chapter 10)
- Dimension styles (see Chapter 11)
- Block definitions and xrefs (see Chapter 14)
- Layouts (see Chapter 4)

When you use commands such as LAYER, LINETYPE, and DIMSTYLE, you are creating and editing named objects. After you've created named objects in a drawing, AutoCAD DesignCenter gives you the tools to copy them to other drawings.

Using AutoCAD DesignCenter

DesignCenter is a dumb name for a useful, if somewhat busy, palette. (Chapter 2 describes how to turn on and work with palettes.) The DesignCenter palette is handy for borrowing data from all kinds of drawings. Whereas the Properties palette, described earlier in this chapter, is concerned with object properties, the DesignCenter palette deals primarily with named objects: layers, linetypes, block (that is, symbol) definitions, text styles, and other organizational objects in your drawings.

The DesignCenter palette (shown in Figure 5-10) consists of a toolbar at the top, a set of tabs below that, a tree view pane on the left, and a content pane on the right. The tree view pane displays a Windows Explorer–like navigation panel, showing drawing files and the symbol tables contained in each drawing. The content pane usually displays the contents of the selected drawing or symbol table.

Toolbar   Tabs

Figure 5-10:
The
AutoCAD
DesignCent
er palette.

Tree view pane   Content pane

The four tabs just below the DesignCenter toolbar control what you see in the tree view and content panes:

- ✔ **Folders:** This tab shows the folders on your local and network drives, just like the Windows Explorer Folders pane does. Use this tab if the drawing you want to copy from isn't currently open in AutoCAD.

- ✔ **Open Drawings:** This tab shows the drawings that are currently open in AutoCAD. Use this tab to copy named objects between open drawings.

✔ **History:** This tab shows drawings that you've recently browsed in DesignCenter. Use this tab to jump quickly to drawings that you've used recently on the Folders tab.

✔ **DC Online:** This tab shows parts libraries that are available on Autodesk's and other companies' Web sites. This tab is essentially an advertising vehicle for software companies offering to sell you symbol libraries and manufacturers encouraging you to specify their products. Browse the offerings on this tab to see whether any of the online libraries can be useful in your work.

The toolbar buttons further refine what you see in the tree view and content panes. A few of these buttons toggle different parts of the panes.

The following steps outline the procedure for using DesignCenter to copy named objects from one drawing to another. See the next section, "Copying layers between drawings," for a specific example.

1. **If it isn't already open, choose Tools⇨Palettes⇨DesignCenter to open the DesignCenter palette.**

   You can also click DesignCenter on the Standard toolbar or press Ctrl+2.

2. **Select or load the drawing(s) whose content you want to view or use into the navigation pane on the left.**

   If the source drawing is already open, you can access its content from the Open Drawings tab. If the source drawing is not open but is stored on your hard drive or network, click Load on the DesignCenter toolbar and navigate to the file's location in the Folders tab.

3. **In the Open Drawings tab (if the source drawing is currently open) or the Folders tab (if the source drawing is not open) of the tree view pane, click the + sign beside the source file to expand the list of named object categories.**

   The list of named object categories appears in a list in the tree view pane on the left and as icons in the content pane on the right.

4. **In the tree view pane, select the category of named object you want to copy.**

   The content pane now displays the individual named objects within the named object category. For example, in Figure 5-10 (shown previously), the Layers category is selected in the tree view pane, and icons for each named layer are shown in the content pane.

5. **In the content pane, select the objects you want to copy. Right-click and choose Add [object] to drawing, or simply drag-and-drop them into the drawing area.**

   Use Shift or Ctrl to select multiple named objects.

Copying layers between drawings

The previous set of steps outlined the general procedure for copying named objects from one drawing to another by using DesignCenter. The following steps show a specific example: copying layers from one drawing to another. You can use the same technique to copy dimension styles, layouts, linetypes, table styles, and text styles.

1. **Toggle the DesignCenter palette on by clicking the DesignCenter button on the Standard toolbar or by pressing Ctrl+2.**

2. **Open a drawing (the *source* drawing) containing named objects you want to copy.**

   You can also use the Folders tab, the Load button, or the Search button to load a drawing into DesignCenter without opening it in AutoCAD.

3. **Open or create a second drawing (the *destination* drawing) into which you want to copy the named objects. Make this the current drawing.**

   If you used the Folders tab, the Load button, or the Search button in Step 2, skip to Step 5; DesignCenter already displays the drawing you selected on the Folders tab.

4. **Click the Open Drawings tab to display your currently opened drawings in DesignCenter's tree view pane on the left.**

5. **If DesignCenter doesn't display the list of named objects indented underneath the source drawing (the one you opened in Step 2), as shown in Figure 5-10, click the plus sign next to the drawing's name to display that list.**

6. **Click Layers in the tree view pane to display the source drawing's layers in the content pane.**

7. **Select one or more layers in the content pane.**

8. **Right-click a selected layer in the content pane and choose Add Layer(s), or drag-and-drop them into the drawing.**

   AutoCAD copies the layers into the current drawing, using the colors, linetypes, and other settings from the source drawing.

If the current drawing contains a layer whose name matches the name of one of the layers you're copying, AutoCAD doesn't change the current drawing's layer definition. For example, if you add a layer named Doors whose color is red into a drawing that already includes a layer called Doors whose color is green, the destination drawing's Doors layer remains green. Named objects from DesignCenter never overwrite objects with the same name in the destination drawing. AutoCAD always displays the message `Duplicate definitions will be ignored` even if there aren't any duplicates.

If you're repeatedly copying named objects from the same drawings or folders, add them to your DesignCenter favorites list. On the Folders tab, right-click the drawing or folder and choose Add to Favorites from the menu. This procedure adds another shortcut to your list of favorites.

- ✔ To see your favorites, click the DesignCenter toolbar's Favorites button.
- ✔ To return to a favorite, double-click its shortcut in the content pane.

Controlling Your Precision

Drawing precision is vital to good CAD drafting practice, even more than for manual drafting. If you think CAD managers get testy when you assign properties by object instead of by layer, wait until they berate someone who doesn't use precision techniques when creating drawings in AutoCAD.

In CAD, lack of precision makes later editing, hatching, and dimensioning tasks much more difficult and time consuming.

- ✔ Small errors in precision in the early stages of creating or editing a drawing often have a big effect on productivity and precision later.
- ✔ Drawings may guide manufacturing and construction projects; drawing data may drive automatic manufacturing machinery. Huge amounts of money, even lives, can ride on a drawing's precision.

CAD precision versus accuracy

You often hear the words *precision* and *accuracy* used interchangeably, but it's useful to understand the difference. In this book, when I use the word *precision*, I mean controlling the placement of objects so they lie exactly where you want them to lie in the drawing. For example, lines whose endpoints meet must meet exactly, and a circle that's supposed to be centered on the coordinates 0,0 must be drawn with its center exactly at 0,0. I use *accuracy* to refer to the degree to which your drawing matches its real-world counterpart. An accurate floor plan is one in which the dimensions of the CAD objects equal the dimensions of the as-built house. In a sense, then, it's not the drawing that should be accurate — it's the house!

CAD precision usually helps produce accurate drawings, but that's not always the case. You can produce a precise CAD drawing that's inaccurate because you started from inaccurate information (for example, the contractor gave you a wrong field measurement). Or you might deliberately exaggerate certain distances to convey the relationship between objects more clearly on the plotted drawing. Even where you must sacrifice accuracy, aim for precision.

In recognition of these facts, a passion for precision permeates the profession. Permanently. Precision is one of the characteristics that separates CAD from ordinary illustration-type drawing work. The sooner you get fussy about precision in AutoCAD, the happier everyone is.

In the context of drawing objects, to use *precision* means to designate points and distances exactly, and AutoCAD provides a package of tools for doing so. Table 5-2 lists the more important AutoCAD precision techniques, plus the status bar buttons that you click to toggle some of the features.

Precision is especially important when you're drawing or editing *geometry* — the lines, arcs, and so on that make up whatever you're representing in the CAD drawing. Precision placement usually is less important with notes, leaders, and other *annotations* that describe, not show.

Table 5-2	Precision Techniques	
Technique	*Status Bar Button*	*Description*
Coordinate entry	—	Enables you to type exact X,Y coordinates.
Object snap overrides	—	Enables you to pick points on existing objects (lasts for one point pick).
Running object snaps	OSNAP	Enables you to pick points on existing objects (lasts for multiple point picks).
Snap	SNAP	Enables you to pick points on an imaginary grid of equally spaced hot spots.
Ortho	ORTHO	Enables you to constrain the crosshairs to move at an angle of 0, 90, 180, or 270 degrees from the previous point.
Direct distance entry	—	Enables you to point the crosshairs in a direction and type a distance.
Object snap tracking	OTRACK	Helps the crosshairs locate points based on multiple object snap points.

Technique	Status Bar Button	Description
Polar tracking	POLAR	Makes the crosshairs jump to specified angles.
Polar snap	—	Causes the crosshairs to move specific distances along polar tracking angles.

Before you draw objects, always check the status bar's SNAP, ORTHO, POLAR, OSNAP, and OTRACK buttons and set the buttons according to your precision needs.

- ✔ A button that looks depressed (not sad, just *pushed in*) indicates that the feature is *on*.
- ✔ A button that looks *popped out* indicates that the feature is *off*.

Keyboard capers: Coordinate entry

The most direct way to enter points precisely is to type numbers at the keyboard. AutoCAD uses these keyboard coordinate entry formats:

- ✔ Absolute Cartesian (X,Y) coordinates in the form *X,Y* (for example, 7, 4)
- ✔ Relative X,Y coordinates in the form *@X,Y* (for example, @3, 2)
- ✔ Relative polar coordinates in the form *@distance<angle* (for example, @6<45)

Cartesian coordinates are named for French philosopher René Descartes (who reasoned, "I think, therefore I am"). In his *Discourse on Method,* Descartes came up with the idea of locating any point on a planar surface by measuring its distance from a pair of axes (that's *axes* as in more than one axis, not the tool for chopping wood). In this book, I refer to Cartesian coordinates as X,Y coordinates.

AutoCAD locates *absolute X,Y coordinates* with respect to the 0,0 point of the drawing — usually its lower-left corner. AutoCAD locates *relative X,Y coordinates* and *relative polar coordinates* with respect to the previous point that you picked or typed. Figure 5-11 demonstrates how to use all three coordinate formats to draw a pair of line segments that start at absolute coordinates 2,1; go 3 units to the right and 2 units up; then go 4 units at an angle of 60 degrees.

AutoCAD also understands *absolute polar coordinates* in the form *distance<angle,* but this format is almost never useful.

Figure 5-11: Coordinating from the keyboard.

Relative polar coordinates   Relative X,Y coordinates   Absolute X,Y coordinates

You can view coordinate locations by moving the crosshairs around in the drawing area and reading the Coordinates area at the left end of the status bar. The X,Y coordinates should change as you move the crosshairs. If the coordinates don't change, click the Coordinates area until the command line says <Coords on>. Although it's not apparent at first, there are, in fact, two <Coords on> display modes: absolute coordinates and polar coordinates. If you start a command such as LINE, pick a point, and then click the Coordinates area a few times, the display changes from coordinates off to live absolute coordinates (X,Y position) to live polar coordinates (distance and angle from the previous point). The live polar coordinates display mode is the most informative most of the time.

When you type coordinates at the command line, do *not* add any spaces because AutoCAD interprets a space as though you've pressed Enter. This "Spacebar = Enter" weirdness is a productivity feature that's been in AutoCAD forever. It's easier to find the spacebar than the Enter key when you're entering lots of commands and coordinates in a hurry — and it's especially handy for touch typists who are all thumbs.

If you're working in architectural or engineering units, the default unit of entry is _inches,_ not feet.

- To specify feet, you must enter the symbol for feet after the number. For example:

    6' for 6 feet

- You can enter a dash to separate feet from inches, as architects often do:

    6'–6" is 6 feet, 6 inches.

- Both the dash and the inch mark are optional when you're entering coordinates and distances.

    AutoCAD understands **6'6"** and **6'6** as the same as **6'–6"**.

- If you're typing a coordinate or distance that contains fractional inches, you _must_ enter a dash — not a space — between the whole number of inches and the fraction.

    6'6–1/2 (or **6'–6–1/2**) represents 6 feet, 6½ inches.

- If all this dashing about confuses you, enter partial inches by using decimals instead.

    6'6.5 is the same as **6'6–1/2"** to AutoCAD, whether you're working in architectural or engineering units.

Grab an object and make it snappy

After you've drawn a few objects precisely in a new drawing, the most efficient way to draw more objects with equal precision is to grab _points,_ such as endpoints, midpoints, or quadrants, on the existing objects. AutoCAD calls these points _object snap points_ because the program pulls, or snaps, the crosshairs to a point on an existing object. The object snap feature in general, and object snap points in particular, are informally called _osnaps._

AutoCAD provides two kinds of object snapping modes.

- **Object snap _overrides_:** An object snap override is active for a single pick.
- **_Running_ object snaps:** A running object snap stays in effect until you turn it off.

Grabbing points with object snap overrides

Here's how you draw precise lines by using object snap overrides:

1. **Open a drawing containing some geometry.**

2. **Turn off running osnap mode by clicking the OSNAP button on the status bar until the button appears to be pushed out and the words `<Osnap off>` appear on the command line.**

Although you can use object snap overrides while running object snap mode is turned on, you should turn off running osnap mode while you're getting familiar with object snap overrides. After you've gotten the hang of each feature separately, you can use them together.

3. **Start the LINE command by clicking the Line button on the Draw toolbar or typing LINE (or L) and pressing Enter.**

AutoCAD prompts you to select the starting point of the line:

```
Specify first point:
```

4. **Hold down the Shift key, right-click anywhere in the drawing area, and release the Shift key.**

The object snap menu appears, as shown in Figure 5-12.

If you find the Shift+right-click sequence awkward, you can avoid it by using the Object Snap toolbar instead. To turn the toolbar on, point to any toolbar button, right-click, and choose Object Snap. Now you can activate an object snap override by clicking its toolbar button.

Figure 5-12:
The object snap right-click menu.

```
⊶ Temporary track point
⌐° From
   Mid Between 2 Points
   Point Filters          ▸
──────────────────────────
∕ Endpoint
∕ Midpoint
✕ Intersection
✕ Apparent Intersect
┈ Extension
──────────────────────────
◎ Center
✪ Quadrant
○ Tangent
──────────────────────────
⊥ Perpendicular
∥ Parallel
∘ Node
⊠ Insert
⊬ Nearest
Ⓧ None
──────────────────────────
ⴖ Osnap Settings...
```

5. **Choose an object snap mode, such as Endpoint, from the object snap menu.**

The object snap menu disappears, and the command line displays an additional prompt indicating that you've directed AutoCAD to seek out, for example, endpoints of existing objects:

```
_endp of:
```

6. **Move the crosshairs slowly around the drawing, pausing over various lines and other objects without clicking yet.**

   When you move the crosshairs near an object with an endpoint, a colored square icon appears at the endpoint, indicating that AutoCAD can snap to that point. If you stop moving the crosshairs for a moment, a tooltip displaying the object snap mode (for example, Endpoint) appears to reinforce the idea.

7. **Click when the Endpoint object snap square appears on the point you want to snap to.**

   AutoCAD snaps to the endpoint, which becomes the first point of the new line segment that you're about to draw. The command line prompts you to select the other endpoint of the new line segment:

   ```
   Specify next point or [Undo]:
   ```

   When you move the crosshairs around the drawing, AutoCAD no longer seeks out endpoints because object snap overrides last only for a single pick. Use the object snap right-click menu again to snap the other end of your new line segment to another point on an existing object.

8. **Use the Shift+right-click sequence described in Step 4 to display the object snap menu again, and then choose another object snap mode, such as Midpoint, from the object snap menu.**

   The command line displays an additional prompt indicating that you've directed AutoCAD to seek, for example, midpoints of existing objects:

   ```
   _mid of:
   ```

   When you move the crosshairs near the midpoint of an object, a colored triangle appears at the snap point. Each object snap type (endpoint, midpoint, intersection, and so on) displays a different symbol. If you stop moving the crosshairs, the tooltip text reminds you what the symbol means. Figure 5-13 shows what the screen looks like during this step.

9. **Draw additional line segments by picking additional points. Use the object snap right-click menu to specify a single object snap type before you pick each point.**

   Try the Intersection, Perpendicular, and Nearest object snaps. If your drawing contains arcs or circles, try Center and Quadrant.

10. **When you're finished experimenting with object snap overrides, right-click anywhere in the drawing area and choose Enter from the menu to end the LINE command.**

    There's a difference between right-clicking and Shift+right-clicking in the drawing area:

    - *Right-clicking* displays menu options for the current command (or common commands and settings when no command is active).

    - *Shift+right-clicking* always displays the same object snap menu.

Already object-snapped to endpoint   New line segment

About to object-snap to midpoint

Figure 5-13:
A snappy
line.

Running with object snaps

Often, you use an object snap mode (such as Endpoint) repeatedly. Use running object snaps to address this need. The following steps set a running object snap:

1. **Right-click the OSNAP button on the status bar.**

2. **Choose the Settings option.**

    The Object Snap tab on the Drafting Settings dialog box appears, as shown in Figure 5-14.

3. **Select one or more object snap modes by checking the appropriate boxes.**

4. **Click OK to close the dialog box.**

Figure 5-14:
Grabbing
multiple
object
features is
an osnap.

You click the OSNAP button on the status bar to toggle running object snap mode. After you turn on running object snap, AutoCAD hunts for points that correspond to the object snap modes you checked in the Drafting Settings dialog box. As with object snap overrides, AutoCAD displays a special symbol — such as a square for an endpoint object snap — to indicate that it has found an object snap point. If you keep the crosshairs still, AutoCAD also displays a tooltip that lists the kind of object snap point.

Use object snap overrides or running object snaps to enforce precision by making sure that new points you pick coincide *exactly* with points on existing objects. In CAD, it's not good enough for points to *almost* coincide or to look like they coincide. You lose points, both figuratively and literally, if you don't use object snaps or one of the other precision techniques covered in this chapter to enforce precision.

Most, but not all, object snap overrides have running object snap equivalents. For example, Endpoint, Midpoint, and Center work as either overrides or running object snaps, but Mid Between 2 Points works only in override mode.

Other precision practices

The following are some other AutoCAD precision techniques (refer to Table 5-2, earlier in this chapter):

✔ **Snap:** If you turn on snap mode, AutoCAD constrains the crosshairs to an imaginary rectangular grid of points at the spacing that you've specified. Follow these steps to turn on snap mode:

1. *Right-click the SNAP button on the status bar.*

2. *Choose the Settings option.*

   The Snap and Grid tab on the Drafting Settings dialog box appears.

3. *Enter a snap spacing in the Snap X Spacing field and click OK.*

Click the SNAP button on the status bar or Press F9 to toggle snap mode off and on. To use snap effectively, change the snap spacing frequently — changing to a smaller spacing as you zoom in and work on smaller areas. You often need to toggle snap off and on because selecting objects and some editing tasks are easier with snap off.

✔ **Ortho:** Ortho mode constrains the crosshairs to move at right angles (orthogonally) to the previous point. Click the ORTHO button on the status bar or Press F8 to toggle ortho mode. Because technical drawings often include lots of orthogonal lines, you may use ortho mode a lot.

✔ **Direct distance entry (DDE):** This point-and-type technique is an easy and efficient way to draw with precision. You simply point the crosshairs in a particular direction, type a distance at the command line, and press Enter. You can use DDE any time the crosshairs are anchored to a point, and the command line or dynamic input tooltip prompts you for another point or a distance.

You'll usually use DDE with ortho mode turned on to specify a distance in an orthogonal direction (0, 90, 180, or 270 degrees). You also can combine DDE with polar tracking to specify distances in non-orthogonal directions (for example, in angle increments of 45 degrees).

✔ **Object snap tracking:** This feature extends running object snaps so that you can locate points based on more than one object snap point. For example, you can pick a point at the center of a square by tracking to the midpoints of two perpendicular sides. Click OTRACK on the status bar or press F11 to toggle object snap tracking.

✔ **Polar tracking:** When you turn on polar tracking, the crosshairs jump to increments of the angle you selected. When the crosshairs jump, a tooltip label starting with `Polar:` appears. Right-click the POLAR button on the status bar and choose the Settings option to display the Polar Tracking tab on the Drafting Settings dialog box. Select an angle from the Increment Angle drop-down list and then click OK. Click the POLAR button on the status bar or press F10 to toggle polar tracking mode.

✔ **Polar snap:** You can force polar tracking to jump to specific incremental distances along the tracking angles by changing the snap type from grid snap to polar snap. For example, if you turn on polar tracking and set it to 45 degrees and turn on polar snap and set it to 2 units, polar tracking jumps to points that are at angle increments of 45 degrees and distance increments of 2 units from the previous point. Polar snap has a similar effect on object snap tracking.

To activate polar snap, follow these steps:

1. *Right-click the SNAP button on the status bar.*

2. *Choose the Settings option.*

    The Snap and Grid tab on the Drafting Settings dialog box appears.

3. *Click the Polar Snap radio button, type a distance in the Polar Distance text box, and then click OK.*

When you want to return to ordinary rectangular snap, as described at the beginning of this list, select the Grid Snap radio button in the Drafting Settings dialog box.

✔ **Temporary overrides:** Settings such as SNAP, ORTHO, and POLAR remain on until you turn them off. You can also use *temporary overrides,* which last only as long as you hold down their key or key combination. For example, with ortho turned off, holding down the Shift key puts AutoCAD into a temporary ortho mode for as long as you press Shift. For additional information, look up "temporary override keys" in the online help system.

If you're new to AutoCAD, its wide range of precision tools probably seems overwhelming at this point. Rest assured that there's more than one way to skin a cat precisely (with cats, accuracy is unimportant), and not everyone needs to understand all the ways. You can make perfectly precise drawings with a subset of AutoCAD's precision tools. I recommend these steps:

1. Get comfortable with typing coordinates, ortho mode, direct distance entry, and object snap overrides.

2. Become familiar with running object snaps and try Snap mode.

3. After you have all these precision features under your belt, feel free to experiment with polar tracking, polar snap, and object snap tracking.

It's easy to confuse the names of the snap and object snap (osnap) features. Remember that *snap* limits the crosshairs to locations whose coordinates are multiples of the current snap spacing. *Object snap (osnap)* enables you to grab points on existing objects, whether those points happen to correspond with the snap spacing or not.

Chapter 6

Where to Draw the Line

As you probably remember from your crayon and coloring book days, drawing stuff is *fun*. CAD imposes a little more discipline, but drawing stuff with AutoCAD is still fun. In computer-aided drafting, you usually start by drawing *geometry* — shapes such as lines, circles, rectangles, and so on — that represents the real-world object that you're documenting. This chapter shows you how to draw geometry.

After you've created some geometry, you'll probably need to add some dimensions, text, and hatching, but those elements come later (in Part III of this book). Your first task is to get the geometry right; then you can worry about labeling things.

Drawing geometry properly in AutoCAD depends on paying attention to object properties and the precision of the points that you specify to create the objects. I cover these matters in Chapter 5, so if you eagerly jumped to this chapter to get right to the fun stuff, take a moment to review that chapter first.

Introducing the AutoCAD Drawing Commands

For descriptive purposes, this chapter divides the drawing commands into three groups:

- ✔ Straight lines and objects composed of straight lines
- ✔ Curves
- ✔ Points

Table 6-1 offers an overview of the most important 2D drawing commands in AutoCAD. It describes the major command options and shows you how to access them from the command line (with the shortcut keys, or an "alias," in parentheses), the Draw menu, and the Draw toolbar. (Don't worry if not all the terms in the table are familiar to you; they become clear as you read through the chapter and use the commands.)

Table 6-1	AutoCAD Drawing Commands			
Button	*Command*	*Major Options*	*Toolbar Button*	*Draw Menu*
	LINE (L)	Start, end points	Line	Line
	RAY	Start point, point through which ray passes	None	Ray
	XLINE (XL)	Two points on line	Construction line	Construction line
	PLINE (PL)	Vertices	Polyline	Polyline
	POLYGON (POL)	Number of sides, inscribed/ circumscribed	Polygon	Polygon

Button	Command	Major Options	Toolbar Button	Draw Menu
	RECTANG (REC)	Two corners, dimensions, area, rotation	Rectangle	Rectangle
	ARC (A)	Various methods of definition	Arc	Arc; submenu for definition methods
	CIRCLE (C)	Three points, two points, tangent	Circle	Circle; sub-menu for definition methods
	REVCLOUD	Arc length	Revision Cloud	Revision Cloud
	DONUT (DO)	Inside, outside diameters	None	Donut
	SPLINE (SPL)	Convert polyline or create new	Spline	Spline
	ELLIPSE (EL)	Arc, center, axis	Ellipse	Ellipse; sub-menu for definition methods
	POINT (PO)	Point style	Point	Point; sub-menu for definition methods

If you're using the 2D Drafting & Annotation workspace in either AutoCAD 2008 or AutoCAD LT 2008, you'll find the first seven icons shown in Table 6-1 in the 2D Draw control panel of the Dashboard. There's a tiny down arrow at the end of the row, and clicking it gives you access to the remaining tool buttons in the Draw toolbar. For a quick practice lap with this workspace, look at Chapter 3, where I guide you along on a test drive. For most of this book, I use the AutoCAD Classic workspace; if you want to use 2D Drafting & Annotation and the Dashboard, just mouse over the tool buttons and read the tooltips to find out which one does what.

Many of the choices on the AutoCAD Draw menu open submenus containing several variations on each drawing command.

AutoCAD's drawing commands are highly interactive. You need to read and respond to the prompts at the dynamic tooltip next to the crosshairs or the command line. (If *command line* sounds to you like a military operation, not an essential AutoCAD concept, see Chapter 2.) Many of the command options that you see in command line prompts are available as well by pressing the up- and down-arrow keys to display the options at the dynamic tooltip. You can also right-click and select command options from the context-specific shortcut menu.

AutoCAD's Dynamic Input system displays a lot of the information that you used to have to look down to the command window to see. To use Dynamic Input, make sure the DYN button on the status bar is pressed in. Don't turn the command window off just yet though, especially if you're new to AutoCAD. I recommend that you keep the command window open and docked at all times.

So what's the best course: to enter drawing commands from the command line or to choose them from the menus or toolbars? I suggest that you start a drawing command the first few times by clicking its button on the Draw toolbar — until you remember its command name. After you click the button, fasten your eyes on the command window so that you see the name of the command and its command line options. Use the keyboard or the right-click menus to select options. After you're acquainted with a drawing command and decide that you like it enough to use it often, find out how to type its keyboard shortcut.

A few drawing commands, such as DONUT, aren't on the Draw toolbar; you have to type those or choose them from the Draw menu.

The Straight and Narrow: Lines, Polylines, and Polygons

As I harp on a bunch of times elsewhere in this book, CAD programs are for precision drawing, so you'll spend a lot of your AutoCAD time drawing objects composed of straight-line segments. This section covers these commands:

- ✔ **LINE (L):** Draws a series of straight line segments; each segment is a separate object.

- ✔ **PLINE (PL):** Draws a *polyline* — a series of straight and/or curved line segments; all the segments remain connected to each other as a single object.

- ✔ **RECTANG (REC):** Draws a polyline in the shape of a rectangle.
- ✔ **POLYGON (POL):** Draws a polyline in the shape of a regular polygon (that is, a closed shape with all sides equal and all angles equal).

The following additional straight-line drawing commands are also available in AutoCAD:

- ✔ **RAY:** Draws a *semi-infinite line* (a line that extends infinitely in one direction).
- ✔ **XLINE (XL):** Draws an *infinite line* (a line that extends infinitely in both directions).

The RAY and XLINE commands are used to draw *construction lines* that guide the construction of additional geometry. Drawing construction lines is less common in AutoCAD than in some other CAD programs. AutoCAD's many precision techniques often provide more efficient methods for creating new geometry than adding construction lines to your drawing does.

Toe the line

The LINE command in AutoCAD draws a series of one or more connected line segments. Well, it *appears* to draw a series of connected segments. In fact, each *segment,* or piece of a line with endpoints, is a separate object. This construction doesn't seem like a big deal until you try to move or otherwise edit a series of segments that you drew with the LINE command; you must select every piece separately. To avoid such a hassle, use polylines (described later in this chapter), not lines and arcs, when you want the connected segments to be a single object.

If you're used to drawing lines in other programs, you may find it confusing at first that AutoCAD's LINE command doesn't stop after you draw a single segment. AutoCAD keeps prompting you to specify additional points so that you can draw a series of (apparently) connected segments. When you're finished drawing segments, just press Enter to finish the LINE command.

Unlike a lot of the AutoCAD drawing commands, LINE doesn't offer a bunch of potentially confusing options. It has a Close option to create a closed polygonal shape and an Undo option to remove the most recent segment that you drew.

Like all drawing commands, LINE puts the line segments that it draws on the current layer and uses the current color, linetype, lineweight, and plot style properties. When you're doing real drafting, as opposed to just experimenting, make sure of the following:

- ✔ Make sure that you've set these properties correctly before you start drawing. (I recommend that you set color, linetype, lineweight, and, if you're using named plot styles, plot style to ByLayer.) See Chapter 5 for information on setting the current properties with the Properties toolbar.

✔ Make sure that you use one of AutoCAD's precision tools, such as object snaps, typed coordinates, and tracking, to ensure that you specify each object point precisely. Chapter 5 describes these tools.

Follow these steps to draw a series of line segments by using the LINE command:

1. **Set the desired layer current, and set other object properties that you want applied to the line segments that you'll draw.**

2. **Click the Line button on the Draw toolbar.**

   AutoCAD starts the LINE command and prompts you to select the first point.

3. **Specify the starting point by clicking a point or typing coordinates.**

   Remember to use one of the precision techniques I describe in Chapter 5 if you're doing real drafting. For the first point, object snap, snap, tracking, and typing coordinates all work well.

   AutoCAD prompts you to specify the other endpoint of the first line segment. The command line shows

   ```
   Specify next point or [Undo]:
   ```

   You can also see command prompts at the Dynamic Input tooltip beside the crosshairs by pressing the down-arrow key. The arrow icon on the dynamic tooltip is your indicator that there are options available.

4. **Specify additional points by clicking or typing.**

   Again, use one of the AutoCAD precision techniques if you're doing real drafting. For the second and subsequent points, all the techniques mentioned in the previous step work well, as do ortho and direct distance entry.

   After you specify the third point, AutoCAD adds the Close option. The command line shows

   ```
   Specify next point or [Close/Undo]:
   ```

5. **When you're finished drawing segments, end with one of these steps:**

   • Either press Enter or right-click anywhere in the drawing area and choose Enter from the right-click menu to leave the figure open.

   • Type **C** and press Enter or press the down arrow on your keyboard and choose Close from the menu (as shown in Figure 6-1) to close the figure.

   In either case, the empty command prompt indicates that the LINE command is finished.

Figure 6-1:
Line it up —
drawing line
segments
with the
LINE
command.

Connect the lines with polyline

The LINE command is fine for some drawing tasks, but the PLINE command is a better, more flexible choice in many situations. The PLINE command draws a special kind of object called a *polyline*. You may hear CAD drafters refer to a polyline as a *pline* because of the command name. (By the way, *pline* rhymes with *beeline* — in other words, it sounds like the place you stand after you drink a lot of beer at the ball game.)

The most important differences between the LINE and PLINE commands are these:

✔ **The LINE command draws a series of single-line segment objects.** Even though they appear to be linked on the screen, each segment is a separate object. If you move one line segment, the other segments that you drew at the same time don't move with it. The PLINE command, on the other hand, draws a single, connected, multi-segment object. If you select any segment for editing, your changes affect the entire polyline. Figure 6-2 shows how the same sketch drawn with the LINE and the PLINE commands responds when you select one of the objects.

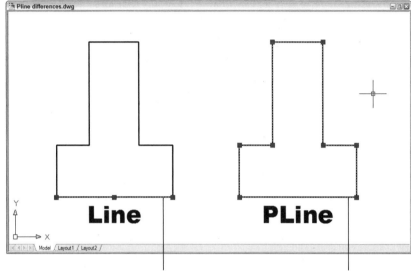

Figure 6-2:
Results of
drawing
with the
LINE and
PLINE
commands.

Each segment is a separate object   All segments form one object

Use the PLINE command instead of LINE in most cases where you need to draw a series of connected line segments. If you're drawing a series of end-to-end segments, there's a good chance that those segments are logically connected — for example, they might represent the outline of a single object or a continuous pathway. If the segments are connected logically, it makes sense to keep them connected in AutoCAD. The most obvious practical benefit of grouping segments together into a polyline is that many editing operations are more efficient when you use polylines. When you select any segment in a polyline for editing, the entire polyline is affected.

✔ **The PLINE command can draw curved segments as well as straight ones.**

✔ **You can add width to each segment of a polyline.** Polyline segment width is visually similar to lineweight, except that polyline segment width can be uniform or tapered. The ability to create polyline segments with line widths was more important in the old days, before AutoCAD had lineweight as an object property. People used to draw polylines with a small amount of width to show the segments as just slightly bolder than regular lines, which are always displayed as a single pixel wide. Nowadays, it's easier and more efficient to achieve this effect with object lineweights (as described in Chapter 5) or plot styles (as described in Chapter 13).

After you create a polyline, you can adjust its segments by grip editing any of the vertex points. (The little squares on the vertices in Figure 6-2 are called *grips;* see Chapter 7 for details on grip editing.) For more complicated polyline editing tasks, you can use the PEDIT command to edit the polyline, or you can convert the polyline to a collection of line and arc segments by using the EXPLODE command — although you lose any width defined for each segment when you explode a polyline.

Drawing polylines composed of straight segments is pretty much like drawing with the LINE command, as demonstrated in the following procedure. The PLINE command has lots of options, so watch the prompts! Use the down-arrow key to see the options listed at the crosshairs, or right-click to display the PLINE shortcut menu, or simply read the command line.

To draw a polyline composed of straight segments, follow these steps:

1. **Set the desired layer current, and set other object properties that you want applied to the polyline object that you'll draw.**

2. **Click the Polyline button on the Draw toolbar.**

   AutoCAD starts the PLINE command and prompts you to specify a start point.

3. **Specify the starting point by clicking a point or typing coordinates.**

   AutoCAD displays the current polyline segment line width at the command line and prompts you to specify the other endpoint of the first polyline segment:

   ```
   Current line-width is 0.0000
   Specify next point or
         [Arc/Halfwidth/Length/Undo/Width]:
   ```

4. **If the current line width isn't zero, change it to zero by typing the commands W, 0, 0, as shown in the following command line sequence:**

   ```
   Specify next point or
         [Arc/Halfwidth/Length/Undo/Width]: W
   Enter Specify starting width <0.0000>: 0
   Enter Specify ending width <0.0000>: 0
   Enter Specify next point or
         [Arc/Halfwidth/Length/Undo/Width]:
   ```

   Despite what you may think, a zero-width polyline segment is not the AutoCAD equivalent of writing with invisible ink. *Zero width* means "display this segment using the normal, single-pixel width on the screen."

5. **Specify additional points by clicking or typing.**

   After you specify the second point, AutoCAD adds the Close option to the prompt. The command line shows

   ```
   Specify next point or
         [Arc/Close/Halfwidth/Length/Undo/Width]:
   ```

   In addition, you can view and choose options from the Dynamic Input menu, as shown in Figure 6-3.

6. **After you finish drawing segments, either press Enter (to leave the figure open) or type C and press Enter (to close it).**

   AutoCAD draws the final segment. The blank command line indicates that the PLINE command is finished.

Figure 6-3:
Getting in
the PLINE.

In the following procedure, I spice things up a bit and give you a preview of coming (curvy) attractions by adding an arc segment to a polyline.

Just so you know, curved segments in polylines are *circular arcs* — pieces of circles that you can draw with AutoCAD's ARC command. AutoCAD can draw other kinds of curves, including ellipses and splines, but not within the PLINE command.

To draw a polyline that includes curved segments, follow these steps:

1. **Repeat Steps 1 though 5 of the previous procedure.**

2. **When you're ready to add one or more arc segments, type A and press Enter to select the Arc option.**

   The prompt changes to show arc segment options. Most of these options correspond to the many ways of drawing circular arcs in AutoCAD; see the "Arc-y-ology" section, later in this chapter. The command line shows

   ```
   Specify endpoint of arc or [Angle/CEnter/CLose/
           Direction/Halfwidth/Line/Radius/Second
           pt/Undo/Width]:
   ```

3. **Specify the endpoint of the arc by clicking a point or typing coordinates.**

   AutoCAD draws the curved segment of the polyline. The prompts continue to show arc segment options.

   Your options at this point include

   • Specifying additional points to draw more arc segments.

• Choosing another arc-drawing method (such as Center or Second pt).

• Returning to drawing straight-line segments with the Line option.

In this example, you return to drawing straight-line segments.

Perhaps the most useful of the alternative arc-drawing methods is Second pt. You can use it to gain flexibility in the direction of the arc, but at the cost of losing tangency of contiguous segments. Sometimes it's best not to go off on a tangent, anyway.

4. **Type** L **and press Enter to select the Line option.**

```
Specify endpoint of arc or
        [Angle/CEnter/CLose/Direction/Halfwidth/Line/
        Radius/Second pt/Undo/Width]: L
```

The prompt changes back to showing straight-line segment options.

```
Specify next point or
        [Arc/Close/Halfwidth/Length/Undo/Width]:
```

5. **Specify additional points by clicking or typing.**

6. **After you're finished drawing segments, either press Enter or type** C **and press Enter.**

Figure 6-4 shows some of the things that you can draw with the PLINE command by using straight segments, arc segments, or a combination of both.

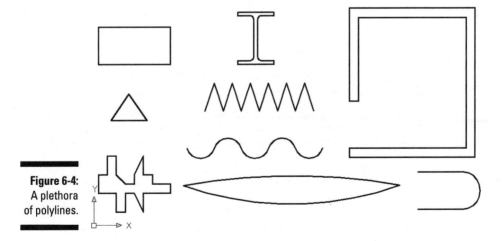

Figure 6-4:
A plethora
of polylines.

The LINE and PLINE commands work well for drawing a series of end-to-end single lines, but what if you want to draw a series of double lines to represent, for example, the edges of a wall or roadway? Here are some options:

- ✔ Use the AutoCAD MLINE command to draw *multilines* — series of two or more parallel straight lines. The AutoCAD multiline feature was full of limitations when it debuted over a decade ago, and despite some minor tweaks in AutoCAD 2006, it hasn't improved significantly since then. Look up the "MLINE" and "MLSTYLE" commands in AutoCAD's online help system if you'd like to tangle with this feature, but be prepared to spend time experimenting and struggling.

- ✔ In AutoCAD LT only, use the DLINE (DL), or Double Line, command to draw pairs of parallel line and/or arc segments. AutoCAD LT doesn't include the MLINE command, which, given MLINE's problems, probably is more of a blessing than a limitation. AutoCAD, on the other hand, doesn't include the DLINE command. (Score one for the little brother!)

- ✔ Use the PLINE command to draw a single set of connected line and/or arc segments, and then use the Offset command to create one or more sets of parallel segments. Chapter 7 covers the Offset command.

Square off with rectangle

You can use the PLINE or LINE command to draw a rectangle segment by segment. In most cases, though, you'll find it easier to use the special-purpose RECTANG command. The following procedure demonstrates how:

1. **Set the desired layer current, and set other object properties that you want applied to the rectangle that you'll draw.**

2. **Click the Rectangle button on the Draw toolbar.**

   AutoCAD starts the RECTANG command and prompts you to specify a point for one corner of the rectangle. The command line shows

   ```
   Specify first corner point or
           [Chamfer/Elevation/Fillet/Thickness/Width]:
   ```

   You can add fancy effects with the additional command options. The default options work best for most purposes. Look up "RECTANG command" in the AutoCAD help system if you want to know more about the options.

3. **Specify the first corner by clicking a point or typing coordinates.**

   AutoCAD prompts you to specify the other corner of the rectangle — the one that's diagonally opposite from the first corner.

   ```
   Specify other corner point or
           [Area/Dimensions/Rotation]:
   ```

4. Specify the other corner by clicking a point or typing coordinates.

If you know the size of the rectangle that you want to draw (for example, 100 units long by 75 units high), type relative coordinates to specify the dimensions (for example, **@100,75**). (Chapter 5 describes how to type coordinates.)

AutoCAD draws the rectangle.

Unlike the neglected MLINE command, the RECTANG command has improved considerably since its debut. You can now specify a rotation angle and — very handy for space planners — you can provide one dimension and an area. RECTANG will calculate the length of the other side and draw the rectangle.

Choose your sides with polygon

Rectangles and other closed polylines are types of *polygons,* or closed figures with three or more sides. The AutoCAD POLYGON command provides a quick way of drawing *regular polygons* — polygons in which all sides and angles are equal. (If regular polygons seem a little square, maybe that's because a square is a special case of a regular polygon!)

The following procedure demonstrates the POLYGON command:

1. Set the desired layer current, and set other object properties that you want applied to the polygon that you'll draw.

2. Click the Polygon button on the Draw toolbar.

AutoCAD starts the POLYGON command and prompts you to enter the number of sides for the polygon.

```
Enter number of sides <4>:
```

3. Type the number of sides for the polygon that you want to draw and press Enter.

The command line prompts you to specify the center point of the polygon.

```
Specify center of polygon or [Edge]:
```

You can use the Edge option to draw a polygon by specifying one side instead of the center and radius of an imaginary inscribed or circumscribed circle. The imaginary circle method is much more common.

4. Specify the center point by clicking a point or typing coordinates.

The command line prompts you to specify whether the polygon will be *inscribed in* (that is, the corners touch the circumference of the circle) or *circumscribed about* (that is, the sides are tangent to the circle) an imaginary circle whose radius you will specify in the following step:

```
Enter an option [Inscribed in circle/Circumscribed
        about circle] <I>:
```

5. **Type** I **or** C **and press Enter.**

   The command line prompts you to specify the radius of an imaginary circle.

   ```
   Specify radius of circle:
   ```

6. **Specify the radius by typing a distance or clicking a point.**

   AutoCAD draws the polygon.

   If you type a distance or you click a point with ortho turned on, the polygon will be aligned orthogonally, as shown in Figure 6-5.

Figure 6-5 shows the results of drawing plenty of polygons — a practice known as *polygony,* which, as far as I know, is still legal everywhere.

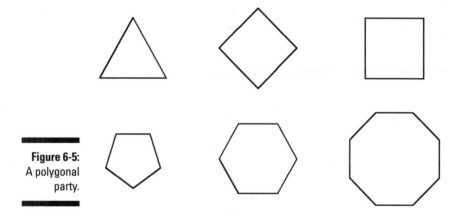

Figure 6-5:
A polygonal
party.

(Throwing) Curves

Although straight-line segments predominate in many CAD drawings, even the most humdrum, rectilinear design is likely to have a few curves. And if you're drawing car bodies or Gaudí buildings, your drawings will be almost nothing but curves! This section shows you how to use the following AutoCAD curve-drawing commands:

- **CIRCLE:** Draws circles (you were expecting rectangles, maybe?).

- **ARC:** Draws circular arcs — arcs cut from circles, not from ellipses, parabolas, or some other complicated curve.

- **ELLIPSE:** Draws ellipses and elliptical arcs.

✔ **SPLINE:** Draws smoothly flowing curves of a variety of shapes.

✔ **DONUT:** Draws filled-in annular rings and circles.

✔ **REVCLOUD:** Draws freeform "clouds," the most common application of which is to indicate revised areas in the drawing.

The following sections describe each command.

Going full circle

AutoCAD offers an easy way to draw circles, and it also offers . . . *other* ways. The easy way is to define the center point of the circle and then to define the radius or diameter. You can also define a circle by entering one of the following options of the command (for those other ways):

✔ **3P (3-Point):** Specify any three points on the circumference.

✔ **2P (2-Point):** Specify the endpoints of a diameter of the circle.

✔ **Ttr (Tangent-Tangent-Radius):** Specify two lines or other objects that are tangent to the circle and then specify its radius.

Whether these additional circle-drawing methods are useful or superfluous depends on the kinds of drawings that you make and how geometry is defined in your industry. Get familiar with the default center point/radius method and then try the other methods to see whether they may be helpful to you. If you find yourself going around in circles, you can always draw them the default way and move them into position with other geometry.

Follow these steps to use the CIRCLE command:

1. **Set the desired layer current and set other object properties that you want applied to the circle that you'll draw.**

2. **Click the Circle button on the Draw toolbar.**

    AutoCAD starts the CIRCLE command and prompts you to specify the center point of the circle. Press the down arrow on your keyboard to see the options at the dynamic input tooltip. The command line shows

    ```
    Specify center point for circle or [3P/2P/Ttr (tan tan
              radius)]:
    ```

    The prompts show the methods other than "center point plus radius" that you can use to draw circles in AutoCAD. (No, tan tan radius is not a mathematician's dance.) Look up "CIRCLE command" in the online help if you think you may have a use for these less common circle-drawing techniques.

3. **Specify the center point by clicking a point or typing coordinates.**

Use one of the precision techniques described in Chapter 5 if you're doing real drafting. Object snap, snap, and typing coordinates all work well for specifying the center point.

AutoCAD then prompts you to specify the circle's radius.

```
Specify radius of circle or [Diameter]:
```

Type **D** and press Enter if you prefer to enter the diameter rather than the radius and you've forgotten your two-times tables — or, more seriously, if the diameter is easier to type exactly than the radius is.

4. **Specify the radius by typing a distance or clicking a point.**

AutoCAD draws the circle, as shown in Figure 6-6.

Cen.-Rad.   **Cen.-Dia.**

Figure 6-6:
Pi R
squared;
circles R
round.

2Point   **3Point**   **Ttr**

Arc-y-ology

Arcs in AutoCAD are, quite simply, pieces of circles. As with circles, AutoCAD offers you an easy way to define arcs. Just specify three points on-screen to define the arc, easy as one-two-three. These points tell AutoCAD where to start the arc, how much to curve it, and where to end it.

Sounds pretty easy, right? So where's the problem? The trouble is that you must nearly always specify arcs more exactly than is possible by using this method. AutoCAD helps you specify such arcs, too, but the procedure ain't easy.

You can start your arc by specifying the center of the arc or the start point. If you choose the Center option, AutoCAD prompts you for the center point first and the start point second. AutoCAD defines arcs counterclockwise, so pick a start point in a clockwise direction from the endpoint. After you specify the center and start point, AutoCAD presents several options you can choose, including the following:

- ✔ **Angle:** This option specifies the included angle that the arc sweeps out. A 180-degree angle, for example, is a semicircle.
- ✔ **Length of chord:** This option specifies the length of an imaginary straight line connecting the endpoints of the arc. Most people seldom or never use this option.
- ✔ **Endpoint:** This option specifies where the arc ends. It's the default option and is often the easiest to use.

If you specify the start point as the first option, you can choose among the following three command line options as well:

- ✔ **Center:** This option prompts you for the arc's center point and then finishes with the three options listed previously.
- ✔ **End:** This option specifies the endpoint of the arc. You then need to define the angle the arc covers, its direction, its radius, or its center point.
- ✔ **Second point:** This is the default option. The second point you choose is not the endpoint; instead, it's a point on the arc that, along with the start and end points, defines how much the arc curves. After you enter the second point, you must enter an endpoint to complete the arc.

To get a feel for how these permutations can be strung together to create different arc-drawing methods, choose Draw⇨Arc and look at the impressive submenu that unfurls, as shown in Figure 6-7.

The following example shows how you draw an arc with the default start point/second point/endpoint method:

1. **Set the desired layer current and set other object properties that you want applied to the arc that you'll draw.**

2. **Click the Arc button on the Draw toolbar.**

    AutoCAD starts the ARC command and prompts you to specify the first endpoint of the arc. The command line shows

    ```
    Specify start point of arc or [Center]:
    ```

3. **Specify the start point by clicking a point or typing coordinates.**

    AutoCAD prompts you to specify a second point on the arc.

Figure 6-7:
A deluge of
Arc options,
with the
results of
using some
of those
options.

4. **Specify a second point on the arc by clicking a point or typing coordinates.**

   The second point lies somewhere along the curve of the arc. AutoCAD determines the exact curvature of the arc after you choose the final endpoint in the following step. To align the second point with an existing object, use an object snap mode.

   AutoCAD prompts you to specify the other endpoint of the arc; as you move the crosshairs around, AutoCAD shows how the arc will look.

5. **Specify the other endpoint of the arc by clicking a point or typing coordinates.**

   AutoCAD draws the arc, as shown previously in Figure 6-7.

As you may recall, pressing Enter repeats the last command. What often throws new AutoCAD users is that Enter does not repeat the *options* of the last command. If you go through the command prompts or the Draw menu to draw an arc using the Center, Start, End option, for example, pressing Enter is not going to repeat that method — it's going to repeat the ARC command in its default form, and the three points you pick will probably not give you the arc you meant to draw. Luckily though, AutoCAD has you covered. If you right-click instead of pressing Enter to repeat the ARC command, the first option is Repeat Start, Center, End.

Solar ellipses

An *ellipse* is like a warped circle with a *major* (long) axis and a *minor* (short) axis. These axes determine the ellipse's length, width, and degree of curvature. An *elliptical arc* is an arc cut from an ellipse.

The AutoCAD ELLIPSE command provides a straightforward way of drawing an ellipse: You specify the two endpoints of one of its axes and then specify an endpoint on the other axis. But like the ARC command, the ELLIPSE command offers a bunch of other options:

- ✔ **Arc:** This option generates an elliptical arc, not a full ellipse. You define an elliptical arc just as you do a full ellipse. The following methods for creating an ellipse apply to either.

- ✔ **Center:** This option requires that you define the center of the ellipse and then the endpoint of an axis. You can then either enter the distance of the other axis or specify that a rotation around the major axis defines the ellipse. If you choose the latter, you can enter (or drag the ellipse to) a specific rotation for the second axis that, in turn, completely defines the ellipse.

- ✔ **Rotation:** With this option, you specify an angle, which defines the curvature of the ellipse — small angles make fat ellipses (0 degrees creates a circle, in fact), and large angles make skinny ellipses. The name of the option, Rotation, has something to do with rotating an imaginary circle around the first axis. If you can figure out the imaginary circle business, then you have a better imagination than I do.

The following command line example creates an ellipse by using the default endpoints of the axes method. Figure 6-8 shows an ellipse and an elliptical arc.

```
Command: ELLIPSE
Specify axis endpoint of ellipse or [Arc/Center]: pick or
        type the first endpoint of one axis
Specify other endpoint of axis: pick or type the other
        endpoint of one axis
Specify distance to other axis or [Rotation]: pick or type
        the endpoint of the other axis
```

You can create elliptical arcs (as opposed to the circular arcs that the AutoCAD ARC command draws) by using the Arc option of the ELLIPSE command; it's perfect for drawing those cannonball trajectories! Alternatively, you can draw a full ellipse and use the TRIM or BREAK command to cut a piece out of it.

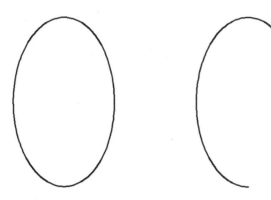

Figure 6-8:
An ellipse
and
elliptical
arc.

Splines: The sketchy, sinuous curves

Most people use CAD programs for precision drawing tasks: straight lines, carefully defined curves, precisely specified points, and so on. AutoCAD is not the program to free your inner artist — unless your inner artist is Mondrian. Nonetheless, even meticulously created CAD drawings sometimes need freeform curves. The AutoCAD *spline object* is just the thing for the job.

You can use AutoCAD splines in two ways:

✔ Eyeball the location and shape of the curve and don't worry too much about getting it just so. That's the freeform, sketchy, not-too-precise approach that I describe here.

✔ Specify their control points and curvature characteristics precisely.

Beneath their easygoing, informal exterior, AutoCAD splines are really highly precise, mathematically defined entities called *NURBS curves* (NonUniform Rational B-Spline curves). Mathematicians and some mechanical and industrial designers care a lot about the precise characteristics of the curves they work with. For those people, the AutoCAD SPLINE and SPLINEDIT commands include a number of advanced options. Look up "spline curves" in the AutoCAD online help if you need precision in your splines.

Drawing splines is straightforward, if you ignore the advanced options. The following procedure draws a freeform curve with the SPLINE command:

1. **Set the desired layer current and set other object properties that you want applied to the spline that you'll draw.**

2. **Click the Spline button on the Draw toolbar.**

AutoCAD starts the SPLINE command and prompts you to specify the first endpoint of the spline. The command line shows:

```
Specify first point or [Object]:
```

3. **Specify the start point by clicking a point or typing coordinates.**

   AutoCAD prompts you to specify additional points:

```
Specify next point:
```

4. **Specify additional points by clicking or typing coordinates.**

   After you pick the second point, press the down-arrow key to display additional options at the dynamic input tooltip. The command line shows

```
Specify next point or [Close/Fit tolerance] <start
         tangent>:
```

   Because you're drawing a freeform curve, you usually don't need to use object snaps or other precision techniques when picking spline points.

5. **Press Enter after you've chosen the final endpoint of your spline.**

   AutoCAD prompts you to specify tangent lines for each end of the spline:

```
Specify start tangent:
Specify end tangent:
```

   The Specify start tangent and Specify end tangent prompts can control the curvature of the start points and endpoints of the spline. In most cases, just pressing Enter at both prompts to accept the default tangents works fine.

6. **Press Enter twice to accept the default tangent directions.**

   AutoCAD draws the spline.

Figure 6-9 shows some examples of splines.

Figure 6-9:
A slew of
splines.

After you've drawn a spline, you can grip edit it to adjust its shape. See Chapter 7 for information about grip editing. If you need finer control over spline editing, look up the SPLINEDIT command in the AutoCAD online help.

Donuts: The circles with a difference

Creating a *donut* is a simple way to define a single object that consists of two concentric circles with the space between them filled.

When you start the DONUT command, AutoCAD prompts you for the inside diameter and the outside diameter — the size of the hole and the size of the donut — as measured across their widest points. After you've entered these values, AutoCAD prompts you for the center point of the donut. But one donut is rarely enough, so AutoCAD keeps prompting you for additional center points until you press Enter (the AutoCAD equivalent of saying, "no, really, I'm full now!").

The following example draws a regulation-size donut, with a 1.5-inch hole and 3.5-inch outside diameter. Figure 6-10 shows two kinds of donuts.

```
Command: DONUT
Specify inside diameter of donut <0.5000>: 1.5
Specify outside diameter of donut <1.0000>: 3.5
Specify center of donut or <exit>: pick or type the center
          point of one or more donuts
```

You can use the DONUT command to create a filled circle — also known as a jelly-filled donut. Just specify an inside diameter of 0.

Figure 6-10:
Donuts, plain and jelly-filled.

Plain   **Jelly-Filled**

Revision clouds on the horizon

It's customary in many industries to submit a set of drawings at a stage of completion and then submit them again later with *revisions* — corrections, clarifications, and requested changes. Often, the recipients like to locate changed stuff easily. A common drafting convention in many industries is to call attention to revised items by drawing freeform clouds around them. The REVCLOUD command makes quick work of drawing such clouds.

Drawing revision clouds is easy, after you understand that you click with the mouse only once in the drawing area. That one click defines the starting point for the cloud's perimeter. After that, you simply move the crosshairs around, and the cloud takes shape. When you return to near the point that you clicked in the beginning, AutoCAD automatically closes the cloud.

The following command line example shows you how to draw a revision cloud. Figure 6-11 shows what revision clouds look like.

```
Command: REVCLOUD
Minimum arc length: 0.5000   Maximum arc length: 0.5000
          Style: Normal
Specify start point or [Arc length/Object/Style] <Object>:
          pick a point along the perimeter of your future
          cloud
Guide crosshairs along cloud path... sweep the crosshairs
          around to define the cloud's perimeter
```

You don't need to click again. Simply move the crosshairs around without clicking. AutoCAD draws the next *lobe* of the cloud when your crosshairs reach the Minimum arc length distance from the end of the previous lobe.

Continue moving the crosshairs around until you return to the point where you clicked first.

Here are a few tips for using revision clouds:

✔ It's a good idea to put revision clouds on their own layer so that you can choose to plot with or without the clouds visible.

✔ You'll probably find it easier to control the shape of revision clouds if you turn off ortho mode before you start the command.

✔ You may need to add a triangle and number, as shown in Figure 6-11, to indicate the revision number. A block with an attribute is a good way to handle this requirement: Chapter 14 covers blocks and attributes.

Figure 6-11:
Cloud cover.

Min. arc length = 0.5
Max. arc length = 0.5

Min. arc length = 0.5
Max. arc length = 1.0

Min. arc length = 1.0
Max. arc length = 1.0

If the revision cloud's lobes are too small or too large, erase the cloud, restart the REVCLOUD command, and use the command's Arc Length option to change the minimum and maximum arc lengths. The default minimum and maximum lengths are 0.5 (or 15 in metric drawings) multiplied by the DIM-SCALE (DIMension SCALE) system variable setting. If you make the minimum and maximum lengths equal (which is the default), the lobes will be approximately equal in size. If you make them unequal, there will be more variation in lobe size — you'll get fluffier clouds. Fortunately, all of these options are more than most non-meteorologists will need. If you've set DIMSCALE properly during your drawing setup procedure (see Chapter 4), REVCLOUD should do a pretty good job of guessing reasonable default arc lengths.

Scoring Points

I thought about not covering points in this book, but I didn't want you complaining that *AutoCAD 2008 For Dummies* is pointless.

The word *point* describes two different things in AutoCAD:

- ✔ A *location* in the drawing that you specify (by typing coordinates or clicking with the mouse)
- ✔ An *object* that you draw with the POINT command

Throughout this chapter and most of the book, I tell you to specify points — that's the location meaning. This section tells you how to draw point objects.

A *point object* in AutoCAD can serve two purposes:

- ✓ **Points often identify specific locations in your drawing to other people who look at the drawing.** A point can be something that displays on the screen, either as a tiny dot or as another symbol, such as a cross with a circle around it.

- ✓ **You can use points as precise object snap locations.** Think of them as construction points. For example, when you're laying out a new building, you might draw point objects at some of the engineering survey points and then snap to those points as you sketch the building's shape with the polyline command. You use the *Node* object snap mode to snap to AutoCAD point objects.

What makes AutoCAD point objects complicated is their almost limitless range of display options, provided to accommodate the two different kinds of purposes just described (and possibly some others that I haven't figured out yet). You use the Point Style dialog box, shown in Figure 6-12, to specify how points should look in the current drawing.

DDPTYPE is the command that opens the Point Style dialog box. You can access it from the menus by choosing Format⇨Point Style. The top portion of the dialog box shows the available point display styles. Most of the choices do pretty much the same thing. Just click one of the squares that says "hey, that's a point!" to you.

Figure 6-12:
The Point Style dialog box controls the way point objects appear on-screen.

The first choice, a single-pixel dot, is hard to see on the screen, and the second choice, invisible (a stealth point?), is impossible to see. Avoid these choices if you want your point objects to show up on the screen and on plots. The single-pixel dot, which is the default display style, works well if you use point objects as object snap locations and don't want obtrusive points on plots.

The remaining settings in the Point Style dialog box control the size at which points appear on the screen at different zoom resolutions. The default settings often work fine, but if you're not satisfied with them, click the Help button to find out how to change them.

After you specify the point style, placing points on-screen is easy; the following example shows you how.

```
Command: POINT
Current point modes: PDMODE=0 PDSIZE=0.0000
Specify a point: pick or type the coordinates of a
             location in the drawing
```

PDMODE and PDSIZE in the command prompt are system variables that correspond to the point display mode and display size options in the Point Style dialog box. If you want to know exactly how the system variables correspond to the dialog box choices, you have all the makings of a successful CAD nerd. Click the Help button in the Point Style dialog box to find out more (about the system variables — not about yourself).

If you start the POINT command from the Draw toolbar or the Draw⇨Point⇨ Multiple Point menu, it will repeat automatically — that is, the command line will prompt you repeatedly to Specify a point. When you're finished drawing points, press Esc to finish the command for good. If the command doesn't repeat automatically, and you want to draw more points, press the Enter key to repeat the POINT command and pick another location on the screen. Repeat as required: Enter, pick, Enter, pick, Enter, pick . . . you get the point.

Chapter 7

Edit for Credit

· ·

In This Chapter

▶ Using command-first editing

▶ Selecting objects with maximum flexibility

▶ Moving, copying, and stretching objects

▶ Manipulating whole objects

▶ Changing pieces of objects

▶ Editing with grips

▶ Editing object properties

· ·

*E*diting objects is the flip side of creating them, and in AutoCAD, you spend a lot of time editing — far more than drawing objects from scratch. That's partly because the design and drafting process is by its nature repetitive, and also because CAD programs make it easy to edit objects cleanly.

When you edit objects in AutoCAD, you need to be just as concerned about specifying precise locations and distances as you are when you originally create the objects. Make sure that you're familiar with the precision techniques described in Chapter 5 before you apply the editing techniques from this chapter to real drawings.

Commanding and Selecting

AutoCAD offers three styles of editing:

✔ Command-first editing

✔ Selection-first editing

✔ Direct object manipulation (grip editing)

AutoCAD refers to command-first editing as *verb-noun editing* and to selection-first editing as *noun-verb editing*. When you see this terminology — for example, in the Options dialog box or the online help system — don't worry, you haven't dropped back into your fifth-grade English class!

Command-first editing

With *command-first editing*, you start a command and then select the objects on which the command works. This style of editing may seem backward to you at first unless you're a longtime user of AutoCAD. Command-first editing works well for power users who are in a hurry and who are willing to memorize most of the commands they need to do their work. It's also the *only* way to use some of the editing commands. It's no surprise that command-first editing is the classic editing style in AutoCAD, and the one method with which you need to be most comfortable.

Selection-first editing

In *selection-first editing*, you perform the same steps — in the same order — as in most Windows applications: Select the object first and then choose the command.

Selection-first editing tends to be easier to master and makes AutoCAD more approachable for new and occasional users.

Direct object manipulation

Direct manipulation is a refinement of selection-first editing in which you perform common editing operations by using the mouse to grab the selected object and perform an action on it, such as moving all or part of it to a different place in the drawing. No named command is involved; the act of moving the mouse and clicking the mouse buttons in certain ways causes the editing changes to happen. AutoCAD supports direct manipulation through a powerful but somewhat complicated technique called *grip editing*. *Grips* are the little square handles that appear on an object when you select it. You can use the grips to stretch, move, copy, rotate, scale, or otherwise edit the object. These grip-editing techniques can make selection-first editing almost as powerful as command-first editing.

Choosing an editing style

This chapter emphasizes command-first editing. (I also discuss grip editing at the end of the chapter.) AutoCAD is fundamentally a command-first program. AutoCAD started out offering *only* command-first editing and later added selection-first methods; AutoCAD 2008 inherits this ancestral trait. I stress command-first editing for the following reasons:

- ✔ It's the editing style that's been in AutoCAD the longest, and the one with which experienced AutoCAD users are most familiar.
- ✔ It works consistently with all editing commands — some editing commands remain command-first only.
- ✔ It provides added object selection flexibility, which is useful when you work on complicated, busy drawings.

After you know how to do command-first editing, you can simply reverse the order of many editing operations to do them selection-first style instead. But if you don't get familiar with command-first editing in the beginning, you'll be bewildered by a few useful AutoCAD commands that work only in the command-first style, such as FILLET and BREAK. (Commands such as these ignore any already selected objects and prompt you to select objects.)

Much of the information in this chapter assumes that you're using the default AutoCAD selection settings. If object selection or grip editing works differently than I describe in this chapter, choose Tools⇨Options to open the Options dialog box and then check the settings on the Selection tab. The seven check box settings listed next should be turned on, as shown in Figure 7-1. (All other check box settings should be turned off.)

- ✔ Selection Preview When a Command Is Active
- ✔ Selection Preview When No Command Is Active
- ✔ Noun/Verb Selection
- ✔ Implied Windowing
- ✔ Object Grouping
- ✔ Enable Grips
- ✔ Enable Grip Tips

For information on what these options do, click the small question mark button beside the Close button at the top-right corner of the Options dialog box and then click one of the options.

Figure 7-1:
Setting
selection
options in
the Options
dialog box.

Grab It

Part of AutoCAD's editing flexibility comes from its object selection flexibility. For example, command-first editing offers 16 selection modes! (I describe the most useful ones in this chapter.) Don't worry, though; you can get by most of the time with three selection modes:

- Selecting a single object
- Enclosing objects in a window selection box (pick left corner and then right corner)
- Including part or all objects in a crossing selection box (pick right corner and then left corner)

One-by-one selection

The most obvious way to select objects is to pick (by clicking) them one at a time. You can build up a selection set cumulatively with this pick-one-object-at-a-time selection mode, but this cumulative convention may be different from what you're used to. In most Windows programs, if you select one object and then another, the first object is *de*selected, and the second one selected; only the object you select last remains selected. In AutoCAD, *all* the objects you select, one at a time, remain selected and are added to the selection set, no matter how many objects you pick. (You can change this behavior to make AutoCAD work like Windows does by turning on the Use Shift to Add to Selection option on the Option dialog box's Selection tab, but I suggest that you don't change it.) Most editing commands affect the entire group of selected objects.

Selection boxes left and right

Selecting objects one at a time works great when you want to edit a small number of objects, but many CAD editing tasks involve editing lots of objects. Do you really want to pick 132 lines, arcs, and circles, one at a time?

Like most Windows graphics programs, AutoCAD provides a selection window feature for grabbing a bunch of objects in a rectangular area. As you may guess by now, the AutoCAD version of this feature is a bit more powerful than the similar feature in other Windows graphics programs and, therefore, slightly confusing at first. AutoCAD calls its version *implied windowing*.

If you click a blank area of the drawing — that is, not on an object — you're *implying* to AutoCAD that you want to specify a selection window, or box. If you move the crosshairs to the right before picking the other corner of the selection box, you're further implying that you want to select all objects that reside *completely* within the selection box. If you move the crosshairs to the left before picking the other corner of the selection box, you're implying that you want to select all objects that reside completely *or partially* within the selection box.

The AutoCAD terminology for these two kinds of selection boxes gets a little confusing:

- The move-to-the-right, only-select-objects-completely-within-the-box mode is called *window* object selection.
- The move-to-the-left, select-objects-completely-or-partially-within-the-box mode is called *crossing* object selection.

Fortunately, AutoCAD gives you visual cues that there's a difference. As you move to the right, the window box appears as a rectangle with blue fill and a solid border. As you move to the left, the crossing box appears as a rectangle with green fill and a dashed border.

Figures 7-2 and 7-3 show a window box and a crossing box in action.

Pick point 2

Figure 7-2:
A window
selection
box, drawn
left to right,
selects only
objects
completely
within
the box.

Pick point 1   Selection box

You can mix and match selecting individual objects, specifying a window box, and specifying a crossing box. Each selection adds to the current selection set, allowing you to build up an enormously complicated selection of objects and then operate on them with one or more editing commands.

You can press the Shift key in combination with any of the three standard selection modes — single object, window box, and crossing box — to *remove* already-selected objects from the selection set. This feature is especially useful when you're building a selection set in a crowded drawing; you can select a big batch of objects by using Window or Crossing, and then hold down the Shift key while selecting to remove the objects that you want to exclude from the editing operation.

Pick point 2

Figure 7-3:
A crossing
selection
box, drawn
right to left,
selects
objects
that are
completely
or partially
within
the box.

Selection box   Pick point 1

Perfecting Selecting

When you edit in command-first mode, you have all the selection options
described in the previous section — single object, window box, and crossing
box — plus a slew of others. If you type **?** and press Enter at any Select
objects prompt, AutoCAD lists all the selection options at the command line:

```
Window/Last/Crossing/BOX/ALL/Fence/WPolygon/CPolygon/
     Group/ Add/Remove/Multiple/Previous/Undo/AUto/
     SIngle/SUbobject/Object
```

Subobject and Object apply specifically to 3D solids and are therefore not
available in AutoCAD LT. In any event, this book doesn't cover 3D construction, but for information on viewing 3D drawings, see Chapter 9.

Table 7-1 summarizes the most useful command-first selection options.

Table 7-1	Some Useful Command-First Selection Options
Option	*Description*
Window	All objects completely within a rectangle that you specify by picking two points
Last	The last object you drew that's still visible in the drawing area
Crossing	All objects within or crossing a rectangle that you specify by picking two points
ALL	All objects on layers that aren't frozen or locked and that are in the current space (model space or paper space)
Fence	All objects touching an imaginary polyline whose vertices you specify by picking points
WPolygon	All objects completely within a polygonal area whose corners you specify by picking points
CPolygon	All objects within or crossing a polygonal area whose corners you specify by picking points
Previous	The previous selection set that you specified

To use any of the command-first selection options at the `Select objects` prompt, type the uppercase letters indicated in Table 7-1 that correspond to the desired option and press Enter. After you're finished selecting objects, you must press Enter again to tell AutoCAD that you've finished selecting objects and want to start the editing operation.

AutoCAD's *Selection preview* features remove any doubt about which objects you're selecting. *Rollover highlighting* displays individual objects with a thick dashed lineweight as the crosshairs are moved over them. *Area selection* displays a transparent, colored highlight over multiple selections using window and crossing options. You can enable and disable both features on the Selection tab of the Options dialog box (refer to Figure 7-1).

The following example demonstrates how to use the ERASE command in command-first mode with several different selection options. The selection techniques used in this example apply to most AutoCAD editing commands.

1. Press Esc to make sure that no command is active and no objects are selected.

If any objects are selected when you start an editing command, the command, in most cases, will operate on those objects (selection-first editing) instead of prompting you to select objects (command-first editing). For the reasons that I describe earlier in this chapter, you should use the command-first editing style until you're thoroughly familiar with it.

Later, you can experiment with selection-first editing if you like. (Just reverse the sequence of commanding and selecting that I describe in this chapter.)

2. **Click the Erase button on the Modify toolbar.**

   AutoCAD displays the `Select objects` prompt at the command line and, if the DYN status bar button is pressed in, the dynamic input tooltip.

3. **Select two or three individual objects by clicking each one.**

   AutoCAD adds each object to the selection set. All the objects you select remain ghosted. AutoCAD displays the `Select objects` prompt.

4. **Specify a window selection box that completely encloses several objects.**

   Move the crosshairs to a point below and to the left of the objects, click, release the mouse button, move the crosshairs above and to the right of the objects, and click again.

   All objects that are completely within the box are selected.

5. **Specify a crossing selection box (Crossing) that encloses a few objects and cuts through several others.**

   Move the crosshairs to a point below and to the right of some of the objects, click, release the mouse button, move the crosshairs above and to the left of some of the objects, and click and release again.

   All objects that are completely within or cross through the box are selected. AutoCAD displays the `Select objects` prompt.

6. **Type WP and press Enter to activate the WPolygon selection option.**

   AutoCAD prompts you to pick points that define the selection polygon.

7. **Pick a series of points and press Enter.**

   Figure 7-4 shows an example. After you press Enter, AutoCAD selects all objects that are completely within the polygon.

8. **Press Enter to end object selection.**

   AutoCAD erases all the selected objects.

Notice how you were able to use a combination of object selection methods to build up a selection set and then press Enter to execute the command on the selected objects. Most AutoCAD editing commands work this way in command-first mode.

If, after erasing a selection set, you immediately realize that you didn't really mean to do away with so many objects, you can use the Undo button on the Standard toolbar to restore all of them. But AutoCAD has one additional unerase trick up its sleeve — the aptly named OOPS command. When you type **OOPS** and press Enter, AutoCAD restores the last selection set that you erased — even if you've run other commands after ERASE.

Figure 7-4:
Lassoing
objects
with a
WPolygon.

Ready, Set, Edit!

The following sections cover the most important AutoCAD editing commands, using command-first editing mode.

Table 7-2 lists AutoCAD's most frequently used editing commands. It describes the major command options and shows how to access them from the command line (with the shortcut keys, or *alias,* in parentheses), the Modify menu, and the Modify toolbar.

Button	Command	Major Options	Toolbar Button	Modify Menu
Table 7-2		**AutoCAD Modify Commands**		
	ERASE (E)	—	Erase	Erase
	COPY (CO)	Base point, Displacement	Copy	Copy

Button	Command	Major Options	Toolbar Button	Modify Menu
	MIRROR (MI)	Keep/Erase source objects	Mirror	Mirror
	OFFSET (O)	Distance, through point, erase, layer	Offset	Offset
	ARRAY (AR)	Rectangular, polar	Array	Array
	MOVE (M)	Base point, Displacement	Move	Move
	ROTATE (RO)	Specify angle, reference angle, copy	Rotate	Rotate
	SCALE (SC)	Scale factor, reference, copy	Scale	Scale
	STRETCH (S)	Base point, displacement	Stretch	Stretch
	LENGTHEN (LEN)	Delta, percent, total, dynamic	None	Lengthen
	TRIM (TR)	Projection, edge	Trim	Trim
	EXTEND (EX)	Projection, edge	Extend	Extend
	BREAK (BR)	At point, second point, pick two points	Break	Break
	JOIN (J)	Select lines, arcs, splines, polylines, elliptical arcs	Join	Join
	CHAMFER (CHA)	Distance, angle, polyline, multiple	Chamfer	Chamfer
	FILLET (F)	Radius, polyline, multiple	Fillet	Fillet
	EXPLODE (X)	Select objects	Explode	Explode

Whether you start an AutoCAD editing command by clicking a toolbar button, choosing a pull-down menu command, or typing a command name, in almost all cases, the command prompts you for points, distances, and options at the command line. Read the prompts during every step of the command, especially when you're figuring out how to use a new editing command. Otherwise, you're unlikely to complete the command successfully.

AutoCAD's dynamic input system displays command options at the crosshairs. When you see a dynamic input tooltip with a down arrow icon, press the down-arrow key on the keyboard to display the command options in a menu. You then can use the mouse to select an option (see Figure 7-5). Pressing the up-arrow key displays previous input.

As I describe in Chapter 5, maintaining precision when you draw and edit is crucial to good CAD work. If you've used a drawing program and are accustomed to moving, stretching, and otherwise editing objects by eye, you'll need to suppress that habit when you edit in AutoCAD. Nothing ruins a drawing faster than by-eyeball editing, in which you shove objects around until they look okay, without worrying about precise distances and points.

Figure 7-5: Choosing command options from the dynamic input menu.

The big three: Move, Copy, and Stretch

Moving, copying, and stretching are, for many drafters, the three most common editing operations. AutoCAD obliges this need with the MOVE, COPY, and STRETCH commands.

Base points and displacements

The MOVE, COPY, and STRETCH commands all require that you specify how far and in what direction you want the objects moved, copied, or stretched. After you've started the command and selected the objects to be edited, AutoCAD prompts you for two pieces of information:

```
Specify base point or [Displacement] <Displacement>:
Specify second point or <use first point as displacement>:
```

In a not-so-clear way, these prompts say that two possible methods exist for you to specify how far and in what direction you want the objects copied, moved, or stretched:

- ✔ **The most common way is to pick or type the coordinates of two points that define a displacement vector.** AutoCAD calls these points the *base point* and the *second point* (hence, it's called the *base point method*). Imagine an arrow pointing from the base point to the second point — that arrow defines how far and in what direction the objects get copied, moved, or stretched.

- ✔ **The other way is to type an X,Y pair of numbers that represents a distance rather than a point.** This distance is the absolute displacement that you want to copy, move, or stretch the objects (thus it's called the *displacement method*).

How does AutoCAD know whether your response to the first prompt is a base point or a displacement? It depends on how you respond to the second prompt. (Is that confusing, or what?) First, you pick a point on-screen or enter coordinates at the Base point prompt. Next, there are a couple of possibilities:

- ✔ If you then pick or type the coordinates of a point at the second point prompt, AutoCAD says to itself, "Aha — displacement vector!" and moves the objects according to the imaginary arrow pointing from the base point to the second point.

- ✔ If you press Enter at the second prompt (without having typed anything), AutoCAD says, "Aha — displacement distance," and uses the X,Y pair of numbers that you typed at the first prompt as an absolute displacement distance.

What makes this displacement business even more confusing is that AutoCAD lets you pick a point at the first prompt and press Enter at the second prompt. AutoCAD still says, "Aha — displacement distance," but now it treats the coordinates of the point you picked as an absolute distance. If the point you picked has relatively large coordinates, the objects can get moved way outside the normal drawing area as defined by the limits. The objects fly off into space, and you probably won't see where they've gone because you're zoomed into part of your normal drawing area; it just looks to you like the objects have vanished! In short, be careful when you press Enter during the MOVE, COPY, and STRETCH commands. Press Enter in response to the second prompt only if you want AutoCAD to use your response to the first prompt as an absolute displacement. If you make a mistake, click the Undo button to back up and try again. You can use Zoom Extents (described in Chapter 8) to look for objects that have flown off into space.

Move

The following steps demonstrate command-first editing with the MOVE command, using the base point method of indicating how far and in what direction to move the selected objects. This procedure also gives detailed recommendations on how to use precision techniques when you edit.

1. Press Esc to make sure that no command is active and no objects are selected.

2. Click the Move button on the Modify toolbar.

The command line displays the `Select objects` prompt.

3. Select one or more objects.

You can use any of the object selection techniques described in the "Perfecting Selecting" section, earlier in this chapter.

4. Press Enter when you're finished selecting objects.

AutoCAD displays the following prompt:

```
Specify base point or [Displacement] <Displacement>:
```

5. Specify a base point by clicking a point or typing coordinates.

This point serves as the tail end of your imaginary arrow indicating how far and in what direction you want the objects moved. After you pick a base point, it's fairly easy to see what's going on because AutoCAD displays a temporary image of the object that moves around as you move the crosshairs. Figure 7-6 shows what the screen looks like.

Specify a base point somewhere on or near the object(s) that you're moving. You can use an object snap mode to choose a point exactly on one of the objects.

AutoCAD displays the following prompt:

```
Specify second point or <use first point as
        displacement>:
```

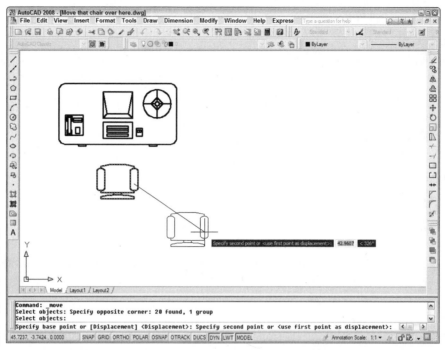

Figure 7-6:
Dragging
objects in
the middle
of the MOVE
command.

6. Specify the second point by clicking a point or typing coordinates.

The second point serves as the arrow end of your imaginary displacement arrow. After you specify the second point, AutoCAD moves the objects.

Don't press Enter alone at this prompt! If you do, AutoCAD treats the X,Y coordinates of the first point you picked as an absolute displacement, and the objects fly off unpredictably. *I repeat: Don't press Enter alone at this prompt!* Pressing Enter without picking a point or typing coordinates at this prompt is one of the most common errors new AutoCAD users make, and it can really pollute your drawing with unwanted objects.

These are common precision techniques for specifying the second point:

✔ Use an object snap mode to pick a second point exactly on another object in the drawing.

✔ Type a relative or polar coordinate, as described in Chapter 5. For example, if you type **@6,2**, AutoCAD moves the objects 6 units to the right and 2 units up. If you type **@3<45**, AutoCAD moves the objects 3 units at an angle of 45 degrees.

Use direct distance entry to move objects in an orthogonal or polar tracking direction. See Chapter 5 for instructions.

Copy

The COPY command works almost identically to the MOVE command, except that AutoCAD leaves the selected objects in place and makes new copies of them in the new location. The COPY command creates multiple copies by default. If you want only one copy, press Enter after placing it in the drawing.

AutoCAD 2008's COPY command has a new option. Choosing mOde at the command prompt or the dynamic input menu lets you switch between making a single copy and multiple copies. This may sound like a trivial change, but if you mostly make multiple copies, or mostly make single copies, you'll appreciate being able to change the default setting.

The COPY command includes an Undo option with which you can roll back multiple copies within a single COPY operation.

Copy between drawings

You can't copy objects from one drawing to another with the COPY command. Instead, you use the COPYCLIP command together with its companion command, PASTECLIP.

COPYCLIP and PASTECLIP use the Windows Clipboard to temporarily store drawing objects from one file so they can be pasted into another file. The Standard toolbar contains Cut, Copy, and Paste tools, the three standard Clipboard buttons you find in every Windows program.

If you're using AutoCAD 2008's new 2D Drafting & Annotation workspace, you'll find that the Standard toolbar has been replaced by a truncated version called Standard Annotation. It's missing the three Clipboard tool buttons (as well as the Zoom flyout tool buttons), so you'll have to use either the Edit menu or the Ctrl+X (cut), Ctrl+C (copy), and Ctrl+V (paste) keyboard shortcuts.

You can use the Windows Clipboard cut-and-paste method to copy or move objects within a single drawing, but using the AutoCAD COPY and MOVE commands usually gives you better control and precision.

Table 7-3 summarizes AutoCAD's Clipboard-related commands, along with the equivalent choices on the right-click menu and the Standard toolbar.

Table 7-3	AutoCAD Clipboard Commands	
Crosshairs Menu Choice	*Command Name*	*Toolbar Button Name*
Cut	CUTCLIP	Cut (Ctrl+X)
Copy	COPYCLIP	Copy (Ctrl+C)

Crosshairs Menu Choice	Command Name	Toolbar Button Name
Copy with Base Point	COPYBASE	None (Ctrl+Shift+C)
Paste	PASTECLIP	Paste (Ctrl+V)
Paste as Block	PASTEBLOCK	None (Ctrl+Shift+V)
Paste to Original Coordinates	PASTEORIG	None

Stretch

The STRETCH command is superficially similar to COPY and MOVE; it has the same inscrutable base point and displacement prompts, and it shifts objects — or parts of objects — to other locations in the drawing. But it also has important differences that often confound new AutoCAD users to the point that they give up trying to figure out how to use STRETCH. That's a mistake because STRETCH is a valuable command. With it, you can perform editing operations in seconds that would take many minutes with other commands. Here are the things you need to know to make STRETCH your friend:

✔ To use STRETCH, you must select objects by using a crossing selection box (or crossing polygon), as described in the section, "Perfecting Selecting," earlier in this chapter. See Figure 7-7.

✔ STRETCH operates on the defining points of objects — endpoints of a line, vertices of a polyline, the center of a circle, and so on — according to the following rule: If a defining point is within the crossing selection box that you specify, AutoCAD moves the defining point and updates the object accordingly.

Figure 7-7:
Use a crossing selection box to select objects for stretching.

For example, if your crossing selection box surrounds one endpoint of a line but not the other endpoint, STRETCH moves the first endpoint and redraws the line in the new position dictated by the first endpoint's new location. It's as though you have a rubber band tacked to the wall with two pins, and you move one of the pins.

✔ STRETCH can make lines longer or shorter, depending on your crossing selection box and displacement vector. In other words, the STRETCH command really combines stretching and compressing.

✔ You usually want to turn on ortho or polar tracking mode before stretching. Otherwise, you'll end up stretching objects in strange directions, as shown in Figure 7-8.

Figure 7-8:
The hazards of stretching without ortho or polar tracking turned on.

The following steps describe how to stretch lines:

1. **Draw some lines in an arrangement similar to the dark lines shown in Figure 7-9.**

   Start your stretching with simple objects. You can work up to more complicated objects — polylines, circles, arcs, and so on — after you've limbered up with lines.

2. **Press Esc to make sure that no command is active and no objects are selected.**

 3. **Click the Stretch button on the Modify toolbar.**

   The command line displays the `Select objects` prompt with a warning to use the Crossing or CPolygon object selection mode:

```
Select objects to stretch by crossing-window or
        crossing-polygon...
Select objects:
```

Original location   Displacement vector

Figure 7-9:
Dragging
objects in
the middle
of the
STRETCH
command.

Crossing window pick point 2   Crossing window pick point 1

4. **Specify a crossing selection box that encloses some, but not all, end-points of the lines.**

   Figure 7-9 shows a sample crossing selection box that completely encloses the two vertical lines on the right side of the figure. This cross-ing selection box cuts through the four horizontal lines, enclosing only one endpoint of each.

   You specify a crossing selection box by picking a point, moving your mouse to the *left,* and picking a second point.

5. **Press Enter to end object selection.**

   AutoCAD displays the following prompt:

   ```
   Specify base point or [Displacement] <Displacement>:
   ```

6. **Specify a base point by object snapping to a point on an existing object or by typing absolute X,Y coordinates.**

   AutoCAD displays the following prompt:

   ```
   Specify second point or <use first point as
           displacement>:
   ```

Toggle ortho mode on and then off by clicking the ORTHO button on the status bar; try moving the crosshairs around first with ortho mode on and then with it off to see the difference.

Figure 7-9 shows what the screen looks like as you move the crosshairs around with ortho off.

7. **Toggle ortho mode on (if it isn't already) and then specify the second point — usually by using direct distance entry, object snapping to a point on an existing object, or typing relative X,Y coordinates.**

    After you pick the second point, AutoCAD stretches the objects. Notice that the STRETCH command *moved* the two vertical lines because the crossing selection box contained both endpoints of both lines. STRETCH lengthened or shortened the four horizontal lines because the crossing selection box enclosed only one endpoint of each.

The STRETCH command takes some practice, but it's worth the effort. Draw some additional kinds of objects and practice stretching with different crossing selection box locations as well as different base points and second points.

More manipulations

The commands in this section — ROTATE, SCALE, ARRAY, and OFFSET — provide other ways (in addition to MOVE, COPY, and STRETCH) of manipulating objects or creating new versions of them. The procedures for each command assume that you're familiar with the object selection and editing precision techniques presented in the MOVE, COPY, and STRETCH procedures (see the previous sections in this chapter).

Rotate

The ROTATE command swings one or more objects around a point that you specify. Follow these steps to use the ROTATE command:

1. **Press Esc to make sure that no command is active and no objects are selected.**

2. **Click the Rotate button on the Modify toolbar.**

3. **Select one or more objects and then press Enter to end object selection.**

    AutoCAD prompts you for the base point for rotating the selected objects:

    ```
    Specify base point:
    ```

4. **Specify a base point by clicking a point or typing coordinates.**

    The base point becomes the point around which AutoCAD rotates the objects. You also have to specify a rotation angle:

    ```
    Specify rotation angle or [Copy/Reference] <0>:
    ```

5. **Specify a rotation angle by typing an angle measurement and pressing Enter, or just press Enter to accept the default value shown in angle brackets.**

   Alternatively, you can indicate an angle on the screen by moving the crosshairs until the Coordinates section of the status bar indicates the desired angle and then clicking. If you choose this alternative, you will need to use ortho mode or polar tracking to indicate a precise angle (for example, 90 or 45 degrees) or an object snap to rotate an object so that it aligns precisely with other objects.

   After you specify the rotation angle by typing or picking, AutoCAD rotates the objects into their new position. The ROTATE command's copy option makes a rotated copy while leaving the source object in place.

Scale

If you read all my harping about drawing scales and drawing scale factors in Chapter 4, you may think that the SCALE command performs some magical scale transformation on your entire drawing. No such luck. It merely uniformly scales one or more objects up or down by a factor that you specify. Here's how it works:

1. **Press Esc to make sure that no command is active and no objects are selected.**

2. **Click the Scale button on the Modify toolbar.**

3. **Select one or more objects and then press Enter to end object selection.**

   AutoCAD prompts you for the base point about which it will scale all the selected objects:

   ```
   Specify base point:
   ```

4. **Specify a base point by picking a point or typing coordinates.**

   The base point becomes the point about which the objects are scaled. AutoCAD prompts you for the scale factor:

   ```
   Specify scale factor or [Copy/Reference] <1.0000>:
   ```

   AutoCAD doesn't scale each object individually around its own base point (because most AutoCAD drawing objects don't have individual base points). Instead, AutoCAD uses the base point that you specify to determine how to scale *all* objects in the selection set. For example, if you select a circle to scale, pick a point outside the circle as the base point, and then specify a scale factor of 2. AutoCAD not only makes the circle twice as big, but also moves the circle twice as far away from the base point that you specified.

5. **Type a scale factor and press Enter.**

   AutoCAD then scales the objects by the factor that you type, using the base point that you specified. Numbers greater than 1 increase the objects' sizes. Numbers smaller than 1 decrease the objects' sizes.

Just like the ROTATE command, the SCALE command also has a copy option with which you can make enlarged or reduced duplicates of selected objects without altering the source objects. And both the SCALE and ROTATE commands remember the last scale factor or rotation angle entered throughout the drawing session.

Changing the drawing scale factor of a drawing after you've drawn it is a tedious and complicated process in AutoCAD. In brief, you need to change the scale-dependent system variables described in Chapter 4 and then scale some, but not all, drawing objects. You don't scale the real-world geometry that you've drawn because its measurements in the real world remain the same. You do scale objects such as text and hatching that have a fixed height or spacing regardless of drawing scale factor. (The SCALETEXT command can help with this operation; see Chapter 10 for more information.) Because of these complications, try to make sure that you choose a proper scale and set up the drawing properly for that scale before you begin drawing. See Chapter 4 for details.

Array

The ARRAY command is like a supercharged COPY: You use it to create a rectangular grid of objects at regular X and Y spacings or a polar wheel of objects at a regular angular spacing. For example, you can use rectangular arrays to populate an auditorium with chairs or a polar array to draw bicycle spokes.

The following steps describe how to create a rectangular array, which you'll probably do more often than creating a polar array:

1. **Press Esc to make sure that no command is active and no objects are selected.**

2. **Click the Array button on the Modify toolbar.**

   The Array dialog box appears, as shown in Figure 7-10.

Figure 7-10:
ARRAY
makes
duplicates
of objects
in a
rectangular
or circular
pattern.

3. **Click the Select Objects button and then select one or more objects. Press Enter to end object selection and return to the Array dialog box.**

4. **Make sure that the Rectangular Array radio button is selected.**

   If rectangular arrays seem too square, choose the cool Polar Array radio button instead and experiment with the other array option.

5. **Fill in the five text boxes: Rows, Columns, Row Offset, Column Offset, and Angle of Array.**

   The Rows and Columns numbers include the row and column of the original objects themselves. In other words, entries of 1 don't create any new objects in that direction. The Row Offset and Column Offset measurements are the distances between adjacent rows and columns. The Angle of Array is the rotation angle of the rectangular array; when the angle is 0 degrees, the array is aligned with the crosshairs.

6. **Click the Preview button.**

   AutoCAD shows what the array will look like with your current settings and displays a dialog box with Accept, Modify, and Cancel buttons.

7. **Click the Accept button if you're satisfied with the array or the Modify button if you want to change the array parameters.**

Offset

You use Offset to create parallel copies of lines, polylines, circles, arcs, or splines. Follow these steps to use Offset:

1. **Click the Offset button on the Modify toolbar.**

   AutoCAD displays the current command settings and prompts you for the *offset distance* — the distance from the original object to the copy you're creating:

   ```
   Current settings: Erase source=No  Layer=Source
           OFFSETGAPTYPE=0
   Specify offset distance or [Through/Erase/Layer]
           <Through>:
   ```

2. **Type an offset distance and press Enter.**

   Alternatively, you can indicate an offset distance by picking two points on the screen. If you choose this method, you should normally use object snaps to specify a precise distance from one existing object to another.

   AutoCAD prompts you to select the object from which you want to create an offset copy:

   ```
   Select object to offset or [Exit/Undo] <Exit>:
   ```

   3. **Select a single object, such as a line, polyline, or arc.**

   Note that you can select only one object at a time with the OFFSET command. AutoCAD asks where you want the offset object.

   ```
   Specify point on side to offset or
           [Exit/Multiple/Undo] <Exit>:
   ```

   4. **Point to one side or the other of the object and then click.**

   It doesn't matter how far away from the object the crosshairs are when you click. You're simply indicating a direction.

   AutoCAD repeats the `Select object` prompt, in case you want to offset other objects by the same distance:

   ```
   Select object to offset or [Exit/Undo] <Exit>:
   ```

   5. **Go back to Step 3 if you want to offset another object, or press Enter if you're finished offsetting objects for now.**

   Figure 7-11 shows the OFFSET command in progress.

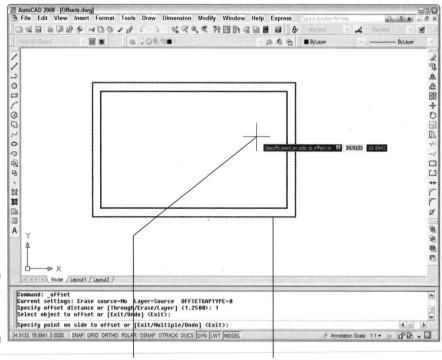

Figure 7-11:
Offsetting a
polyline.

Point on side of offset   Object to offset

If you want to offset a series of connected lines (for example, a rectangular house plan outline or one side of a pathway on a map), make sure that you either draw it as a polyline or convert the individual line and/or arc segments into a polyline with the PEDIT command. If you draw a series of line segments with the LINE command and then try to offset it, you have to pick each segment and offset it individually. Even worse, the corners usually aren't finished off in the way that you'd expect because AutoCAD doesn't treat the segments as connected. You avoid all these problems by offsetting a polyline, which AutoCAD does treat as a single object. Figure 7-11 shows an offset polyline. See Chapter 6 for more information about the differences between lines and polylines.

Slicing, dicing, and splicing

The commands in this section — TRIM, EXTEND, BREAK, FILLET, CHAMFER, and JOIN — are useful for shortening and lengthening objects, for breaking them in two, and for putting them back together again.

Trim and Extend

TRIM and EXTEND are the twin commands for making lines, polylines, and arcs shorter and longer. They're the yin and yang, the Laurel and Hardy, the Jack Sprat and his wife of the AutoCAD editing world. The two commands and their prompts are almost identical, so the following steps cover both. I show the prompts for the TRIM command; the EXTEND prompts are similar:

1. **Click the Trim or Extend button on the Modify toolbar.**

   AutoCAD prompts you to select cutting edges that will do the trimming (or, if you chose the EXTEND command, boundary edges for extending to):

   ```
   Current settings: Projection=UCS, Edge=None
   Select cutting edges ...
   Select objects or <select all>:
   ```

2. **Press Enter to accept the default option to select all drawing objects, or select individual objects by picking them. Press Enter to end object selection.**

   The objects you select in this step become the cutting edge of the TRIM command or the boundary to which objects will be extended by the EXTEND command.

   Figure 7-12 shows a cutting edge (for TRIM) and a boundary edge (for EXTEND).

   AutoCAD prompts you to select objects that you want to trim or extend (EXTEND does not have the eRase option):

   ```
   Select object to trim or shift-select to extend or
           [Fence/Crossing/Project/Edge/eRase/Undo]:
   ```

Cutting edge (for trim)

Boundary edge (for extend)

Figure 7-12:
Anatomy of
the TRIM
and
EXTEND
operations.

Objects to trim

Objects to extend

3. **Select a single object to trim or extend. Choose the portion of the object that you want AutoCAD to trim away or the end of the object that's closer to the extend-to boundary.**

   AutoCAD trims or extends the object to one of the objects that you selected in Step 2. If AutoCAD can't trim or extend the object — for example, if the trimming object and the object to be trimmed are parallel — the command line displays an error message such as Object does not intersect an edge.

   You can select multiple objects to trim and extend by typing **F** and pressing Enter to use the Fence object selection mode or by entering **C** to use Crossing selection. Even better, you can use implied windowing and drag a right-to-left selection box to select multiple objects. Refer to "Selection boxes left and right" and Table 7-1, earlier in the chapter, for more on multiple object selection.

The command line continues to prompt you to select other objects to trim or extend:

```
Select object to trim or shift-select to extend or
        [Fence/Crossing/Project/Edge/eRase/Undo]:
```

4. **Choose additional objects, or press Enter when you're finished trimming or extending.**

If you accidentally trim or extend the wrong object and you're still in the TRIM or EXTEND command, type **U** and press Enter to undo the most recent trim or extend. If you find yourself with a remnant that won't trim because it doesn't cross the cutting edge, type **R** (for eRase) and press Enter to erase it without leaving the TRIM command.

The example in Figure 7-12 shows trimming to a single cutting edge, in which the end of each trimmed line gets lopped off. Another common use of the TRIM command is for trimming out a piece of a line between two cutting edges. In the two-cutting-edges scenario, TRIM cuts a piece out of the middle of the trimmed line. The default option for selecting cutting edges or boundaries is ALL, which works well in this scenario. Pressing Enter to accept the default option selects all objects in the drawing as a cutting edge if you're in the TRIM command, or a boundary if you're in the EXTEND command.

The LENGTHEN (LEN) command provides other useful ways to make lines, arcs, and polylines longer (or shorter). You can specify an absolute distance (or *delta*) to lengthen or shorten by, a percentage to lengthen or shorten by, or a new total length. Look up "LENGTHEN command" in AutoCAD's help system for more information.

Break

The BREAK command isn't what you use before heading out for coffee. (AutoCAD doesn't have a command for that yet, but I keep hoping.) It's for creating gaps in lines, polylines, circles, arcs, or splines. BREAK also comes in handy if you need to split one object into two without actually removing any visible material.

If you want to create regularly spaced gaps in an object — so that it displays dashed, for instance — don't use BREAK. Use an AutoCAD dash-dot linetype instead. See Chapter 5 for more linetype information.

The following example shows how you BREAK an object (don't worry — in AutoCAD, you won't have to pay for it):

1. **Click the Break button on the Modify toolbar.**

   AutoCAD prompts you to select a single object that you want to break.

2. **Select a single object, such as a line, polyline, or arc.**

The point you pick when selecting the object serves double duty: It selects the object, of course, but it also becomes the default first break point (that is, it defines one side of the gap that you'll create). Thus, you should either use one of the AutoCAD precision techniques, such as an object snap, to pick the object at a precise point, or use the First point option (described in the next step) to repick the first break point.

AutoCAD prompts you to specify the second break point or to type **F** and press Enter if you want to respecify the first break point:

```
Specify second break point or [First point]:
```

3. **If the point that you picked in the preceding step doesn't also correspond to a break point (see the previous tip), type F and press Enter to respecify the first break point, and then pick the point with an object snap or other precision technique.**

   If you do type **F** and press Enter and then respecify the first break point, AutoCAD prompts you to select the second break point:

```
Specify second break point:
```

4. **Specify the second break point by picking a point or typing coordinates.**

   AutoCAD cuts a section out of the object, using the first and second break points to define the length of the gap.

If you want to cut an object into two pieces without removing anything, click the Break at Point button on the Modify toolbar. You first select the object and then choose a point that defines where AutoCAD breaks the object in two. You can then move, copy, or otherwise manipulate each section of the original object as a separate object.

Fillet and chamfer

Whereas TRIM, EXTEND, and BREAK alter one object at a time, the FILLET and CHAMFER commands modify a pair of objects. As Figure 7-13 shows, FILLET creates a curved corner between two lines, whereas CHAMFER creates a beveled corner. (In case you wondered, it's pronounced *FILL-et,* not *fill-AY.* Saying that you know how to *fill-AY* may get you a job in a butcher shop, but it will get you strange looks in a design office.)

Figure 7-13:
Cleaning up those corners with FILLET and CHAMFER.

Original lines   Filleted lines   Chamfered lines   Lines filleted with zero radius

The following steps describe how to use the FILLET command. The CHAMFER command works similarly except that, instead of specifying a fillet radius, you specify either two chamfer distances or a chamfer length and angle.

1. **Click the Fillet button on the Modify toolbar.**

    AutoCAD displays the current fillet settings and prompts you to select the first object for filleting or specify one of three options:

    ```
    Current settings: Mode = TRIM, Radius = 0.0000
    Select first object or [Undo/Polyline/Radius/Trim/
            Multiple]:
    ```

2. **Type R and press Enter to set the fillet radius.**

    AutoCAD prompts you to specify the fillet radius that it uses for future fillet operations:

    ```
    Specify fillet radius <0.0000>:
    ```

3. **Type a fillet radius and press Enter.**

    The number you type will be the radius of the arc that joins the two lines.

    AutoCAD then asks you to select the first object:

    ```
    Select first object or [Undo/Polyline/Radius/Trim/
            Multiple]:
    ```

4. **Select the first line of the pair that you want to fillet.**

    AutoCAD prompts you to select the second object for filleting:

    ```
    Select second object or shift-select to apply corner:
    ```

5. **Select the second line of the pair that you want to fillet.**

    AutoCAD fillets the two objects, drawing an arc of the radius that you specified in Step 3.

You can fillet two lines and specify a radius of zero to make them meet at a point. If you have lots of lines to fillet, whether with a zero or the same nonzero radius, use the FILLET command's Multiple option to speed the process.

Holding down the Shift key before picking the second line automatically gives you a clean intersection, the same as if you'd explicitly set the fillet radius to 0. The CHAMFER command has the same Shift-select option.

Join

Use the JOIN command to fill gaps in lines, arcs, elliptical arcs, splines, and polylines. If the lines are collinear (that is, they lie in the same straight line), or the arcs, splines, polylines, or elliptical arcs are on a similarly curved path, JOIN will create a single new entity to replace the existing separate pieces, as shown in Figure 7-14.

Select lines to join to source:

Figure 7-14:
Joining
sundered
pieces.

The following steps describe how to use the JOIN command:

1. **Click the Join button on the Modify toolbar.**

   AutoCAD prompts you to select the source object.

2. **Select the object whose properties you want the joined line to assume.**

   AutoCAD prompts according to the object type selected. If you select a line, the command prompt or dynamic input tooltip shows

   ```
   Select lines to join to source:
   ```

3. **Continue selecting collinear lines to join to the original source line.**

   AutoCAD continues prompting for additional collinear lines until you press Enter to end object selection.

4. **Press Enter to end the command.**

   AutoCAD joins the selected objects into a single object. The new object will inherit relevant properties of the source object.

You can turn an arc into a circle or an elliptical arc into a full ellipse with JOIN's cLose option.

Get a Grip

Although command-first editing is the most flexible and widespread editing style in AutoCAD, it's not the only way. *Grip editing* is a useful adjunct to command-first editing, especially when you want to modify just one or two objects. You may have encountered grip editing when using other kinds of graphics programs. Even if you're an experienced user of other graphics programs, you've never seen grips used in quite the way that AutoCAD uses them.

Anything that you can do with grip editing can be done with command-first editing as well. In some situations, grip editing is a little more efficient or convenient than command-first editing, but command-first editing always gets the job done. If you master only one style of editing, make it command-first style. In other words, feel free to skip this section — at least until you're comfortable with command-first editing.

About grips

Grips are those little square or triangular handles that appear on an object after you select it.

In their simplest guise, AutoCAD grips work similarly to the little squares on graphical objects in other Windows programs. But in AutoCAD, instead of clicking and dragging a grip, you must click, release the mouse button, move the crosshairs, and click again at the new location. (By separating the selection of beginning and ending points into two different operations, AutoCAD allows you to use different techniques — such as different object snap modes — to select each point.)

AutoCAD grips are, for sophisticated users, better than the grips found in most other programs because you can do so much more with them. You can, for example, use AutoCAD grips to move, stretch, or copy an object. You also can use them to rotate an object, scale it to a different size, or *mirror* an object — that is, create one or more backward copies. Grips also act as *visible object snaps,* or little magnets that attract the crosshairs.

A gripping example

The following sections cover in detail the five grip-editing modes: STRETCH, MOVE, ROTATE, SCALE, and MIRROR. Follow these steps to explore the grip-editing modes:

1. **Press Esc to make sure that no command is active and no objects are selected.**

AutoCAD displays a blank command prompt — that is, no command is currently active.

2. **Click an object on-screen to select it and display its grips.**

   Grips — solid blue squares on the selected object — appear at various points on the object. Note that the AutoCAD command prompt remains blank; you haven't started a command or grip-editing operation yet.

3. **Click another object.**

   Both the newly selected object and the previously selected object display grips.

4. **Click one of the grips on either object.**

   The blue square turns to a red square. This grip is now *hot,* or ready for a grip-editing operation.

   Grip-editing options now appear on the command line. The first option to appear is STRETCH.

5. **Press the spacebar repeatedly to cycle through the five grip-editing options on the command line.**

   ```
   ** STRETCH **
   Specify stretch point or [Base point/Copy/Undo/eXit]:
   ** MOVE **
   Specify move point or [Base point/Copy/Undo/eXit]:
   ** ROTATE **
   Specify rotation angle or [Base
           point/Copy/Undo/Reference/eXit]:
   ** SCALE **
   Specify scale factor or [Base
           point/Copy/Undo/Reference/eXit]:
   ** MIRROR **
   Specify second point or [Base point/Copy/Undo/eXit]:
   ```

   The grip-editing option displayed on the command line and the dynamic input tooltip changes as you press the spacebar. If you move the crosshairs (without picking) in between each press of the spacebar, the appearance of your selected object changes as you display each option. As you can see, each of the grip-editing operations resembles the ordinary AutoCAD command of the same name. Choosing STRETCH, for example, causes a stretched version of the object to appear on-screen.

Pressing the spacebar a bunch of times is a good way to become familiar with the grip-editing modes, but there's a more direct way to choose a particular mode. After you click a grip to make it hot, right-click to display the grip-editing menu. That menu contains all the grip-editing options plus some other choices, as shown in Figure 7-15.

If dynamic input is enabled (via the DYN status bar button), pressing the down-arrow key while cycling through the grip-editing options displays a dynamic menu at the crosshairs from which you can choose options specific to the current grip-editing function.

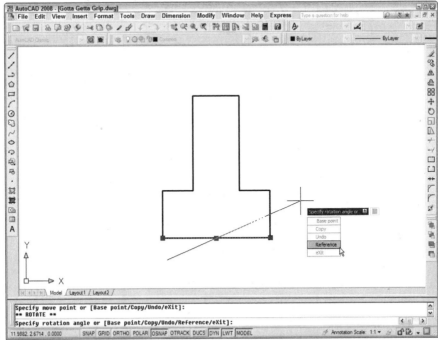

Figure 7-15:
The grip-
editing
crosshairs
menu.

6. **Press the spacebar until STRETCH (or the option you want) reappears as the grip-editing option.**

7. **Move the hot grip in the direction in which you want to stretch (or otherwise manipulate) your object.**

    AutoCAD dynamically updates the image of the object to show you what the modified object will look like before you click the final location.

8. **Click again to finish the grip-editing operation.**

    The selected object with the hot grip updates.

9. **Click the same grip that you chose in Step 4 (now in a different location) to make it hot.**

10. **This time, move the crosshairs near one of the grips on the other object. When you see the magnetic pull of the grip on the other object, click again to connect the hot grip with the other grip.**

    The object point represented by the hot grip now coincides exactly with the grip on the other object.

11. **Press Esc to deselect all objects and remove all grips.**

Figure 7-16 shows a hot (red) endpoint grip of a line being connected to the cold (blue) endpoint grip of another line. The angled line shows the original position of the line being edited, and the thin vertical line shows the new position. Using a grip in this way as a visible object snap offers the same advantage as using object snap overrides, as described in Chapter 5: It ensures precision by making sure that objects meet exactly.

Red (hot) grip   Blue (cold) grip

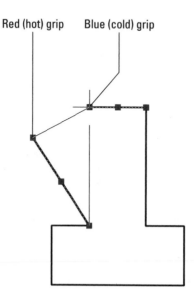

Figure 7-16:
Using grips
to connect
two objects.

You can experiment with all the grip-editing options to find out how they affect a selected object.

Because MOVE and STRETCH are the most useful grip-editing modes, I cover them more specifically.

Move it!

Back in the days of manual drafting, moving objects was a big pain in the eraser. You had to erase the stuff you wanted to move and redraw the objects in their new location. In the process, you usually ended up erasing parts of other stuff that you didn't want to move and left smudged lines and piles of eraser dust everywhere. CAD does away with all the fuss and muss of moving objects, and AutoCAD grip editing is a great way to make it happen. The following steps describe how to move objects:

1. **Select one or more objects.**

Use any combination of the three editing modes — single object, window box, and crossing box — described in the "Grab It" section, earlier in this chapter.

2. **Click one of the grips to make it hot.**

   At this point in your editing career, it doesn't matter which grip you click. As you become more familiar with grip editing, you'll discover that certain grips serve as better reference points than others for particular editing operations.

3. **Right-click anywhere in the drawing area and choose Move from the crosshairs menu.**

4. **Move the crosshairs to a different location and click.**

   As you move the crosshairs around, AutoCAD displays the tentative new positions for all the objects, just as it does for the regular Move command, as shown previously in Figure 7-6. After you click, the objects assume their new positions.

5. **Press Esc to deselect all objects and remove all grips.**

Copy, or a kinder, gentler Move

If you were paying attention during the section "A gripping example," earlier in the chapter, you may have noticed while pressing the spacebar that copy was not among the five grip-editing modes. Why not? Because every grip mode includes a copy option (as the command-line prompts shown in the "A gripping example" section indicate). In other words, you can STRETCH with copy, MOVE with copy, ROTATE with copy, SCALE with copy, and MIRROR with copy.

The copy option leaves the selected objects in place and does the editing operation on a new copy of the objects.

By far the most common use for the copy option is with the MOVE grip-editing mode. If you think about "MOVE with copy" for about two seconds, you'll realize that it's just a complicated way of saying "copy." The following steps show how to copy objects quickly by using grip editing:

1. **Select one or more objects.**

2. **Click any one of the grips to make it hot.**

3. **Right-click anywhere in the drawing area and choose Move from the menu.**

4. **Right-click again and choose Copy from the menu.**

5. **Move the crosshairs to a different location and click.**

   After you click, new objects appear in the new location.

6. **Move the crosshairs to additional locations and click there if you want to make additional copies.**

7. **Press Esc twice — once to end the copying operation and once to deselect all objects and remove all grips.**

A warm-up Stretch

The STRETCH grip-editing mode works differently from the other modes. By default, it affects only the object with the hot grip on it, not all objects with grips on them. You can override this default behavior by using the Shift key to pick multiple hot grips. Follow these steps to get acquainted with using the STRETCH grip-editing mode to stretch one or more objects:

1. **Turn off ortho mode by clicking the ORTHO button on the status bar until the button appears to be pushed out and the words `<Ortho off>` appear on the command line.**

Polishing those properties

When you think of editing objects, you probably think first about editing their *geometry:* moving, stretching, making new copies, and so on. That's the kind of editing I cover in this chapter.

Another kind of editing is changing objects' *properties*. As I describe in Chapter 5, every object in an AutoCAD drawing has a set of non-geometrical properties, including layer, color, linetype, and lineweight. Sometimes, you need to edit those properties — when you accidentally draw something on the wrong layer, for example. Four common ways of editing objects' properties in AutoCAD are

✔ **The Properties palette:** This is the most flexible way to edit properties. Select any object (or objects), right-click in the drawing area, and choose Properties from the menu. The Properties palette displays the names and values of all properties. Click in the appropriate value cell to change a particular property.

✔ **Layers and Properties toolbars:** Another way to change properties is to select objects and then choose from the drop-down lists (Layer, Color, and so on) on the Layers and the Properties toolbars. See Chapter 5 for more information.

✔ **Match Properties:** You can use the Match Properties button on the Standard toolbar — the button with the paintbrush on it — to paint properties from one object to another. Match Properties works similarly to the Format Painter button in Microsoft applications. Match Properties works even when the objects reside in different drawings.

✔ **Change Space:** I introduce the concepts of model space and paper space in Chapter 4. Sometimes you add some geometry to paper space and then realize it should have been in model space, or vice versa. The former CHSPACE Express Tool is now part of core AutoCAD and AutoCAD LT — you'll find it on the Modify menu. For more information, look up CHSPACE in the Command Reference of the online help.

Ortho mode forces stretch displacements to be orthogonal — that is, parallel to lines running at 0 and 90 degrees. During real editing tasks, you'll often want to turn on ortho mode, but while you get acquainted with stretching, leaving ortho mode off makes things clearer.

2. **Select several objects, including at least one line.**

3. **On one of the lines, click one of the endpoint grips to make it hot.**

All the objects remain selected, but as you move the crosshairs, only the line with the hot grip changes. Figure 7-17 shows an example.

Original location   Displacement vector

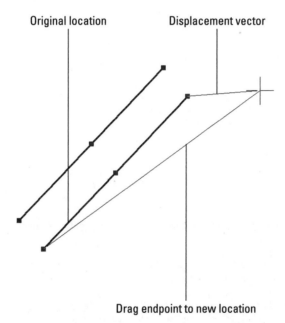

Figure 7-17:
Dragging
a line's
endpoint in
the middle
of the
STRETCH
grip-editing
operation.

Drag endpoint to new location

4. **Click a new point for the hot endpoint grip.**

The line stretches to accommodate the new endpoint location.

5. **On the same line, click the midpoint grip to make it hot.**

As you move the crosshairs, the entire line moves. Using the STRETCH grip-editing mode with a line's midpoint "stretches" the entire line to a new location.

6. **Click a new point for the hot midpoint grip.**

The line moves to the new midpoint location.

7. **Hold down the Shift key. On one of the lines, click one of the endpoint grips to make it hot.**

8. **Still holding down the Shift key, click one of the endpoint grips on a different line to make it hot.**

   Two grips on two different lines are now hot because you held down the Shift key and then clicked both grips.

   You can create more hot grips by holding down the Shift key and clicking more grips.

9. **Release the Shift key and re-pick any one of the hot grips.**

   Releasing the Shift key signals that you're finished making grips hot. Re-picking one of the hot grips establishes it as the base point for the stretch operation.

10. **Click a new point for the grip.**

    All the objects with hot grips stretch based on the displacement of the grip that you clicked in Step 9 (see Figure 7-18).

11. **Turn on ortho mode by clicking the ORTHO button on the status bar until the button appears to be pushed in and the words <Ortho on> appear on the command line. Repeat Steps 2 through 10 to see the effect of ortho mode on stretching.**

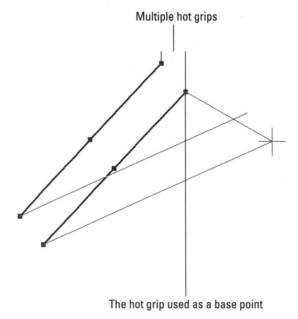

Multiple hot grips

Figure 7-18:
Stretching
multiple
objects with
multiple hot
grips.

The hot grip used as a base point

Chapter 8

A Zoom with a View

*O*ne of the advantages of CAD over manual drawing is CAD's capability to give you different ways to view your drawing. You can zoom in close, zoom out to a great distance, and pan around. In fact, not only *can* you zoom and pan in your drawing, but in most kinds of drawings, you *must* do it frequently to be able to draw, edit, and view effectively.

Technical drawings are jam-packed with lines, text, and dimensions. Zooming and panning frequently enables you to see the details better, draw more confidently (because you can see what you're doing), and edit more quickly (because object selection is easier when there aren't a zillion objects on the screen). This chapter covers AutoCAD's most useful display control features.

Zoom and Pan with Glass and Hand

Moving your viewpoint in to get a closer view of your drawing data is called *zooming in;* moving your viewpoint back to get a more expansive view is called *zooming out.*

Zooming in and out of your drawing is one of the big advantages that AutoCAD offers over manual drawing. You can do detailed work on tiny objects and then zoom out and move around rooms, houses, or neighborhoods from an Olympian perspective.

Panning is closely related to zooming. If you zoom in enough that some of your drawing no longer shows up on-screen, you're going to want to *pan* around — move left, right, up, and down in your drawing — without zooming in and out. AutoCAD makes panning easy with scroll bars and *real-time* panning. And in case you're wondering what *real-time* panning might be (as opposed to *pretend-time* panning, maybe?), it simply means you can see the objects moving around the screen as you drag the mouse up and down or back and forth. (Of course, it's your viewpoint that's moving, not the objects!)

Both panning and zooming change what is known as the view. The *view* is the current location and magnification of the AutoCAD depiction of your drawing. Each time you zoom or pan, you establish a new view. You can give a name to a specific view to make returning to that view easy, as I demonstrate later in this chapter.

You'll get a better sense of panning and zooming around a drawing if you actually have a drawing to look at. Draw some objects on the screen, open one of your own existing drawings, or open one of AutoCAD's sample drawings located in the C:\Program Files\AutoCAD 2008\Sample folder. (If you're using AutoCAD LT, the sample drawings are located in the C:\Program Files\AutoCAD LT 2008\Sample folder.)

Fortunately, zooming and panning in AutoCAD is as simple as it is necessary. The following steps describe how to use AutoCAD's Zoom and Pan Realtime feature, which is easy to operate and provides a lot of flexibility:

1. **Click the Zoom Realtime button on the Standard toolbar.**

   If you're using the 2D Drafting & Annotation workspace, you'll find Zoom Realtime at the bottom of the Dashboard, but see my upcoming warning about this workspace.

   The Realtime option of the ZOOM command starts. The crosshairs change to a magnifying glass, and AutoCAD prompts you at the command line:

   ```
   Press ESC or ENTER to exit, or right-click to display
              shortcut menu.
   ```

2. **Move the crosshairs near the middle of the screen, press and hold down the left mouse button, and drag the crosshairs up and down until the objects you want to see almost fill the screen.**

   Dragging up increases the zoom magnification, and dragging down decreases it.

3. **Right-click in the drawing area and choose Pan from the menu that appears (shown in Figure 8-1).**

   The magnifying glass cursor changes to a hand.

4. **Click and drag to pan the drawing in any direction.**

   You can use the right-click menu to toggle between Zoom and Pan as many times as you like. If you get lost in your drawing, choose Zoom Original or Zoom Extents to return to a recognizable view.

5. **Right-click in the drawing area and choose Exit.**

   The Zoom or Pan Realtime cursor returns to the normal AutoCAD crosshairs.

Figure 8-1:
The Zoom/
Pan
Realtime
right-click
menu.

Exit
Pan
✔ Zoom
3D Orbit
Zoom Window
Zoom Original
Zoom Extents

In the preceding example, you started with zooming and ended with panning. You also have the option of doing the reverse: Click the Pan Realtime button (in either the AutoCAD Classic Standard toolbar or the Dashboard), and after you've panned, use the right-click menu to switch to zooming. However you start it, the important thing to realize is that Zoom and Pan Realtime is a single AutoCAD function. At any time, you can switch between panning and zooming (or switch to a related function, such as Zoom Window) by using the right-click menu.

You also can pan and zoom by using your mouse's scroll wheel (if it has one) or the middle button of a three-button mouse:

✔ To zoom in and out, roll the scroll wheel forward and backward.

✔ To zoom to the extents of your drawing, double-click the scroll wheel or the middle button.

✔ To pan, hold down the scroll wheel or the middle button as you move the mouse.

You can adjust the zoom direction of your wheel mouse by changing the value of the ZOOMWHEEL system variable. (See Chapter 2 for a description of what system variables are and how to change them.) When ZOOMWHEEL = 0 (the default), scrolling the wheel forward zooms in, and scrolling backward zooms out; change the value of ZOOMWHEEL to 1 to reverse directions.

The scroll wheel or middle mouse button zoom and pan operations described in the preceding list depend on an obscure AutoCAD system variable named MBUTTONPAN. When MBUTTONPAN is set to 1 — the default value — you can use the middle button to pan and zoom as I describe in the preceding list. Unless your system has been customized by someone, if you change MBUTTONPAN to 0, clicking the middle mouse button displays an object snap menu at the crosshairs, as it did in older AutoCAD versions. If you're not able to zoom or pan with your middle mouse button, set MBUTTONPAN back to 1. (With MBUTTONPAN set to 1, you use Shift+right-click to display the object snap menu at the crosshairs.)

Realtime zooming and panning is the easiest, most interactive way to get around in your drawings. In some situations, though, this method is less efficient or precise than the old-fashioned methods, the most important of which are described in the next section.

AutoCAD 2008's new 2D Drafting & Annotation workspace has some dandy features, but its version of the Standard toolbar — called Standard Annotation — is not one of them. The latter toolbar is missing all the Zoom tool buttons described as follows, although four of them can be found at the bottom of the Dashboard. If you want to use this workspace, I suggest you replace the Standard Annotation toolbar for the old Standard version — just right-click any tool button, uncheck Standard Annotation, and check Standard.

Out of the frying pan . . .

Another way to pan in AutoCAD should be familiar from other Windows programs — the scroll bars in the drawing area. Scrolling is the same in AutoCAD as in any other Windows program; click the arrows in the right and bottom scroll bars on the borders of the drawing window to scroll, or pan, a step at a time; or click and drag the little scroll boxes to pan as little or as much as you want to.

By default, scroll bars are turned on in the AutoCAD (LT) Classic and 2D Drafting & Annotation workspaces in both AutoCAD and AutoCAD LT. If you want to turn them off, choose Tools⇨Options to display the Options dialog box. On the Display tab, uncheck the box next to Display Scroll Bars in Drawing Window.

Time to zoom

Because zooming is such a frequent necessity in AutoCAD, it's worth knowing some alternative ways of doing it.

Of the following options, Zoom Realtime and Zoom Previous have full-time tool buttons on the Standard (but not the Standard Annotation) toolbar. The middle of the three magnifying-glass buttons is a *flyout* button. Click and hold on it, and buttons for the other Zoom options fly out. Because, theoretically, you may want to use an option again soon, the most recently used flyout button floats to the top of the pile.

The ZOOM command has several different options, the most important of which are the following:

- **All and Extents:** Zoom Extents (the button with the four-headed arrow) zooms out just far enough to show all the objects in the current drawing. Zoom All (the button showing the sheet with the folded-over corner) does the same thing, unless the drawing's limits are larger than the extents, in which case Zoom All zooms to show the entire rectangular area defined by the limits. If you've defined your limits properly (see

Chapter 4), Zoom All is a good way to see your whole drawing area. These two options are especially useful when you zoom in too small or pan off into empty space and want to see your entire drawing again.

It's a good idea to Zoom All or Zoom Extents and then save the drawing before you close it. By performing these steps, you ensure the following:

- The next person who opens the drawing — whether it's you or someone else — can see the full drawing as soon as they start working.

- If you've accidentally copied some objects way beyond where they should be, Zoom All or Extents will make them show up so you can delete them.

- The drawing preview that appears in the Select File dialog box displays the full drawing, instead of just a tiny, unidentifiable corner of it.

✔ **Window:** This option is great for zooming in quickly and precisely. It zooms to a section of your drawing that you specify by clicking two points. The two points define the diagonal of a window around the area you want to look at.

Note that the ZOOM command's Window option is not a click-and-drag operation — unlike in some other Windows programs and, confusingly, unlike in the Zoom/Pan Realtime Zoom Window option. With the ZOOM command's Window option, you click one corner, release the mouse button, and then click the other corner.

✔ **Scale (X/XP):** The X option zooms by a percentage of the current display; values less than 1 cause you to zoom in, values greater than 1 cause you to zoom out. You can also think of the value as a scaling factor: 0.5X causes the screen image to shrink to half its apparent size, and 2X causes the screen image to double its apparent size. (The XP option after a number is for zooming model space objects in a viewport relative to paper space; see Chapter 4 for information about paper space.)

✔ **Realtime:** Realtime zooming, the technique described previously, enables you to zoom in and out by starting a realtime zoom and then moving the crosshairs up (to zoom in) or down (to zoom out).

✔ **Previous:** This option undoes the last zoom and/or pan sequence, taking you back to where you started.

✔ **Object:** This option zooms in close enough to show selected objects as large as they can be displayed on-screen. Using ZOOM Object is like putting the selected objects under AutoCAD's microscope.

AutoCAD provides *smooth view transitions* whenever you use the non-real-time pan and zoom commands. Sometimes you can get lost if you do a ZOOM All from a small, highly magnified area. It's a bad idea to leave a trail of breadcrumbs across your screen, so these slow-motion pans and zooms may be fine, at least until you do know your way out of the forest . . . or your drawing.

If, like me, you find that this feature gets old fast, there's a View Transitions dialog box (type **VTOPTIONS** to open it) in which you can turn it off. Just uncheck the Enable Animation for Pan & Zoom option.

Some of the zoom options take some getting used to. I recommend that you use realtime zoom and pan for most of your zooming and panning. Supplement it with Zoom Window to move quickly into a precise area, Zoom Previous to back up in zoom/pan time, and Zoom All or Zoom Extents to view your whole drawing.

A View by Any Other Name . . .

If you find yourself repeatedly zooming and panning to the same area, you can probably get there faster with a named view. After you name and save a view of a particular area of your drawing, you can return to that area quickly by restoring the view. You use the VIEW command, which displays the View Manager dialog box, to create and restore named views.

Follow these steps to create a named view:

1. **Zoom and pan until you find the area of the drawing that you want to assign a name to.**

2. **Choose View⇨Named Views.**

   The View Manager dialog box appears.

3. **Click the New button.**

   The New View dialog box appears, as shown in Figure 8-2.

4. **Type a name in the View Name text box.**

5. **(Optional) Type a new category in the View Category box or select an existing one from the drop-down list.**

   You use View Categories to organize views and certain display characteristics of views in sheet sets. Until you use the sheet sets feature, you can leave this box blank.

   AutoCAD LT doesn't support view categories. The New View dialog box in LT is missing the View Category list box and the Background area shown in Figure 8-2.

6. **Select the Current Display radio button, if it's not selected already.**

   If you want to save a region other than the currently displayed view, select the Define Window radio button instead, click the Define View Window button to the right of it, and pick two corners of the region's rectangle (as if you were zooming windows).

Figure 8-2:
Create a
new view
for you.

7. Confirm or change the choices in the Settings area.

If you check the Save Layer Snapshot with View option, when you later restore the view, AutoCAD also will restore the layer visibility settings (on/off and freeze/thaw) that were in effect when you created the view. (Chapter 5 describes the layer visibility settings.) The UCS, Live Section, and Visual Style settings are primarily for 3D drawings; the latter two settings are not included in AutoCAD LT.

8. Click OK.

The New View dialog box disappears, and you see your new named view in the list in the View Manager dialog box.

9. Click OK.

The View Manager dialog box disappears.

To restore a named view, choose View⇨Named Views or enter **VIEW** (or type **V**) at the command line to display the View Manager dialog box. In the Views list, expand either Model Views or Layout Views (depending on where you saved your view). Click the name of the view that you want to restore, click the Set Current button, and then click OK to close the dialog box.

You also can plot the area defined by a named view. See Chapter 13 for instructions on plotting views.

Looking Around in Layout Land

All the zoom, pan, and view operations I describe in this chapter apply to paper space layouts as well as to model space. (Chapter 4 describes the difference between model space and paper space and how to navigate between the two.) One little complication exists, though: In a *paper space layout* — that is, any drawing area tab except for the Model tab — it's possible for the crosshairs to be in either paper space or in model space inside a viewport. Zooming and panning have a different effect depending on which space your crosshairs are in at the moment. Experiment with the different effects by following these steps:

1. **Open a drawing that contains at least one paper space layout with a title block and one or more viewports.**

   If you don't have any such drawings handy, try using the AutoCAD sample drawing located at `C:\Program Files\AutoCAD 2008\Sample\ Sheet Sets\Architectural\A-05.dwg`. AutoCAD LT users can try `C:\Program Files\AutoCAD LT 2008\Sample\Tallship.dwg`.

2. **Click one of the layout tabs — that is, any tab other than the Model tab.**

   AutoCAD displays the paper space layout for that tab, including any title block and viewports.

3. **Click the PAPER/MODEL button on the status bar until it says PAPER.**

   Alternatively, you can double-click in the gray part of the drawing area outside the layout.

   The crosshairs are now in paper space, so zooming and panning changes the appearance of all the objects in the layout, including the title block.

4. **Choose View⇨Zoom⇨All.**

   AutoCAD displays the entire layout, as shown in Figure 8-3.

5. **Zoom and pan by using any of the techniques described in this chapter.**

   Zooming and panning change the appearance of the title block, as shown in Figure 8-4. The effect is similar to moving a plotted sheet in and out and all around in front of your face.

6. **Choose View⇨Zoom⇨All.**

   AutoCAD displays the entire layout again.

7. **Click the PAPER/MODEL button on the status bar until it says MODEL.**

   Alternatively, you can double-click with the crosshairs over a viewport.

   The crosshairs are now in model space, inside the viewport, so zooming and panning change only the display of the objects that are visible in the viewport. The display of the title block doesn't change.

Figure 8-3:
The full
layout.

Figure 8-4:
Zooming
in paper
space.

8. **Zoom and pan by using any of the techniques described in this chapter.**

   Zooming and panning don't change the appearance of the title block, as shown in Figure 8-5. The result looks as if you're moving a picture of the model space geometry in and out and all around behind a frame.

   In real drawings, you usually shouldn't zoom and pan inside viewports after they've been set up (see Chapter 4). Doing so changes the scale of the viewport, which messes up plotting. I'm asking you to do it here to illustrate the difference between zooming in paper space and zooming in a model space viewport.

   If the title block changes when you zoom and pan, someone has locked the viewport to prevent the kind of mischief that I warn against in the previous paragraph. (You also see the command prompt `Viewport is view-locked. Switching to Paper space.`) See "viewports, floating, locking" in the AutoCAD online help system if you need to lock — or unlock — viewports.

9. **Choose View⇨Zoom⇨Previous one or more times until you've restored the original view.**

Figure 8-5:
Zooming in a model space viewport.

10. **Click the PAPER/MODEL button on the status bar until is says PAPER.**

    Always leave the crosshairs in paper space when you're ready to call a drawing finished.

11. **Choose File⇨Close and click the No button to close the drawing without saving changes.**

    In this example, I have you close the drawing without saving changes just in case you did mess up the viewport zoom scale.

In most cases, you set up a paper space layout once, as described in Chapter 4, and then just return to it to plot. You shouldn't be spending a lot of time zooming and panning in paper space layouts. You zoom and pan to get a better view of what you're drawing and editing, and that's what the Model tab is for. But if you do want to zoom in paper space — to get a better look at part of your title block, for example — make sure that you're doing it with the PAPER/MODEL button set to PAPER.

The VPMAX and VPMIN commands allow you to maximize and minimize a viewport in the current layout. These commands provide an alternative to switching between the Model and Layout tabs without the potential problems of zooming inside of paper space viewports. The easiest way to run VPMAX or VPMIN is to click the Maximize Viewport/Minimize Viewport button located on the status bar, just to the right of the PAPER button.

Degenerating and Regenerating

As you zoom and pan around your drawing, you may wonder how the image that you see on-screen is related to the DWG file that AutoCAD saves on the hard disk. Well, maybe you don't wonder about that, but I'm going to tell you anyway!

When you draw and edit objects, AutoCAD stores all their geometrical properties (that is, location and size) in a highly precise form — technically, *double floating-point precision*. The program always maintains that precision when you save the DWG file. For computer performance reasons, however, AutoCAD does *not* use that high-precision form of the data to display your drawing on-screen. Instead, AutoCAD converts the highly precise numbers in the DWG file into slightly less precise *integers* in order to create the view that you see on-screen.

The happy consequence of this conversion is that zooming, panning, and other display changes are a lot faster than they would be otherwise. The unhappy consequence is that the conversion, which is called a *regeneration* (or *regen* for short), occasionally leaves you with some artifacts to deal with.

In most cases, AutoCAD performs regenerations automatically when it needs to. You will sometimes see command line messages like `Regenerating model` or `Regenerating layout`, which indicate that AutoCAD is taking care of regens for you.

If, on the other hand, you see the command line message `Regen queued`, then AutoCAD is warning you that it's *not* performing a regeneration, even though one might be advisable now. In addition, you might see a warning dialog box with the message `About to regen -- proceed?` These messages are AutoCAD's way of saying, "What your drawing looks like on the screen at the moment may not exactly match the real version of the drawing database that gets stored when you save the drawing. I'll update the display version at the next regeneration."

The REGENAUTO command (not in AutoCAD LT) controls whether or not AutoCAD performs most regenerations automatically by setting the system variable REGENMODE. (See Chapter 2 if you're unfamiliar with system variables or how to change them.)

 ✔ The default REGENAUTO mode in new drawings, On, tells AutoCAD to regenerate your drawing automatically if it's required to synchronize the screen display with the drawing database.

 ✔ The other REGENAUTO mode, Off, tells AutoCAD not to regenerate automatically but instead to display `Regen queued` on the command line and let you force a regeneration with the REGEN command if you want to.

The REGENAUTO off option is for the most part a holdover from much slower computers and older versions of AutoCAD. You probably don't need to subject yourself to the mental contortion of trying to avoid regens unless you work on huge drawings and/or use a painfully slow computer.

Don't confuse the REGEN command with the REDRAW command. REGEN (View➪Regen) forces the synchronization process described in this section. Redraw (View➪Redraw) simply refreshes the screen, without attempting to synchronize the screen with the drawing database. The REDRAW command was useful in the days of very slow computers and older versions of AutoCAD, which didn't handle the display as effectively, but it's essentially a useless command now.

The REGENALL command (View➪Regen All) regenerates all viewports in a paper space layout. If you run the REGENALL command in model space, it has the same effect as the ordinary REGEN command.

Chapter 9

On a 3D Spree

*A*utodesk's programmers completely revamped the 3D interface in AutoCAD 2007 (the previous release), modernizing what had been essentially unchanged for over a decade. Creating 3D models is now a lot simpler and more intuitive than it used to be.

Unfortunately, I simply don't have the space in this book to cover every aspect of 3D in AutoCAD 2008, so I focus here on visualization and navigation, two facets you'll need to know before you can go far in 3D object creation. I start off by showing you how to navigate in AutoCAD 2008's 3D environment. Then, I show you how to change the appearance of your models on-screen.

A book like this one can only begin to cover some of the specialized areas involved in working in 3D in AutoCAD. Among the areas I pass over are

- ✔ 3D object creation
- ✔ Camera functions
- ✔ Animations and walkthroughs
- ✔ Solid and surface modeling
- ✔ Lighting
- ✔ Materials
- ✔ Rendering

For these and other facets of working in AutoCAD 2008's powerful and complex 3D environment, have a look at *AutoCAD 2008 3D Modeling Workbook For Dummies* by Lee Ambrosius, from Wiley Publishing (available in late 2007).

If you're an AutoCAD LT user, you're going to have to sit out most of this chapter. One of the major areas where LT differs from regular AutoCAD is in its extremely limited 3D functionality. You do have the Dashboard, however, and the "Go Dashboarding" section later in this chapter explains how you use it.

The new 3D visualization and rendering abilities of AutoCAD 2008 have upped the system requirements substantially from AutoCAD 2006 and earlier versions. The full version of AutoCAD will run if your computer has 512MB of RAM, but if you want to work in 3D, Autodesk recommends 2GB of RAM and a video card with at least 128MB of its own memory. If you're thinking of buying a new video card (or a whole new system), check Autodesk's Web site (www.autodesk.com) for a list of supported video cards.

Two features in AutoCAD 2008 help you get your 3D feet wet:

✔ The 3D Modeling workspace

✔ The Dashboard

Before you start making stuff, or even looking at already-made stuff, it's important to get a firm grasp on these two features. A *workspace* is a named collection of toolbars and tool palettes that you use for specific processes. The 3D Modeling workspace, like the 2D Drafting & Annotation workspace, opens the Dashboard with task-specific control panels and adjusts some of the other tool palettes.

Entering the Third Dimension

If you're new to the 3D game, and you've been working in 2D up until now, there are a couple of things you need to do in order to start a new 3D model in AutoCAD. You have to change the workspace, and then you have to open a new file using a 3D template. The following steps explain how:

1. **Open the drop-down list in the Workspaces toolbar (see Figure 9-1) and choose 3D Modeling.**

   Toolbars and palettes flash on and off, and eventually AutoCAD settles down and displays the Dashboard and the Modeling tool palette.

   Whether you're working with the full version or LT, you'll more than likely see a toolbar labeled Impressions appear when you switch workspaces. Impressions is a separate program from Autodesk that lets you dress up 2D drawings for presentation purposes. I recommend you close this toolbar for now. To find out more about Impressions, point your Web browser to http://labs.autodesk.com/Impressionlanding.html.

AutoCAD may want to open the tool palettes and the Dashboard docked side by side, which really takes up a lot of drawing area. To stack them one above the other and regain a bit of room, double-click the grab handles at the top of the tool palettes or the Dashboard to float the palette in the drawing area; then double-click the now-floating palette's title bar — the panels should rearrange themselves as they appear in Figure 9-1.

You now have a 3D Modeling workspace, but you're likely still in a 2D drawing.

2. **Choose File⇨New.**

   The Select Template dialog box appears.

3. **Choose acad3d.dwt if you're working in imperial units or acadiso3d.dwt if you're working in metric. Click OK.**

   A 3D modeling space appears (see Figure 9-1).

Workspaces toolbar   Palette handles   Dashboard

Figure 9-1:
Ascending
the z-axis.

Modeling tool palette

To switch from 3D to the AutoCAD Classic 2D world, simply reverse the steps, as follows:

1. **Open the drop-down list in the Workspaces toolbar and choose AutoCAD Classic.**

   After more flashing toolbars and palettes, AutoCAD settles down and displays (by default) the Tool Palettes window. If the Impressions toolbar opens, move it out of the way or close it.

   Again, you need to start a new drawing to complete the process.

2. **Choose File⇨New.**

   The Select Template dialog box appears.

3. **Choose an appropriate template file and click OK.**

   If you want to work in imperial units, choose `acad.dwt` for color-dependent plotting or `acad -Named Plot Styles.dwt` for named plot styles. For metric, choose `acadiso.dwt` or `acadISO -Named Plot Styles.dwt`.

Go Dashboarding!

If you've gotten this far, you can't help but notice that large palette-like area over at the right side of the screen. It's called the *Dashboard,* and it contains a number of panels that give access to different aspects of working in 3D (see Figure 9-2).

Figure 9-2:
The Dashboard ready for some 3D Modeling.

— Layers control panel

— 3D Make control panel

— Visual Styles control panel

— Light control panel

— Materials control panel

— Render control panel

— 3D Navigate control panel

TIP

Each section of the Dashboard contains an additional hidden set of tool buttons and controls. To access them, move your mouse pointer over the vertical border area at the left side of the panel. When a downward-pointing double arrow appears, click to expand the panel (see Figure 9-3). The vertical bar in the expanded panel turns orange; to collapse the panel, click the upward-pointing double arrow (see Figure 9-4). Note that the Materials panel doesn't have room to show the downward-pointing area, but you can click the icon itself (it's the paintbrush on a sphere) to expand this panel.

Figure 9-3: Click the double arrows to expand a control panel . . .

Figure 9-4: . . . and click again to collapse it.

The default 3D Modeling Dashboard is divided into seven control panels as follows:

✔ **Layers control panel:** Contains tool buttons for managing layers and layer states. The expanded panel contains a slider and drop-down list for controlling the amount of fade for locked layers and filtering which layers to apply the setting to.

✔ **3D Make control panel:** Contains tools for creating 3D primitive solids (for example, cubes, spheres, cones, and so on), freeform solids, and surfaces (that is, lofts and sweeps), and for performing Boolean and other 3D object modification. The expanded control panel contains additional 3D editing tools.

- ✔ **Visual Styles control panel:** Contains tools for configuring display type (for example, x-ray mode, shadows on or off, and so on) and a drop-down list for selecting preconfigured visual styles. See the "Get some (visual) style" section, coming up.

- ✔ **Lights control panel:** Contains tools for enabling or disabling default ambient light or sunlight. Sliders control time of year and hour of day for shadow generation. The expanded panel contains tools for adding new point, spot, and distant lights, changing global location (unless you live in San Francisco, in which case you're already home!). If you really want to play master of the universe, click the Edit the Sun button.

- ✔ **Materials control panel:** Select materials from a dialog box and apply them to the surfaces of your 3D model.

- ✔ **Render control panel:** You have your lights, you have your camera, and you have your action — now create your final renderings here.

- ✔ **3D Navigate control panel:** Contains tools for standard display commands like PAN and ZOOM as well as camera creation and modification tools, animation walkthrough setup tools, and perspective/parallel toggles. The expanded panel contains sliders and additional controls for varying camera focal length and setting up and recording animations.

The bottom half of the Dashboard, including lights, materials, and rendering tools, is beyond the scope of this book. For more information, check out the online help system or the companion title that I wrote with Lee Ambrosius, *AutoCAD and AutoCAD LT All-in-One Desk Reference For Dummies,* from Wiley Publishing.

The Dashboard can be set up to display in three different configurations. By default, when you apply the 3D Modeling workspace, the Dashboard is docked at the right side of the screen. You can also anchor the Dashboard so that it appears as a vertical title bar; when you move your mouse pointer over the title bar, the Dashboard expands. Finally, the Dashboard can float in the drawing area, just like any other palette.

Unless you have way more screen space than I do, I suggest you anchor your Dashboard. To anchor a docked Dashboard, click on the "handles" (the two raised horizontal bars) at the top of the Dashboard and drag it into the drawing area. Then right-click the title bar and choose Anchor Right or Anchor Left to reduce the Dashboard palette to a vertical title bar. Figure 9-5 shows both Dashboard and Tool Palettes anchored at the right side of the display and the Properties palette anchored at the left. Pausing the mouse pointer over the title bar has opened the Dashboard to its full size.

Figure 9-5:
Anchor the
Dashboard
to reclaim
some
screen
space.

If you've accidentally closed the Dashboard, you can reopen it by choosing Tools➪Palettes➪Dashboard.

Working out with the Dashboard

The following steps show you some of the functions built into the Dashboard (and, once again, I refer you to our sister volume, *AutoCAD and AutoCAD LT All-in-One Desk Reference For Dummies,* for more information on working in 3D in AutoCAD 2008).

1. **Open a drawing containing some 3D objects.**

   If you don't have such a drawing, open one of AutoCAD 2008's sample drawings — for example, `C:\Program Files\AutoCAD 2008\ Sample\3D House`.

   A 3D model of a single-story house opens, displayed from an elevated southeasterly point of view (that is, "southeasterly" relative to the x- and y-axes).

2. **If the Dashboard is not already open, open it by choosing Tools➪ Palettes➪Dashboard.**

For this exercise, it might be worth turning off Autohide or un-anchoring the Dashboard so you don't have to keep mousing over the title bar to open it.

3. Move the mouse pointer over the gray bar at the left side of the 3D Navigate control panel (the one with the clock icon) and click the double downward-pointing arrows.

The 3D Navigate control panel expands, displaying additional tool buttons and controls for moving about in 3D.

4. In the Dashboard's 3D Navigate control panel, click Perspective Projection.

The two buttons at the right end of the 3D Navigate toolbar switch between Perspective and Parallel Projection. One or the other of these buttons is always orange to show you which mode you're in — not that there's any doubt when you're in perspective mode! (See Figure 9-6.)

5. Drag the Lens Length/Field of View slider bar to the left to reduce the focal length of the camera lens.

The farther to the left you drag the slider, the wider the apparent focal length. Stop when you've had enough distortion!

Figure 9-6:
A new
perspective
on things.

6. **Click Parallel Projection on the 3D Navigate control panel's toolbar.**

   The view of the model returns to Parallel Projection mode.

7. **Move the mouse pointer over the gray bar at the left side of the Visual Styles control panel and click the double downward-pointing arrows.**

   The expanded 3D Navigate panel rolls up, and the Visual Styles control panel expands to show a number of additional buttons and controls.

8. **Click the arrow in the Visual Styles drop-down list.**

   A schematic representation of five preconfigured visual styles appears (see Figure 9-7). I discuss visual styles in the next section.

Figure 9-7:
Some new styles to try on.

Get some (visual) style

Visual styles are collections of settings that build on the SHADEMODE settings found in earlier versions of AutoCAD. There are five default visual styles in AutoCAD 2008:

- ✓ **2D Wireframe:** Old Faithful! AutoCAD's classic 2D viewing mode: full wireframe, dot-based grid, the 2D UCS icon, and no steenkin' perspective.

- ✓ **3D Hidden:** You can still run the old HIDE command from the command line and get a hidden-line-removed (HLR) view in the 2D Wireframe visual style, but selecting 3D Hidden switches you to a gray background and linear grid.

- ✓ **3D Wireframe:** AutoCAD uses two different display systems, one for 2D and one for 3D. You can actually view 3D objects in the 2D system (are you confused yet?) but you don't get gray backgrounds, linear grids, and a flashy 3D UCS icon; for that, you need to call upon the 3D display system. And functionally, kids, that's the only difference between 2D Wireframe and 3D Wireframe.

✔ **Conceptual:** This is the more artistic of the two shaded visual styles in AutoCAD 2008. The objects tend to look a little chunkier and more sketch-like than in the Realistic mode.

✔ **Realistic:** Choosing the Realistic visual style displays the model in fully shaded (but not rendered) mode.

AutoCAD's 2D display system is a cleaner-looking environment, and display changes do seem to go faster than in the 3D display system. However, you can't view in perspective mode using the 2D display system.

AutoCAD 2008's five preconfigured visual styles are only the beginning. You can modify any of the styles or create new ones in the Visual Styles Manager palette (see Figure 9-8).

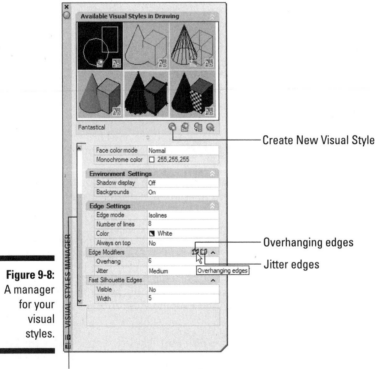

Figure 9-8:
A manager
for your
visual
styles.

Create New Visual Style

Overhanging edges

Jitter edges

Properties of selected Visual Style

To display the Visual Styles Manager, click the Visual Styles Manager button on the Visual Styles control panel toolbar. To modify an existing visual style, change the values in the Visual Styles Manager's Properties area.

The following steps explain how to create a new visual style:

1. **In the Visual Style Manager, click Create New Visual Style.**

   The Create New Visual Style dialog box opens.

2. **Enter a name and optional description for the new visual style and then click OK to return to the Visual Style Manager.**

3. **Enter new values in the appropriate fields of the Properties area.**

   For example, to create a sketchy appearance to your model, in the Edge Settings section of the Visual Style Manager, turn on Overhanging Edges and Jitter Edges by clicking the two buttons on the Edge Modifiers title bar.

   Overhanging Edges extends edges so they extend beyond the objects they meet; Jitter Edges applies a hand-drawn effect to object edges. You can increase the overhang amount by changing the numeric value. You can increase the jitter effect by selecting High — or by drinking more coffee. See Figure 9-9 for a rather extreme example of overhanging jitters.

Figure 9-9:
A pretty
sketchy
design.

Navigating in Three Dimensions

If you're brand new to 3D AutoCAD, you may be wondering how to look at the back of the house — or whatever it is you're modeling from whatever angle you desire.

The easiest way to change viewpoints is to use the View➪3D Views submenu (shown in Figure 9-10) to switch to one of the standard orthographic 3D views or an isometric view.

- ✔ The six standard orthographic (straight-on) views are Top, Bottom, Left, Right, Front, Back.

- ✔ The four standard isometric views are SW (left-front), SE (right-front), NE (right-back), and NW (left-back). (An *isometric view* is one in which you see the object from above — or below, but AutoCAD's standard views don't do below.)

Figure 9-10:
The 3D
Views
submenu.

An isometric view is a not quite realistic kind of 3D view where lines that are parallel in reality are also parallel in the view. In a perspective view, lines that are parallel in reality appear to meet at a vanishing point, as parallel lines *appear* to do in reality (think of railroad tracks heading across the prairie). The isometric views I mention previously are parallel projection views, and you can view 3D models using those views in either the full version of

AutoCAD or AutoCAD LT. The views of the 3D house in Figures 9-6 and 9-9 are perspective views, which you can set up only from the Dashboard's 3D Navigation control panel or the 3DORBIT command, neither of which is included in AutoCAD LT.

The six orthographic and four isometric views are called *standard* because they're often used in manual drafting and rendering work. They work well for showing 3D models of common objects such as mechanical components and buildings. (You can also change to *plan view*, which is a top-down view of either the world coordinate system or a user coordinate system.)

You can specify nonstandard viewpoints by choosing View⇨3D Views⇨ Viewpoint Presets. In the Viewpoint Presets dialog box that appears, specify the following settings:

✓ **A viewing angle *in* the XY plane:** Imagine your camera circling around an object while keeping the camera at the same elevation.

✓ **An angle *from* the XY plane:** Imagine using a boom to swoop the camera up to a different height so that you're looking at the object from increasingly steep angles.

AutoCAD LT includes limited 3D viewing capabilities. The same preset views are in both LT and AutoCAD, and there's also a Viewpoint Presets dialog box in which you set a viewing position by specifying angles in and from the XY plane. Finally, there's the really ugly VPOINT command (View⇨3D Views⇨Viewpoint). Refer to the online help for directions on . . . er, viewing directions.

Going into Orbit

Standard views and the Viewpoint Presets dialog box are fine for many 3D construction tasks, but if you really want to have fun with a model, 3DORBIT (not in AutoCAD LT) is your ticket to it. There are two orbiter modes: Constrained and Free. The Constrained mode is pretty much like the Free mode with training wheels.

Free Orbit displays an *arcball* on the screen — a circle representing a sphere around your object (see Figure 9-11). You click various places inside, outside, and on the arcball and then drag to change the 3D view. The idea is that you're spinning an imaginary sphere containing your model. As you drag the cursor, AutoCAD updates the screen dynamically.

In case you're wedded to the command line, there are two different command names you need before you can enter orbit: 3DORBIT (3DO) starts Constrained orbiting (no arcball), and 3DFORBIT runs the arcball-enhanced Free orbiting mode.

3DOrbit provides many other options through its right-click shortcut menu. You can change the shading mode and projection type, and you can turn on several visual aids that help you understand where you are in 3D space. Additional shortcut menu options enable you to pan, zoom, and restore standard or named views.

The following steps show some of the things that you can do with 3DOrbit:

1. **Open or continue in a drawing file containing some 3D objects.**

   `C:\Program Files\AutoCAD 2008\Sample\3D House` is a good example.

2. **Choose View⇨Orbit⇨Free Orbit.**

   The 3DOrbit arcball appears, as shown in Figure 9-11.

3. **Move the cursor inside the arcball.**

   The 3DOrbit *full orbit cursor* appears (two oval arrows circling a sphere).

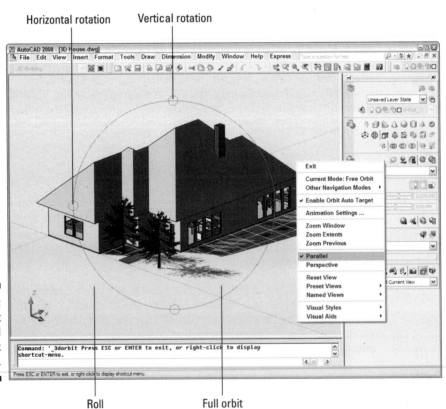

Horizontal rotation   Vertical rotation

Roll   Full orbit

Figure 9-11:
The 3DOrbit arcball and right-click menu.

4. **Click and drag, keeping the cursor inside the arcball.**

   You can rotate the model in all directions. Imagine that the cursor is your finger pushing on a globe that rotates freely in all directions.

   Pay attention to the shaded UCS (user coordinate system) icon at the lower-left corner of the drawing area as you change the view. The UCS icon helps you visualize how each orbiting operation works. If your UCS icon is not displayed, choose View➪Display➪UCS Icon➪On.

5. **Release the mouse button and move the cursor outside the arcball.**

   The 3DOrbit *roll cursor* appears (a circular arrow circling a tiny sphere).

6. **Click and drag, keeping the cursor outside the arcball.**

   You can rotate the model around an axis at the center of the circle, coming out of the screen. Imagine that you're turning the steering wheel on a car, with the steering column pointing into the screen.

7. **Release the mouse button and move the cursor over one of the small circles at the quadrant points (that is, 12 o'clock, 3 o'clock, 6 o'clock, and 9 o'clock) of the arcball.**

   The 3DOrbit *horizontal or vertical rotation cursor* appears (an elliptical arrow circling a sphere).

8. **Click and drag away from the small circle.**

   You can rotate the model around a horizontal axis (if you clicked the circle at 3 o'clock or 9 o'clock) or a vertical axis (if you clicked the circle at 12 o'clock or 6 o'clock) passing through the little circle. Imagine that you're turning a piece of meat on a spit (vegetarians, imagine it's an eggplant), with the spit located horizontally or vertically in the plane of the screen.

9. **Release the mouse button and right-click in the drawing area.**

   The 3DOrbit shortcut menu, shown in Figure 9-11, appears.

10. **Experiment with different Projection modes.**

    • *Parallel projection* is the default AutoCAD projection — lines that are parallel in the 3D object remain parallel in the projected view on the screen.

    • *Perspective projection* makes objects look more realistic (for example, train tracks appear to converge in the distance), but lines that are parallel in the model don't appear parallel in perspective projection.

    If you manage to 3DOrbit out of control so that you no longer see your model, right-click to display the 3DOrbit shortcut menu and choose Zoom Extents. The Zoom, Pan, and Preset Views options offer other ways of getting your model back in your sights.

11. **When you're finished orbiting, right-click in the drawing area and choose Exit.**

When you start orbiting with no objects selected, AutoCAD tries to update the display of everything in your model, and this can take some time. To speed things up or to simply regain your bearings, try selecting some objects before you start orbiting. Then, AutoCAD updates the display of the selected models only. When you exit orbit mode, the entire model redisplays based on the new viewpoint.

Hungry for More?

AutoCAD 2008's 3D features are logical, intuitive, and (relatively) easy to use. And, unfortunately, more than I can cover in a 400-page book. To find out about solid and surface modeling, AutoCAD 2008 includes a number of options:

- ✔ **New Features Workshop:** Choose Help⇨New Features Workshop. Open the drop-down list in the upper left and choose AutoCAD 2007. The Create, Produce, and Present headings cover 3D features. The New Features Workshop includes animations and tutorials to help get you up to speed quickly.

- ✔ **Online help system:** Choose Help⇨Help or press the F1 key. In the left pane of the Help window, expand User's Guide and then click Work with 3D Models. Figure 9-12 shows a help section on lofts and sweeps. (I know, once upon a time this would have been in a printed manual!)

- ✔ **"Building Your World":** This PDF file comes on the AutoCAD 2008 CD and covers object creation, 3D navigation, and visualization, including lighting and rendering. (Is this a case of "Print your own darned manual?")

Figure 9-12:
Help is at
hand.

Part III
If Drawings Could Talk

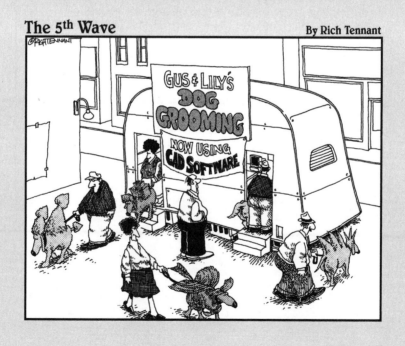

The 5th Wave   By Rich Tennant

GUS & LILY'S DOG GROOMING
NOW USING CAD SOFTWARE

In this part . . .

Text, dimensions, and hatching have long been important clarifying elements in drafting. In AutoCAD, these elements are flexible almost to a fault, and you can edit and update them quickly as you change the geometry beneath them. The text, dimension, and hatching annotations that you add "speak" about the geometry so that others can understand exactly what, how big, and how far.

After you've made some drawings that talk, you'll probably send the message around by printing — or as CAD users call it, *plotting* — them. Chapter 13 is your guidebook to navigating the plot process, understanding how the legacy of AutoCAD plotting influences current practice, and most of all, getting a good-looking, properly scaled plot onto paper.

Chapter 10

Text with Character

*I*t used to be said that "a picture is worth a thousand words." (What with inflation and cost of living increases, a picture is now actually worth 3,780 words!) The opposite is often true as well: Adding a few words to your drawing can save you from having to draw thousands of lines and arcs. It's a lot easier to write `Simpson A35 framing clip` next to a simple, schematic representation of a clip than to draw one in microscopic detail and hope that the contractor can figure out what it is!

Most CAD drawings include some text in the form of explanatory notes, object labels, and titles. This chapter demonstrates how to add text to drawings. It shows you how to take advantage of AutoCAD's annotative text objects and text styles, as well as how to find specific text and check your drawing for spelling errors. Chapter 11 covers text that's connected with dimensions and leaders.

Although most sensible people would think of leader notes as text (since that's what they are!), AutoCAD considers them — or at least formats them — as if they were dimensions. That's why I cover them in Chapter 11, "Entering New Dimensions," instead of in this chapter.

In most cases, adding text, dimensions, and other descriptive symbols is something that you should do later in the drafting process, after you've drawn at least some of the geometry. In CAD drawings, text and other annotations are usually intended to complement the geometry, not to stand alone. Thus, you generally need to have the geometry in place before you annotate it. Many drafters find that it's most efficient to first draw as much geometry as possible and then to add text annotations and dimensions to all the geometry at the same time. In this way, you develop a rhythm with the text and dimensioning commands instead of bouncing back and forth between drawing geometry and adding annotations.

AutoCAD 2008's annotative objects present a whole new way of adding notes, dimensions, and other annotations to your drawings. This chapter introduces annotative text, and subsequent chapters cover annotative dimensions and hatches. See the "Annotatively yours" sidebar, later in this chapter, for some background.

Getting Ready to Write

In AutoCAD, adding text to a drawing is only slightly more complicated than adding it to a word processing document. Here are the basic steps, which I explain in more detail in the following sections:

1. **Create a new AutoCAD text style, or select an existing style, that includes the font and other text characteristics you want to use.**

2. **Make an appropriate layer current.**

To make your AutoCAD drawing efficient and easy to edit for both you and others, create text on its own layer. Most drafting offices already have a set of CAD standards that establish specific layers for text and other object types.

3. **Run *one* of these commands to draw text:**
   - MTEXT draws paragraph (also called multiline) text.
   - DTEXT draws single-line text.

4. **Specify the text alignment points, justification, and (if necessary) height.**

5. **Type the text.**

6. **(Optional) For annotative text, assign annotation scales to the text you just typed.**

You're probably familiar with most of these steps already — especially if you've ever used a word processor. In the next few sections of this chapter, I review the particularities of AutoCAD text styles, the two kinds of AutoCAD text, and ways of controlling height and justification.

Annotatively yours

One of the great things about AutoCAD is that it offers multiple ways of accomplishing your drafting tasks. The drawback, of course, is that it's much more complicated to learn. You could master one of the ways and then find yourself working in an office where you're expected to use a different way, one that you've never tried. The solution — one that this book tries to provide — is to give you at least a taste of the most common methods.

AutoCAD 2008 supports three different methods for adding annotations to your drawings:

✔ **Add text and dimensions in model space, multiplying the drawing scale factor (see Chapter 4 for details) times the desired plotted size.** For example, assume that someone has drawn a floor plan at a scale of ¼" = 1'–0" (corresponding to a drawing scale factor of 48), and you want your notes to appear ⅛" high when the drawing is plotted to scale. You need to create text that's 48 times ⅛", or 6", high.

✔ **Add text and dimensions in layouts in paper space.** Because paper space is plotted at 1:1, you create annotations at their actual plotted size. The scale calculations are simple ("What's ⅛" times 1, boss?"), but sometimes it's beneficial to have drawing annotations in the same space as the drawing geometry, and you may have to duplicate notes in each layout.

✔ **Add text and dimensions in model space using annotative text and dimension styles.** Create them at their actual plotted size — referred to as *paper text height* by AutoCAD — and then assign *annotation scales* for all your desired plot scales. Changing the annotation scale on the status bar automatically changes the visible annotation scale in the drawing.

I think that annotative objects are the most compelling new feature in AutoCAD 2008. One of the more difficult concepts for new users to grasp is the necessity of scaling text and dimensions to apparently ludicrous sizes (6" high drawing text, for example) so that they plot correctly. Annotative objects allow you to keep your annotations in model space and specify the paper size; AutoCAD does the scale calculations for you.

Annotative object types include both single-line and multiline text (covered in this chapter), dimensions and leaders (covered in Chapter 11), hatches (see Chapter 12), and blocks and attributes (refer to Chapter 14). By default, only annotative objects at the current annotation scale as set on the status bar are displayed, but a handy toggle beside the Annotation Scale list lets you view annotative objects at all scales if you need to.

The annotative workflow does require an additional step compared with the other two methods listed previously. Instead of just creating your text (or other annotative object), you create it as usual and then add annotation scales to the objects. I describe the process in detail in the steps in this chapter and in the following chapters.

Simply stylish text

AutoCAD assigns text properties to individual lines or paragraphs of text based on *text styles*. These text styles are similar to the paragraph styles in a word processor; they contain font and other settings that determine the look and feel of text. An AutoCAD text style includes

- ✔ The font

- ✔ A text height, which you can set or leave at 0 for later flexibility

- ✔ Special effects (where available), such as italic

- ✔ *Really* special effects, such as vertical and upside down, which almost nobody uses

Before you add text to a drawing, use the Text Style dialog box — choose Format⇨Text Style to open it — to select an existing style or create a new one with settings that are appropriate to your purpose. Your AutoCAD notes may generate strange responses (or no response at all) if they appear in Old Persian Cuneiform or Cyrillic.

Text styles in AutoCAD 2008 have a new Annotative property, set in the Text Style dialog box. You can also assign the annotative property to text styles in old drawings by opening the Text Style dialog box in the drawing, checking the Annotative box, and saving the drawing in AutoCAD 2008.

Most drawings require very few text styles. You can create a style for all notes, object labels, and annotations and another text style for special titles. You may also want to create a unique text style for your dimensions (refer to Chapter 11 for more on dimension text). A title block may require one or two additional fonts, especially if you want to mimic the font used in a company logo or project logo.

As with layers, your office may have its own text style standards. If so, you'll make everyone happy by following those standards. One of the best ways to make your use of text styles efficient and consistent is to create them in a template drawing that you use to start new drawings. (If your office is well organized, it may already have a template drawing with the company-approved styles defined in it.) See Chapter 4 for information about creating and using templates. Another handy technique is to copy existing text styles from one drawing to another by using the DesignCenter palette. See Chapter 5 for instructions.

Font follies

When you create a text style in AutoCAD, you have a choice of a huge number of fonts. AutoCAD can use two different kinds of fonts: native AutoCAD SHX (compiled shape) fonts and Windows TTF (TrueType) fonts:

- ✔ **SHX:** In the Text Style dialog box, SHX font names appear with a drafting compass to the left of the name and display the .shx file extension. SHX fonts usually provide better performance because they're optimized for AutoCAD's use.

✔ **TTF:** In the Text Style dialog box, TrueType font names appear with a TT symbol to the left of name without any file extension. TTF fonts give you more and fancier font options, but they can slow down AutoCAD when you zoom, pan, and select and snap to objects. TrueType fonts also can cause greater complications when you exchange drawings with other AutoCAD users. Chapter 15 describes the special procedure that you need to use in order to install custom TrueType fonts.

It's okay to use a TrueType font sparingly for something like a title block logo, but in general, you should stick with standard AutoCAD SHX fonts whenever possible.

The most popular AutoCAD font is Romans.shx (Roman Simplex). (You may also run into Simplex.shx, an older version of Roman Simplex.) Romans.shx is a good, general-purpose font for drafting in AutoCAD. Avoid complicated, thick fonts. They can slow down AutoCAD, and they're usually more difficult to read than the simpler fonts. Remember, you're doing CAD here, not fancy graphic design or reproductions of medieval manuscripts!

Whenever possible, avoid *custom fonts,* which are font files that don't come with AutoCAD or AutoCAD LT (both programs come with the same fonts). AutoCAD installs its standard SHX fonts in the `C:\Program Files\ AutoCAD 2008\Fonts` folder; as long as you haven't added any custom fonts to that folder, you can refer to it for a list of standard fonts. AutoCAD does not embed font files in drawings; instead, it must refer to the font files installed locally under either AutoCAD (for SHX fonts) or Windows (for TrueType fonts). If you use a custom font of either type, exchanging your drawings with other people will be more complicated. If you must use a custom font, make a note of it and remember either to send it whenever you send the DWG file (assuming that the font isn't copyrighted, which many custom fonts are) or to warn the recipients that the text will appear different on their systems. It's far less hassle to avoid custom fonts altogether. See Chapter 15 for additional information about how to deal with fonts when you send and receive drawings.

Get in style

The following steps describe how to select an existing text style or create a new one before you enter text into a drawing. (If you want to experiment with an existing drawing that contains a variety of text styles, you can use `C:\Program Files\AutoCAD 2008\Sample\Architectural - Annotation Scaling and Multileaders.dwg`.) LT users have the same drawing file in LT's sample folder.

1. **Choose Format⇨Text Style.**

   The Text Style dialog box appears, as shown in Figure 10-1.

2. **In the Styles list, select each style in turn to examine the properties of the text styles that have been created in this drawing.**

   Note the font name and look at the Preview panel in the lower-left corner of the dialog box to get a feel for what the different fonts look like.

3. **If you find a suitable text style, select it in the Styles list, click Set Current, and then skip to Step 8.**

   What constitutes a suitable text style depends on industry practices, office standards, and personal preferences about how the text should look. The information in preceding sections may help you decide. If not, ask an experienced drafter in your office or look at some printed drawings and try to match the text on those. If you're starting from scratch, I highly recommend that you use annotative styles — look for the triangular symbol beside the style name.

4. **If you don't find a suitable text style, or if you prefer to create your own text style, click New.**

   Pay attention to the style that's current when you click New. If it's an annotative style, your new style will automatically be annotative; if it's not annotative, it won't. It's easy enough to check or uncheck the Annotative check box, but you may overlook this action at first.

   The New Text Style dialog box appears, with a text box for you to type a name.

5. **Type a name for your new text style and then click OK.**

   Your new text style is added to the Styles list and becomes the current style.

6. **Choose a font from the Font Name list.**

   Romans.shx is the best all-purpose font for most drafting work. If you'd like to use a different font, review the font suggestions and warnings in the previous section.

   The font that you choose becomes the font that's assigned to your new text style.

7. **To create an annotative text style, check the Annotative box. Clear the check box for non-annotative text.**

   Click the little *i* icon next to the Annotative label to find out more.

8. **Adjust the remaining text style settings.**

   The text style shown in Figure 10-1 has the following setup:

   - *Paper Text Height* (just Height for non-annotative styles) = 0.0
   - *Width Factor* = 1.0
   - *Oblique Angle* = 0
   - All check boxes other than Annotative are unchecked.

   A text style height of 0.0 makes the style *variable height,* which means that you can specify the height separately for each text object. Assigning a *fixed* (that is, nonzero) height to a text style forces all text using the style to be the same height. Variable height styles are more flexible, but fixed height styles usually make it easier to draw text of consistent height. The decision to use variable height versus fixed height styles is another aspect of text that depends on office practice, so if you work with other AutoCAD users, ask around.

   Dimensions use text styles to format the appearance of the dimension text. When you create a text style that you think you might use for your dimensions, you *must* set a height of 0. Otherwise, the setting that controls the dimension text will not work, and your dimension text is likely to be either enormous or microscopic. This one should be a double warning because it's one of the most common mistakes made by new AutoCAD drafters.

9. **Click Apply and then click Close.**

   The Text Style dialog box closes, and the text style that you selected or created is now the current style for new text objects.

Taking your text to new heights

On the off chance that you're choosing not to use annotative text styles, this section shows you why you might want to change your mind.

In Chapter 4, I describe the importance of choosing an appropriate drawing scale when you set up a drawing. I warn you that you need to know the drawing scale factor for tasks described in other chapters of this book. This is one of those chapters, and I'm about to explain one of those tasks! And when I'm done, remember — you can avoid all the arithmetic by using annotative text — it's just a check box away!

Drawing scale is the traditional way of describing a scale with an equal sign or colon — for example ¼" = 1'–0", 1:20, or 2:1. The *drawing scale factor* represents the same relationship with a single number, such as 48, 20, or 0.5. The drawing scale factor is the multiplier that converts the first number in the drawing scale into the second number. Make it a point to determine the drawing scale factor of a drawing before you add non-annotative text to it.

Plotted text height

Most industries have plotted text height standards (AutoCAD 2008 refers to *paper* text height, which means the same thing). A plotted text height of ⅛" or 3 mm is common for notes. Some companies use slightly smaller heights (for example, ³⁄₃₂" or 2.5 mm) to squeeze more text into small spaces.

Calculating non-annotative AutoCAD text height

To calculate non-annotative text height, you need to know the drawing scale factor, the desired plotted text height, and the location of the multiplication button on your calculator. Use the following steps to figure out text height:

1. **Determine the drawing scale factor.**

   If you set up the drawing, you should know its drawing scale, as described in Chapter 4. If someone else set up the drawing, and they're still around, ask them!

   Other methods of figuring out a drawing's scale factor include searching the drawing for a bar scale or text note that indicates the drawing scale, or if a printout is available, measuring dimensioned distances on the hard copy with an architectural or engineering scale. Finally, if the drawing dimensions are in model space, you can check the value of the DIM-SCALE variable (the system variable that controls dimension scale), as described in Chapter 11.

2. **Determine the height that your notes should appear when you plot the drawing to scale.**

   See the preceding "Plotted text height" section for suggestions.

3. **Multiply the numbers that you figured out in Steps 1 and 2.**

   The Cheat Sheet at the front of this book includes drawing scale factor and text height charts for both millimeters and feet and inches.

After you know the AutoCAD text height, you can use it to define the height of a text style or of an individual text object. If you assign a nonzero height to a text style (Step 8 in the "Get in style" section, earlier in this chapter), all text that you create with that style will use the fixed height. If you leave the text style's height set to 0, AutoCAD asks you for the text height when you draw each single-line text object.

This discussion of text height assumes that you're adding non-annotative text in model space. In addition to annotative text in model space, there's a third alternative. You can add annotative or non-annotative text to a paper space layout — for example, when you draw text in a title block or add a set of sheet notes that doesn't directly relate to the model space geometry. When you create text in paper space, you specify the actual, plotted paper height instead of the scaled-up height.

One line or two?

For historical reasons (namely, because the AutoCAD text capabilities used to be much more primitive than they are now), AutoCAD offers two different kinds of text objects and two corresponding text-drawing commands. Table 10-1 explains the two commands, with their aliases shown in parentheses.

Table 10-1	The Two Kinds of AutoCAD Text	
Text Object	*Command*	*Comments*
Paragraph text	MTEXT (T)	Designed for multiple lines, with word-wrapping. AutoCAD keeps the multiple lines together as a single object. Other special formatting, such as numbered or bulleted lists and columns, is possible.
Single-line text	DTEXT (DT)	Designed for creating single lines. Although you can press Enter to create more than one line of text, each line becomes a separate text object.

Although you may be inclined to ignore the older single-line text option, it's worth knowing how to use both kinds of text. The DTEXT command is quite a bit simpler than the MTEXT command, and it's still useful for entering short, single-line pieces of text such as object labels and one-line notes. And it's the command of choice for CAD comedians who want to document their one-liners!

Your text will be justified

Both the DTEXT and MTEXT commands offer a bewildering array of text *justi-fication* options — in other words, which way the text flows from the point or points that you pick in the drawing to locate it. For most purposes, the default

Left justification for single-line text or Top Left justification for paragraph text works fine. Occasionally, you may want to use a different justification, such as Center for labels or titles. Both commands provide options for changing text justification. I point out these options when I demonstrate the commands later in this chapter.

Using the Same Old Line

Despite its limitations, the DTEXT command is useful for labels and other short notes for which MTEXT would be overkill. The following procedure shows you how to add text to your drawing by using the AutoCAD DTEXT command.

You *can* use DTEXT for multiple lines of text: Just keep pressing Enter after you type each line of text, and DTEXT puts the new line below the previous one. The problem with this approach is that DTEXT creates each line of text as a separate object. If you later want to add or remove words in the multiple lines, AutoCAD can't do any word-wrapping for you; you have to edit each line separately, cutting words from one line and adding them to the adjacent line.

The DTEXT command does not use a dialog box or a fancy formatting toolbar like the MTEXT command's In-Place Text Editor. You set options by typing them into the command line or the dynamic input tooltip.

Here's how you add text with the DTEXT command:

1. **Set an appropriate layer current, as described in Chapter 5.**

2. **Set an appropriate text style current, as described in the section "Simply stylish text," earlier in this chapter.**

3. **(Optional) Use the OSNAP button on the status bar to turn off running object snap mode.**

   You may or may not want to snap text to existing objects. For example, you'd want to use a Middle object snap to locate a letter or number precisely at the center of a circle.

4. **Choose Draw⇨Text⇨Single Line Text to start the DTEXT command.**

   If this is the first annotative object you're creating in this drawing session, AutoCAD displays a Select Annotation Scale dialog box warning you that you are indeed creating an annotative object and asking you to set the scale at which you want the annotation to appear.

   Don't click the Text button on the Draw toolbar — that starts the multi-line text command, MTEXT, which I cover in the next section.

AutoCAD tells you the current text style and height settings and prompts you to select a starting point for the text or to choose an option for changing the text justification or current text style first:

```
Current text style: "Standard" Text height: 0.2000
     Annotative: Yes
Specify start point of text or [Justify/Style]:
```

If the text style is annotative, the text height displayed in the prompt is the model space height, not the ultimate plotted text height. For example, if the text style is created with a fixed paper text height of 0.2000, and the annotation scale is set to 1:2, the AutoCAD prompt will read `Text height: 0.4000`.

5. **If you want to change justification from the default (Left), type J, press Enter, and choose one of the other justification options.**

   Look up "single-line text, aligning" in the online help system index if you need help with the justification options.

6. **Specify the insertion point for the first text character.**

   You can enter the point's coordinates from the keyboard, use the mouse to click a point on-screen, or press Enter to locate new text immediately below the most recent single-line text object that you created.

   AutoCAD prompts you for the text height:

   ```
   Specify height <0.2000>:
   ```

7. **Specify the height for the text.**

   This prompt doesn't appear if you're using a text style with a fixed (that is, nonzero) height. See the "Simply stylish text" section, earlier in this chapter, for information about fixed versus variable text heights.

   AutoCAD prompts you for the text rotation angle:

   ```
   Specify rotation angle of text <0>:
   ```

8. **Specify the text rotation angle by typing the rotation angle and pressing Enter or by rotating the line on-screen with the mouse.**

   AutoCAD prompts you to type the text.

9. **Type the first line of text and press Enter.**

10. **Type additional lines of text, pressing Enter at the end of each line.**

    Figure 10-2 shows text appearing on-screen as you type it.

11. **To complete the command, press Enter at the start of a blank line.**

    AutoCAD adds the new single-line text object — or objects, if you typed more than one line — to the drawing.

Figure 10-2:
Single-line
text appears
letter-by-
letter.

To align lines of text exactly, make sure that you type all the lines in one instance of the DTEXT command, pressing Enter after each line to make the next line appear just after it. Otherwise, aligning different lines of text precisely is harder to do (unless you set your snap just right or use a complicated combination of object snaps and point filters). To edit single-line text after you've created it, select the text, right-click, and choose Edit to open the In-Place Text Editor. ("In-Place" simply means that you edit text at its exact size and location in the drawing.) I tell you more about in-place text editing later in this chapter.

An in-place editing box highlights the selected text object, enabling you to edit the contents of the text string. If you want to edit other text properties, such as text height, select the text, right-click, and choose Properties to display the Properties palette. Use the Properties palette to change parameters as needed.

Turning On Your Annotative Objects

As I describe in the "Annotatively yours" sidebar, you have a couple of extra steps in the workflow in order to take advantage of single-line or multiline text you create using annotative styles. You have to assign the scales you're likely to use in your drawing to the text objects and then set the annotation scale accordingly. The following steps explain how to assign annotation scales to text that has been created using an annotative text style:

1. **Make sure the text *is* annotative by hovering the crosshairs over it.**

   Text created with an annotative style but that has not had any annotation scales applied to it displays a single triangular symbol beside the crosshairs (the symbol represents the end view of a triangular engineering scale). If there's no symbol, the text is not annotative.

You can make individual text objects annotative even if they've been created using a non-annotative style by selecting the text, pressing Ctrl+1 to open the Properties palette, and changing the Annotative property from No to Yes. There may be times when you would want to do this, but they're probably few and far between. Until you become very familiar with annotative objects and decide how you want to use them in both new and old drawings, I recommend that you stick to creating your annotative text by using annotative text styles rather than assigning the annotative property on individual text objects created with non-annotative styles.

2. **Right-click over a text object and choose Annotative Object Scale⇨ Add/Delete Scales.**

   The Annotation Object Scale dialog box appears and shows a list of all annotative scales assigned to the selected object. In the case of a new text or other annotative object, the only scale listed will be whatever annotation scale is set current on the status bar.

3. **In the Annotation Object Scale dialog box, click Add.**

   The Add Scales to Object dialog box appears, displaying a list of all drawing scale values stored in the drawing.

4. **Select the desired scales from the list, holding down the Ctrl key to select more than one, and then click OK.**

   The Annotation Object Scale dialog box reappears, with the scales you added displayed in the list box.

   AutoCAD will happily let you select all the scales in the box, but your drawings will be easier to manage if you select only the scales you're likely to use — you can always go back and add another scale later.

   As I point out in Chapter 4, you can edit the scale list (choose Format⇨ Scale List) to remove the scales you never use. If you make a mistake, just click the Reset button in the Edit Scale List dialog box to restore all the default scales.

5. **Click OK.**

   After you assign annotative scales to text (or any annotative object), you'll see a pair of triangular annotative object symbols. Don't worry — although you *are* seeing double, you've done it right!

6. **Open the Annotation Scale list on the application or drawing status bar and select one of the scales you added to the object.**

   The annotative objects (text in this case) will change their size as you change the annotation scale. If you select a scale from the list that you did not assign to the object in Step 3, the annotative objects disappear unless you turn on the Annotation Visibility toggle on the status bar. There are a lot of options, a mess of settings, and a slew of system variables in this complex new feature. To find out more about annotative objects, refer to the New Features Workshop: Select AutoCAD 2008 from the drop-down list and then choose Scale Annotations.

Figure 10-3 shows two versions of the same drawing, with the same text objects (the bulleted notes and windows sizes) displaying at the different annotation scales specified in the two status bars. The non-annotative text (the room label) remains unchanged.

Saying More in Multiline Text

When you just can't shoehorn your creative genius into one or more one-line pieces of text, AutoCAD's multiline text object gives you room to go on and on and on. The following procedure shows you how to create multiline text with the MTEXT command.

Making it with Mtext

The first part of the MTEXT command prompts you for various points and options. The order is a bit confusing, so read these steps and the prompts carefully.

Figure 10-3: Annotative text scales automatically as the annotation scale changes.

Here's how you use the MTEXT command:

1. **Set an appropriate layer and text style current and (optionally) turn off running object snap mode, as described in Steps 1 through 3 in the "Using the Same Old Line" section.**

2. **Click the Multiline Text button on the Draw toolbar.**

   The command line displays the current text style and height settings and prompts you to select the first corner of an imaginary rectangle that will determine the word-wrapping width for the text object:

   ```
   Current text style:  "S-NOTES"  Text height:  0.2000
         Annotative:  Yes
   Specify first corner:
   ```

3. **Pick a point in the drawing.**

   The command line prompts you for the opposite corner of the text rectangle that will determine the word-wrapping width and gives you the option of changing settings first:

   ```
   Specify opposite corner or [Height/Justify/Line
         spacing/Rotation/Style/Width/Columns]:
   ```

4. **Type H and press Enter to change the default text height.**

   The command line prompts you for a new default text height:

   ```
   Specify height <0.2000>:
   ```

5. **Type an appropriate text height.**

   See the "Taking your text to new heights" section, earlier in this chapter, for information. If you're adding text in model space, I highly recommend that you use annotative text.

   The prompt for the opposite corner of the Mtext rectangle reappears. The command line shows

   ```
   Specify opposite corner or [Height/Justify/Line
         spacing/Rotation/Style/Width/Columns]:
   ```

6. **If you want to change justification from the default (top left), type J, press Enter, and choose one of the other justification options.**

   Look up "multiline text, aligning, Justify Multiline Text" in the index of the online help system if you want an explanation of the other justification options.

7. **Pick another point in the drawing.**

   Don't worry about the height of the rectangle that you create by choosing the second point; the width of the rectangle is all that matters. AutoCAD adjusts the height of the text rectangle to accommodate the number of lines of word-wrapped text. Don't worry too much about the width, either; you can adjust it later.

The In-Place Text Editor frameless window appears with the tab and indent ruler above it and the Text Formatting toolbar above that, as shown in Figure 10-4.

In-Place Text Editor frameless window   Text Formatting toolbar   Tab and indent ruler

Figure 10-4:
Adding
multiline
text.

8. **Verify the text font and height.**

   The text font and height should be right if you correctly performed Steps 1, 4, and 5. If not, you can change these settings in the Font drop-down list and the Text Height text box on the Text Formatting toolbar.

9. **Type text into the text area of the In-Place Text Editor.**

   AutoCAD word-wraps multiline text automatically. If you want to force a line break at a particular location, press Enter.

   By convention in most industries, text in drawings is always uppercase. How many times have you forgotten to press the Caps Lock key before entering drawing text? How many times have you forgotten to turn Caps Lock off again when it's time to type your e-mail? To save yourself some agony, right-click in the In-Place Text Editor and choose AutoCAPS from the menu.

10. **If you want other formatting, select text, right-click, and choose the appropriate option from the menu (as shown in Figure 10-5).**

Edit	▶
Learn about MTEXT	
Display Options	▶
Insert Field...	Ctrl+F
Symbol	▶
Import Text...	
Columns	▶
Paragraph...	
Bullets and Lists	▶
Background Mask...	
MText Justification	▶
Find and Replace...	Ctrl+R
Select All	Ctrl+A
Change Case	▶
AutoCAPS	
Remove Formatting	▶
Combine Paragraphs	
Character Set	▶
Help	F1
Cancel	

Columns submenu:
✓ No Columns	
Dynamic Columns	▶
Static Columns	▶
Insert Column Break Alt+Enter	
Column Settings...	

Dynamic Columns submenu:
Auto height
Manual height

Figure 10-5:
More
multiline
text
formatting
options in
the right-
click menu.

11. Click OK in the Text Formatting toolbar (or press Ctrl+Enter).

The In-Place Text Editor window closes, and AutoCAD adds your text to the drawing.

12. Add annotation scales to the new multiline text object.

The steps are the same for multiline text as for single-line text. Refer to the "Turning On Your Annotative Objects" section, earlier in this chapter, if you need a refresher.

As you can tell by looking at the Text Formatting toolbar and multiline text right-click menu, the MTEXT command gives you plenty of other options. You can show or hide the toolbar, the ruler, or the Options buttons, and you can give the In-Place Text Editor an opaque background. Right-clicking gives you access to columns and numbered or bulleted lists and a shortcut to the New Features Workshop entry on multiline text (choose "Learn about MTEXT").

Between them, the Text Formatting toolbar and the right-click menu also include a Stack/Unstack button for fractions, a Find and Replace utility, tools for changing between lowercase and uppercase, options for applying background masks and inserting fields, a special Symbol submenu, and an Import Text option for importing text from a TXT (ASCII text) file or RTF (Rich Text Format) file. I discuss background masks and fields in the next section. If you think you may have a use for any of these other features, choose Contents➪ Command Reference➪Commands➪M Commands➪MTEXT in AutoCAD's online help to find out more about them.

In AutoCAD 2008, multiline text objects can be set up in columns *or* paragraphs. (I cover columns in more detail later in the chapter.) The new Paragraph dialog box, which you open from the right-click menu, lets you set indents and tab stops as well as control line spacing both within and between paragraphs.

It slices, it dices . . .

Two more useful options on the multiline text right-click menu are Background Mask and Insert Field.

Mtext dons a mask

When you turn on background masking, AutoCAD hides the portions of any objects that lie underneath the multiline text. Use these steps to turn on and control this feature:

1. **Right-click in the In-Place Text Editor and choose Background Mask from the menu.**

   The Background Mask dialog box appears.

2. **Click the Use Background Mask check box so that this option is turned on.**

3. **Either click Use Drawing Background Color (to make the mask the same color as the drawing area's background color) or choose a color from the drop-down list (to make the text appear in a solid rectangle of the specified color).**

4. **Click OK to return to the In-Place Text Editor.**

If you've turned on background masking but it isn't having the desired effect, use the DRAWORDER or TEXTTOFRONT command to move text on top of other objects.

Mtext plays the field

The Insert Field option (not available in AutoCAD LT) creates a text field that updates automatically every time you open, save, plot, or regenerate the drawing. These fields can contain data such as the date, filename, or author. Fields draw information from the operating system settings, Drawing Properties dialog box, sheet sets feature, and AutoCAD system variables. (For more information about system variables, see Chapter 2.) Use the following procedure to add a field while you're creating multiline text:

1. **Right-click in the In-Place Text Editor and choose Insert Field from the menu.**

   The Field dialog box appears.

2. **Choose a Field Name in the left column.**

3. **Choose a Format in the right column, or for date fields, type a format in the Date Format box.**

4. **Click OK.**

   AutoCAD adds the field to the Mtext object that you're creating or editing.

If you see four dashes instead of a valid field value, you probably need to do one of the following things:

✔ Regenerate the drawing (see Chapter 8).

✔ Save the drawing.

✔ Fill in Drawing Properties dialog box values (see Chapter 4) and then regenerate the drawing.

✔ Configure sheet sets (see Chapter 13).

Figure 10-6 shows fields and background masking in action.

Figure 10-6:
Mtext plays
the field
and dons
a mask.

Doing a number on your Mtext lists

Another advantage of Mtext is that it supports bulleted and numbered lists. This feature is especially useful for creating general drawing notes, as shown in Figure 10-7. AutoCAD automates the process of creating numbered lists almost completely. Here's how:

1. **Follow Steps 1 through 8 in the previous section, "Making it with Mtext," to open the In-Place Text Editor.**

2. **Type a title — for example,** DESIGN CRITERIA.

   If you'd like to have your title underlined, click Underline on the Text Formatting toolbar before you type the title; click Underline again to turn it off. Press Enter to go to the next line and Enter again to leave a little more space.

3. **Right-click inside the text editing window and choose Bullets and Lists from the menu; then reopen the menu and enable Allow Bullets and Lists, Allow Auto-List, Use Tab Delimiter Only, and Numbered.**

   The number 1 followed by a period appears on the current line, and the cursor jumps to the tab stop visible in the ruler at the top of the In-Place Text Editor window.

   Enabling *Numbered* places numerals followed by periods in front of items in a list. (*Bulleted* places bullet characters in front of items in a list.) *Auto-list* enables automatic numbering — each time you press Enter to move to a new line, AutoCAD increments the number.

4. **Type the text corresponding to the current number or bullet.**

   As AutoCAD wraps the text, the second and subsequent lines align with the tab stop — that is, the text is automatically indented.

5. **Press Enter at the end of the paragraph to move to the next line.**

   Just like creating numbered lists in your favorite word processor, AutoCAD automatically inserts the next number at the beginning of the new paragraph, with everything perfectly aligned, as shown in Figure 10-7.

   To create nested numbered or bulleted items as seen in Figure 10-7, simply press Tab at the start of the line. If you change your mind, you can bump a nested text item up a level by selecting the item in the In-Place Text Editor and pressing Shift+Tab.

6. **Repeat Steps 4 and 5 for each subsequent numbered or bulleted item.**

   For legibility, you sometimes want to add spaces between the notes. If you press Enter twice to give yourself a blank line, AutoCAD — like every good word processor — thinks you're finished with your list and turns numbering off. AutoCAD is smart, so you need to be smarter. If you put the cursor at the end of the first note and press Enter, you get a blank line. The problem is, the blank line is now numbered, and your intended Note 2 is now Note 3. Just press the Backspace key. The number on the blank line disappears, and Note 2 is back to being Note 2 again. When you delete a numbered item, the remaining numbers automatically adjust.

If you don't like the horizontal spacing of the numbers or the alignment of subsequent lines, you can adjust them easily by manipulating the tab and indent markers in the In-Place Text Editor's ruler.

 7. **In the ruler, drag the upper slider (the triangle pointing down) to the right a short distance. Drag the lower slider (the triangle pointing up) to the right a slightly greater distance.**

The upper slider controls the indentation of the first line in each paragraph. The lower slider controls the indentation of the second and subsequent lines. An indent of one to two of the short, vertical tick marks usually works well for the first line. An indent of two to four tick marks works well for the second and subsequent lines.

Indention of second and subsequent lines

Indention of first line   Tab

Figure 10-7:
Tabs, indents, and automatic numbering set to create numbered lists.

8. **Click in the ruler just above the lower slider.**

   A small triangle (pointing right) appears above the lower slider. This triangle shows the tab stop.

   Make sure that the corner of the tab stop (right-pointing) triangle aligns horizontally with the point of the lower slider triangle. If not, click and drag the tab stop until it aligns.

If you prefer to type tab and indent distances, not adjust them with the cursor, open the Paragraph dialog box from the Mtext right-click menu. Whichever way you do it, if you select text first, the tab and indent changes apply to the selected text. If you don't select text first, the changes apply to new text from that point in the multiline text object forward.

Line up in columns — Now!

AutoCAD is getting more word processor–like with every release. Two versions back, it was simple indents, then in AutoCAD 2007 came numbered lists and bulleted lists.

AutoCAD 2008 continues the longer-wider-shinier tradition with columns in multiline text. Columns come in two flavors: *static* and *dynamic*.

- With **static columns**, you specify the number of columns into which to flow your text. Columns are always the same height, and text is allowed to overflow the final column if there's too much of it.

- **Dynamic columns,** as you might expect, are friendlier and more flexible. Column heights can be individually adjusted, and new columns are added automatically to accommodate the text.

Selecting either column type also offers you a Column Settings dialog box where you can specify values numerically instead of by dragging grips.

Figure 10-8 shows a block of multiline text imported as an RTF file from a word processor and then formatted in dynamic columns with the Manual Height option.

Setting up columns is pretty straightforward — the following steps explain how:

1. **Open a drawing that contains a large multiline text object, or create a large multitext object in a new drawing.**

If you already have drawing specifications or general notes in a word processor document, or even a text file, you can right-click inside the MTEXT command's In-Place Text Editor and choose Import Text. The Select File dialog box opens, giving you the choice of Rich Text Format (RTF) or ASCII text (TXT) files.

Figure 10-8:
Dynamically
columnizing
your text.

2. **If the In-Place Text Editor is not already open, double-click the text, or right-click it and choose Mtext Edit.**

3. **Click Columns in the Text Formatting toolbar and choose either Dynamic Columns or Static Columns.**

   If you choose Dynamic Columns, select either Automatic Height or Manual Height. Selecting Manual Height puts grips on each column so you can adjust their height individually, as shown in Figure 10-8. Automatic height displays a single grip, so the heights of all columns remain the same, but new columns are still added as required by the amount of text.

   If you choose Static Columns, select the number of columns you want from the menu. Clicking **2**, for example, creates two columns regardless of the length of your text — you may end up with overflowing text or empty columns.

4. **Click OK in the Text Formatting toolbar when you're satisfied with the column arrangement.**

   You can revert to a non-columnar arrangement by clicking the Columns button in the Text Formatting toolbar and choosing No Columns.

Modifying Mtext

After you create a multiline text object, you edit it like a single-line text object: Select the object, right-click, and choose Mtext Edit or Properties.

✔ The Mtext Edit option opens the In-Place Text Editor window so that you can change the text contents and formatting.

✔ The Properties option opens the Properties palette, where you can change overall properties for the text object.

The easiest way to change the word-wrapping width of a paragraph text object is to *grip edit* it. Select the text object, click one of the corner grips, release the mouse button, move the crosshairs, and click again. Chapter 7 describes grip editing in detail.

Just like any good word processor or text editor, AutoCAD includes both a spell checker and a find-and-replace tool for text or dimensions. To check the spelling of selected objects or the entire drawing, choose Tools➪Spelling to display the Check Spelling dialog box. Choosing Edit➪Find or typing FIND and pressing Enter displays the Find and Replace dialog box. Handily, Find and Replace is also accessible from within the MTEXT command's In-Place Text Editor — in case you just want to replace text within a single multiline text object. Look up SPELL or FIND in the online help index if you need more information on either command.

Gather Round the Tables

You don't know the meaning of the word *tedious* unless you've tried to create a column-and-row data table in older versions of AutoCAD with the Line and DTEXT commands. AutoCAD's table object and the TABLESTYLE and TABLE commands for creating it make the job almost fun.

Surprisingly, and despite the emphasis on the feature in this chapter, table objects in AutoCAD 2008 are *not* annotative, so you have just two methods of adding them to drawings. You can create them in model space, scaling them up by the drawing scale factor (see Chapter 4 for a refresher), or — and this seems more sensible to me — you can create them in a layout, in paper space, defining them by their actual plotted (paper) dimensions.

Tables have style, too

You control the appearance of tables — both the text and the gridlines — with *table styles* (just as you control the appearance of standalone text with text styles). Use the TABLESTYLE command to create and modify table styles. Follow these steps to create a table:

1. **Choose Format➪Table Style.**

   The Table Style dialog box appears.

2. **In the Styles list, select the existing table style whose settings you want to use as the starting point for the settings of your new style.**

For example, select the default table style named Standard.

3. **Click the New button to create a new table style that's a copy of the existing style.**

The Create New Table Style dialog box appears.

4. **Enter a New Style Name and click Continue.**

The New Table Style dialog box appears, as shown in Figure 10-9.

Figure 10-9:
Setting
the table.

5. **In the Cell Styles area, with "Data" showing in the list box, specify settings for the data alignment, margins, text, and borders.**

The settings you are likely to want to change are Text Style, Text Height, and perhaps either Text Color (all three are on the Text tab) or Grid Color (on the Borders tab). If you leave colors set to ByBlock, then the text and grid lines will inherit the color that's current when you create the table. That color will be the current layer's color, if you follow my advice in Chapter 5.

6. **In the Cell Styles area, open the drop-down list and repeat Step 5 for the Headers (that is, the column headings) and the Title.**

7. **Click OK to close the New Table Style dialog box.**

The Table Style dialog box reappears.

8. **(Optional) Select your new table style from the Styles list and then click Set Current.**

Your new table style becomes the current table style that AutoCAD uses for future tables in this drawing.

9. **Click Close.**

   The Table Style dialog box closes. Now you're ready to create a table, as described in the next section.

You can access the Table Cell Format dialog box directly from the Title, Column Head, or Data pages of the New Table Style dialog box. The Table Cell Format dialog box provides a number of additional options for formatting cells by data type.

AutoCAD stores table styles in the DWG file, so a style that you create in one drawing isn't immediately available in others. You can copy a table style from one drawing to another with DesignCenter. (Use the procedure for borrowing dimension styles outlined in Chapter 11, but substitute Table Styles for Dimstyles.)

Creating and editing tables

After you create a suitable table style, adding a table to your drawing is easy with the TABLE command. Here's how:

1. **Set an appropriate layer current.**

   Assuming that you leave the current color, linetype, and lineweight set to ByLayer, as I recommend in Chapter 5, the current layer's properties will control the properties of any parts of the table that you left set to ByBlock when you defined the table style. (See Step 5 in the preceding section, "Tables have style, too.")

2. **Choose Draw⇨Table.**

   The Insert Table dialog box appears.

3. **Choose a table style from the Table Style Name drop-down list.**

4. **Choose an Insertion Behavior:**

   • *Specify Insertion Point* is the easiest method and means that you pick the location of the table's upper-left corner (or lower-left corner if you set Table Direction to Up in the table style). With this method, you specify the default column width and number of rows in the Insert Table dialog box.

   • *Specify Window* means that you pick the upper-left corner and then the lower-right corner. With this method, AutoCAD automatically scales the column widths and determines how many rows to include.

5. **Specify Column & Row Settings.**

   If you chose Specify Window in Step 4, AutoCAD sets the Column Width and number of Data Rows to Auto, which means that AutoCAD will figure them out based on the overall size of the table that you specify in Steps 7 and 8.

6. **Click OK.**

   AutoCAD prompts you to specify the insertion point of the table.

7. **Click a point or type coordinates.**

   If you chose Specify Insertion Point in Step 4, AutoCAD draws the table grid lines, places the cursor in the title cell, and displays the Text Formatting toolbar.

8. **If you chose Specify Window in Step 4, specify the diagonally opposite corner of the table.**

   AutoCAD draws the table. Based on the table size that you indicated, AutoCAD chooses the column width and number of rows.

9. **Type a title for the table.**

10. **Type values in each cell, using the arrow keys or Tab key to move among cells.**

    The cell right-click menu offers many other options, including copying contents from one cell to another, merging cells, inserting rows and columns, changing formatting, and inserting a *block* (that is, a graphical symbol — see Chapter 14 for information about blocks).

   The fields feature described earlier in this chapter works for table text, too — you can insert a field into a table cell. For example, you might use this feature to create part of a title block, with fields serving as the "date" and "drawn by" data.

11. **Click OK on the Text Formatting toolbar.**

    Figure 10-10 shows a completed table, along with the Insert Table dialog box.

You can edit cell values later simply by double-clicking in a cell. To change column width or row height, click on the table grid and then click and move the blue grips. (To change the width of one column without altering the over-all width of the table, hold down the Ctrl key while you move the grip.) If you want to change other aspects of a table or individual cells in it, select the table or cell and use the Properties palette to make changes.

Tables got a thorough overhaul in AutoCAD 2008. In addition to manually entering text and blocks in an empty table, AutoCAD 2008 tables can display content from a data link or from object data in the drawing (see Figure 10-10). There's a cool new Table toolbar, but don't go looking for it on the regular toolbar menu; to open it, you have to click inside a table cell. If these new fea-tures sound like something you can't live without, check out "Annotate Drawings, Tables" in the online help User's Guide.

Figure 10-10:
The Insert Table dialog box and the result of using it.

You can import tables from Microsoft Excel instead of using the Insert Table dialog box. To import Excel data, in Excel, select the desired cells and choose Edit⇨Copy. Then in AutoCAD, choose Edit⇨Paste Special and choose AutoCAD Entities in the Paste Special dialog box. AutoCAD attempts to copy the Excel spreadsheet's formatting along with the cell data, but you'll probably have to adjust column widths and perform other cleanup on the imported table.

You can go the other direction — from AutoCAD to Excel or another program — via a CSV (Comma Separated Value) file. Look up "TABLEEXPORT command" in AutoCAD's online help index.

You can extract attribute data to tables. See Chapter 14 for information about blocks and attributes. You can also perform simple calculations in tables by using predefined functions or your own arithmetical expressions. Look up "Use Formulas in Table Cells" in AutoCAD's online help Search page.

Chapter 11

Entering New Dimensions

· ·

· ·

*I*n drafting — either CAD or manual drafting — *dimensions* are special text labels with attached lines that together clearly indicate the size of something. Although it's theoretically possible to draw all the pieces of each dimension by using AutoCAD commands such as LINE and MTEXT, dimensioning is so common a drafting task that AutoCAD provides special commands for doing the job more efficiently. These dimensioning commands group the parts of each dimension into a convenient, easy-to-edit package. Even better, as you edit an object — by stretching it, for example — AutoCAD automatically updates the measurement displayed in the dimension text label to indicate the object's new size, as shown in Figure 11-1. And perhaps best of all, AutoCAD 2008's new annotative dimensions automatically change their size as you change the annotation scale on the model tab or the viewport scale in a layout.

As I mention in Chapter 10, I consider AutoCAD 2008's new annotative objects to be the most significant new feature in this release. In Chapter 10, I explain the general principles of annotative objects; in this chapter, I take a closer look at annotative dimensions.

AutoCAD controls the look of dimensions by means of *dimension styles,* just as it controls the look of text with text styles. (AutoCAD also uses text styles to control the appearance of the text in dimensions.) But dimension styles are much more complicated than text styles because dimensions have so many more pieces that you need to control. After you find or create an appropriate dimension style, you use one of several dimensioning commands to draw dimensions that point to the important points on an object (the two endpoints of a line, for example).

Original dimension

Figure 11-1:
Changing
objects auto-
matically
updates
dimensions.

Dimension updates when you change the object   Current annotation scale

AutoCAD dimensioning is a big, complicated subject. (It's so complicated, in fact, that Autodesk has an especially wise person in charge of dimensioning in AutoCAD — this person is called the *dimwit.*) Every industry has its own dimensioning conventions, habits, and quirks. As usual, AutoCAD tries to support them all and, in so doing, makes things a bit convoluted for everyone. This chapter covers the essential concepts and commands that you need to know to start drawing dimensions. Be prepared to spend some additional time studying how to create any specialized types of dimensions that your industry uses. Who knows — if you work hard, you could become your own company's resident dimwit!

You add dimensions to a drawing *after* you've drawn at least some of the geometry; otherwise, you won't have much to dimension! Your dimensioning and overall drafting efficiency improve if you add dimensions in batches, rather than draw a line, draw a dimension, draw another line, draw another dimension. . . .

Discovering New Dimensions

Before digging into the techniques that you use to create dimension styles and dimensions, I review some AutoCAD dimensioning terminology that you need to understand. If you're already familiar with CAD dimensioning lingo, just skim this section and look at the figures in it. Otherwise, read on.

Why dimensions in CAD?

You may think that CAD would have rendered text dimensions obsolete. After all, you comply with all my suggestions about using AutoCAD precision techniques when you draw and edit, and you're careful to draw each object at its true size, right? The contractor or machinist can just use AutoCAD to query distances and angles in the CAD DWG file, right? Sorry, but no (to the last question, anyway). Here are a few reasons why the traditional dimensioning that CAD drafting has inherited from manual drafting is likely to be around for a while:

✔ **Some people need to or want to use paper drawings when they build something.** We're still some time away from the day when contractors haul computers around on their tool belts (never mind mousing around a drawing while hanging from scaffolding).

✔ **In many industries, paper drawings still rule legally.** Your company may supply both plotted drawings and DWG files to clients, but your contracts probably specify that the plotted drawings govern in the case of any discrepancy. The contracts probably also warn against relying on any distances that the recipient of the drawings measures — using measuring commands in the electronic drawing file or a scale on the plotted drawing. The text dimensions are supposed to supply all the dimensional information that's needed to construct the object.

✔ **Dimensions sometimes carry additional information besides the basic length or angle.** For example, dimension text can indicate the allowable manufacturing tolerances or show that a particular distance is typical of similar situations elsewhere on the drawing.

So remember the old rule of drafting prowess: "It's not the size of the drawn object that matters, but the dimensions that are on it."

Anatomy of a dimension

AutoCAD uses the names shown in Figure 11-2 and described in the following list to refer to the parts of each dimension:

✔ **Dimension text:** Dimension text is usually the number that indicates the actual distance or angle. Dimension text can also include other text information in addition to or instead of the number. For example, you can add a suffix such as TYP. to indicate that a dimension is typical of several similar configurations, or you can insert a description such as See Detail 3/A2.

✔ **Dimension lines:** In dimensions that indicate length or distance, the dimension lines go from the dimension text outward, either horizontally, vertically, rotated at a specified angle, or parallel to the object being measured, to indicate the extent of the dimensioned distance. (For other dimension types — for example, the radius and diameter dimensions shown in Figure 11-3 — the dimension line simply points at the object being dimensioned.) AutoCAD's default dimension style settings center the dimension text vertically and horizontally on the dimension lines (see Figure 11-2), but you can change those settings to cause the text to appear in a different location — sitting over an unbroken dimension line as shown previously in Figure 11-1, for example. See the section, "Adjusting style settings," later in this chapter, for instructions.

✔ **Dimension arrowheads:** The dimension arrowheads appear at the ends of the dimension lines and clarify the extent of the dimensioned length. AutoCAD's default arrowhead style is the closed, filled type shown in Figure 11-2, but you can choose other symbols, such as tick marks, to indicate the ends of the dimension lines. (Don't get ticked off, but AutoCAD calls the line ending an *arrowhead* even when, as in the case of a tick mark, it doesn't look like an arrow.)

✔ **Extension lines:** Extension lines extend outward from the extension line origin points that you select (usually by snapping to points on an object) to the dimension lines. By drafting convention, a small gap usually exists between the extension line origin points and the beginning of the extension lines. You can also make a set of dimensions look tidier by assigning fixed lengths for the extension lines. And if you need to dimension to circles or centerlines, you can assign dash-dot linetypes to either or both extension lines. The extension lines usually extend just beyond where they meet the dimension lines.

Figure 11-2:
The parts of a dimension.

A field guide to dimensions

AutoCAD provides several types of dimensions and commands for drawing them. Figure 11-3 shows the most common types, and the following list describes them:

- **Linear dimensions:** A *linear* dimension measures the linear extent of an object or the linear distance between objects. Most linear dimensions are either horizontal or vertical, but you can draw dimensions that are rotated to other angles, too.

- **Aligned dimensions:** An *aligned* dimension is similar to a linear dimension, but the dimension line tilts to the same angle as a line drawn through the origin points of its extension lines.

- **Radial dimensions:** A *radius* dimension calls out the radius of a circle or arc, and a *diameter* dimension calls out the diameter of a circle or arc. You can position the dimension text inside or outside the curve, as shown in Figure 11-3. If you position the text outside the curve, AutoCAD (by default) draws a little cross at the center of the circle or arc.

- **Angular dimensions:** An *angular* dimension calls out the angular measurement between two lines, the two endpoints of an arc, or two points on a circle. The dimension line appears as an arc that indicates the sweep of the measured angle.

Figure 11-3: Common types of dimensions.

Other types of dimensions and dimension-like annotations you can add to AutoCAD objects include arc length and ordinate dimensions, tolerances, center marks, and leaders. See the "Bring Out Your Inner Leader" section at the end of this chapter for instructions on how to draw leaders. Look up "dimensions, creating" on the Index tab in the AutoCAD online help system for more information about other kinds of dimensions.

Dimension associativity

By default, AutoCAD groups all the parts of each dimension — the extension lines, dimension lines, arrowheads, and text — into a special *associative dimension* object. *Associative* means two things:

- ✓ **The different parts of the dimension function as a single object.** When you click any part of the dimension, AutoCAD selects all of its parts.

- ✓ **The dimension is connected to the points on the object that you specified when you drew the dimension.** If you change the size of the object (for example, stretch a line), the dimension updates appropriately — the lines and arrows move, and the text changes to reflect the line's new size.

The associative dimensions I'm talking about here first appeared in AutoCAD 2002. Before that, AutoCAD had a more primitive kind of dimensioning. Dimensions were single objects, and they did update if you stretched an object while being very careful to include the dimension itself in the crossing selection for the STRETCH command. Here's where things can get a bit confusing: AutoCAD used to call these old-style, single-object dimensions *associative* but now calls them *non-associative*, and what used to be called non-associative dimensions before AutoCAD 2002 are now called *exploded* dimensions. For more information about how to determine which kind of dimension AutoCAD draws, see the "Controlling and editing dimension associativity" section, later in this chapter.

Finding your dimension tools

The AutoCAD Dimension menu provides access to dimensioning commands. If you find yourself adding dimensions in batches, the Dimension toolbar is more efficient because it makes the dimensioning commands more accessible. You toggle the Dimension toolbar off and on by right-clicking any AutoCAD toolbar icon and choosing Dimension from the menu. As with other toolbars, you can move the Dimension toolbar to a different location on the screen or dock it on any margin of the drawing area.

If you choose to work in the 2D Drafting & Annotation workspace, the Dashboard's default Dimensions control panel contains all the Dimension toolbar buttons with the minor exceptions of Dimension Edit and Dimension Text Edit — both of whose functions are available in the Properties palette. By default, the Dashboard also contains a Multileaders panel. (I discuss multi-leaders at the end of this chapter.)

All dimensioning commands have long command names (such as DIMARC, DIMLINEAR, and DIMRADIUS) and corresponding command aliases (such as DAR, DLI, and DRA, respectively) that you can type at the command prompt. If you do lots of dimensioning and don't want to toggle the Dimension toolbar on and off repeatedly, memorize the abbreviated forms of the dimension commands that you use frequently. You'll find a list of the long command names on the Contents tab in the AutoCAD online help system. Choose Command Reference⇨Commands⇨D Commands.

Doing Dimensions with Style (s)

Creating a usable dimension style that gives you the dimension look you want is the biggest challenge in using AutoCAD's dimensioning features. Each drawing contains its own dimension styles, so changes you make to a dimension style in one drawing affect only that drawing. However, after you get the dimension styles right in a drawing, you can use it as a template or starting point for later drawings.

A *dimension style* (or *dimstyle* for short) is a collection of drawing settings called *dimension variables,* which are a special class of the *system variables* that I introduce in Chapter 2.

If you want to see a list of the dimension variable names and look up what each variable controls, see Contents⇨Command Reference⇨System Variables⇨ D System Variables in the AutoCAD online help system. All the system variables that begin with *DIM-* are dimension variables.

In AutoCAD 2008, you can create dimension styles with the new *annotative* property — the steps to creating both annotative and non-annotative dimension styles are spelled out in the following sections. Although it's possible to change individual non-annotative dimensions to annotative in the Properties palette, it's far more efficient to assign the annotative property to a dimension style so that all dimensions created in that style will be annotative.

Borrowing existing dimension styles

If you're lucky enough to work in an office where someone has set up dimension styles that are appropriate for your industry and project, you can skip the pain and strain of creating your own dimension styles. Bear in mind, however, that dimension styles copied from pre–AutoCAD 2008 drawings are not going to be annotative. If the ready-made dimension style that you need lives in another drawing, you can use the DesignCenter palette to copy it into your drawing, as described in the following steps:

1. **Open the drawing that contains the dimension style you want to copy (the *source* drawing).**

2. **Open the drawing to which you want to copy the dimension style (the *destination* drawing).**

   If you already had both drawings open, make sure that you can see the destination drawing. If you can't, either open the Window menu and choose the destination drawing in order to bring it to the foreground or tile the windows, as shown in Figure 11-4.

3. **Click the DesignCenter button on the Standard toolbar.**

   The DesignCenter palette appears. (I describe this palette in detail in Chapter 5.)

4. **In the DesignCenter palette, click the Open Drawings tab.**

   DesignCenter's tree view pane on the left side of the palette displays a list of drawings that you currently have open in AutoCAD.

5. **In the tree view pane of the DesignCenter palette, click the plus sign (+) next to the name of the source drawing that you opened in Step 1.**

   A list of object categories that you can copy, including Dimstyles, appears in the tree view pane.

6. **Click Dimstyles in the list in the tree view pane.**

   The display in the content pane at the right changes to show the individual dimension styles that are stored in the source drawing.

7. **Click and drag the desired dimension style from the content pane of the DesignCenter palette into the window containing the destination drawing that you opened in Step 2, as shown in Figure 11-4.**

   If the name of the dimension style that you copy duplicates the name of an existing dimension style in the destination drawing, AutoCAD will not overwrite the existing dimension style. In that case, you must first rename the existing dimension style in the destination drawing by using the information in the next section.

Drag from source drawing's Dimstyles in AutoCAD DesignCenter

Figure 11-4:
Copying a
dimension
style from
one drawing
to another.

Drop in destination drawing

If you want a dimension style to be available in new drawings, copy the style to a template drawing and use that template to create your new drawings. See Chapter 4 for more information about template drawings.

Creating and managing dimension styles

If you *do* need to create your own dimension styles, or you want to tweak ones that you copied from another drawing, you use the Dimension Style Manager dialog box, shown in Figure 11-5.

Every drawing comes with a default dimension style named Standard (for imperial [feet and inches] drawings) or ISO-25 (for metric drawings). Although you can use and modify the Standard or ISO-25 style, I suggest that you leave them as-is and create your own dimension style(s) for the settings that are appropriate to your work. This approach ensures that you can use the default style as a reference. More important, it avoids a potential naming conflict that can change the way your dimensions look if the current drawing gets inserted into another drawing. (Chapter 14 describes this potential conflict.)

Figure 11-5:
Yet another manager, this one for dimension styles.

New drawings created in AutoCAD 2008 or AutoCAD LT 2008 using either the imperial template (`acad.dwt` or `acadlt.dwt` in AutoCAD LT) or the metric template (`acadiso.dwt` or `acadltiso.dwt in LT`) contain *two* dimension styles. As noted previously, imperial drawings have a style named Standard, and metric drawings sport a style named ISO-25 — what's new is that both have a new style called *Annotative*. The Annotative style is a clone of Standard or ISO-25 with the single difference being the values of the overall scale factor (also known as the DIMSCALE system variable).

The following steps describe how to create your own dimension style(s):

1. **Choose Format⇨Dimension Style or click the Dimension Style button on the Styles toolbar.**

   The Dimension Style Manager dialog box appears.

2. **In the Styles list, select the existing dimension style whose settings you want to use as the starting point for the settings of your new style.**

   For example, select the default dimension style named Standard or ISO-25.

3. **Click the New button to create a new dimension style that's a copy of the existing style.**

   The Create New Dimension Style dialog box appears.

4. **Enter a New Style Name and check or uncheck Annotative. Click Continue.**

   Check the Annotative box to create an annotative dimension style, or uncheck it for a non-annotative style. Refer to Chapter 10 for more about annotative objects.

The New Dimension Style dialog box appears. (This dialog box is virtually identical to the Modify Dimension Style dialog box shown in Figure 11-6 in the following section.)

5. **Modify dimension settings on any of the seven tabs in the New Dimension Style dialog box.**

   See the descriptions of these settings in the next section of this chapter.

6. **Click OK to close the New Dimension Style dialog box.**

   The Dimension Style Manager dialog box reappears.

In AutoCAD 2008, your new dimension style becomes the current dimension style that AutoCAD uses for future dimensions in this drawing. (In previous versions, you had to click Set Current to make your newly created style the current style.)

7. **Click Close.**

   The Dimension Style Manager dialog box closes.

8. **Draw some dimensions to test your new dimension style.**

Avoid changing existing dimension styles that you didn't create unless you know for sure what they're used for. When you change a dimension style setting, all dimensions that use that style change to reflect the revised setting. Thus, one small dimension variable setting change can affect a large number of existing dimensions! To play it safe, instead of modifying an existing dimension style, create a new style by copying the existing one and modifying the new one.

A further variation on the already convoluted dimension style picture is that you can create dimension *substyles* (also called *style families*) — variations of a main style that affect only a particular type of dimension, such as radial or angular. You probably want to avoid this additional complication if you can, but if you open the Dimension Style Manager dialog box and see names of dimension types indented beneath the main dimension style names, be aware that you're dealing with substyles.

Adjusting style settings

After you click New or Modify in the Dimension Style Manager dialog box, AutoCAD displays a tabbed New/Modify Dimension Style dialog box with a mind-boggling — and potentially drawing-boggling if you're not careful — array of settings. Figure 11-6 shows the settings on the Lines tab, which I've modified from the AutoCAD defaults to conform to one office's drafting standards.

Figure 11-6:
Modifying
dimension
settings.

Fortunately, the dimension preview that appears on all tabs — as well as on the main Dimension Style Manager dialog box — immediately shows the results of most setting changes. With the dimension preview and some trial-and-error changing of settings, you can usually home in on an acceptable group of settings. For more information, use the dialog box help feature: Click the question mark button on the title bar and then click the setting that you want to know more about.

Before you start messing with dimension style settings, it's important to know what you want your dimensions to look like when they're plotted. If you're not sure how it's done in your industry, ask others in your office or profession or look at a plotted drawing that someone in the know represents as being a good example.

The following sections introduce you to the more important New/Modify Dimension Style tabs and highlight useful settings. Note that whenever you specify a distance or length setting, you should enter the desired *plotted* size. For dimensions created with annotative styles, these are the actual paper (plotted) sizes. For dimensions with non-annotative styles, AutoCAD scales all these numbers by the overall scale factor that you enter on the Fit tab.

Following lines and arrows

The settings on the Lines and the Symbols and Arrows tabs control the basic look and feel of all parts of your dimensions except text. Use these tabs to change the type and size of arrowheads or the display characteristics of the dimension and extension lines.

Tabbing to text

Use the Text tab to control how your dimension text looks — the text style and height to use (see Chapter 10) and where to place the text with respect to the dimension and extension lines. You'll probably want to change the Text Style setting to something that uses a more pleasing font than the ugly default Txt.shx font, such as the Romans.shx font. The default Text Height is too large for most situations — set it to ⅛", 3 mm, or another height that makes sense. Figure 11-7 shows one company's standard text settings.

Figure 11-7: Whip your dimension text into shape.

If you're not opposed to defacing books, get out a bright red marker and put a circle around this warning (unless you borrowed the book from the library, of course) because this is one of the most common mistakes made by new AutoCAD users. Here goes: You must define the text style that you specify for a dimension style with a height of 0 in the Text Style dialog box. (See Chapter 10 for more information about variable-height and fixed-height text styles.) If you specify a fixed-height text style for a dimension style, the text style's height will override the Text Height setting in the New/Modify Dimension Style dialog box. Use a zero-height style to avoid the problem — and bear in mind that using nonzero-height text styles in dimensions is one of the most common mistakes made by new AutoCAD users.

Industry or company standards usually dictate the size of dimension text. (For example, ⅛" or 3 mm is common in the architectural industry.) In any case, make sure you pick a height that's not too small to read on your smallest check plot.

Getting fit

The Fit tab includes a bunch of confusing options that control when and where AutoCAD shoves the dimension text if it doesn't quite fit between the dimension lines. The default settings leave AutoCAD in "maximum attempt at being helpful" mode — that is, AutoCAD moves the text, dimension lines, and arrows around automatically so that things don't overlap. If these guesses seem less than satisfactory to you, try the modified settings shown in Figure 11-8: Select the Over Dimension Line, Without Leader radio button under Text Placement and the Draw Dim Line Between Ext Lines check box under Fine Tuning. (You can always move the text yourself by grip editing it, as I describe later in this chapter.)

Even at its most helpful, AutoCAD sometimes makes a bad first guess about how you want your dimension text and arrows arranged. If you're having problems getting the look you want, don't flip your wig — flip your arrows to the other side of the dimension lines by selecting the dimension, right-clicking, and choosing Flip Arrow from the menu.

Most important, the Fit tab includes the Annotative check box, as shown in Figure 11-8. Using annotative dimensions, as I recommend in this chapter, will make your dimensioning go a lot more smoothly!

Figure 11-8: Keep Fit and don't forget the Scale for dimension features setting.

Annotative check box

With AutoCAD 2008's annotative objects, you can now choose between three different methods for dimensioning your drawings:

✔ **You can dimension in model space using annotative dimensions.** Assign annotation scales to the dimensions, and they change size as you change scales in the Annotation scales list on the status bar. I think this system has the most to offer both new and experienced users.

✔ **You can dimension in model space with non-annotative dimensions.** If your drawing includes areas of different scales, you can create multiple dimension styles, one for each scale. This is probably the least convenient method, especially in a drawing with multiple scale views.

✔ **You can dimension in paper space using either annotative or non-annotative dimensions.** Select the Scale Dimensions to Layout radio button on the Dimension Style Manager's Fit tab and draw dimensions in a paper space layout.

I recommend that you get comfortable with annotative dimensioning in model space first. If you later want to try dimensioning in paper space, look up "dimensioning, methods" in the AutoCAD online help system. As for old-style (that is, non-annotative) dimensioning, it's still part of the program, and many offices will probably keep doing it that way for a while to come.

The Use Overall Scale Of setting corresponds to the DIMSCALE system variable, and you'll hear AutoCAD drafters refer to it as such. When either Scale Dimensions to Layout (for paper space layout dimensioning) or Annotative (for rescalable model space dimensioning) is selected, DIMSCALE is automatically set to 0. Look up the DIMSCALE system variable in the AutoCAD online help system for more information about additional dimension scale options.

Using primary units

The Primary Units tab gives you incredibly detailed — or maybe overly detailed — control over how AutoCAD formats the characters in the dimension text string. You usually want to set the Unit format and Precision and maybe specify a suffix for unitless numbers if it's not clear from your drawing what units you're using. You may also change the Zero Suppression settings, depending on whether you want dimension text to read 0.5000, .5000, or 0.5. ("Zero Suppression!" also makes a great rallying cry for organizing your fellow AutoCAD drafters.)

Other style settings

If your work requires that you show dimensions in two different units (such as inches and millimeters), use the Alternate Units tab to turn on and control alternate units. If your work requires listing construction tolerances (for example, 3.5 +/-0.01), use the Tolerances tab to configure the tolerance format that you want.

The New/Modify Dimension Style dialog box Tolerances tab settings are for adding manufacturing tolerances (for example, +0.2 or -0.1) to the text of ordinary dimensions — the kind of dimensions I cover in this chapter. AutoCAD also includes a separate TOLERANCE *command* that draws special symbols called *geometric tolerances*. If you need these symbols, you probably know it; if you've never heard of them, just ignore them. Look up "Geometric Tolerance dialog box" on the Index tab in the AutoCAD online help system for more information.

Drawing Dimensions

After you've copied or created a suitable dimension style, you're ready to dimension. Fortunately, adding dimensions to a drawing with existing dimension styles is usually pretty straightforward.

When you want to dimension something in AutoCAD, you can either select the object, such as a line or polyline segment, or select *points* on that object, such as the endpoints of the line or polyline segment. If you select an object, AutoCAD finds the most obvious points on it to dimension, such as the endpoints of a line. If you choose to select individual points instead, use object snaps (see Chapter 5). The points that you pick — or that AutoCAD finds for you — are called the *origins* of the dimension's extension lines. When you change the size of the object (for example, by stretching it), AutoCAD automatically moves the dimension's origin points and updates the dimension text to show the new length.

If you don't use object snaps or another AutoCAD precision technique to choose dimension points, the dimension text probably won't reflect the precise measurement of the object. This lack of precision can cause serious problems. When in doubt, OSNAP to it!

When you set up a new drawing, and you want to use annotative dimensions, make sure the Annotative box is checked on the Fit tab in the New/Modify Dimension Style dialog box (refer to Figure 11-8). For a new drawing with non-annotative dimensions, change the Use Overall Scale Of setting on the Fit tab so that it matches the drawing scale factor. Before you draw any dimensions in a drawing that you didn't set up, check this setting to make sure it's correct.

The AutoCAD dimensioning commands prompt you with useful information at the command line. Read the command line prompts during every step of the command, especially when you're trying a dimensioning command for the first time.

Lining up some linear dimensions

Linear dimensions are the most common type of dimensions, and horizontal and vertical are the most common of those. The following example demonstrates all the important techniques for creating horizontal and vertical linear dimensions, as well as aligned dimensions (which are similar to linear dimensions):

1. **Use the LINE command to draw a non-orthogonal line — that is, a line segment that's not horizontal or vertical.**

   An angle of about 30 degrees works well for this example.

   If you want to apply dimensioning to an object other than a line, use these steps as a general guideline, filling in the appropriate commands and data as applicable to your drawing.

2. **Set a layer that's appropriate for dimensions as current.**

   Just as with text, it's a good idea to have a dedicated layer for dimensions in every drawing. See Chapter 5 for details on setting a layer as current.

3. **Set a dimension style that's appropriate for your needs as current.**

   Choose an existing dimension style from the Dim Style Control drop-down list on the Styles toolbar or create a new style by using the procedure in the section, "Creating and managing dimension styles," earlier in this chapter.

4. **Choose Dimension⇨Linear, click the Linear button on the Dimension toolbar, or type DLI and press Enter.**

   AutoCAD prompts you:

   ```
   Specify first extension line origin or <select
           object>:
   ```

5. **To specify the origin of the first extension line, snap to the lower-left endpoint of the line by using endpoint object snap.**

   If you don't have endpoint as one of your current running object snaps, specify a single endpoint object snap by holding down the Shift key, right-clicking, and choosing Endpoint from the menu. (See Chapter 5 for more about object snaps.)

   AutoCAD prompts you:

   ```
   Specify second extension line origin:
   ```

6. **To specify the origin of the second extension line, snap to the other endpoint of the line by using endpoint object snap again.**

   AutoCAD draws a *horizontal* dimension — the length of the displacement in the left-to-right direction — if you move the crosshairs above or below the line. It draws a *vertical* dimension — the length of the displacement in the up-and-down direction — if you move the crosshairs to the left or right of the line.

   AutoCAD prompts you:

   ```
   Specify dimension line location or
   [Mtext/Text/Angle/Horizontal/Vertical/Rotated]:
   ```

7. **Move the mouse to generate the type of dimension you want, horizontal or vertical, and then click wherever you want to place the dimension line.**

   AutoCAD draws the dimension.

When you're specifying the dimension line location, you usually *don't* want to object snap to existing objects — you want the dimension line and text to sit in a relatively empty part of the drawing rather than bump into existing objects. If necessary, temporarily turn off running object snap (for example, click the OSNAP button on the status bar) in order to avoid snapping the dimension line to an existing object.

If you want to be able to align subsequent dimension lines easily, turn on snap and set a suitable snap spacing — more easily done than said! — before you pick the point that determines the location of the dimension line. See Chapter 4 for more information about snap.

 8. **Repeat Steps 4 through 7 to create another linear dimension of the opposite orientation (vertical or horizontal).**

 9. **Choose Dimension⇨Aligned, click the Aligned button on the Dimension toolbar, or type DAL and press Enter.**

The prompt includes an option to select an object instead of picking two points (you can use this technique with the Linear Dimension command, too):

```
Specify first extension line origin or <select
        object>:
```

10. **Press Enter to choose the Select Object option.**

AutoCAD prompts you:

```
Select object to dimension:
```

11. **Select the line or other object that you want to dimension.**

AutoCAD automatically finds the endpoints of the line and uses them as the extension line origin points, as shown in Figure 11-9.

AutoCAD prompts you:

```
Specify dimension line location or
[Mtext/Text/Angle]:
```

12. **Click wherever you want to place the dimension line.**

AutoCAD draws the dimension.

Making dimensions annotative

If you've created your dimensions using an annotative style, you can set them up so that they change to the appropriate plotted (paper) size when you change the drawing's annotation scale. The process is the same for dimensions as it is for text (covered in Chapter 10) or for hatching (covered in Chapter 12). Refer to Chapter 10 for details.

AutoCAD uses endpoints as dimension origin points

Figure 11-9:
Drawing an aligned dimension by selecting an object.

Select a line   Broken extension line using DIMBREAK

Specify dimension line placement

Drawing other kinds of dimensions

After you have the hang of ordinary linear dimensions, you should be able to master other common dimension types quickly. Draw some lines, arcs, and circles and try the other dimension commands on the Dimension toolbar or menu.

To draw a series of side-by-side dimensions whose dimension lines are perfectly aligned, use the DIMCONTINUE command. To draw an overall dimension above one or more smaller dimensions, use DIMBASELINE. If you use these commands often in your work, you may find that the QDIM (Quick DIMension) command provides a quick way to draw lots of dimensions in one fell swoop. (And wouldn't you know it — QDIM is not included in AutoCAD LT.)

AutoCAD 2008 has four new commands for tweaking existing dimensions and creating new types of dimension:

✔ **DIMBREAK:** In manual drafting, it's considered bad form to cross object lines (that is, real geometry) with dimension lines or extension lines. Dimension Break prompts you to select a dimension and then an object to break it. In Figure 11-9, the right extension line of the 3.50 horizontal dimension is broken by the lower extension line of the 1.50 vertical dimension. You can use DIMBREAK on the new multileader objects as well.

✔ **DIMINSPECT:** Inspection dimensions are like a combination of linear dimensions and the annotation objects created by the TOLERANCE command described earlier. This type of dimension is highly specific to mechanical drafting, and like tolerance objects, you'll already know if you need to use it.

✔ **DIMJOGLINE:** Jogged linear dimensions indicate that a dimension object does not show the actual measured distance that's indicated by the dimension value. The topmost dimension in Figure 11-10 displays a dimension value that would actually place the other end of the dimension well off the sheet.

✔ **DIMSPACE:** The Dimension Space command applies a specified separation between existing linear or angular dimensions. Prior to AutoCAD 2008, spacing dimensions equally — other than by using the DIMBASELINE command as they are created — required tedious manipulation with Snap and MOVE.

For more information on any of these commands, look them up by command name in the index of the online help system.

Figure 11-10 shows some results of using some of the additional dimensioning commands (the command aliases are shown in parentheses).

Figure 11-10:
Examples of additional dimensioning commands.

DIMRADIUS (DRA)   DIMDIAMETER (DDI)   DIMANGULAR (DAN)
DIMJOGLINE (DJL)   DIMCONTINUE (DCO)

DIMJOGGED (DJO)   DIMLINEAR (DLI)   DIMARC (DAR)   DIMBASELINE (DBA)

Arc dimensions created with the DIMARC command measure the length along the circumference of the arc, not the radius. Make sure your industry or office standards agree with this type of dimensioning — the standard way of dimensioning arcs is with a radius dimension like the one in Figure 11-3.

Editing Dimensions

After you draw dimensions, you can edit the position of the various parts of each dimension and change the contents of the dimension text. AutoCAD groups all the parts of a dimension into a single object.

Editing dimension geometry

The easiest way to change the location of dimension parts is to use grip editing, which I describe in Chapter 7. Just click a dimension, click one of its grips, and maneuver away. You'll discover that certain grips control certain directions of movement. Experiment for a few minutes to see how they work.

If you want to change the look of a component of a specific, individual dimension (for example, substitute a different arrowhead or suppress an extension line), use the Properties palette. (See Chapter 7 for more on the Properties palette.) All the dimension settings in the New/Modify Dimension Style dialog box (see "Adjusting style settings," earlier in this chapter) are available in the Properties palette when you select one or more dimensions.

If you select one or more dimensions and right-click, the menu displays a number of useful options for overriding dimension settings or assigning a different style.

When you change a setting in the Properties palette, you're *overriding* the default style setting for that dimension. If you need to make the same change to a bunch of dimensions, it's better to create a new dimension style and assign that style to them. You can use the Properties palette or the right-click menu to change the dimension style that's assigned to one or more dimensions.

You can use the Properties palette to turn on AutoCAD's background mask feature, described in Chapter 10, for the text of individual dimensions: Select the dimensions, display the Text area in the Properties palette, and find the Fill Color item. Click in the list box, scroll down, and select Background to use the drawing background color (which usually gives the best results). To ensure that dimension text lies on top of other objects, use the DRAWORDER or TEXTTOFRONT command — see Chapter 10 for more information.

The AutoCAD EXPLODE command on the Modify toolbar will blow a dimension to smithereens — or at least into a bunch of line and multiline text objects. Don't do it! Exploding a dimension makes it much harder to edit cleanly and eliminates AutoCAD's ability to update the dimension text measurement automatically.

Editing dimension text

In most cases, you shouldn't have to edit dimension text. Assuming that you drew your geometry accurately and picked the dimension points precisely, AutoCAD displays the right measurement. If you change the size of the associated object, AutoCAD updates the dimension and its measurement. However, you may occasionally want to *override* the dimension text (that is, replace it with a different measurement) or *add* a prefix or a suffix to the true measurement.

AutoCAD creates dimension text as a multiline text (Mtext) object, so dimension text has the same editing options as ordinary text. Unfortunately, the right-click menu for dimension objects doesn't include a Text Edit option. You can use the Text Override field in the Properties palette or type **ED** (the keyboard shortcut for the DDEDIT command) to edit dimension text in the In-Place Text Editor.

AutoCAD displays the true dimension length as text in the actual dimension (and keeps the text up to date if you change the distance between the dimension's origin points). You can override the true length by typing a specific length or other text string. You can preserve the true length but add a prefix or suffix by inserting <> (that is, the left and right angled bracket characters) as a placeholder for the dimension value. For example, if you enter <> **Max.**, and the actual distance is 12.00, AutoCAD displays 12.00 Max. for the dimension text. If you later stretch the object so that the actual distance changes to 14.50, AutoCAD automatically changes the dimension text to read 14.50 Max. Now you can appreciate the importance of drawing and editing geometry precisely!

Avoid the temptation to override the default dimension text by replacing the angled brackets with a numeric value. Doing so eliminates AutoCAD's ability to keep dimension measurements current, but even worse, you get no visual cue that the default distance has been overridden (unless you edit the dimension text). If you're overriding dimension text a lot, it's probably a sign that the creator of the drawing didn't pay enough attention to using precision techniques when drawing and editing. I'm not going to point any fingers, but you probably know whom to talk to.

Controlling and editing dimension associativity

When you add dimensions by selecting objects or picking points on the objects by using object snap modes, AutoCAD normally creates associative dimensions, which are connected to the objects and move with them. This is the case in new drawings that were originally created in any version of AutoCAD starting with 2002.

If you have to work on drawings created or last edited in versions older than AutoCAD 2002, you must set the DIMASSOC system variable to 2 before AutoCAD 2008 will create associative dimensions. An easy way to make this change for the current drawing is to open the Options dialog box (choose Tools⇨Options), click the User Preferences tab, and turn on the Make New Dimensions Associative setting. Be aware that this setting affects only new dimensions that you draw from now on — to make existing non-associative dimensions associative, use the DIMREASSOCIATE command described in the following list. Look up "DIMASSOC system variable" in the AutoCAD online help system for more information.

You aren't likely to need any of these three commands very often, but if you do, look up the command name in the online help system:

- **DIMREASSOCIATE:** If you have dimensions that aren't currently associative (probably because they were created in older versions of AutoCAD) or are associated with the wrong objects, you can use the DIMREASSOCI-ATE command (Dimension⇨Reassociate Dimensions) to associate them with points on the objects of your choice.

- **DIMDISASSOCIATE:** You can use the DIMDISASSOCIATE command to sever the connection between a dimension and its associated object.

- **DIMREGEN:** In a few special circumstances, AutoCAD doesn't automatically update geometry-driven associative dimensions (maybe Autodesk should call them "usually fully awake but occasionally asleep at the wheel associative dimensions"). In those cases, the DIMREGEN command will fix things.

Bring Out Your Inner Leader

Don't worry; I'm not going to give you a sales pitch about office politics or personal growth opportunities! No, I'm talking about those notes with arrows that point to drawing objects that you need to embellish with some verbiage.

AutoCAD 2008 brings a new kind of leader to the forefront. Multileaders — *mleaders* for short — are a vast improvement over old-style leaders available before now. In fact, they're so good, they should be running the United Nations! Mleaders, unlike the old-style leaders, are single objects. They are also able to point in multiple directions at once (just don't ask them which way is the bus station). Finally, multileaders — just like text, dimensions, hatching, and other objects you use to document your drawing in AutoCAD 2008 — can be annotative. This section concentrates on multileaders, so the New in AutoCAD 2008 icon up there on the left applies to everything from here to the end of the chapter.

There are two older style leaders stored in AutoCAD's attic (Autodesk hates to throw anything away). These semi-retired leaders are no longer accessible on menus or toolbars, but they're still lurking up there waiting to . . . er, lead you astray. If you've become attached to typing commands, you may be inclined to type either LEADER or LE to create those pointy-headed thingies. If you do, be aware that LEADER runs the positively ancient command for creating notes-with-arrows. There are no options, so only straight leader lines and infinitely long text strings are what you get. LE (the alias for the QLEADER command) runs the merely elderly command for creating notes-with-arrows; this one has a Settings dialog box where you can set some options, and it does ask you to specify a width for your Mtext note. However, unlike multileaders, both LEADER and LE create the leader lines and the text as two separate objects.

Electing a leader

Most people would think that this topic belongs with text in Chapter 10 because I'm talking about text notes that happen to have arrows (or leader lines) associated with them. However, AutoCAD treats leaders as a special kind of dimension object (no jokes about dim-witted leaders, please!). You can draw multileader objects that consist of leader lines and multiline text at the same time by using the MLEADER command, as described in the following steps:

1. **Set a layer — one that's appropriate for annotations — current.**

   See Chapter 5 for the details on setting a layer as current.

   AutoCAD lumps leaders with dimensions because the DIMSCALE variable sets the sizes of their components, the same as for dimensions. But that doesn't mean that leaders have to go on the same layer as your dimensions; many office standards place them on a text layer instead.

2. **Set a multileader style — one that's appropriate for your needs — current.**

   Choose an existing multileader style from the drop-down list on the Styles or Multileaders toolbar, or create a new style by choosing Format⇨

Multileader Style. Visit the online help for tips on creating new multi-leader styles.

3. **Choose Dimension⇨Multileader or click the Multileader button on the Multileaders toolbar.**

The command line prompts you to select the location for the pointy end of the leader arrowhead:

```
Specify leader arrowhead location or [leader Landing
first/Content first/Options] <Options>:
```

The initial default method is to locate the arrowhead followed by the leader landing (that is, the short horizontal line between the leader line and the text), at which point AutoCAD displays the In-Place Text Editor, and you enter the text of your note. If you'd rather place the leader landing first, type **L** and press Enter. If you'd rather type the content first, type **C** and press Enter.

If you want to draw spline-curved rather than straight leader lines, specify the number of pick points for the leader lines and press Enter to display multileader options at the command line or the dynamic input tooltip. Refer to the online help for more information on the command options.

4. **Pick a location in the drawing that you want the leader to point to.**

If you use an object snap mode, such as Nearest or Midpoint, to pick a point on an object, AutoCAD associates the leader with the object. If you later move the object, AutoCAD updates the leader so that it points to the new location.

The command line prompts you for the next point.

5. **Pick a second point.**

AutoCAD draws a shaft from the arrowhead to this point.

If you pick a second point that's too close to the arrowhead point, and AutoCAD doesn't have enough room to draw the arrowhead, it omits the arrowhead.

By default, AutoCAD lets you pick two points for the leader line: the first point locates the arrowhead, and the second point locates the start of the short horizontal leader landing. If you need more points than that, restart the command and choose Options, Maxpoints and set a new value.

After you pick the point for the leader landing, AutoCAD opens the In-Place Text Editor.

6. **Enter your comment.**

You're now in the same In-Place Text Editor I describe in Chapter 10, with the same Text Formatting toolbar and all the options described in that chapter.

7. Click OK.

The In-Place Text Editor window closes and adds your comment to the drawing, next to the leader.

Figure 11-11 shows several different leaders with notes.

Figure 11-11:
No loss
for (multi)
leaders.

Multi options for multileaders

Multileaders are a major improvement to old-style leaders in AutoCAD. In addition to the MLEADER command itself, which I walk you through in the preceding steps, they come with a slew of new formatting, drawing, and editing commands:

- ✔ **MLEADEREDIT:** Use this command to add or remove leader lines from multileader objects. You'll find a button for each of those functions on the Multileaders toolbar and the Dashboard, or choose Modify➪Object➪Multileader➪Add (or Remove).

- ✔ **MLEADERSTYLE:** Multileaders, like text, tables, and dimensions, are formatted according to named styles. To display the Multileader Style Manager dialog box (which looks a lot like a simplified version of the Dimension Style Manager), choose Format➪Multileader Style.

- ✔ **MLEADERALIGN:** A tedious chore in AutoCAD 2007 and earlier was getting all the leaders to line up; it usually involved drawing a construction line and then using object snaps to move common points on the leaders to the construction line. To line up mleaders, type **MLEADERALIGN** (or **MLA** for short) and press Enter or choose Align Multileaders from the Multileaders toolbar.

✓ **MLEADERCOLLECT:** Multileaders can contain blocks as well as text (I cover blocks in Chapter 14). Type **MLEADERCOLLECT** (or **MLC** for short) to gather a group of leaders containing blocks; they'll rearrange themselves as a single multileader containing the multiple blocks.

For more information on any of these commands, look them up by name in the Command Reference section of the online help.

Multileaders and multileader styles can be annotative or non-annotative. Making them annotative and assigning appropriate annotation scales is a huge time saver for detail views that you might want to plot at different scales. If you haven't read it yet, refer to Chapter 10.

Chapter 12

Down the Hatch

● ●

● ●

*I*f you were hoping to hatch a plot (or plot a hatch), see Chapter 13 instead. If you want to hatch an egg, look for *Raising Chickens For Dummies.* If you need to fill in closed areas of your drawings with special patterns of lines or solid fills, this is your chapter.

Drafters often use hatching to represent the type of material that makes up an object, such as insulation, metal, concrete, and so on. In other cases, hatching helps emphasize or clarify the extent of a particular element in the drawing — for example, showing the location of walls in a building plan or highlighting a swampy area on a map so you know where to avoid building a road. Figure 12-1 shows an example of hatching in a structural detail.

As I mention in Chapter 10, hatching is another component of AutoCAD 2008's new annotative objects. Hatch patterns have a scale factor (as I explain in the "Getting it right: Hatch angle and scale" section), and can be created so that the hatch scale updates as the annotation scale changes.

An AutoCAD hatch is a separate object that fills a space, that has an appearance dictated by the hatch pattern assigned to it, and that is associated with the objects that bound the space, such as lines, polylines, or arcs. If you move or stretch the boundaries, AutoCAD normally updates the hatching to fill the resized area.

Batch-o-Hatch.dwg

Model / Layout1

Annotation Scale: 6" = 1'-0"

Figure 12-1:
A big batch
o' hatch.

Don't go overboard with hatching. The purpose of hatching is to clarify, not overwhelm, the other geometry in the drawing. If your plots look like a patchwork quilt of hatch patterns, it's time to simplify.

Hatching is another kind of annotation of your geometry, similar in purpose to text and dimensions. As I describe at the beginning of Chapter 10, you'll usually be more efficient if you save annotation for later in the drafting process. Draw as much geometry as possible first and *then* hatch the parts that require it. In other words, batch your hatch.

Hatch . . . Hatch . . . Hatchoo

This section outlines the steps you use to add hatching to a drawing with the Hatch and Gradient dialog box, shown in Figure 12-2. (AutoCAD LT doesn't do gradients, so the dialog box is simply labeled Hatch.)You can use this information to get started quickly with hatching. When you need more information about any part of the process, jump to the relevant sections of "Pushing the Boundary (of) Hatch," later in this chapter.

To see the additional hatch options at the right side of the dialog box in Figure 12-2, click the More Options arrow beside the Help button.

Figure 12-2:
The Hatch
tab of the
Hatch and
Gradient
dialog box.

The following steps show you how to hatch an enclosed area by using the "pick points" method of selecting the hatch area:

1. **Open a drawing containing geometry that forms fully closed boundaries, or draw some boundaries by using the drawing commands described in Chapter 6.**

   The areas you want to hatch should be completely enclosed. The CIRCLE, POLYGON, and RECTANG commands, and the LINE and PLINE commands with the Close option, make great hatch boundaries (see Chapter 6 for details).

2. **Set an appropriate layer current, as described in Chapter 5.**

   It's usually best to put hatching on its own layer.

3. **Start the HATCH command by clicking the Hatch button on the Draw toolbar.**

   The Hatch and Gradient dialog box (or the Hatch dialog box in AutoCAD LT) appears.

4. **Choose Predefined, User Defined, or Custom from the Type drop-down list.**

   Predefined or User Defined works best for most purposes. See the next section for details.

5. **If you chose Predefined or Custom in the previous step, select any predefined or custom hatch pattern from the Pattern drop-down list or the Pattern button just to the right of it. If you chose User Defined, you don't need to choose a pattern.**

6. **Specify an Angle and Scale for the hatch pattern. (Or, if you chose User Defined in Step 4, specify Angle and Spacing.)**

   See the section, "Getting it right: Hatch angle and scale," later in this chapter, for more information.

7. **Select hatch options as required.**

   Check the Annotative check box if you want your hatch patterns to rescale themselves when you change the annotation scale in model space or in a viewport. Associative hatches (enabled by default) will update to the new area when you change the hatch boundary. By default, when you select a number of closed areas and then click OK, the hatched areas will be created as a single object; check the Create Separate Hatches check box if you want to be able to modify each hatched area individually. Set the Draw Order drop-down list to specify whether the hatch objects are in front of or behind the hatch boundary or other drawing objects.

8. **Click the Add: Pick Points button.**

   The Hatch and Gradient dialog box (temporarily) disappears, and your drawing reappears with the following prompt at the command line:

   ```
   Pick internal point or [Select objects/remove
           Boundaries]:
   ```

9. **Pick a point inside the boundary of the area you want to hatch.**

   AutoCAD analyzes the drawing and decides which boundaries to use. In a complex drawing, this analysis can take several seconds. AutoCAD highlights the boundary that it finds.

   If AutoCAD highlights the wrong boundary, right-click, choose Clear All from the menu, and try again.

10. **Right-click anywhere in the drawing area and choose Enter from the menu to indicate that you're finished selecting points.**

    The Hatch and Gradient dialog box reappears.

11. **Click the Preview button to preview the hatch.**

    The Hatch and Gradient dialog box (temporarily) disappears again, and AutoCAD shows you what the hatch will look like:

    ```
    Pick or press Esc to return to dialog or <Right-click
            to accept hatch>:
    ```

12. **Click anywhere in the drawing area to return to the Hatch and Gradient dialog box.**

13. **Adjust any settings and preview again until you're satisfied with the hatch.**

14. **Click OK.**

    AutoCAD hatches the area inside the boundary.

Catch a hatch: Copying hatch properties

One slick way to hatch is by using the Inherit Properties button in the Hatch and Gradient dialog box to copy hatch properties from an existing hatch object. Think of it as point-and-shoot hatching. If someone — such as you — added some hatching in the past that's just like what you want to use now, click the Inherit Properties button and pick the existing hatching.

Inherit Properties updates the hatch pattern settings in the Hatch and Gradient dialog box to make them the same as the existing hatch pattern object that you picked. You can use the cloned hatch pattern specifications as is or modify them by making changes in the Hatch and Gradient dialog box.

Consistency is a good thing in drafting, especially in computer-aided drafting, in which some or all of your drawing may be used for a long time. Thus, it's good to use the same hatch patterns, scales, and angles for the same purposes in all your drawings. Find out whether your project, office, company, or profession has hatching standards that apply to your work.

Occasionally, AutoCAD gets confused and doesn't resize a hatch after you resize the boundary. If that happens, erase and then re-create the hatch in the resized area.

Pushing the Boundary (of) Hatch

The remainder of this chapter shows you how to refine the techniques presented in the preceding section. I describe how to copy existing hatching, take advantage of the various options in the Hatch and Gradient dialog box (including annotative hatches), and choose more complicated hatching boundaries.

Hatch from scratch

You can use predefined, user-defined, or custom hatch patterns. Most of the time, you'll choose either predefined or user-defined hatch patterns, unless some generous soul gives you a custom pattern.

Pick a pattern, any pattern: Predefined hatch patterns

To use AutoCAD's *predefined* hatch patterns, select Predefined from the Type drop-down list at the top of the Hatch tab in the Hatch and Gradient dialog box. This selection sets the stage for choosing the hatch pattern.

You specify a predefined hatch pattern in one of two ways:

- ✔ If you know the name of the hatch pattern, select it from the Pattern drop-down list. The list is alphabetical, except that SOLID (that is, a solid fill) is at the very beginning.

- ✔ If you don't know the pattern's name, or if you prefer the visual approach, click the Pattern button (the tiny button with the ellipsis [three dots] to the right of the Pattern drop-down list and pattern name) to display the Hatch Pattern Palette with pattern previews and names.

AutoCAD has about 80 predefined hatch patterns from which to choose. The list includes ANSI (American National Standards Institute) and ISO (International Organization for Standardization) standard hatch patterns. Figure 12-3 shows the some of the Other Predefined hatch patterns, which cover everything from Earth to Escher to Stars. Hatch patterns whose names begin with *AR-* are intended for architectural and related industries and use different scaling factors than the non-AR patterns.

Figure 12-3:
Plenty
of hatch
patterns.

After you've selected a pattern, specify angle and scale, as I describe in the section, "Getting it right: Hatch angle and scale," later in this chapter.

It's up to you: User-defined hatches

A *user-defined* hatch pattern makes a hatch pattern out of parallel lines. Use this option to create a simple pattern and specify the space between the lines in drawing units. For example, you can hatch a wall in a building plan with a user-defined pattern and specify that the hatch lines be three inches apart.

Make it solid, man

Although you may not guess it, AutoCAD treats filling an area with a solid color as a type of hatching. Simply choose SOLID from the top of the Pattern drop-down list.

Like any other object, a solid hatch takes on the current object color — or the current layer's color if you leave color set to ByLayer. Therefore, check whether the current object layer and color are set appropriately before you use the Solid hatching option (see Chapter 5 for details).

You can create the effect of a solid fill in AutoCAD in several other ways:

✔ If you want a solid-filled circle, use the DONUT command and specify an inside diameter of 0. (See Chapter 6.)

✔ If you want one or more line segments with either uniform or tapered widths, use the PLINE command's Width option. (See Chapter 6.)

✔ If you want a pattern that starts out solid but then fades away (or transitions to a different color) in one or more directions, use the Gradient tab on the Hatch and Gradient dialog box (not included in AutoCAD LT). This option creates a gradient fill. You can control the color(s), direction(s), and angle of the gradient.

Solid and gradient fills are a good way to mimic *poché* — an old, hand-drafting technique in which you shade areas with a lighter colored pencil (usually red) to make those areas appear lightly shaded on blueline prints. The following figure shows some examples of solid and gradient fills.

After you choose User Defined from the Type drop-down list in the Hatch and Gradient dialog box, you specify the angle and spacing of the lines. You can select the Double check box to achieve a crosshatching effect (two perpendicular sets of hatching lines). User-defined patterns require that you enter an angle and spacing, not angle and scale. Spacing is expressed in the current drawing units.

Getting it right: Hatch angle and scale

Predefined and custom hatch patterns require that you enter the angle and scale for AutoCAD to generate the hatching. Usually, you won't have any trouble deciding on an appropriate angle, but a suitable scale can be tricky. Because (with a few exceptions) AutoCAD's hatch patterns don't represent real objects, you don't have to be that precise about scaling them — you can just make them look good. But where do you start?

The answer to that question depends on whether you're using AutoCAD 2008's new annotative hatching or the old-style, non-annotative hatching. For non-annotative hatching, you need to calculate the hatch scale based on the drawing scale factor, as described in Chapter 4. As a general rule, hatch patterns look best at somewhere between one-half and three-quarters of the drawing scale factor. For example, the EARTH pattern (in the Other Predefined tab of the Hatch Pattern Palette, as shown in Figure 12-3 and as used in an actual drawing in Figure 12-1) looks pretty good in a full-scale (1 = 1) drawing with a hatch scale of 0.75. If you're adding EARTH pattern hatching to a 1" = 1'–0" detail (drawing scale factor equals 12), try using a hatch scale of 0.75 × 12, or 9.0. Using a consistent multiplier like 0.5 or 0.75 applied to the drawing scale factor ensures that hatching looks consistent (that the spaces between the lines are the same) at all scales when you plot.

Autodesk created the hatch patterns whose names begin with *AR-* particularly for use in architectural drawings, and unlike the non-AR patterns, they *do* represent real objects. The AR-patterns were designed with a final hatch scale of 1.0 in mind, but in some cases, you'll have to adjust up or down in order to achieve a suitable scale.

Hatching for the 21st Century

With annotative hatching, you can ignore those ugly scale factor calculations. Instead, you start with the paper scale (since that's where all your fancy CAD geometry is going to end up) of 1:1. Once again, most patterns look better at between half and three-quarters of the paper scale, so try setting the hatch scale to, say, 0.75. The following steps explain how to create annotative hatching:

1. **Follow Steps 1 to 6 in the "Hatch . . . Hatch . . . Hatchoo" section earlier in the chapter.**

   Open the Hatch and Gradient (just plain Hatch in AutoCAD LT) dialog box and choose a pattern, angle, and scale.

2. **In the Options area of the dialog box, check the Annotative check box.**

   This time, you're going to create annotative hatch objects, so make sure you check the Annotative box in the Hatch and Gradient dialog box.

3. **Continue following Steps 8 to 14 in the "Hatch . . . Hatch . . . Hatchoo" section.**

   The Hatch and Gradient dialog box appears and disappears as you adjust settings and preview the pattern. When you're in preview mode, AutoCAD prompts:

   ```
   Pick or press Esc to return to dialog or <Right-click
        to accept hatch>:
   ```

4. **When your hatch looks good, right-click to place the hatch and end the command.**

   AutoCAD hatches the area inside the boundary. If you've correctly created an annotative hatch object, you'll see the annotative object symbol (the end of a triangular drawing scale) beside the crosshairs if you move your mouse over the hatch.

5. **Select the hatch object; then right-click and choose Annotative Object Scale⇨Add/Delete Scales to assign annotative scales to the hatch object.**

   The Annotation Object Scale dialog box appears and shows a list of all annotative scales assigned to the selected object. In the case of a new hatch object, the only scale listed will be the current annotation scale; if you're doing this in a new drawing, that will probably be 1:1, the default value.

6. **In the Annotation Object Scale dialog box, click Add.**

   The Add Scales to Object dialog box appears, displaying a list of all drawing scale values stored in the drawing.

7. **Select the desired scales from the list, holding down the Ctrl key to select more than one, and then click OK.**

   The Annotation Object Scale dialog box reappears, with the scales you added displayed in the list box.

   Don't go overboard and select every scale in the list — select only the scales you're likely to use.

8. **Click OK.**

   After you've assigned annotative scales to a hatch (or any annotative) object, you'll see a pair of triangular annotative object symbols. Don't worry — although you *are* seeing double, you've done it right!

9. **Open the Annotation Scale drop-down list on the application or drawing status bar and select one of the scales you added to the object.**

The annotative hatch objects will change their spacing as you change the annotation scale. If you select a scale from the list that you did not assign to the object in Step 7, the hatch will revert to the default 1:1 scale.

Figure 12-4 shows two versions of the same drawing, dressed up with annotative and non-annotative hatch patterns. As the annotation scales displayed on the drawing status bars show, the annotative hatches change their scale while the non-annotative hatches remain unchanged. Before AutoCAD 2008, the only way to get the effect in these two views was to create two separate layers, one for each hatch scale, and hatch the object twice.

Do fence me in: Defining hatch boundaries

After you specify the hatch pattern, angle, and scale you want to use, you define the boundary (or boundaries) into which you want to pour that hatch pattern in one of two ways:

✔ Picking points within the area(s) you want hatched

✔ Selecting objects that surround those areas

Figure 12-4: Hatches annotative (and not).

The actual operation involved in using either of these options is confusing to most people. You'll probably need a little practice before you get used to it.

The idea behind either definition option is simple when applied to simple areas — that is, closed areas with no additional objects inside them. To define the hatch boundary for a simple area, do one of these two things:

✔ Click the Add: Pick Points button in the Hatch and Gradient dialog box and then click a point *inside* the boundary.

✔ Click the Add: Select Objects button and select one or more objects that form a fully closed boundary.

This simple hatching gets more complicated if you have one closed object inside another, as in Figure 12-5. The AutoCAD hatch preview and a bit of experimentation will clarify all these potentially puzzling permutations.

Pick a point inside a simple area.   Pick Points inside both areas.

Pick one point between two areas.

Figure 12-5:
Get picky
about your
hatching (X
indicates a
pick point).

Select a single boundary object.   Select both boundary objects.

Select one boundary object with another nested inside.

As I warn earlier in this chapter, boundaries should be *completely* closed before AutoCAD will hatch them. That's one of the reasons you should employ the precision techniques from this book whenever you draw or edit objects. If the lines surrounding your boundary don't either meet *exactly* or cross, AutoCAD scolds you with a `Valid boundary not found` error message.

The Valid boundary not found error message means that you need to repair lines or other objects so they are a fully closed boundary. Sometimes you can use the FILLET command with a zero fillet radius to force two lines to meet exactly. Another possibility is to use grip editing to align one endpoint precisely with another. Chapter 7 discusses these two editing techniques.

Have palette, will hatch

With Tool Palettes, described in Chapter 2, you can create click-and-drag hatch palettes. With a hatch palette, you click a tool (a swatch) and drag into an enclosed boundary to hatch the area. If your hatching needs are simple, you can create a Tool Palette for the patterns and scales you often use. See "hatches, adding to tool palettes" in AutoCAD's online help for more information.

Editing Hatch Objects

Editing an existing hatch pattern is simple after you're familiar with the Hatch and Gradient dialog box. Follow these steps:

1. **Double-click the hatch object.**

   AutoCAD opens the Hatch Edit dialog box and displays the hatch object's current settings.

2. **Make any desired changes, use the Preview button to look them over, and click OK to keep the changes.**

Alternatively, you can use the Properties palette (described in Chapter 7) to make most existing hatch pattern changes. The Properties palette is especially good for changing several hatches at once.

To make one hatch look like another, use the Match Properties button on the Standard toolbar.

The multitude of options in the Hatch and Gradient and Hatch Edit dialog boxes let you tweak your hatch patterns in all sorts of useful and semi-useful ways. You can easily set a new origin point for hatch objects, you can hatch areas that are not fully visible on-screen, and you can optionally hatch multiple boundaries at one go and have the hatches treated as individual objects.

You can find the area of any hatch object by simply selecting the hatch object and then opening the Properties palette. The area is listed in the Geometry section, near the bottom of the palette.

Chapter 13

The Plot Thickens

Despite the increasing number of offices with a computer (or two) on every desk, many people still need to or want to work with printed drawings. Perhaps you thought that using AutoCAD means you don't have to rely on hard-copy versions of drawings because you can view them on-screen instead. Even if that's true, you may need to give hard-copy prints to your less savvy colleagues who don't have AutoCAD. You may want to make some quick prints to pore over during your bus ride home. You may find that checking drawings the old-fashioned way — with a hard-copy print and a red pencil — turns up errors that managed to remain hidden on the computer screen.

Whatever the reason, you'll want to print drawings at some point — probably sooner rather than later. Depending on where you are in a project, plotting is the pop quiz, mid-term, or final exam of your drawing-making semester. This chapter helps you ace the test.

You Say Printing, I Say Plotting

Plotting originally meant creating hard-copy output on a device that was capable of printing on larger sheets, such as D size or E size (or A1 or A0 for the metrically inclined), that measure several feet (or one or more meters) on a side. (See Chapter 4 for information about drafting paper sizes.) These plotters often used pens to draw, robot-fashion, on large sheets of vellum or drafting film. The sheets could then be run through *diazo blueline machines* — copying machines that create blueline prints — in order to create less-expensive copies. *Printing* meant creating hard-copy output on ordinary printers that used ordinary-sized paper, such as A size (letter size, 8½ x 11 inches) or B size (tabloid or ledger size, 11 x 17 inches) — that's A4 or A3 for you metric folk.

Nowadays, AutoCAD and most CAD users make no distinction between plotting and printing. AutoCAD veterans usually say "plotting," so if you want to be cool, you can do so, too.

Whatever you call it, plotting an AutoCAD drawing is considerably more complicated than printing a word processing document or a spreadsheet. CAD has a larger range of different plotters and printers, drawing types, and output procedures than other computer applications. AutoCAD tries to help you tame the vast jungle of plotting permutations, but you'll probably find that you have to take some time to get the lay of the land and clear a path to your desired hard-copy output.

Get with the system

One of the complications you face in your attempts to create a hard copy is that AutoCAD has two distinct ways of communicating with your plotters and printers. Operating systems, and the programs that run on them, use a special piece of software called a *printer driver* to format data for printing and then send it to the printer or plotter. When you configure Windows to recognize a new printer connected to your computer or your network, you're actually installing the printer's driver. ("Bring the Rolls around front, James. And bring me a gin and tonic and a D-size plot while you're at it.") AutoCAD, like other Windows programs, works with the printers you've configured in Windows. AutoCAD calls these *system printers* because they're part of the Windows system.

But AutoCAD, unlike other Windows programs, can't leave well enough alone. Some output devices, especially some larger plotters, aren't controlled very efficiently by Windows system printer drivers. For that reason, AutoCAD comes with specialized *non-system drivers* (that is, drivers that are not installed as part of the Windows system) for plotters from companies such as Hewlett-Packard, Xerox, and Océ. These drivers are kind of like non-union workers. They ignore the tidy rules for communicating with Windows printers in order to get things done a bit more quickly and flexibly.

Using already-configured Windows system printer drivers usually is easiest, and they work well with many devices — especially devices such as laser and inkjet printers that print on smaller paper. However, if you have a large plotter, you *may* be able to get faster plotting, better plot quality, or more plot features by installing a non-system driver. To find out more, choose Contents⇨Driver and Peripheral Guide⇨Use Plotters and Printers in the AutoCAD online help system.

Configure it out

For now, you should simply make sure that AutoCAD recognizes the devices that you want to use for plotting. The following steps show you how:

1. **Launch AutoCAD and open an existing drawing or start a new, blank drawing.**

2. **Choose Tools⇨Options to open the Options dialog box; then click the Plot and Publish tab.**

3. **Click the drop-down arrow to view the list just below the Use as Default Output Device option, as shown in Figure 13-1.**

   The list includes two kinds of device configurations, designated by two tiny, difficult-to-distinguish icons to the left of the device names:

   - A little laser printer icon with a sheet of white paper coming out the top indicates a Windows system printer configuration.

   - A little plotter icon with a piece of paper coming out the front indicates a non-system (that is, AutoCAD-specific) configuration.

   The non-system configuration names always end in .pc3 because they're stored in special AutoCAD Plotter Configuration version 3 files. So, if you can't tell the difference between the icons, look for the .pc3 at the end of the name.

4. **Verify that the list includes the printers and plotters that you want to have available in AutoCAD.**

   If not, how you add one depends on your operating system. In Windows XP, choose Start⇨Printers and Faxes and click the Add a Printer link under Printer Tasks on the left side of the window. In Windows Vista, choose Start⇨Control Panel⇨Hardware and Sound⇨Printers⇨Add a Printer and then click Add a Local Printer. In Windows 2000, choose Start⇨Settings⇨Printers, launch the Add Printer Wizard, and follow the instructions. If your printer isn't in the default Windows list, cancel the wizard and hunt down a driver disk that came with your printer, or better yet, download the current driver from the printer manufacturer's Web site.

5. **Choose the output device that you want to make the default for new drawings.**

6. **Click OK to close the dialog box and retain any changes that you made in the previous step.**

Non-system printers   List of devices

System printers

You use the AutoCAD Plotter Manager's Add-a-Plotter Wizard to create non-system driver configurations. (Choose File⇨Plotter Manager to display a window containing a shortcut to the wizard.) This wizard is similar to the Windows Add Printer Wizard; if you can handle adding an ordinary printer in Windows, you can probably handle adding a non-system plotter configuration to AutoCAD. When you complete the wizard steps, AutoCAD saves the information in a PC3 (Plotter Configuration version 3) file. If you add an HP Designjet plotter, you will be advised by the Add-a-Plotter Wizard to install the device as a Windows system printer (see the online help for more information). Many people find that the standard drivers work fine, but as I mention later in this chapter, custom drivers may include additional paper sizes as well as other handy settings.

A Simple Plot

Okay, so you believe me. You know that you're not going to master AutoCAD plotting in five minutes. That doesn't change the fact that your boss, employee, wife, husband, construction foreman, or 11-year-old son wants a quick check plot of your drawing.

Plotting success in 16 steps

Here's the quick, cut-to-the-chase procedure for plotting a simple drawing —
a mere 16 steps! This procedure assumes that you plot in model space — that
is, that the Model tab at the bottom of the drawing area shows the drawing in
a way that you want to plot. (I cover plotting paper space layout tabs in the
section, "Plotting the Layout of the Land," later in this chapter.) This procedure doesn't deal with controlling plotted lineweights. (See the "Plotting
Lineweights and Colors" section later in this chapter for those details.) It
should, however, result in a piece of paper that bears some resemblance to
what AutoCAD displays on your computer monitor.

Follow these steps to make a simple, not-to-scale, monochrome (black-and-
white) plot of a drawing:

1. **Open the drawing in AutoCAD.**

2. **Click the Model tab at the bottom of the drawing area to ensure that
   you're plotting the model space contents.**

   I explain model space and paper space in Chapter 4 and how to plot
   paper space layouts later in this chapter.

3. **Zoom to the drawing's current extents (choose View⇨Zoom⇨Extents)
   so you can verify the area you're going to plot.**

   The extents of a drawing consist of a rectangular area just large enough
   to include all the objects in the drawing.

4. **To display the Plot dialog box, click the Plot button on the Standard
   toolbar (or the Standard Annotation toolbar if you're in the 2D
   Drafting & Annotation workspace).**

   The Plot dialog box appears, as shown in Figure 13-2.

5. **In the Printer/Plotter area, select a device from the Name drop-down
   list.**

6. **In the Paper Size area, select a paper size that's loaded in your printer
   or plotter.**

   Make sure that the paper size is large enough to fit the drawing at the
   scale at which you want to plot it. For example, if you want to plot a
   D-size drawing, but you have only a B-size printer, you're out of luck —
   unless you resort to multiple pieces of paper and lots of tape.

7. **In the Plot Area area (sponsored by the Department of Redundancy
   Department), choose Extents from the What to Plot drop-down list.**

   If you set limits properly, as I suggest in Chapter 4, you can choose
   Limits instead to plot the drawing area that you defined. The Window
   option — that is, plot a window whose corners you pick — is useful
   when you want to plot just a portion of your drawing.

Figure 13-2:
The Plot
dialog box,
with a
tooltip to
show you
the printable
area.

More Options button   Printable area

8. **In the Plot Offset (Origin Set to Printable Area) area, select the Center the Plot check box.**

    Alternatively, you can specify offsets of zero or other amounts in order to position the plot at a specific location on the paper.

9. **In the Plot Scale area, either select the Fit to Paper check box or uncheck Fit to Paper and specify a scale (by choosing from the drop-down list or typing into the two text boxes).**

    For most real plotting, you'll plot to a specific scale, but feel free to select the Fit to Paper check box for now. If you do want to plot to a specific scale, see the "Instead of fit, scale it" section later in this chapter for guidance.

10. **Click the More Options button (at the bottom-right corner of the dialog box, next to the Help button).**

    The Plot dialog box reveals additional settings, as shown in Figure 13-3.

11. **In the Plot Style Table (Pen Assignments) area, choose monochrome.ctb or monochrome.stb from the drop-down list.**

    AutoCAD may ask you if you want to "Assign this plot style table to all layouts?" Answer Yes to make monochrome.ctb (or monochrome.stb) the default plot style table for the paper space layout tabs as well as the Model tab, or answer No to make the change apply only to the current tab.

The "Plotting with style" section, later in this chapter, describes plot style tables.

12. **In the Plot Options area, make sure that the Plot with Plot Styles check box is selected and that the Save Changes to Layout check box is deselected, as shown in Figure 13-3.**

    Leaving the Save Changes to Layout check box deselected tells AutoCAD to use any plot settings changes that you make only for this plot — AutoCAD will revert to the original plot settings the next time you plot the drawing.

    After you become confident with plotting, you may want to select this check box so that AutoCAD *does* save your plotting settings changes as the default. Alternatively, click the Apply to Layout button to make the current plot settings the default for future plotting of this tab (that is, the Model tab) in this drawing.

13. **In the Drawing Orientation area, choose Portrait or Landscape.**

    The icon (the letter A on a sheet) in the lower-right corner may help you decide on the right orientation. If not, the full preview in the next step will tell you for sure.

14. **Click the Preview button and check that the drawing displays on the paper at the correct orientation and size, as shown in Figure 13-4; then right-click and choose Exit to return to the Plot dialog box.**

15. **If you found any problems in the preview, adjust the plot settings (for example, Plot Area, Plot Scale, or Drawing Orientation) and repeat the preview until the plot looks right.**

Figure 13-4:
Preview of
coming plot-
tractions.

16. Click OK to create the plot.

When AutoCAD finishes generating and sending the plot, it displays a
Plot and Publish Job Complete balloon notification from the status bar. If
you decide that you don't want to see these notifications, right-click the
Plot/Publish Details Report Available icon near the right end of the
status bar and deselect Enable Balloon Notification.

There — 16 steps, as promised. If for some reason your plot didn't work, well,
I warned you that AutoCAD plotting was complicated and temperamental!
Read the rest of this chapter for all the details about the numerous other
plotting options that can cause plotting to go awry. If you're in a big hurry,
turn directly to the troubleshooting section, "Troubles with Plotting," at the
end of this chapter.

Preview one, two

One of the keys to efficient plotting is liberal use of AutoCAD's preview feature. (To maintain political balance, I recommend conservative use of some
other AutoCAD options elsewhere in the book.)

The postage stamp–sized partial preview in the middle of the Plot dialog box is a quick reality check to make sure your plot fits on the paper and is turned in the right direction. If the plot area at the current scale is too large for the paper, AutoCAD displays thick red warning lines along the side(s) of the sheet where the drawing will be truncated.

Click the Preview button to see a full preview in a separate window. You see exactly how your drawing lays out on the paper and how the various line-weights, colors, and other object plot properties will appear. You can zoom and pan around the preview by using the right-click menu. (Any zooming or panning that you do does not affect what area of the drawing gets plotted — zooming and panning is just a way to get a better look at different areas of the plot preview.)

Instead of fit, scale it

In most real plotting situations, you want to plot to a specific scale rather than let AutoCAD choose an oddball scale that just happens to maximize the drawing on the paper. And if you're going to plot the Model tab of a drawing to scale, you need to know its drawing scale factor. Chapter 4 describes setup concepts, and Chapter 10 provides some tips for determining the scale factor of a drawing that someone else created.

If your drawing was created at a standard scale, such as 1:50 or ¼"=1'–0", then you simply choose the scale from the handy Scale drop-down list in the Plot dialog box. If your scale is not in the list, type the ratio between plotted distance and AutoCAD drawing distance into the two text boxes below the Scale drop-down list, as shown in Figure 13-5. The easiest way to express the ratio usually is to type **1** in the upper box and the drawing scale factor in the lower box. (See Chapter 4 for more information.)

Your CAD manager may have added uncommon scales or removed scales from the Scale drop-down list that your company never uses. If you're designing espresso machines in Milano, for example, you'll probably never need to plot your drawings at ¹⁄₁₂₈"=1'–0".

Creating half-size plots for some purposes is common in some industries. To plot model space half-size, double the drawing scale factor. For example, a ⅛"=1'–0" drawing has a drawing scale factor of 96, which is equivalent to a plot scale of 1=96. To make a half-size model space plot of it, specify a plot scale of 1=192 (or choose ¹⁄₁₆"=1'–0" from the Scale drop-down list).

Figure 13-5:
Lots of ways
to scale.

Type a ratio   Or choose a predefined scale

Even if you work with drawings that are created to be plotted at a specific scale, plotting with a Fit to Paper scale may be the most efficient way to make a reduced-size check plot. For example, drafters in your office might create drawings that get plotted on D-size sheets (24 x 36 inches), whereas you have access to a laser printer with a B-size (11 x 17 inches) paper tray. By plotting the D-size drawings scaled to fit on B-size paper, you end up with check plots that are slightly smaller than half size ($\frac{11}{24}$ size, to be exact). You won't be able to measure distances on the check plots with a scale, but you probably will be able to check them visually for overall correctness.

Plotting the Layout of the Land

In the previous section, I show you how to plot the model space representation of your drawing by making sure that the Model tab is active when you open the Plot dialog box. However, paper space gives you many additional options for controlling the look of your output without having to modify the underlying geometry. So in some drawings, you may want to plot a paper space layout instead.

About paper space layouts and plotting

As Chapter 4 describes, you can use AutoCAD's paper space feature to compose one or more *layouts* for plotting your drawing in particular ways. Each layout lives on a separate tab, which you click at the bottom of the drawing area. In addition, AutoCAD saves plot settings (plot device, paper size, plot scale, and so on) separately for each of the tabs — that is, for each of the layout tabs as well as the Model tab.

Whether to plot model space or a paper space layout in a drawing depends entirely on how the drawing was set up. If you or someone else went through a layout setup procedure similar to the one in Chapter 4, then you probably should plot the paper space layout. If not, then plot the Model tab.

Don't confuse the Model tab at the bottom of the drawing area with the MODEL/PAPER button on the status bar. The tabs control which view of the drawing (model space or a paper space layout) fills the drawing area. When a paper space layout fills the drawing area, the status bar button controls whether drawing and editing take place in paper space or in model space inside a viewport. When you plot a layout, it doesn't matter whether the MODEL/PAPER button says *MODEL* or *PAPER* — AutoCAD always plots the paper space layout (not just the contents of model space in the viewport).

The presence of a Layout1 tab next to the Model tab at the bottom of the drawing area doesn't necessarily mean that the drawing contains an already-set-up paper space layout. AutoCAD always displays a Layout1 tab when you open a drawing created in AutoCAD Release 14 or earlier, and it displays a Layout1 and Layout2 tab when you open a drawing created in AutoCAD 2000 or later. Layout1 and Layout2 are simply AutoCAD's default names; the creator of the drawing may have renamed them something more descriptive.

You can regain a teensy bit of drawing space along the bottom of the drawing area by turning off the layout tabs. You can either right-click the model tab or a layout tab and select Hide Layout and Model tabs, or you can choose Tools⇨Options⇨Display and clear the Display Layout and Model Tabs check box. The tabs vanish, and the Model/Paper button is replaced with two buttons on the status bar. To put things back the way they were, check the Display Layout box in the Options dialog box or right-click one of the new status bar buttons and choose Display Layout and Model tabs.

If you don't have any paper space drawings handy, you can use one of the AutoCAD sample drawings, such as the mechanical drawing stored in `C:\Program Files\AutoCAD 2008\Sample\Blocks and Tables - Imperial.dwg` or `Blocks and Tables - Metric.dwg`. AutoCAD LT users, check out `C:\Program Files\AutoCAD LT 2008\Sample\Elevations.dwg`.

The path to paper space layout plotting success

Plotting a paper space layout is pretty much like plotting model space except that you need to find the appropriate layout first and make sure that its tab is selected before you open the Plot dialog box, as follows:

1. **Click the layout tabs at the bottom of the drawing area until you find a suitably set-up layout.**

   If no one has set up the layout yet, AutoCAD creates a default layout. (If the Show Page Setup Manager for New Layouts setting on the Display tab of the Options dialog box is turned on, you'll see the Page Setup Manager dialog box first — just click the Close button.) The default layout probably won't be useful for real projects, but you can use it to find out about the layout plotting procedure. Refer to Chapter 4 for instructions on creating a real layout.

2. **Click the Plot button on the Standard toolbar.**

   The Plot dialog box appears.

3. **Specify a Printer/Plotter Name and a Paper Size.**

   If you don't have a printer capable of outputting larger than letter- or tabloid-sized sheets, you can still experiment by selecting a device that outputs to file, such as `DWF6 ePlot.pc3`.

4. **In the What to Plot drop-down list, choose Layout, as shown in Figure 13-6.**

   The Layout option is available only when plotting a layout tab; Limits is available only when plotting the Model tab.

5. **Specify the Plot Offset (such as 0 in both the X and Y directions).**

   Specifying the Plot Offset as 0 in both X and Y directions places the lower-left corner of the plotted drawing at the lower-left corner of the printable area.

6. **In the Plot Scale area, select 1:1 from the Scale drop-down list, as shown in Figure 13-6.**

   One of the big advantages of layouts is that you don't need to know anything about drawing scale in order to plot the drawing — hence the name *paper* space. Figure 13-6 shows the proper settings for plotting a layout.

   To create a half-size plot of a layout, select 1:2 from the Scale drop-down list. In addition, select the Scale Lineweights check box in order to reduce lineweights proportionally. (I cover plotting lineweights in the next section.)

Figure 13-6:
Settings for
plotting a
paper space
layout.

If you find that the layout is too big for your plotter's largest paper size at a plot scale of 1:1, you can select Extents from the What to Plot drop-down list and then select the Fit to Paper check box in the Plot Scale area. Alternatively, you can close the Plot dialog box and fix the problem if you want to have a paper space layout that permanently reflects a new paper size. Use the Page Setup dialog box to modify the layout settings, or copy the layout and modify the new copy.

7. Click the More Options button and change any additional plot options that you want to.

Refer to Steps 11 through 13 in the section, "Plotting success in 16 steps."

8. Click the Preview button, ensure that the drawing displays on the paper at the correct orientation and size, and then right-click and choose Exit to return to the Plot dialog box.

If you found any problems in the preview, change your plot settings and preview again until it looks right.

9. Click OK to create the plot.

Plotting Lineweights and Colors

In previous sections of this chapter, I help you gain some plotting confidence. Those sections show you how to create scaled, monochrome plots with uniform lineweights in model space or paper space. Those skills may be all you need, but if you care about controlling plotted lineweights and colors, or adding special effects such as *screening* (plotting shades of gray), read on.

Plotting with style

Plot styles provide a way to override object properties with alternative plot properties. (See Chapter 5 for information about object properties.) The properties include plotted lineweight, plotted color, and screening (plotting shades of gray). Figure 13-7 shows the full range of options. Plot styles come in two exciting flavors:

- Color-dependent plot styles
- Named plot styles

Figure 13-7:
Editing a color-dependent plot style table.

Color-dependent plot styles are based on the standard way of plotting in earlier versions of AutoCAD (before AutoCAD 2000), whereas named plot styles provide a newer way.

It's remotely possible that you won't need to bother with plot styles. If the drawings you want to plot have layer and object properties (especially line-weight) that reflect how you want objects to plot, you can dispense with plot styles. But most people and most drawings use plot styles, so you should at least be familiar with them.

A couple of common reasons for using plot styles are to

> ✔ **Map screen colors to plotted lineweights.** If this idea seems completely loony to you, try to suspend judgment until you've read the "Plotting through thick and thin" section, a bit later in this chapter.

> ✔ **Create screened lines on monochrome plots.** Lines that are screened display in various shades of gray, not black. Drafters sometimes use screened lines to de-emphasize secondary objects that otherwise would overwhelm the main objects in the drawing. Screening is expressed as a percentage, with 100 percent being completely black and 0 percent being invisible.

Using plot styles

If you want objects in your drawing to plot with properties that differ from their display properties, you need plot styles. For example, you can plot with different lineweights or colors from the ones you're using for display pur-poses. Or, as I mention in the preceding section, you may need to map dis-play colors to plotted lineweights. AutoCAD groups plot styles into plot style tables, each of which is stored in a separate file.

Color-dependent plot style tables live in Color TaBle (CTB) files, and they map the 255 AutoCAD display colors to 255 plot styles. AutoCAD automatically attaches the color-dependent plot styles to every object, based on — you guessed it — the object's color. (Are those AutoCAD programmers brilliant, or what?) Color-dependent plot style tables are especially handy for mimicking the old color-mapped-to-lineweight plotting approach of AutoCAD R14 and ear-lier releases; this remains the most common method in most companies.

Named plot style tables live in Style TaBle (STB) files. After you've created a named plot style table, you create one or more plot styles and give them any names you like. Then you can assign the named plot styles to layers or to individual objects. (See Chapter 5 for more information about object and layer properties.)

Named refers to the plot styles, not to the tables. Both color-dependent plot style *tables* and named plot style *tables* have names because both are stored in files, and files have to have names. But color-dependent plot *styles* don't have names, and named plot *styles* do have names.

To use a plot style table and its included plot styles (whether they're color-dependent or named), you must attach it to model space or a paper space layout. The plot style table then affects plotting only for that tab. This approach lets you plot the same drawing in different ways by attaching different plot styles to different tabs.

You can attach a plot style to model space or a paper space layout by selecting its tab at the bottom of the drawing area, opening the Plot dialog box or Page Setup Manager dialog box, and choosing the plot style table name in the Plot Style Table (Pen Assignments) area of the expanded Plot dialog box. See the section, "Controlling plotted lineweights with screen colors," later in this chapter, for an example.

When you start a new drawing in the usual way — that is, by using a template drawing (see Chapter 4), the template drawing's plot style behavior determines whether you can choose CTB or STB files. (That's why most of AutoCAD's stock template drawings come in Color Dependent Plot Styles and Named Plot Styles versions.) If you want to change from color-dependent plot styles to named plot styles (or vice versa) in a particular drawing, use the CONVERTPSTYLES command.

Creating plot styles

If you're really lucky, you won't need to use plot styles. If you're somewhat lucky, you'll need to use plot styles, but someone will provide the plot style table files for you. If that's the case, you must put the CTB or STB files in your Plot Styles folder in order for AutoCAD to recognize them. (To find the location of your Plot Styles folder, open the Options dialog box, choose the Files tab, and look for the Printer Support File Path⇨Plot Style Table Search Path setting.)

If you're not lucky at all, then you'll need to be smart — that is, you'll want to know how to create your own plot style table files. Here's how:

1. **Choose File⇨Plot Style Manager.**

   The Plot Styles folder opens in a separate window.

2. **Double-click the Add-a-Plot Style Table Wizard program shortcut.**

3. **Read the opening screen and then click Next.**

4. **Choose the Start from Scratch option or one of the other three options if you want to start with settings from another file. Then click Next.**

   The remaining steps in this procedure assume that you chose Start from Scratch. If you chose another option, simply follow the wizard's prompts.

If the creator of a drawing provides you with an AutoCAD R14/AutoCAD LT 98 PC2 (version 2) or AutoCAD R12/AutoCAD LT 95 PCP (version 1) file, choose the Use a PCP or PC2 File option. With this option, the wizard imports color-to-plotted-lineweight settings automatically.

 5. **Choose whether you want to create a color-dependent plot style table (CTB file) or a named plot style table (STB file). Then click Next.**

    Choose Color-Dependent Plot Style Table in order to map screen colors to plotted lineweights. Choose Named Plot Style Table in order to leave screen colors alone (so that the colors plot as you see them on-screen) and to create named plot styles that you can apply to layers or objects.

 6. **Type a name for the new CTB or STB file and then click Next.**

 7. **Click the Plot Style Table Editor button.**

    The Plot Style Table Editor dialog box opens (refer to Figure 13-7).

 8. **If you created a color-dependent plot style table, assign Lineweight, Screening, or other plot properties to each color that's used in the drawing. If you created a named plot style table, click the Add Style button and then assign plot properties to each of the named styles that you create.**

    To determine which colors are used in a drawing, switch to the AutoCAD window and open the Layer Properties Manager dialog box by clicking the Layer Properties Manager button located on the Layers toolbar.

    To change a setting for all colors or named styles, select all of them first by clicking the first color or named style, holding down the Shift key, scrolling to the end of the list, and then clicking the last color or named style. Any subsequent changes you make get applied to all the selected colors or named styles.

 9. **Click the Save & Close button to close the Plot Style Table Editor dialog box. Then click Finish to complete the steps for the wizard.**

    The Plot Styles folder now displays your new CTB or STB file.

 10. **Close the Plot Styles folder by clicking the X in its title bar.**

Creating your first plot style table can be a harrowing experience because you have so many options. Just remember that your most likely reason for creating one is to map screen colors to plotted lineweights (as I describe in greater detail in the next section). Also remember that you may be able to minimize your effort by getting a CTB file from the person who created the drawing that you want to plot.

In Chapter 5, I recommend that you limit yourself to the first 9 Standard AutoCAD Colors when defining layers, and not a patchwork of the 255 colors that AutoCAD makes available. If you follow my advice, your work to create a color-dependent plot style table will be much reduced because you'll have to assign plot properties for only 9 colors, rather than worrying about 255 of them.

You can use the file found in `C:\Program Files\AutoCAD 2008\Sample\ Plot Screening and Fill Patterns.dwg` for systematic testing of your CTB files. This drawing shows an array of color swatches for all 255 AutoCAD colors. Some of the other tabs (such as Grayscale and Screening 25%) also demonstrate how different CTB files attached to the same layout produce radically different results.

Named plot styles hold a lot of promise, but there are at least a couple of places — dimensions and tables — where they don't work as well as traditional color-based plotting. Dimension properties allow you to assign different colors to dimension lines, extension lines, and text. The purpose for this is to allow different parts of a dimension object to print with different lineweights; for example, you can have your dimension text print with a medium lineweight, the same as your annotation text, while keeping extension and dimension lines to a fine lineweight. But because named plot styles are based on objects or layers, you don't have that lineweight control over individual dimension components. The same limitation applies to tables, where you can set your text to be one color and your grid lines to be another.

Plotting with plodders

Color-as-color and lineweight-as-lineweight seem like great ideas, but Autodesk knew when it added object lineweights back in 1999 that longtime users of AutoCAD weren't going to abandon the old colors-mapped-to-lineweights approach overnight. Thus, you can still control plotted lineweight by display color in AutoCAD.

AutoCAD veterans, by and large, have chosen to stick with the Old Way for now. They've done so for a variety of reasons, including inertia, plotting procedures and drawings built around the Old Way, third-party applications that don't fully support the newer methods, and the need to exchange drawings with clients and subcontractors who haven't upgraded. In summary, the ripple effect of those who need to or want to continue using colors-mapped-to-lineweights is lasting a long time. Don't be surprised if you find yourself going with the flow for a while.

The default setting in AutoCAD 2008 is to plot object lineweights, so that's the easiest method if you don't have to consider the historical practices or predilections of other people with whom you exchange drawings. Mapping screen colors to lineweights requires some initial work on your part, but after you've set up the mapping scheme, the additional effort is minimal.

If you *really* get carried away and decide to take advantage of the 16 million-odd colors in AutoCAD's True Color or Color Book modes, you're not going to be controlling lineweights with color-dependent plot styles. CTB plot styles affect the lineweights only of objects that use the traditional 255 colors of the AutoCAD Color Index palette. If you want true color or Color Book colors, use object lineweights or named plot styles to control plotted lineweight.

Your life is simpler if you use AutoCAD LT. Only the full version of AutoCAD supports True Color and Color Books modes.

Plotting through thick and thin

Long ago, manual drafters developed the practice of drawing lines of different thicknesses, or *lineweights,* in order to distinguish different kinds of objects. Manual drafters did it with different technical ink pen nib diameters or with different hardnesses of pencil lead and varying degrees of pressure on the pencil. Because a computer mouse usually doesn't come with different diameters of mouse balls, the AutoCAD developers had to figure out how to let users indicate lineweights on-screen and on a plot. They came up with two different ways to indicate lineweight:

- Mapping on-screen colors to plotted lineweights. I describe this common approach in Chapter 5.
- Displaying lineweights on-screen to match what the user can expect to see on the plot. This approach first appeared in AutoCAD 2000.

Controlling plotted lineweights with object lineweights

Plotting object lineweights is trivial, assuming that the person who created the drawing took the trouble to assign lineweights to layers or objects (see Chapter 5 for details). Just make sure that the Plot Object Lineweights check box in the expanded Plot dialog box is checked. You may also want to deselect the Plot with Plot Styles check box because plot styles can override the object lineweights with different plotted lineweights. (You can also make these settings in the Page Setup dialog box for the appropriate layout or Model tab. To access Page Setup, right-click the Model tab or any layout tab and choose Page Setup Manager; if you've chosen to hide the Model and Layout tabs, choose File⇨Page Setup Manager.)

If you want object lineweights to control plotted lineweights, make sure that Plot Object Lineweights is checked in the Plot Options area of the Plot or Page Setup dialog box. If you *don't* want to plot the lineweights assigned to objects, you must uncheck both the Plot Object Lineweights and Plot with Plot Styles check boxes in the Plot or Page Setup dialog box. Checking Plot with Plot Styles checks Plot Object Lineweights as well.

Controlling plotted lineweights with screen colors

To map screen colors to plotted lineweights, you need a color-dependent plot style table (CTB file), as I describe in the section "Plotting with style," earlier in this chapter. If you're plotting a drawing created by someone else, that someone else may be able to supply you with the appropriate CTB file or, at least, with a PCP or PC2 file from which you can create the CTB file quickly. At the very least, the creator of the drawing should be able to give you a printed chart showing which plotted lineweight to assign to each AutoCAD screen color. Use the instructions in the "Plotting with style" section to copy or create the required CTB file.

Unfortunately, no industry-wide standards exist for mapping screen colors to plotted lineweights. Different offices do it differently. That's why it's so useful to receive a CTB, PCP, or PC2 file with drawings that someone sends you.

After you have the appropriate CTB file stored in your Plot Styles folder, follow these steps to use it:

1. **Click the tab that you want to plot — the Model tab or the desired paper space layout tab.**

2. **Click the Plot button on the Standard toolbar.**

3. **In the Plot Style Table (Pen Assignments) area on the expanded Plot dialog box, select the CTB file from the drop-down list, as shown in Figure 13-8.**

   This action attaches the plot style table (CTB file) to the tab that you clicked in Step 1.

Figure 13-8: Selecting a plot style table that maps screen colors to plotted lineweights.

4. **Click the Apply to Layout button.**

   AutoCAD records the plot setting change with the current tab's configuration information. Assuming that you save the drawing, AutoCAD uses the CTB that you selected as the default plot style when you (or other people) plot that tab in the future.

5. **Continue with the plotting procedures described earlier in this chapter.**

If your drawing uses a named plot style table instead of a color-dependent plot style table, you follow the same procedure, except that you select an STB file instead of a CTB file in Step 3.

You can tell whether the current drawing was set up to use color-dependent plot styles or named plot styles by looking at the Properties toolbar. If the last drop-down list (Plot Style Control) is grayed out, the drawing uses color-dependent plot styles. If this list is not grayed out, the drawing uses named plot styles.

Plotting in color

Plotting the colors that you see on-screen requires no special tricks. In the absence of a plot style table (that is, if you selected None from the drop-down list in the Plot Style Table (Pen Assignments) area in the Plot or Page Setup dialog box), AutoCAD sends color information as it appears on-screen to the plotter. As long as your output device can plot in color, what you see should be what you get.

If you attach a plot style table to the tab that you're plotting (as described in the previous section), you can — if you really want to — map screen colors to different plotted colors. In most cases, you don't want that kind of confusion. Instead, leave the Color property in the plot style table set to Use Object Color.

If your goal is *not* to plot color, make sure that you set the Color property for all plot styles to Black. If you try to plot colors on a monochrome device, you may find that objects appear in various shades of gray, with lighter colors mapped to lighter shades of gray and darker colors to darker shades of gray. This process of mapping colors to shades of gray is called *monochrome dithering,* and it usually is *not* what you want in a CAD drawing. To override it, use the Plot Style Table Editor, as described in the section "Creating plot styles," earlier in this chapter, to set the Color option for all colors to Black (the default setting is Use Object Color). If you don't already have a plot style table that you want to use, choose monochrome.ctb (for color-based plot styles) or monochrome.stb (for named plot styles) — both of which come with AutoCAD — from the drop-down list in the Plot Style Table (Pen Assignments) area of the Plot dialog box.

When in doubt, send it out

Whether you plot to scale or not, with different lineweights or not, in color or not, consider using a service bureau for some of your plotting. In-house plotting on your office's output devices is great for small check plots on faster laser or inkjet printers. Large-format plotting, on the other hand, can be slow and time consuming. If you need to plot lots of drawings, you may find yourself spending an afternoon loading paper, replenishing ink cartridges, and trimming sheets.

Good plotting service bureaus have big, fast, expensive plotters that you can only dream about owning. Also, *they're* responsible for babysitting those fancy devices, feeding them, and fixing them. As a bonus, service bureaus can make blueline prints from your plots if you need to distribute hard-copy sets to other people.

The only downside is that you need to coordinate with a service bureau to make sure it gets what it needs from you and can deliver the kinds of plots you need. Some service bureaus plot directly from your DWG files, while others ask you to make PLT (plot) files. Some service bureaus specialize in color plotting, while others are more comfortable with monochrome plotting and making blueline copies.

When you're choosing a service bureau, look for one that traditionally has served drafters, architects, and engineers. These service bureaus tend to be more knowledgeable about AutoCAD, and they should have more plotting expertise than the desktop publishing, printing, and copying shops.

Whomever you choose, do some test plots well before the day that important set of drawings is due. Talk to the plotting people and get a copy of their plotting instructions. Have the service bureau create some plots of a couple of your typical drawings and make sure they look the way you want them to.

If you do lots of plotting with a service bureau, look into whether you can charge it to your clients as an expense (just like bluelines or copying).

To see the full range of AutoCAD colors available on your plotter, or to see how a particular plot style table affects plotting, open and then plot the file `C:\Program Files\AutoCAD 2008\Sample\Plot Screening and Fill Patterns.dwg`. The Screening 100% layout in this drawing contains color swatches for all 255 AutoCAD colors.

It's a (Page) Setup!

Page setups specify the plotter, paper size, and other plot settings that you use to plot a particular tab of a particular drawing. AutoCAD maintains separate page setups for model space and for each paper space layout (that is, for each tab you see in the drawing area). When you click the Apply to Layout button in the Plot dialog box (or select the Save Changes to Layout check box and then click OK to plot), AutoCAD stores the current plot settings as the page setup for the current tab.

You also can give page setups names and save them. The advantage of doing so is that you can switch quickly between different plot settings and copy plot settings from one drawing tab to another. Named page setups are stored with each drawing, but you can copy them from another drawing into the current one with the Page Setup Manager dialog box (described later in this section).

If you want to get fancier, you can create named page setups in order to plot the same layout (or the Model tab) in different ways, or to copy plot settings from one tab to another or one drawing to another. Click the Add button in the Plot dialog box to create a named page setup from the current plot settings. After you create a named page setup, you can restore its plot settings by choosing it from the Page Setup Name drop-down list.

For even greater control, choose File⇨Page Setup Manager to create, change, and copy page setups. In the Page Setup Manager dialog box, shown in Figure 13-9, you can create new page setups and modify existing ones. Click the Modify button to open the Page Setup dialog box, which is almost identical to the Plot dialog box. The primary difference is that you're changing plot settings rather than actually plotting. The Set Current button copies the page setup that you've selected on the Page Setups list to the current layout tab. With the Import button, you can copy a layout from another drawing or drawing template (DWT) file.

Figure 13-9:
The Page
Setup
Manager
dialog box.

Continuing the Plot Dialog

In previous sections of this chapter, I cover most of the important options in the Plot dialog box. This section reveals a few more fine points that will make your plotting life easier. I don't cover every minute, obscure, useful-only-at-cocktail-party-discussions detail. (And if this sounds like your kind of cocktail party, remind me that I'm busy that night!) I do point out some occasionally useful options that will increase your vocabulary when you're communicating with the Plot dialog box.

Use the Plot dialog box's quick help to find out more about any part of the dialog box:

1. **Click the question mark next to the Close button in the dialog box's title bar.**

2. **Point the arrow at the part of the dialog box that you want to know more about and click.**

3. **Click the Help button at the bottom of the dialog box if the pop-up help isn't enough.**

4. **For a more conceptual take on plotting, click the Learn about Plotting link to view the Quick Start to Plotting section of the online help.**

The following list explains most of the remaining controls, check boxes, and lists in the Plot dialog box:

✔ **Printer/Plotter:** As I describe in the section "Configure it out," earlier in this chapter, you use the Name drop-down list to select the Windows system printer or non-system driver configuration that you want to use for plotting.

Clicking the Properties button opens the Plotter Configuration Editor dialog box, with which you can change media (type of paper) and other properties that are unique to the currently selected plotter or printer. In particular, you can define custom paper sizes.

As if AutoCAD's Plot dialog box settings weren't overwhelming enough, depending on your plot device, you may also have to deal with the Plotter Configuration Editor dialog box. Some plotter drivers hide important settings in this dialog box. To access them, you typically click the Custom Properties button near the bottom of the Plotter Configuration Editor dialog box. For example, if you're using the enhanced Windows system driver for HP plotters, available at www.designjet.hp.com, you can click the Custom Properties button and then the More Sizes button to specify which paper sizes are available to you on the Paper Size drop-down list of the main Plot dialog box.

To make matters even *more* confusing, if you make any changes in the Plotter Configuration Editor dialog box, AutoCAD prompts you to save the changes to a separate PC3 file. You should choose Save Changes to the Following File (that is, create a new AutoCAD-specific configuration that includes the revised settings) and type a configuration name that you'll recognize later. When you want to plot with custom settings, remember to choose the AutoCAD-specific PC3 configuration near the end of the Printer/Plotter Name drop-down list, and not the original Windows system printer configuration near the beginning of the list.

✔ **Plot to File:** If you need to plot to a file rather than directly to your plotter or network printer queue, select the Plot to File option. When you click OK to plot, AutoCAD asks you for a plot filename and location.

This option is especially useful when you want to use the ePlot feature to publish a DWF file on a Web site. You also may need to use this option to create files to send to a plotting service bureau.

Plotting to the `DWG to PDF.pc3` file creates versions of your drawing files that can be opened and viewed in the free and widely available Adobe Reader software.

✔ **Plot Stamp On:** Use this option to turn on and off and configure the contents of a text string that AutoCAD adds automatically to the corner of each plot. The plot stamp can include useful information such as the drawing filename and plot date and time.

✔ **Plot Area:** Specify the area of the drawing to plot. Your choices include Display, Extents, and Window, regardless of whether you're plotting a paper space layout or the model space tab. If you defined named views in the drawing, AutoCAD adds a View option. The additional choice is Layout for a paper space layout tab or Limits for the model space tab.

- *Display* means the drawing as it's currently displayed in the drawing window (including any empty space around the drawing objects).

- *Extents* means the rectangular area containing all the objects in the drawing.

- *Limits* (Model tab only) means the model space area that you specified (you did tell your drawing its limits, didn't you?) when you set up the drawing. (See Chapter 4 for details.)

- *Layout* (Layout tabs only) means the paper space area you defined when you set up the layout.

- *Window* means a rectangular area that you specify.

- *View* means a named view, which you select from the drop-down list. (Chapter 8 describes named views and how to create them.)

TIP

Usually, you'll choose to plot Layout in paper space. For model space, the choice depends on whether the drawing was set up properly and what you want to plot. If you set limits properly, as I describe in Chapter 4, then plot Limits in order to get the whole drawing area. If you're trying to plot a drawing in which the limits weren't set properly, try Extents instead. Use Window or View if you want to plot just a portion of model space.

Sheet sets without regrets

A typical AutoCAD project could include dozens of drawings, scores of sheets, lots of layouts, copious cross-drawing references, and more than a few people working on those components at once. How do you create, manage, update, plot, and generally keep a handle on all that stuff without going crazy? The sheet sets feature is AutoCAD's response to this challenge.

Sheet sets were introduced in AutoCAD 2005, and it's probably fair to say that the feature hasn't caught on like wildfire just yet. It's a whole new paradigm for creating and out-putting drawing sets, and many individuals and companies apparently haven't felt the need to make the switch. (Maybe they're still trying to get their heads around named plot styles!)

Sheet sets rely on several relatively sophisti-cated AutoCAD features, so make sure you have at least a nodding acquaintance with these items before you start to grapple with sheet sets:

✔ Paper space layouts (covered in Chapter 4)

✔ Named views (Chapter 8)

✔ Tables and text fields (Chapter 10)

✔ Blocks and attributes (Chapter 14)

✔ External references (Chapter 14)

Understanding external references and layouts is especially important because these features are central to the way the Sheet Set Manager (shown in the accompanying figure) creates and organizes sheets. You can create a sheet list automatically, and labels and callouts also automatically update as you add and remove sheets from the sheet set.

An AutoCAD sheet set is treated as a single unit for ease in publishing drawings to paper or the Web, for electronically transmitting complete sets of drawing sheets, and for archiving pro-jects at milestones or on completion.

For more information on sheet sets, look at the User's Guide in AutoCAD's online help system — select Choose a Work Process before You Begin and then select Work with Sheets in a Sheet Set.

Sheet sets are a feature of full AutoCAD only — they're not included in AutoCAD LT.

✔ **Plot Offset:** A plot offset of X=0 and Y=0 positions the plot at the lower-left corner of the plottable area. If you want to move the plot from this default position on the paper, enter non-zero numbers or select the Center the Plot check box. (The Center the Plot check box is available only when you haven't selected Layout from the What to Plot drop-down list.)

✔ **Shaded Viewport Options:** If your drawing includes viewports showing shaded or rendered 3D models, use this area to control the plotted appearance.

✔ **Plot Options:** The Plot Object Lineweights and the Plot with Plot Styles check boxes control whether AutoCAD uses the features described in the "Plotting with style" and "Plotting through thick and thin" sections, earlier in this chapter.

The Hide Paperspace Objects check box controls whether AutoCAD hides objects that are behind other objects when a 3D model is displayed in a viewport. If your drawing is entirely 2D, then this option doesn't matter. If your drawing includes 3D objects, then selecting this setting is like applying the 3DORBIT command's Hidden option to the plot. Look up "3DORBIT command" on the Index tab in the AutoCAD online help system for more information.

✔ **Plot Upside-Down:** Select this check box if you want to rotate the plot 180 degrees on the paper (a handy option for plotting in the southern hemisphere or for avoiding having to cock your head at an uncomfortable angle as you watch plots come out of the plotter).

AutoCAD normally generates plots in the foreground — that is, the plotting process takes over the program for the entire time that the program is creating the plot. AutoCAD 2008 includes a background plotting feature that returns control of the program to you more quickly. If you have a reasonably fast computer with adequate memory, turn on this feature in the Options dialog box: Choose Tools⇨Options, click the Plot and Publish tab, and in the Background Processing Options area, select Plotting.

If you want to automate plotting for a batch of drawings, check out AutoCAD's *sheet sets* feature. One of the tasks that sheet sets are designed to accomplish is the publishing of a set of drawing sheets at one fell swoop. See the "Sheet sets without regrets" sidebar for a brief overview.

Troubles with Plotting

No matter how many times you read this chapter or how carefully you study the AutoCAD documentation, you'll occasionally run into plotting problems. You're especially likely to encounter problems when trying to plot other people's drawings because you don't always know what plotting conventions they had in mind. (*Plotting conventions* aren't where spies meet; they're a standardized approach to plotting issues.) Table 13-1 describes some of the more common plotting problems and solutions.

Table 13-1	Plotting Problems and Solutions
Problem	*Possible Solution*
Nothing comes out of the plotter (system printer driver).	Check whether you can print to the device from other Windows applications. If not, it's not an AutoCAD problem. Try the Windows Print Troubleshooter (**Windows 2000:** Start⇨Help⇨Contents⇨Troubleshooting and Maintenance; **Windows XP:** Start⇨ Help and Support⇨Printing and Faxing⇨ Fixing a Printing Problem⇨Printing Troubleshooter; **Windows Vista:** Start⇨ Help and Support, type **printing trouble-shooting** in the Search box and press Enter, then click Troubleshoot Printer Problems).
Nothing comes out of the plotter (non-system printer driver).	Choose File⇨Plotter Manager, double-click the plotter configuration, and check the settings.
Objects don't plot the way they appear on-screen.	Check for a plot style table with weird settings or try plotting without a plot style table.
Objects appear ghosted or with washed-out colors.	In the plot style table, set Color to Black for all colors.
Scaled to Fit doesn't work right in paper space.	Change the What to Plot drop-down list from Layout to Extents.
The HP-enhanced Windows system driver that you downloaded from HP's Web site doesn't have the right paper sizes (for example, no architectural paper sizes).	In the Plot dialog box's Printer/Plotter area, click the Properties button to display the Plotter Configuration Editor dialog box, click the Custom Properties button (near the bottom), and then click the More Sizes button to specify the standard and custom paper sizes.
Something else is wrong.	Check the plot log: Click the Plot/Publish Details Report Available icon near the right end of the status bar and look for error messages.

Part IV
Share and Share Alike

In this part . . .

After you get the lines and text right, you may be justified in thinking that your work in AutoCAD is done. But AutoCAD enables you to do so much more! Blocks and external references help you manage data within drawings, between drawings, and across a network. If you plan to share drawings (whether among your own projects, with people in your office, or with folks in other companies), you need to think about consistency in presentation and drawing organization.

The Internet is the biggest ongoing swap meet in human history, and AutoCAD offers some unique trading possibilities — and potential pitfalls — via e-mail and the Web. With the information in this part, you'll be teaching AutoCAD how to give and receive in no time.

Chapter 14

Playing Blocks and Rasteroids

In This Chapter

▶ Introducing blocks, external references (xrefs), and raster images

▶ Creating block definitions

▶ Inserting blocks

▶ Using attributes in blocks

▶ Authoring dynamic blocks

▶ Attaching and managing xrefs and DWFs

▶ Controlling xref paths

▶ Attaching and managing raster image files

Chapter 7 shows you how to copy objects within a drawing or even to another drawing. That's one way to use AutoCAD to improve drafting efficiency. You can copy a DWG file and then modify it to create a similar drawing — an even better productivity booster, as long as you're in the habit of making similar drawings. But all those are baby steps compared to the techniques that I cover in this chapter: treating drawings, parts of drawings, drawings saved in Web format (DWF, or Design Web Format), and raster images as reusable and updateable modules. If you want to make drafting production more efficient with CAD, you want to know how to use blocks, xrefs, DWFs, and raster files.

A *block* is a collection of objects grouped together to form a single object. You can *insert* this collection more than once in the same drawing, and when you do, all instances of the block remain identical. By redefining the *block definition,* you can automatically change all instances of the block insertion at once. Although a block lives within a specific drawing, you can transfer copies of it into other drawings. And you can add fill-in-the-blank text fields, called *attributes,* to blocks.

In earlier versions, block attribute values were limited to a single line of variable text with a maximum of 255 characters. AutoCAD 2008 introduces multiline attributes; in addition to having more than one line, multiline attributes have many of the formatting options of multiline text. And blocks both with and without attributes can be defined as annotative objects to boot. (See Chapter 10 for a rundown on annotative objects.)

Blocks don't have to be static creations. Instead of having a half-dozen regular blocks for a half-dozen different door sizes, you can create a single *dynamic block* that includes all those sizes. Unlike a regular block, in which every instance of a particular block is geometrically identical, each instance of a dynamic block can display geometric variations. For example, you can insert one furniture block three times and have one instance display as a sofa, one as a loveseat, and one as an armchair. I introduce *block authoring* — the process for creating and editing dynamic blocks — in this chapter.

An *external reference drawing,* or *xref,* is like an industrial-strength block. An xref is a pointer to a separate drawing outside the drawing you're working on. When you attach a reference drawing, it appears on-screen and on plots as part of your drawing, but it continues to live as a separate document on your hard disk. If you edit the externally referenced drawing, the appearance of the drawing changes in all drawings that reference it.

A *raster image* file stores a graphical image as a series of dots. Raster files are good for storing photographs, logos, and other images, whereas CAD *vector* files are good for storing geometrical objects such as lines and arcs, along with text and other annotations for describing the geometry. Sometimes it's handy to combine raster images with CAD vector files by attaching them to your drawing files, and AutoCAD's External References palette makes the process straightforward.

Before AutoCAD 2007, *external references* were drawing files that you attached to your current drawing. Images were (and still are) raster graphics files that you attached in a similar way but with a different command. In AutoCAD 2007 and later, *External References* is the name of the palette with which you attach and manage not only external reference drawings (xrefs), but also image files, DWF underlays, and MicroStation DGN files. (A *DWF* file is a lightweight version of a DWG file; I discuss DWFs [you can call them *dwiffs* if you don't mind being thought of as a dweeb] in Chapter 15.)

Both AutoCAD 2008 and AutoCAD LT 2008 enable you to attach DGN files to current drawings via the External References palette. *DGN* files are drawing files created by one of AutoCAD's major competitors: MicroStation from Bentley Systems. (You can also import and export DGN drawing data in both AutoCAD and AutoCAD LT.) If you're new to AutoCAD, you're not so likely to encounter DGN files unless you're working for a large company that exchanges a lot of drawings with partners and consultants. For more information on DGN files in AutoCAD 2008, look up "DGN Files, About" in the online help system index.

Blocks, external references, DWF underlays, raster images, and DGN files enable you to reuse your work and the work of others, giving you the potential to save tremendous amounts of time — or to cause tremendous problems if you change a file on which other people's drawings depend. Use these features when you can to save time, but do so in an organized and careful way so as to avoid problems.

How you use blocks and especially xrefs depends a lot on the profession and office in which you work. Some disciplines and companies use these drawing organization features heavily and in a highly organized way, while others don't. Ask your colleagues what the local customs are and follow them.

Rocking with Blocks

First, a little more block theory, and then you can rock right into those blocks. To use a block in a drawing, you need two things: a block *definition* and one or more block *inserts.* AutoCAD doesn't always make the distinction between these two things very clear, but you need to understand the difference to avoid terminal confusion about blocks. (Maybe this syndrome should be called *blockheadedness?*)

A block definition lives in an invisible area of your drawing file called the *block table.* (It's one of those symbol tables that I describe in Chapter 5.) The block table is like a book of graphical recipes for making different kinds of blocks. Each block definition is like a recipe for making one kind of block. When you insert a block, as described later in this chapter, AutoCAD creates a special object called a *block insert.* The insert points to the recipe and tells AutoCAD, "Hey, draw me according to the instructions in this recipe!"

Although a block may look like a collection of objects stored together and given a name, it's really a graphical recipe (the block definition) plus one or more pointers to that recipe (one or more block inserts). Each time you insert a particular block, you create another pointer to the same recipe.

The advantages of blocks include

- ✔ **Grouping objects together when they belong together logically.** You can draw a screw using lines and arcs and then make a block definition out of all these objects. When you insert the screw block, AutoCAD treats it as a single object for purposes of copying, moving, and so on.

- ✔ **Saving time and reducing errors.** Inserting a block is, of course, much quicker than redrawing the same geometry again. And the less geometry you draw from scratch, the less opportunity there is to make a mistake.

- ✔ **Efficiency of storage when you reuse the same block repeatedly.** If you insert the same screw block 15 times in a drawing, AutoCAD stores the detailed block definition only once. The 15 block inserts that point to the block definition take up much less disk space than 15 copies of all the lines, polylines, and arcs.

✔ **The ability to edit all instances of a symbol in a drawing simply by modifying a single block definition.** This one is a biggie. If you decide that your design requires a different kind of screw, you simply redefine the screw's block definition. With this new recipe, AutoCAD then replaces all 15 screws automatically. That's a heck of a lot faster than erasing and recopying 15 screws!

✔ **Varying the appearance of block inserts by using dynamic blocks.** This one is an even bigger biggie. If your design requires a different kind of screw, you simply change the view of the screw to the other kind (assuming, of course, you've defined your screw as a dynamic block). Every instance of the screw in the drawing could show a different kind of screw. And *that's* a heck of a lot more efficient than creating 15 different block definitions!

Blocks *aren't* as great for drawing elements used in multiple drawings, however, especially if several people are working on and sharing parts of drawings with one another. That's because blocks, after they get into multiple drawings, stay in each drawing; a later modification to a block definition in one drawing does not automatically modify all the other drawings that use that block. If you use a block with your company's logo in a number of drawings and then you decide to change the logo, you must make the change within each drawing that uses the block.

If all you need to do is group some objects so that you can more easily select them for copying, moving, and so on, use AutoCAD's *group* feature. Type **GROUP** (or the command alias **G**) and press Enter to open the Object Grouping dialog box in AutoCAD or the Group Manager dialog box in AutoCAD LT. Then select some objects, click the New button in AutoCAD or the Create Group button in AutoCAD LT, and type a name for the group. When you're editing drawings that contain groups, press Ctrl+H to toggle "group-ness" on or off. If you've toggled "group-ness" on, picking any object in a group selects all objects in the group. If you've toggled it off, picking an object selects only that object, even if it happens to be a member of a group.

Creating block definitions

To create a block definition from objects in the current drawing, use the Block Definition dialog box. (The other way to create a block definition is by inserting another drawing file into your current drawing as a block, which I explain in the next section.) The following steps show you how to create a block definition by using the Block Definition dialog box:

1. **Click the Make Block button on the Draw toolbar.**

   The Block Definition dialog box appears (see Figure 14-1).

   Layers matter when you create the objects that make up a block. Block geometry created on most layers retains the characteristics, such as color and linetype, of those layers. But if you create a block using geometry created on Layer 0, that geometry has no characteristics, such as color and linetype, of its own; chameleon-like, it takes on the features of the layer into which it's inserted.

Figure 14-1: The Block Definition dialog box.

2. **Type the block definition's name in the Name text box.**

   If you type the name of an existing block definition, AutoCAD will warn you when you click OK at the end of the process, and ask if you want to replace that block definition with the new objects you select. This process is called *block redefinition*.

   To see a list of the names of all the current blocks in your drawing, open the Name drop-down list.

3. **Specify the base point (also known as the insertion point) of the block, using any of the following methods:**

   - Enter the coordinates of the insertion point in the X, Y, and Z text boxes.

   - Click the Pick Point button and then select a point on the screen. (In this case, use an object snap or other precision technique, as described in Chapter 5, to grab a specific point on one of the block's objects.)

Checking the new Specify On-screen boxes for both Base point and Objects lets you fill in the other information in the dialog box, click OK, and then pick a base point and select objects for the block at the command line.

The *base point* is the point on the block by which you insert it later, as I describe in the next section.

Use an obvious and consistent point on the group of objects for the base point, such as the lower-left corner, so that you know what to expect when you insert the block.

4. **Click the Select Objects button and then select the objects that you want as part of the block.**

AutoCAD uses the selected objects to create a block definition and displays an icon showing those objects next to the block name. Figure 14-2 shows the base point and group of selected objects during the process of creating a new block definition.

Figure 14-2:
Building a
block.

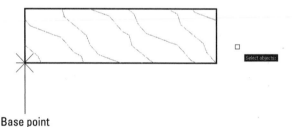

Base point

5. **Select a radio button to tell AutoCAD what to do with the objects used to define the block: retain them in place, convert them into a block instance, or delete them.**

The default choice, Convert to Block, is usually the best. See Step 9 for a description of what happens with each choice.

6. **Specify the insert units to which the block will be scaled in the Block Unit drop-down list.**

When you or someone else drags the block from one drawing into another via the DesignCenter palette (see Chapter 5) or Tool Palettes (described later in this chapter), the units you specify here and the units of the drawing you're dragging into will control the default insertion scale factor.

Three additional features in AutoCAD's Block Definition dialog box give you even more control over what happens to your blocks as they're inserted:

- If the *Annotative* check box is selected, you can assign multiple plotted drawing scales to the block and then display the inserted block at the different scale representations by choosing one from the Annotation scale list on the status bar.

- If the *Scale Uniformly* check box is selected, blocks will be inserted with the same X, Y, or Z scale factors. (Scale Uniformly is automatically checked if Annotative is checked.)

- If the *Allow Exploding* check box is selected, blocks can be exploded during or after their insertion in a drawing.

7. Enter a description for the block in the Description text area.

You don't have to enter a description to create a block, but it's not a bad idea. Think like a database manager and enter a useful description that will identify the block to yourself and others.

8. Make sure that the Open in Block Editor check box is unchecked.

You don't need to use the Edit Block Definition dialog box if you're not going to add dynamic features to the block. I cover defining dynamic blocks later in this chapter.

9. Click OK to complete the block definition process.

AutoCAD stores the block definition in the current drawing's block table. If you selected the Convert to Block radio button (the default) in Step 5, AutoCAD also creates a block insert pointing to the new block definition — the objects look the same on-screen, but now they're an instance of the block rather than existing as separate objects. If you selected the Retain radio button, the objects remain in place but aren't converted into a block insert — they stay individual objects with no connection to the new block definition. If you selected the Delete radio button, the objects disappear (but the block definition still gets created).

When you define a block, you can include a special kind of variable text object called an *attribute definition*. When you insert a block that contains one or more attribute definitions, AutoCAD prompts you to fill in values for the text fields. Attributes are useful for variable title block information (sheet number, sheet title, and so on) and symbols that contain different codes or callouts. I describe how to create and use attribute definitions later in this chapter.

Keep your common symbol drawings in one or more specific folders that you set aside just for that purpose. You may want to use one of the following techniques to develop a library of symbols that you use frequently:

✔ Create a separate DWG file for each block.

✔ Store a bunch of symbols as block definitions in one drawing and use DesignCenter to import block definitions from this drawing when you need them.

Inserting blocks

AutoCAD provides a number of ways to insert a block or a whole drawing file, but the most commonly used and most flexible is the Insert dialog box. Here's the procedure for inserting a block:

1. **Set an appropriate layer current, as described in Chapter 5.**

   It's a good idea to insert each block on a layer that has something to do with the block's geometry or purpose:

   • If all the objects in the block definition reside on one layer, then it's usually best to insert the block on that layer.

   • If the block geometry spans several layers, choose one of them to insert the block on.

   If any of the block definition's geometry was created on Layer 0, that geometry will inherit the color, linetype, and other object properties of the layer that you insert the block on. It's like the chameleon changing color to match its surroundings or a politician changing his position to match the day's opinion polls.

2. **Click the Insert Block button on the Draw toolbar.**

   The Insert dialog box appears, as shown in Figure 14-3.

Figure 14-3:
The Insert
dialog box.

3. **Enter the block definition name or external filename by using one of the following methods:**

   • Use the Name drop-down list to select from a list of block definitions in the current drawing.

   • Click the Browse button to select an external DWG file and have AutoCAD create a block definition from it.

You can use an external drawing to replace a block definition in your current drawing. If you click Browse and choose a file whose name matches the name of a block definition that's already in your drawing, AutoCAD warns you and then updates the block definition in your drawing with the current contents of the external file. This process is called *block redefinition,* and as described in Step 2 in the "Creating block definitions" section, AutoCAD automatically updates all the block inserts that point to the block definition.

4. **Enter the insertion point, scale, and rotation angle of the block.**

   You can either select the Specify On-screen check box in each area to specify the parameters on-screen at the command prompt, or type the values you want in the text boxes in the Insertion Point, Scale, and Rotation areas.

   Check the Uniform Scale check box to constrain the X, Y, and Z scaling parameters to the same value (which is what you want in almost all cases).

5. **If you want AutoCAD to create a copy of the individual objects in the block instead of a block insert that points to the block definition, select the Explode check box.**

6. **Click OK.**

7. **If you checked the Specify On-screen check box for the insertion point, scale, or rotation angle, answer the prompts on the command line to specify these parameters.**

After you insert a block, all the objects displayed in the block insert behave as a single object. When you select any object in the block insert, AutoCAD highlights all the objects in it.

Another way to insert a block is to drag a DWG file from Windows Explorer and drop it anywhere in the current drawing window. AutoCAD then prompts you to choose an insertion point and optionally change the default scale factor and rotation angle. Similarly, you can drag a block definition from the Blocks section of the DesignCenter palette and drop it into the current drawing window. (Chapter 5 describes DesignCenter.)

AutoCAD provides one additional way of inserting blocks: the Tool Palettes window, which is described in Chapter 2. As is true of using a tool palette for hatching (Chapter 12), you first must create and configure appropriate tools. The easiest method is right-clicking a drawing in DesignCenter and choosing Create Tool Palette. A new tabbed page is added to the Tool Palettes window containing all the block definitions from the drawing that you right-clicked. Simply click and drag a tool to insert its corresponding block into a drawing. Dragging blocks from the tool palettes doesn't give you the chance to specify a different insertion scale, nor can you use all AutoCAD's precision tools to specify the insertion point precisely — you may need to move the block into place after inserting it. I recommend that you first master the other block insertion methods described in this chapter — especially the Insert dialog box and DesignCenter palette. Then if you find yourself inserting the same blocks frequently, consider creating a tool palette containing them. See "tool palettes, adding drawings from" in the AutoCAD online help system for more information.

Be careful when inserting one drawing into another. If the host (or parent) drawing and the inserted (or child) drawing have different definitions for layers that share the same name, the objects in the inserted drawing take on the layer characteristics of the host drawing. For example, if you insert a drawing with lines on a layer called Walls that's blue and dashed into a drawing with a layer called Walls that's red and continuous, the inserted lines on the wall layer will turn red and continuous after they're inserted. The same rules apply to linetypes, text styles, dimension styles, table styles, multileader styles, and block definitions that are nested inside the drawing you're inserting.

If you need to modify a block definition after you've inserted one or more instances of it, use the Block Editor (BEDIT command); choose Tools⇨Block Editor. Look up "BEDIT" in the AutoCAD online help system. BEDIT is available in both AutoCAD and AutoCAD LT.

Attributes: Fill-in-the-blank blocks

You may think of attributes as the good (or bad) qualities of your significant other, but in AutoCAD, *attributes* are fill-in-the-blank text fields that you can add to your blocks. When you create a block definition and then insert it several times in a drawing, all the ordinary geometry (lines, circles, regular text strings, and so on) in all the instances are exactly identical. Attributes provide a little more flexibility in the form of text strings that can be different in each block insert.

For example, suppose that you frequently designate parts in your drawings by labeling them with a distinct number or letter in a circle for each part. If you want to create a block for this symbol, you can't simply draw the number or letter as regular text using the MTEXT or DTEXT command. If you create a block definition with a regular text object (for example, the letter A), the text string will be the same in every instance of the block (always the letter A). That's not much help in distinguishing the parts!

Instead, you create an *attribute definition,* which acts as a placeholder for a text string that can vary each time you insert the block. You include the attribute definition when you create the block definition (refer to the "Creating block definitions" section, earlier in this chapter). Then each time you insert the block, AutoCAD prompts you to fill in an *attribute value* for each attribute definition.

In earlier versions, block attribute values were limited to a single line of variable text with a maximum of 255 characters. AutoCAD 2008 introduces multiline attributes; as well as offering more than one line, multiline attributes have many of the formatting options of multiline text. For more information on creating and inserting blocks with multiline attributes, look up "attribute definitions, multiline" in the online help system index.

The AutoCAD documentation and dialog boxes often use the term *attribute* to refer indiscriminately to an *attribute definition* or an *attribute value*. I blame a lot of the confusion about attributes to this sloppiness. Just remember that an attribute definition is the text field or placeholder in the block definition, while an attribute value is the specific text string that you type when you insert the block.

Attribute definitions

You use the Attribute Definition dialog box to create attribute definitions (clever, huh?). The procedure is similar to creating a text string except that you must supply a little more information. Create attribute definitions with the following steps:

1. **Change to the layer on which you want to create the attribute definition.**

2. **Choose Draw⇨Block⇨Define Attributes to run the ATTDEF command.**

   The Attribute Definition dialog box appears, as shown in Figure 14-4.

   You rarely need to use any of the first four Mode settings (Invisible, Constant, Verify, or Preset). Just leave them unchecked. If you're curious about what the modes do, use the dialog box help to find out more.

Figure 14-4:
The
Attribute
Definition
dialog box.

3. **Select or deselect the Lock Position check box.**

   If Lock Position is checked, the attributes cannot be relocated within the block insertion — the whole thing is treated as a single object. Unchecking Lock Position allows attributes to be moved by dragging their grips, without moving the block insertion as a whole.

4. **Select or deselect the Multiple Lines check box.**

   Checking Multiple Lines in the Modes area disables the "Default" text box and displays a button to open the Multiline Editor. You don't get the whole panoply of formatting options that you get in the MTEXT command's In-Place Text Editor, but you can over- or underscore text, and a right-click menu lets you import text, assign a background mask, or choose from a number of other options. Refer to the online help system for more information.

5. **In the Attribute area, type values for the tag (the unique identifier for the attribute), the user prompt, and the default value.**

   The name you type into the Tag text box can't contain any spaces. The Prompt and Default text boxes may contain spaces.

   Attribute values can include automatically updating fields, such as date, filename, or system variable setting. Click the Insert Field button (not in AutoCAD LT) to the right of the Default text box to insert a field. See Chapter 10 for more information.

6. **(Optional) If you selected the Multiple Lines check box in Step 4, click the Open Multiline Editor button (it shows three periods) to enter the multiline default attribute value and add any formatting; then click OK.**

   The value you enter here is the default text stored in the attribute definition, and you can change it when you insert the block.

7. **In the Text Settings area, specify the Justification, Text Style, Height, Rotation, and Boundary Width (the last for multiline attributes only).**

   The text properties for attribute definitions are the same as those for text objects — see Chapter 10.

8. **Select Specify On-screen to choose an insertion point for the attribute definition.**

   An attribute definition's insertion point is like a text string's base point. Remember to use snap, object snap, or another precision tool if you want the eventual attribute values to be located at a precise point.

9. **Click OK to create the attribute definition.**

10. **Repeat Steps 1 through 9 for any additional attribute definitions.**

If you need to create a series of attribute definitions in neat rows, create the first one using Steps 1 through 9 and then select the Align below Previous Attribute Definition check box for the subsequent definitions. To make a series of non-adjacent attributes, create the first one using Steps 1 through 9 and then copy the first attribute definition and edit the copy with the Properties palette. You can prevent your attributes from being dragged around the block by selecting the Lock Position check box in the Attribute Definition dialog box.

Block definition containing attribute definitions

After you create one or more attribute definitions — and any other geometry that you want to include in the block — you're ready to create a block definition that contains them. Follow the steps in the section "Creating block definitions," earlier in this chapter.

At Step 4 in the section "Creating block definitions," you can select any attribute definitions before or after you select the other geometry. However, you should select each attribute definition one by one (clicking on each attribute definition rather than selecting multiple attributes with a selection window) in the order that you want the attribute value prompts to appear in the Edit Attributes dialog box (see Figure 14-5). If you don't select the attributes one by one, your block and attributes will still work, but the order of the attribute prompts in the Edit Attributes dialog box may not be what you want.

You can use the Block Attribute Manager (choose Modify⇨Object⇨Attribute⇨ Block Attribute Manager — not included in AutoCAD LT) to reorder the attribute definitions in a block definition. You also can use this dialog box to edit other attribute definition settings, such as the prompt, text style, or layer.

Insert a block containing attribute definitions

After you create a block definition that contains attribute definitions, you insert it just like any other block. Follow the steps in the section "Inserting blocks," earlier in this chapter. At the end of the steps, AutoCAD displays the Edit Attributes dialog box, shown in Figure 14-5. The dialog box contains one row for each of the attribute definitions and has any default values filled in. You simply edit the values and then click OK.

The ATTDIA (ATTribute DIAlog box) system variable controls whether AutoCAD prompts for attribute values in a dialog box (ATTDIA=1) or at the command line (ATTDIA=0). If you insert a block and see command line prompts for each attribute value, type a value and press Enter for each attribute value. When you return to the Command prompt, type **ATTDIA**, press Enter, type **1**, and press Enter again. When you insert blocks with attributes in this drawing in the future, AutoCAD displays the Edit Attributes dialog box instead of prompting you at the command line.

Figure 14-5:
The Edit
Attributes
dialog box.

Edit attribute values

After you insert a block that contains attributes, you can edit the individual attributes in that block insert with the EATTEDIT command (Enhanced ATTtribute EDIT — once again, not included in AutoCAD LT). Choose Modify⇨ Object⇨Attribute⇨Single and click any object in the block insert. AutoCAD displays the Enhanced Attribute Editor dialog box with the current attribute values, as shown in Figure 14-6. The most common attribute editing operation is to edit the text value — that is, the text string that appears in the block insert. You also can change properties of the attributes, such as layer and text style.

Figure 14-6:
The
Enhanced
Attribute
Editor dialog
box.

Many people use attributes in the way I've described so far — as fill-in-the-blank text fields in blocks. But attributes also can serve as data extraction tools. For example, you can export attribute values, such as part numbers and quantities, to a table object in AutoCAD or to a text, spreadsheet, or database file for analysis or reporting.

Data extraction is a substantial new feature in AutoCAD 2008. Selecting Tools⇨ Data Extraction starts the new Data Extraction Wizard (which replaces the Attribute Extraction Wizard in AutoCAD 2007 — looks like the wizard got a promotion!). You'll find out much more about this specialized function in the online help. Check out User's Guide⇨Share Data Between Drawings and Applications⇨Extract Data from Drawings and Spreadsheets. And, LT users, while you don't have this command, you can still extract attribute information to space- or comma-delimited text files by using the Attribute Extraction dialog box. For more information, look up the ATTEXT command in the online help.

Exploding blocks

In regular block definitions (that is, excluding dynamic blocks), the objects in each block insert act like a well-honed marching squadron: If you move or otherwise edit one object in the block insert, all objects move or change in the same way. Usually this cohesion is an advantage, but occasionally you need to break up the squadron in order to modify one object without affecting the others.

To *explode* a block insert into individual objects, click Explode (the firecracker button) on the Modify toolbar and then select the block insert. When you explode a block insert, AutoCAD replaces it with all the objects — lines, polylines, arcs, and so on — specified in the block definition. You then can edit the objects individually or perhaps use them to make more block definitions.

If you explode a block that contains attributes, the attribute *values* change back to attribute *definitions*. This usually isn't the sort of change that you want. If you really need to explode the block insert, you'll probably want to erase the attribute definitions and draw regular text strings in their place. If you've installed the AutoCAD Express Tools (not available in AutoCAD LT), you can perform this task automatically with the BURST command (Express⇨ Blocks⇨Explode Attributes to Text).

Purging unused block definitions

Each block definition slightly increases the size of your DWG file, as do other named objects such as layers, text styles, and dimension styles. If you delete (or explode) all the block inserts that point to a particular block definition, then that block definition no longer serves any purpose.

You should run the PURGE command periodically in each drawing and purge unused block definitions and other named objects. Choose File⇨Drawing Utilities⇨Purge to display the Purge dialog box. Click the Purge All button in order to purge all unused named objects in the current drawing.

Theme and variations: Dynamic blocks

You can add variety to your blocks by making them dynamic. The two most useful applications for dynamic blocks are multiple presentations of similar objects and manipulation of components within individual block inserts.

There's no question that AutoCAD's dynamic blocks feature gives a great deal of flexibility to block creation and insertion. But it's also a very complicated system, with its own set of commands and system variables. I recommend that you become *very* familiar with the regular block creation and insertion techniques I describe in the previous sections before you tackle dynamic blocks.

Spend some time planning your dynamic blocks. Sketch out the geometry for each variation in appearance (or *visibility state*) and decide where the common base point should be. Unless you're a lot smarter than I am, you'll probably find that creating dynamic blocks is complex enough without trying to design your blocks as you go.

Now you see it . . .

If your drawing shows six different kinds of windows, one approach is to create six different standard blocks to represent them all. Alternatively, you can create a single dynamic block and define *visibility states* to cover all six different types. The following steps show you how to make your blocks do double (or sextuple?) duty by using the Edit Block Definition dialog box:

 1. **Open a drawing that contains some block definitions you'd like to combine or draw some simple geometry to make some similar types of objects.**

    You can create dynamic blocks from scratch, or you can work with exist-ing standard (that is, non-dynamic) block definitions. Figure 14-7 shows a drawing with three non-dynamic blocks.

 2. **Choose Tools⇨Block Editor to open the Edit Block Definition dialog box.**

 3. **In the Block to create or edit box, specify a new block name or click <Current Drawing> and then click OK to display the Block Editor window.**

    The Block Editor is a special authoring environment with its own set of palettes, a toolbar, and a passel of command-line commands. You also have access to the rest of AutoCAD's toolbars, so you can draw and edit just like you're in the regular drawing window.

Dynamic Blocks (chairs).dwg

Figure 14-7:
Three
blocks to
make three
seats.

If you enter a new block name, AutoCAD displays an empty block-authoring environment where you draw geometry or insert existing blocks. If you instead select Current Drawing, AutoCAD places all drawing objects inside the block-authoring environment.

4. **Create some geometry for the first visibility state, or choose Insert⇨ Block and select an existing block definition to serve as the first visibility state.**

When creating geometry from scratch, pay attention to where the common base point should be. Although you use different blocks to assemble a multiple-view block, they should all have the same base point (0,0 is a good one for blocks). You don't want your chairs jumping around between different insertion points!

5. **If you inserted an existing block in Step 4, uncheck all three Specify On-screen check boxes, make sure that the Explode check box is *not* checked, and then click OK.**

6. **Repeat Steps 4 and 5, drawing or inserting all the necessary geometry.**

At this point, your drawing screen may look pretty strange (see Figure 14-8). Don't worry; you're going to fix it up in the next steps.

7. **Click the Parameters tab of the Block Authoring palettes and then click Visibility Parameter.**

If the Block Authoring palettes are not open, click the Authoring Palettes button on the Block Authoring toolbar.

AutoCAD prompts you to specify the parameter location.

Block Authoring toolbar   Visibility States controls

Figure 14-8:
Three seats
in the Block
Editor.

Block Authoring palettes   Visibility Parameter marker

8. **Click to place the parameter marker somewhere other than the base point location you chose in Step 4.**

   The parameter location you specify will be the spot on the block where the dynamic block option grip will be displayed. It's not crucial where you locate this point, but try to pick a sensible location on the object. If you specify the same point for the parameter location as the base point for the block, you may have a hard time selecting the dynamic option grip.

9. **AutoCAD places a parameter marker at the selected point and returns to the command line.**

   As shown in Figure 14-8, the label Visibility appears next to the visibility parameter marker, and a yellow Alert symbol indicates that no action has been assigned to the parameter yet. The Visibility States controls at the right end of the Block Authoring toolbar become active.

10. **Click Manage Visibility States on the Block Authoring toolbar. Click Rename and change VisibilityState0 to something more descriptive. Click OK.**

    As is the case with other named objects in AutoCAD, it's good procedure to assign useful, descriptive names rather than accept the default generic labels.

11. **On the Block Authoring toolbar, click Make Invisible. At the Select objects prompt, select the geometry or block inserts that should be invisible in the current visibility state — that is, those that are *not* associated with the current visibility state — and then press Enter.**

    By default, the invisible objects disappear from the screen. You can view them in a faded appearance by clicking Visibility Mode on the Block Authoring toolbar.

12. **Click Manage Visibility States again and then click New to create a new visibility state. In the New Visibility State dialog box, enter a descriptive name. Select the Show All Existing Objects in New State radio button, and then click OK.**

    All of your geometry should reappear.

13. **Repeat Steps 10, 11 and 12 to create additional visibility states associated with the remaining geometry or blocks.**

    The geometry or block insert associated with the last-created visibility state should be visible on-screen.

14. **From the Block Authoring toolbar, click Close Block Editor. Save the changes to your new block or to <Current Drawing>.**

    AutoCAD displays an alert box asking if you want to save changes to your block. Click Cancel to return to the block editor or No to discard your edits. Click Yes to save. AutoCAD closes the block authoring environment and returns to the standard drawing editor window.

Lights! Parameters!! Actions!!!

You can modify the appearance of individual instances of the same block by defining *parameters* and *actions* to move, rotate, flip, or align parts of them. You can adjust the block's appearance as you insert it or at any time afterward. The following steps show you how to use the Block Editor to add some action to a block definition:

1. **Open a drawing that contains some block definitions whose appearance you'd like to spice up a little, or draw some simple geometry that might make a suitably dynamic block.**

    Action parameters are most effective in block definitions that contain groups of related objects — for example, an office desk and chair or a furniture arrangement.

2. **Choose Tools⇨Block Editor to open the Edit Block Definition dialog box.**

3. **In the Block to create or edit field, type a new block name or click <Current Drawing>, and then click OK.**

4. **Create some geometry or insert some blocks. When inserting blocks, remember to make sure that the Explode check box at the lower-left corner of the Insert dialog box is *not* checked, and then click OK.**

   Draw the geometry or insert the blocks in a group such that you can insert the finished arrangement into your drawings — for example, Figure 14-9 shows the creation of a dynamic block for a coffee shop or cafeteria.

5. **Repeat Step 4 until you've drawn all the needed geometry or inserted all the necessary blocks.**

6. **Click the Parameters tab of the Block Authoring palettes and then click Rotation Parameter.**

   If the Block Authoring palettes are not open, click the Authoring Palettes button on the Block Authoring toolbar.

   AutoCAD prompts you to specify the parameter location.

7. **Click to place the parameter marker somewhere on the object geometry other than the base point location.**

   If you specify the same point for the parameter location as the base point for the block, you may have a hard time selecting the dynamic option grip.

8. **AutoCAD places a parameter marker at the selected point and returns to the command line, prompting you to specify the radius of the rotation parameter, the default rotation angle, and finally the parameter label location.**

   The parameter marker's label appears next to the rotation parameter marker.

   If you type **D** and press Enter, you can add a brief description to the parameter. Then when you hover over the dynamic block's custom grip that's associated with that parameter, AutoCAD displays a grip tip (as shown later in Figure 14-10).

9. **Click the Actions tab of the Block Authoring palettes and then click Rotate Action. Select the Rotate Parameter, select the objects that should be modified when the grip is used, and specify a point for the action's label.**

   AutoCAD returns to the command prompt. At this point, it's fine to go with default values and on-screen pick points.

10. **Repeat Steps 6 through 9, trying different parameters and actions. For example, choose a Point Parameter and a Move Action.**

    Figure 14-9 shows a set of block components, several of which have action parameters assigned to them. After the block is inserted, you can manipulate the components to which you've added parameters to vary the appearance of the blocks. I explain how a little later in this chapter.

Learn about Dynamic Blocks

Figure 14-9:
A passel of
parameters
ready for
action.

Point Parameter marker   Rotation Parameter marker

11. **From the Block Authoring toolbar, click Close Block Editor.**

An AutoCAD alert box asks if you want to save changes to your block.
Click Yes to save changes to your new block or <Current Drawing>.

AutoCAD closes the block-authoring environment and returns to the
standard drawing editor window.

Manipulating dynamic blocks

After a dynamic block has been inserted in a drawing, you can select it and
modify its display through a special set of *custom grips*. (That's what
AutoCAD is calling them, so I'm following suit.)

When you select a standard (that is, non-dynamic) block, you see a single
grip at the insertion point. When you select a dynamic block, you see at least
two — and maybe more — custom grips, as well as the insertion point grip.
The custom grips usually look different from the regular object grips, but not
always, so take care when clicking grips.

The following steps show you how to make your dynamic blocks do the
things you just spent all this time teaching them to do:

1. **Insert a few blocks that contain some dynamic parameters such as visibility or action parameters.**

If your block inserts don't have any action parameters, go to Step 4.

2. **Select a block that includes some action parameters.**

   The block insert displays a number of grips (see Figure 14-10). If the insert displays only one grip, it isn't a dynamic block.

3. **Click one of the custom grips — for example, clicking a round grip opens the rotation parameter of the object. Rotate the component as required.**

4. **Select a block that includes a visibility parameter and then click the visibility grip. Choose the desired visibility state from the right-click menu.**

   For additional information on manipulating actions and visibility states, refer to the online help system.

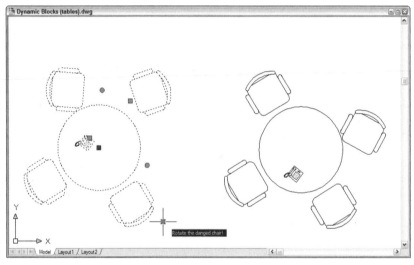

Figure 14-10: Variations on dynamic blocks (original on the right, and a handy grip tip on a chair at left center).

Dynamic blocks, as I've suggested more than once, are a powerful — and complicated — feature. The Block Authoring Palettes contain 10 selectable parameters, 8 actions, and 20 parameter sets. I'm thinking of writing a new book called *AutoCAD Block Authoring For Dummies;* until I do, AutoCAD's online help system is your best resource for more information on all the possibilities of dynamic blocks. The quickest and most direct way to AutoCAD's own help is to click the Learn about Dynamic Blocks button (just left of the Close Block Editor button in Figure 14-9) while you're working in the Block Editor environment.

Going External

In AutoCAD, an *xref,* or external reference, is a reference to another, *external* drawing file — one outside the current drawing — that you can make act as though it's part of your drawing. Technically, a reference is simply a pointer from one file to another. The xref is the actual pointer, but many people call the combination of the pointer and the external file the xref.

In AutoCAD 2008, external drawing files are just one of four different file types you can attach to your current drawing by using the somewhat confusingly named External References palette. You use this palette to attach externally referenced drawings (xrefs), images, DWF files, and MicroStation DGN files. It's really worth getting past the confusion — it's *very* useful to be able to see externally referenced drawing files, attached images, DWF underlays — and maybe even MicroStation drawing files — all in the same window.

Drawings that you include as xrefs in other drawings are called *child* draw- ings. Drawings that contain pointers to the child drawings are called *parent* drawings. This family terminology gets a little weird when you realize that a child drawing can have lots of parent drawings that refer to it — apparently it's the commune version of family relations. If you find such relationships odd, you can, like the AutoCAD online help system, refer to the parent draw- ing as the *host* drawing. I prefer the terms *parent* and *child,* in part because they're easily extendable to describing more complex relationships, such as a parent drawing, which xrefs a child drawing, which in turn xrefs a grandchild drawing. Complicated enough? Luckily, this family arrangement doesn't include grandnieces or second cousins once removed!

Xrefs have a big advantage over blocks: If you change a child drawing, AutoCAD automatically updates all the parent drawings that reference the child drawing upon opening the parent drawings.

When you open a drawing that contains xrefs, AutoCAD displays a little symbol (which looks like papers with a binder clip) on the right end of the status bar. This symbol alerts you to the fact that some of the things you see in the draw- ing are actually parts of other, xrefed drawings. If an xref changes while you have the parent drawing open (because you or someone else opens and saves the child drawing), the status bar xref symbol displays an `External Reference Files Have Changed` balloon notification in AutoCAD, but not in AutoCAD LT. (If you want to change whether the notifications appear and how often AutoCAD checks for changes, look up "XREFNOTIFY" and "XNOTIFYTIME" in the online help.) You can use the Reload option on the External References palette or simply click the Reload link in the balloon notification to show the updated xrefs. See the "Managing xrefs" section, later in this chapter, for details.

Another advantage of xrefs over blocks is that their contents aren't stored in your drawing even once. The disk storage space taken up by the original drawing (that is, the xref) isn't duplicated, no matter how many parent drawings reference it. This characteristic makes xrefs much more efficient than blocks for larger drawings that are reused several times.

You can always buy a larger hard drive, however, so the storage issue isn't crucial. The key benefit of xrefs is that they enable you to organize your drawings in a modular way so that changes you make to a single drawing file automatically "ripple through" all the parent drawings in which it's xrefed. This benefit is even greater on larger projects involving multiple drafters, each of whose work may be incorporated in part or in whole in the work of others.

The automatic update feature of xrefs is a big advantage only if you're organized about how you use xrefs. Suppose that an architect creates a plan drawing showing a building's walls and other major features that are common to the architectural, structural, plumbing, and electrical plan drawings. The architect then tells the structural, plumbing, and electrical drafters to xref this background plan into their drawings so that everyone is working from a consistent and reusable set of common plan elements. If the architect decides to revise the wall locations and updates the xrefed drawing, everyone will see the current wall configuration and be able to change their drawings. But if the architect absentmindedly adds architecture-specific objects, such as toilets and furniture, to the xrefed drawing, or shifts all the objects with respect to 0,0, everyone else will have problems. If different people in your office share xrefs, create a protocol for who is allowed to modify which file when, and what communication needs to take place after a shared xref is modified.

Becoming attached to your xrefs

Attaching an external reference drawing is similar to inserting a block, and almost as easy. Just use the following steps:

1. **Set an appropriate layer current, as described in Chapter 5.**

   I recommend that you insert xrefs on a separate layer from all other objects. Note that if you freeze the layer an xref is inserted on, the entire xref disappears. (This behavior can be either a handy trick or a nasty surprise.)

2. **If the External References palette is not already open, choose Tools⇨ Palettes⇨External References to open it.**

   The toolbar at the top of the palette lets you attach a drawing as an xref, a raster image file, a DWF underlay, or a MicroStation DGN drawing file. I cover attaching images and DWFs later in this chapter. If you need to attach DGN files, visit the online help.

3. **Click Attach DWG (see Figure 14-11) and locate the drawing file you want to attach.**

   The Select Reference File dialog box appears.

Attach DWG   List View

Tree View

Figure 14-11:
Using the
External
References
palette to
attach an
xref.

4. **Browse to find the file you want to attach, select it, and then click Open.**

   The External Reference dialog box appears.

5. **Specify the parameters for the xref in the dialog box.**

   Parameters include the insertion point, scaling factors, and rotation angle. You can set these parameters in the dialog box or specify them on-screen, just as you can do when inserting a block, as described earlier in this chapter.

   You can select the Attachment or Overlay radio button to tell AutoCAD how to handle the xref. The choice matters only if you create a drawing that uses xrefs, and then your drawing is, in turn, used as an xref. Attachment is the default choice, and it means that the xrefed file will always be included with your drawing when someone else uses your drawing as an xref. Overlay, the other choice, means that you see the xrefed drawing, but someone who xrefs your drawing won't see the overlaid file. By choosing Overlay, you can xref a map, for example, to your drawing of a house but not have the map show up when someone else xrefs your house drawing. (That person can xref the map, if need be.) I recommend that you use the default Attachment reference type unless you have a specific reason to do otherwise.

The Path Type drop-down list provides more flexibility in how the xref's path gets stored. See the "Forging an xref path" section, later in this chapter, for more information. For now, I recommend that you choose Relative Path instead of the default Full Path.

 6. **Click OK.**

The externally referenced file appears in your drawing.

Layer-palooza

When you attach or overlay an xref, AutoCAD adds new layers to your current drawing that correspond to the layers in the xrefed DWG file. The new layers are assigned names that combine the drawing name and layer name; for example, if you xref the drawing MYSCREW.DWG, which has the layer names GEOMETRY, TEXT, and so on, the xrefed layers will be named MYSCREW|GEOMETRY, MYSCREW|TEXT, and so on. By creating separate layers corresponding to each layer in the xrefed file, AutoCAD eliminates the potential problem I warned you about with blocks when layers have the same name but different color or linetype in the two drawings.

Creating and editing an external reference file

To create a file that you can use as an external reference, just create a drawing and save it (or use the WBLOCK command to create a new DWG from geometry in the current drawing). That's it. You can then create or open another drawing and create an external reference to the previous one. The xrefed drawing appears in your parent drawing as a single object, like a block insert. In other words, if you click any object in the xref, AutoCAD selects the entire xref. You can measure or object snap to the xrefed geometry, but you can't modify or delete individual objects in the xref — you open the xref drawing in order to edit its geometry.

AutoCAD's XOPEN command (not in AutoCAD LT) provides a quick way to open an xrefed drawing for editing. You just start the command and pick any object in the xref. Alternatively, you can select the xref in the External References palette and then right-click and choose Open to open one or more xrefs for editing. See the "Managing xrefs" section, later in this chapter, for more information.

An alternative to opening the xrefed file when you need to edit it is to use the REFEDIT command (not in AutoCAD LT). Look up "REFEDIT" in the AutoCAD online help system.

Forging an xref path

When you attach an xref, AutoCAD, by default, stores the xref's full path — that is, the drive letter and sequence of folders and subfolders in which the DWG file resides — along with the filename. This default behavior corresponds to the Full Path setting in the Path Type drop-down list. (Figure 14-12 shows the three xref path options.) Full Path works fine as long as you never move files on your hard disk or network and never send your DWG files to anyone else — which is to say, it almost never works fine!

Figure 14-12: Follow the path less traveled when you attach an xref.

At the other end of the path spectrum, the No Path option causes AutoCAD not to store any path with the xref attachment — only the filename is stored. This is the easiest and best option if the parent and child drawings reside in the same folder.

If you prefer to organize the DWG files for a particular project in more than one folder, then you'll appreciate AutoCAD's Relative Path option, shown in Figure 14-12. This option permits xrefing across more complex, hierarchical folder structures but avoids many of the problems that the Full Path option can cause. For example, you may have a parent drawing, H:\Project-X\ Plans\First floor.dwg, that xrefs H:\Project-X\Common\Column grid.dwg. If you choose Relative path, AutoCAD will store the xref path as ..\ Common\Column grid.dwg instead of H:\Project-X\Common\ Column grid.dwg. Now if you decide to move the \Project-X folder and its subfolders to a different drive (or send them to someone else who doesn't have an H: drive), AutoCAD will still be able to find the xrefs.

When you use Relative Path, you'll see xref paths that include the special codes . and . . (single and double period). The single period means "this parent drawing's folder," and the double period means "the folder above this parent drawing's folder."

You can report on and change xref paths for a set of drawings with the AutoCAD Reference Manager (not in AutoCAD LT). See Chapter 15 for more information.

If all these path options and periods leave you feeling punchy, you can keep your life simple by always keeping parent and child drawings in the same folder and using the No Path option when you attach xrefs.

Managing xrefs

The External References palette includes many more options for managing xrefs after you attach them. Many of these options are hiding in right-click menus. Important options include:

- ✔ **List of external references:** You can change between the List view and Tree view of your drawing's external references just by clicking the appropriate button at the top of the palette (see Figure 14-11). You can resize the columns by dragging the column dividers or re-sort the list by clicking the column header names, just as in Windows Explorer.

- ✔ **Detach:** Right-click an xref in the External References palette and choose Detach to completely remove the selected reference to the external file from your drawing.

- ✔ **Reload:** Right-click an xref and choose Reload to force AutoCAD to reread the selected xrefed DWG file from the disk and update your drawing with its latest contents. This feature is handy when you share xrefs on a network and someone has just made changes to a drawing that you've xrefed.

- ✔ **Unload:** Right-click on an xref and choose Unload to make the selected xref disappear from the on-screen display of your drawing and from any plots you do of it, but retain the pointer and attachment information. Right-click again and choose Reload to redisplay an unloaded xref.

- ✔ **Bind:** Right-click an xref and choose Bind to bring the selected xref into your drawing and turn it into a block. You might use this function, for example, to roll up a complex set of xrefs into a single archive drawing.

In many offices, binding xrefs without an acceptable reason for doing so is a crime as heinous as exploding blocks indiscriminately. In both cases, you're eliminating an important data management link. Find out what the policies are in your company. When in doubt, keep yourself out of a bind. And even when you do have a good reason to bind, you generally should do it on a copy of the parent drawing.

> ✔ **Open:** Right-click an xref and choose Open to open one or more xref drawings in separate drawing windows (sorry LT users — you can't do that either). After you edit and save an xref drawing, return to the parent drawing and use the Reload option in the External References palette to show the changes.

None of these options (other than opening and editing the xref) affects the xrefed drawing itself; it continues to exist as a separate DWG file. If you need to delete or move the DWG file that the xref refers to, do it in Windows Explorer.

The fact that the xrefed drawing is a separate file is a potential source of problems when you send your drawing to someone else; that someone else needs *all* the files that your drawing depends on, or it will be useless. Make sure to include xrefed files in the package with your drawing. See Chapter 15 for a procedure.

AutoCAD (but not AutoCAD LT) includes an additional xref feature called *xref clipping.* You can use the XCLIP command to clip an externally referenced file or a block insertion so only part of it appears in the parent drawing. AutoCAD LT doesn't include the XCLIP command, but if you open a drawing containing an xref that was clipped in AutoCAD, the clipped view will be preserved.

XCLIP includes a new Invert option; instead of masking everything *outside* the clip boundary, XCLIP Invert masks everything *inside* the boundary, so you could, for example, mask an existing building on a site plan and show a new building in the "vacant lot."

Blocks, Xrefs, and Drawing Organization

Blocks and xrefs are useful for organizing sets of drawings to use and update repeated elements. It's not always clear, though, when to use blocks and when to use xrefs. Applications for xrefs include

- ✔ The parts of a title block that are the same on all sheets in a project.

- ✔ Reference elements that need to appear in multiple drawings (for example, wall outlines, site topography, column grids).

- ✔ Assemblies that are repeated in one or more drawings, especially if the assemblies are likely to change together (for example, repeated framing assemblies, bathroom layouts, modular furniture layouts).

- ✔ Pasting up several drawings (for example, details or a couple of plans) onto one plot sheet.

- ✔ Temporarily attaching a background drawing for reference or tracing.

On the other hand, blocks remain useful in simpler circumstances. Situations in which you might stick with a block are

- ✔ Components that aren't likely to change.
- ✔ Small components.
- ✔ A simple assembly that's used repeatedly but in only one drawing. (You can easily update a block in one drawing with the REFEDIT command.)
- ✔ When you want to include *attributes* (variable text fields) that you can fill in each time you insert a block. Blocks let you include attribute definitions; xrefs don't.

Everyone in a company or workgroup should aim for consistency as to when and how they use blocks and xrefs. Check whether guidelines exist for using blocks and xrefs in your office. If so, follow them; if not, it would be a good idea to develop some guidelines.

Mastering the Raster

AutoCAD includes three more xref-like features: the ability to attach *raster images,* DWF files, and DGN files to drawings. I cover DWF files in the next section and refer you to the online help if you should find some DGN files on your hands. The image feature is useful for adding a raster logo to a drawing title block or placing a photographed map or scene behind a drawing. A raster, or *bitmapped,* image is one that's stored as a field of tiny points.

Most AutoCAD drawings are vector images. A *vector* image is an image defined by storing geometrical definitions of a bunch of objects. Typical objects include a line, defined by its two endpoints, and a circle, defined by its center point and radius. Vector-based images are typically smaller (in terms of the disk space they occupy) and more flexible than raster images but also are less capable of displaying visually rich images such as photographs.

Raster images often come from digital cameras or from other programs, such as Photoshop. Raster images also can come into the computer from some kind of scanner that imports a blueline print, photograph, or other image.

Whether you're doing your scanning yourself or having a service bureau do it for you, you need to know that AutoCAD — but not AutoCAD LT — handles most of the popular image file formats, including: the Windows BMP format; the popular Web graphics formats GIF and JPEG; common print formats like PCX, PNG, and TIFF; and the less popular DIB, FLC, FLI, GP4, MIL, RLE, RST, TGA, and several even more obscure ones.

Here are three scenarios in which you could incorporate raster images in your drawing:

- ✔ **Small stuff:** You can add logos, special symbols, and other small images that you have in raster files.
- ✔ **Photographs and maps:** You can add photographs (such as a future building site) and maps (for example, showing the project location).
- ✔ **Vectorization:** To convert a raster image into a vector drawing by tracing lines in the raster image, you can attach the raster image in your drawing, trace the needed lines by using AutoCAD commands, and then detach the raster image. (This procedure is okay for a simple raster image; add-on software is available, from Autodesk and others, to support automatic or semiautomatic vectorization of more complex images.)

Using raster images is much like using external references. The raster image isn't stored with your drawing file; a reference to the raster image file is established from within your drawing, like an xref. You can clip the image and control its size, brightness, contrast, fade, and transparency. These controls fine-tune the appearance of the raster image on-screen and on a plot.

When you attach raster images, you have to make sure that you send the raster files along when you send your drawing to someone else.

AutoCAD LT can open, view, and plot drawings containing attached raster images, but LT can't do the attaching. Raster masters require full AutoCAD.

Attaching an image

Follow these steps to bring a raster image into AutoCAD:

1. **If the External References palette is not already open, choose Tools⇨ Palettes⇨External References to open it.**

   Use the drop-down list on the first toolbar button to attach a drawing, an image, a DWF file, or a DGN file.

2. **Click Attach Image and locate the image file you want to attach.**

   The Select Image File dialog box appears, as shown in Figure 14-13.

3. **Browse to find the file you want to attach, select it, and then click Open.**

   The Image dialog box appears.

   Click the Details button in the Image dialog box to see more information about the resolution and image size of the image you're attaching.

Figure 14-13:
The Select
Image File
dialog box.

4. **Specify the parameters for the attached image in the dialog box.**

   Parameters include the insertion point, scale factor, and rotation angle.
   You can set these parameters in the dialog box or specify them on-
   screen, similar to what you can do with blocks and external references,
   as described earlier in this chapter. Use the dialog box quick help (click
   the question mark in the dialog box's title bar and then click the area in
   the dialog box for which you want help) or click the dialog box's Help
   button to find out more about specific options.

   The Image dialog box includes the same Full Path, Relative Path, and No
   Path options as those for attaching xrefs. (See the "Forging an xref path"
   section, earlier in this chapter.)

5. **Click OK.**

   The image appears in your drawing.

6. **If you need to ensure that the raster image floats behind other objects
   in the drawing, select the raster image, right-click, choose Draw
   Order, and then choose Send to Back.**

   The DRAWORDER command provides additional options for which objects
   appear on top of which other objects. If you need this kind of flexibility,
   look up "DRAWORDER command" in the AutoCAD online help system.

Maintaining your image

You manage the images in your drawing with the External References palette.
You can view a list of image files that appear in the current drawing, detach
(remove) image references, and unload and reload images when needed. You
can't bind an image to your drawing; it always remains an external file.

You can clip images so that only part of the image is displayed in your drawing. Choose Modify⇨Clip⇨Image and follow the prompts to clip the image.
You can have multiple overlapping or distinct pieces of any number of images
in your drawing, and only the parts you need are loaded into memory when
you have your drawing open.

Raster image files often are larger than DWG files of corresponding complexity; raster file size can affect performance within AutoCAD because the raster file loads into memory when you are working on your drawing. Some workarounds speed up operations:

- ✔ Attach raster images late in the production process.

- ✔ Create a lower-resolution version of the raster file, just large enough to create the desired effect in your drawing.

- ✔ Right-click over an image in the External References palette and choose Unload to temporarily hide an image without losing the attachment information.

In addition, raster files can increase the time that AutoCAD takes to generate plots (and the plot file sizes) dramatically. Before you settle on using large raster files in your AutoCAD drawing, do some testing on zooming, editing, and plotting.

A DWF Is Just a DWF

DWF stands for Design Web Format. You could think of a DWF as DWG Lite because it looks just like a drawing file and contains some of the actual drawing file data. (Some people call DWF files *dwiffs*, but I'm going to hold off on that one until I start hearing DWG files called *dwiggs*.)

You create DWFs from within AutoCAD in one of two ways. Either choose Plot and select the DWF option in the Printer/Plotter name list, or choose Publish and select DWF in the Publish To area of the Publish dialog box. DWFs are compact and secure: You can't edit a DWF in AutoCAD. The DWF format is ideal for two purposes: You can post DWFs on the Web, and you can send your drawings to consultants and clients in a form that they can't mess up. And as described previously, you can attach DWFs to your drawing files in pretty much the same way you attach drawings as external references. DWFs attached to drawing files are referred to as DWF underlays.

The previous sections show how to attach a DWG and a raster image. Follow these steps to attach a DWF file as an underlay:

1. **If the External References palette is not already open, choose Tools⇨ Palettes⇨External References to open it.**

    The toolbar at the top of the palette lets you attach an external file as an xref, a raster image file, or a DGN or DWF underlay. I cover attaching xrefs and images earlier in this chapter. See the online help for information on attaching DGN files.

2. **Click Attach DWF and locate the file you want to attach.**

   The Select DWF File dialog box appears.

3. **Browse to find the file you want to attach, select it, and then click Open.**

   The Attach DWF Underlay dialog box appears.

4. **Specify the parameters for the DWF in the dialog box.**

   The layout may be different, but the content is mostly the same. Parameters include specifying a sheet, the insertion point, scaling factors, rotation angle, and path type (see Figure 14-14). You can set these parameters in the dialog box or specify them on-screen, just as you can do when inserting a block, attaching an xref, or attaching an image, as described earlier in this chapter.

Figure 14-14:
The Attach DWF Underlay dialog box.

5. **Click OK.**

   The externally referenced DWF file appears in your drawing.

In AutoCAD 2008, you can control the visibility of layers in DWF underlays (assuming that layer data has been saved in the DWF). To do so, select any object in an attached DWF file, right-click, and choose DWF Layers from the right-click menu. AutoCAD displays the DWF Layers dialog box, which you can use to turn individual layers off and on.

DWF files are not as precise as DWGs — that's why they're a lot smaller. When using object snap to locate points in DWFs, you may see the word *approximate* on the object snap tooltip. If this is a problem, you can increase the precision of your DWF file when you create it.

Chapter 15

Drawing on the Internet

*U*nless you've been living under a rock for the past 15 years, you know that the Internet is causing major changes in the way people work. Because of the Net, most of us communicate differently, exchange files more rapidly, and phone out for pizza less frequently.

Many of the features described in this chapter have undergone frequent tinkering, revision, and refocusing in recent AutoCAD versions. AutoCAD 2005 added ETRANSMIT and PUBLISH capabilities to keep up with that version's sheet sets feature, as well as a Markup Set Manager to expedite the process of submitting and reviewing design drawings.

As I explain in Chapter 14, DWFs are not just for the Web. In AutoCAD 2008, you can attach a DWF as a reference "underlay" in the same way you attach regular DWGs as external references. See the "Design Web Format — Not Just for the Web" section, later in this chapter, for more information.

In this chapter, I show you how and when to use AutoCAD's Internet features. I also cover how the Internet features can connect with traditional CAD tasks, such as plotting. The emphasis of this chapter is on useful, no-nonsense ways to take advantage of the Internet in your CAD work.

The Internet and AutoCAD: An Overview

As with all things Webby, the Internet features in AutoCAD are a hodgepodge of the genuinely useful, the interesting but still somewhat immature or difficult to use, and the downright foolish. I steer you toward features and techniques that are reliable and widely used today and away from features that (to put it kindly) might not be ready for prime time. On the other hand, a few of today's questionable features are likely to become the reliable, commonplace ones of tomorrow. I give you enough context to see how everything works and where it may lead. Table 15-1 summarizes AutoCAD's Internet features and tells you where in this book to find more information.

Table 15-1		AutoCAD 2008 Internet Features	
Feature	*Description*	*Comments*	*Where You Can Find More Info*
ETRANSMIT command	Package DWG files for sending via e-mail or FTP or posting on the Web	Useful to most people	The "Send it with ETRANSMIT" section in this chapter
Reference Manager	Report on and modify paths of referenced files	Useful for people who send drawings and use complex, multifolder xref schemes	The "Help from the Reference Manager" section in this chapter
File navigation dialog box	Can save to and open from Web and FTP sites	Potentially useful for people who routinely work with files on Web or FTP sites	Chapter 2
DWF files	A "lightweight" drawing file format for posting drawings on the Web or sharing them with people who don't have AutoCAD	The recipient must have Autodesk Design Review or DWF Viewer installed; potentially useful for sharing drawings with people who don't have AutoCAD	"Design Web Format — Not Just for the Web" in this chapter
PUBLISH command	Create DWF files, plot (PLT) files, or paper plots in batches	Can help automate the traditional plotting procedure; if DWF files ever catch on, will streamline their creation	"Making DWFs (or plots) with PUBLISH" in this chapter

Feature	Description	Comments	Where You Can Find More Info
Publish to Web	A wizard that builds and publishes a Web page containing drawings	Like most wizards, fairly easy to use but limited; possibly useful as a quick-and-dirty Web publishing approach	"PUBLISHTOWEB command" in the AutoCAD online help system
Insert hyperlink	Add hyperlinks to objects in drawings	Of questionable use, except in specialized applications	"Hand-y objects" in this chapter
Password protection	Requires a password in order to open a drawing	Useful for limiting access to sensitive DWG or DWF files	"The Drawing Protection Racket" in this chapter
Digital signatures	Provide electronic confirmation that someone has approved a particular version of a particular drawing	Requires an account with a digital certificate provider; new technology, so look before you leap — and talk to your attorney first	"The Drawing Protection Racket" in this chapter

Sending Strategies

E-mail and FTP (File Transfer Protocol) have largely replaced blueline prints, overnight delivery, floppies, and higher-capacity disks as the standard means of exchanging drawings. Some companies even use specially designed Web-based services, such as Autodesk's Buzzsaw, as a repository for project drawings from all the companies working on a particular project. Whether you're exchanging drawings in order to reuse CAD objects or simply to make hard-copy plots of someone else's drawings, you need to be comfortable sending and receiving drawings electronically.

Sending and receiving DWG files does not differ much from sending and receiving other kinds of files, except for the following:

✔ **DWG files tend to be bigger than word processing documents and spreadsheets.** Consequently, you may need to invest in a faster Internet connection. For instance, if you have dialup modem access to the Internet, you may want to consider upgrading to broadband access, such as DSL or cable.

✔ **You can easily forget to include all the dependent files.** I tell you in the next section how to make sure that you send all the necessary files — and how to pester the people who don't send you all their necessary files.

✔ **It's often not completely obvious how to plot what you receive.** Read Chapter 13 and the "Bad reception?" section later in this chapter to solve plotting puzzles.

Whenever you send DWG files together, follow the Golden Exchange Rule: "Send files unto others as you would have them sent unto you." That means sending all the dependent files along with the main DWG files, sending plotting support files (CTB or STB files — see Chapter 13), and including a description of what you're sending. And ask the recipient to try opening the drawings you sent right away so you both have more time to respond if there's any problem.

Send it with ETRANSMIT

Many people naively assume that an AutoCAD drawing is always contained in a single DWG file, but that's often not the case. Each drawing file created in AutoCAD can contain references to other kinds of files, the most important of which are described in Table 15-2. Thus, before you start exchanging drawings via e-mail or FTP, you need a procedure for assembling the drawings with all their dependent files.

Table 15-2	Other Kinds of Files That DWG Files Commonly Reference		
Description	*File Types*	*Consequences If Missing*	*Explained In*
Custom font files	SHX, TTF	AutoCAD substitutes another font	Chapter 10
Other drawings (xrefs)	DWG, DWF	Stuff in the main drawing disappears	Chapter 14
Raster graphics files	JPG, PCX, TIF, and so on	Stuff in the drawing disappears	Chapter 14
Plot style tables	CTB, STB	Lineweights and other plotted effects won't look right	Chapter 13

As you can see from the table, the consequences of not including a custom font aren't that dire: The recipient will still see your text, but the font will be different. Of course, the new font may look odd or cause text spacing problems within the drawing. If, on the other hand, you forget to send xrefs or raster graphics that are attached to your main drawing, the objects contained on those attached files simply will be gone when the recipient opens your drawing. Not good!

Table 15-2 doesn't exhaust the types of files that your DWG files might refer to. Custom plotter settings (such as custom paper sizes) may reside in PC3 or PMP files. If you use sheet sets (see Chapter 13), a DST file contains information about the sheet structure. An FMP file controls some aspects of font mapping. (Like so much else in AutoCAD, the tools and rules for mapping missing fonts are flexible but somewhat complicated. Look up the FONTALT and FONTMAP system variables in the AutoCAD online help system for detailed information.)

Rapid eTransmit

Fortunately, AutoCAD's ETRANSMIT command pulls together all the files that your main DWG file depends on. Follow these steps to assemble a drawing with all its dependent files by using ETRANSMIT:

1. **Open the drawing that you want to run ETRANSMIT on.**

   If the drawing is already open, save it. ETRANSMIT requires that any changes to the drawing be saved before you proceed.

2. **Choose File⇨eTransmit.**

   The Create Transmittal dialog box appears, as shown in Figure 15-1.

Figure 15-1:
Rapid
eTransmit.

3. **On the Files Tree or Files Table tab, remove the check mark next to any file that you want ETRANMSIT *not* to copy with the main drawing.**

Unless you have assigned custom font mapping, you can omit the `Acad.fmp` file.

4. **Select a transmittal setup from the list.**

Transmittal setups contain settings that control how ETRANSMIT processes the drawings and creates the transmittal package. Click the Transmittal Setups button to create new or modify existing setups. The default Standard transmittal setup works fine for many purposes, except that you probably want to turn on the Include Fonts setting, as described in the next paragraph. In any case, you should view the settings (click the Modify button) just to see what options you can change if you need to later.

If you want AutoCAD to include SHX and TTF font files, including any custom fonts that you're using, you must turn on the Include Fonts setting in the transmittal setup. (Click Transmittal Setups, click Modify, and check the Include Fonts check box.) Note, however, that many SHX and TTF files are custom fonts, which work like licensed software. Sending them to others is just like sharing your AutoCAD program CD with others. No, I don't mean that it's easy and fun; I mean that it's illegal and unethical. Before you send a custom font file to someone else, find out the licensing restrictions on the font and work within them.

5. **Click the View Report button.**

You see a report listing the files that ETRANSMIT will copy, along with warnings about any files that it can't locate.

6. **Review the report and make sure that ETRANSMIT was able to find all the files.**

7. **Click OK.**

ETRANMSIT displays a file dialog box so that you can specify the name and location of the transmittal package.

8. **Click Save.**

ETRANSMIT creates the transmittal package (which is a ZIP file by default).

Although recent versions of AutoCAD automatically compressed DWG files, the AutoCAD 2007 file format — which is used by AutoCAD 2008 — started packing some weight back on. Zipping AutoCAD 2007–format files manages to compress them by up to 50 percent. More importantly, zipping creates a single, tidy package of all your DWG, raster image, plot style table, and font files.

FTP for you and me

FTP, or *File Transfer Protocol,* is a simple but robust protocol for copying files over the Internet. A computer that's connected to the Internet can act as an FTP *server,* which means that part of its hard disk is accessible over the Internet. The person who configures the FTP server can place restrictions so that only people who enter a particular logon name and password can see and download files. FTP overcomes the file size limitations that often occur with e-mail.

Because of all these FTP benefits, it's increasingly common for people at larger companies to place drawing files on their company's FTP site and tell you to go get them. This approach relieves them of having to e-mail you the files, and relieves you of waiting for that 10MB e-mail download when you least expected it.

In most cases, the person making the files available to you via FTP will send you a Uniform Resource Locator (URL) that looks like a Web page address, except that it starts with `ftp://` instead of `http://`. If you open your Web browser and enter the FTP URL into the address field, the browser connects to the FTP site, asks you for a location and name to use for the file when it gets copied to your system, and begins downloading the file. If the FTP site uses password protection, you'll have to enter a logon name and password first.

If you want fancier FTP download options, you can use an FTP utility such as CuteFTP (`www.cuteftp.com`).

Bad reception?

Other sections in this chapter focus on sending files to others. What happens when you're on the receiving end? Not everyone will be as conscientious as you are about following the Golden Exchange Rule. You'll receive drawings with missing dependent files and no information or support files for plotting.

When you receive an e-mail message or FTP download containing drawings (zipped, I hope!), copy the file to a new folder on your hard disk or a network disk and unzip the files.

Check at least a few of the drawings in the package to make sure that all the xrefs, fonts, and raster image files were included. You can perform this check by opening each main drawing in that folder. After you open each file, press the F2 key to view the command line window and look for missing font and xref error messages of the following sort:

```
Substituting [simplex.shx] for [helv.shx].
Resolve Xref "GRID": C:\Here\There\Nowhere\grid.dwg
Can't find C:\Here\There\Nowhere\grid.dwg
```

A Substituting . . . message indicates that AutoCAD couldn't find a font and is substituting a different font for it. A Can't find . . . message indicates that AutoCAD couldn't locate an xref. Any missing raster files appear as rectangular boxes with the names of the image files inside the rectangles. Missing DWFs appear as an error message at the insertion point.

Alternatively, you can open the External References palette, which reveals any missing referenced files. (See Chapter 14 for details.)

Write down each missing file and then tell the sender to get on the ball (in a nice way, of course) and send you the missing pieces. While you're at it, tell that person to buy this book and read this chapter! Or buy it for them yourself!

If you receive drawings with custom TrueType font files (files whose extensions are TTF), you must install those files before Windows and AutoCAD will recognize them. Refer to your Windows version's online help for instructions on installing fonts.

Help from the Reference Manager

In Chapter 14, I warn you about the complications of xref paths and the potential perils of AutoCAD not being able to locate xrefs if you move project folders around or transfer drawings to or from someone else. A similar danger exists for raster image files and DWF and DGN underlays (Chapter 14) and for font files (Chapter 10). The ETRANSMIT command, described earlier in this chapter, does a good job of gathering dependent xrefs, raster files, and font files, but it can't gather what AutoCAD can't locate.

AutoCAD's Reference Manager utility (not available to LT users) is a real life-saver if you find yourself suffering from file path perils — whether they occur in your own company or when sending files to or receiving them from others.

Reference Manager is a separate program, not a command inside AutoCAD. Follow these steps to launch the utility:

1. **Choose Start➪All Programs➪Autodesk➪AutoCAD 2008➪Reference Manager.**

   The Reference Manager program opens, as shown in Figure 15-2.

2. **Click the Add Drawings button to add one or more DWG files to the Drawings pane on the left.**

Figure 15-2:
The
Reference
Manager.

[Reference Manager dialog box]

Type	Status	File Name	Reference Name	Saved Path	Found Path
A Font	✔ Resolved	txt	STANDARD		c:\program files\autocad
A Font	✔ Resolved	ARIBLK.TTF	Fancy		C:\WINDOWS\fonts
A Font	✔ Resolved	txt	STANDARD		c:\program files\autocad
A Font	✔ Resolved	romans.shx	S-TEXT		c:\program files\autocad
A Font	✔ Resolved	txt	STANDARD		c:\program files\autocad
A Font	✔ Resolved	romans.shx	S-TEXT		c:\program files\autocad
A Font	✔ Resolved	txt	STANDARD		c:\program files\autocad
A Font	✔ Resolved	ARIBLK.TTF	Fancy		C:\WINDOWS\fonts
Image	✔ Resolved	Foundation-repair.jpg	Foundation-repair		g:\drawings
Image	✔ Resolved	Iris.tif	Iris		g:\drawings
Image	✔ Resolved	Foundation-repair.jpg	Foundation-repair		g:\drawings
Image	✔ Resolved	Iris.tif	Iris		g:\drawings
Xref Attachment	! Not Found	DT-03.dwg	DT-03	H:\Projects\SE...	
Xref Attachment	! Not Found	S-Detail-03.dwg	S-Detail-03		

Drawings added: 4 · Drawings broken References: 14 · Selected: 0

3. **Click the Export Report button to create a text report listing all the dependent files and their paths, or click the Edit Selected Paths button to modify paths.**

   Click the Help button in Reference Manager to find out more about the utility's capabilities.

If you always keep parent and child DWG files in the same folder — the simplest approach to dealing with xref paths — then you probably won't need to use the Reference Manager.

Design Web Format — Not Just for the Web

Earlier in this chapter, I explain how you can exchange drawings via e-mail and FTP. That's all the Internet connectivity that many AutoCAD users need, but if you're curious about connecting drawings to the Web or sharing drawings with people who don't have AutoCAD, this section is for you.

The AutoCAD Web features are built on three pieces of technology:

✔ A special "lightweight" drawing format called DWF that Autodesk originally developed especially for putting drawings on the Web.

✔ A free program from Autodesk called Autodesk DWF Viewer that enables anyone to view and print DWF files without having AutoCAD.

✔ A not-free program from Autodesk calls Autodesk Design Review, for marking up and reviewing DWF and DWG files.

All about DWF

The AutoCAD DWG format works well for storing drawing information on local and network disks, but the high precision and large number of object properties that AutoCAD uses make for comparatively large files.

To overcome this size problem and encourage people to publish drawings on the Web, Autodesk developed an alternative lightweight vector format for representing AutoCAD drawings: DWF (Design Web Format). A DWF file is a more compact representation of a DWG file. DWF uses less space — and less transfer time over the Web and e-mail — because it's less precise and doesn't have all the information that's in the DWG file.

You can create DWF files from your drawings and send the DWFs to people who don't have AutoCAD. Your recipients can view and plot the DWF files after they download the free Autodesk DWF Viewer program, which is available on Autodesk's Web site, www.autodesk.com.

DWFs can be used just like external references. Here's one more file type — and one more reason — to use Reference Manager or ETRANSMIT to package up your drawings before you send them out. For more on DWF underlays, see Chapter 14.

ePlot, not replot

A DWF file captures a single, plotted view of your drawing, so, unlike a DWG file, it can provide a clear-cut snapshot of what you want to see on paper. With a DWG file, on the other hand, you have to provide lots of information to other people — drawing view, scale, plot style settings, and so on — in order for them to get the same plotting results that you did.

Potential ePlotting scenarios include the following:

✔ Architects and other consultants on a building project periodically upload DWF files to the project Web site. Architects and engineers with some minimal CAD knowledge can review the drawings on-screen and create their own hard-copy plots, if necessary. Principals and clients who don't want anything to do with CAD, or even with computers, can have their employees create hard-copy plots for them to examine.

✔ When Internet-savvy people need hard-copy prints of your drawings, you e-mail a zipped file containing DWF files, along with the URL for Autodesk DWF Viewer and simple instructions for creating plots from the DWF files. (Be ready to walk them through the process by phone the first time or two to reduce anxiety on everyone's part.)

✔ A CAD plotting service bureau encourages its customers to send DWF files instead of DWG files for plotting. The DWF files are much smaller and require less intervention on the part of the service bureau's employees.

Autodesk hopes to establish ePlot and the DWF format as a standard for CAD documents similar to what Adobe's PDF has become for word processing documents. It remains to be seen whether ePlotting will become a popular way to generate hard-copy output. In particular, many people outside of CAD-using companies don't have access to large-format plotters. They're limited to 8½-x-11-inch — or, at best, 11-x-17-inch — reduced-size check plots. Consequently, many people won't be able to plot your DWF files to scale and may not even be able to plot them large enough to read everything.

Don't be afraid to try ePlotting with colleagues inside or outside your company, but don't become too dependent on it until you see whether the rest of the CAD world shares your enthusiasm. Otherwise, you risk becoming the only one who's willing to use your DWF files for plotting — in which case, the next version of the feature will be called mePlot.

AutoCAD 2008 uses version 6 of the DWF format, which Autodesk introduced with AutoCAD 2004. However, the DWF format changes frequently as Autodesk adds new features to AutoCAD and new Design Web Format capabilities; there will probably be a DWF7 format released at some point in 2007, so check AutoCAD's Web site from time to time for updates. The most important new feature in DWF 6 is the ability to save multiple sheets in a single DWF file, as shown in Figure 15-3. It's like stapling together a set of drawings, except that you never have to worry about your stapler being empty.

Making DWFs with ePlot

As I describe in the preceding section, AutoCAD treats DWF files like electronic plots, or ePlots. You create a DWF file from the current drawing just as if you were plotting it to a piece of paper, as I describe in Chapter 13. The only difference is that, in the Plot dialog box's Printer/Plotter area, you choose the plotter configuration named DWF6 ePlot.pc3, as shown in Figure 15-4. When you do so, AutoCAD automatically turns on the Plot to File setting. Then, when you click OK to generate the ePlot, AutoCAD displays a dialog box in which you specify a filename and location for the DWF file that gets created. The location can be a folder on a hard disk or a Web server.

When you make DWFs with ePlot, pay particular attention to the Scale setting in the Plot Scale area. If you're creating a DWF simply for viewing in a browser, you can select the Fit to Paper check box rather than worry about a specific plot scale. If you want to enable others to plot your DWF file to scale, as described earlier in this chapter, you need to choose the desired plot scale factor. Chapter 13 describes how to choose an appropriate plot scale factor.

Figure 15-3:
One DWF
file can
include
multiple
sheets.

Figure 15-4:
"Look ma,
no paper!"
Plotting to a
DWF file.

Making DWFs (or plots) with PUBLISH

The ePlot method of creating DWF files described in the previous section
works fine for single drawings. But if you want to create DWF files for a lot of

drawings or plot a bunch of drawings the good ol' fashioned way (on paper, that is), you can use the Publish dialog box, shown in Figure 15-5, to speed the process.

Although the Publish dialog box is wired to support DWF as well as regular (paper) plotting, for now, more people are likely to use it for paper plotting. (An alternative use is creating plot files to send to a plotting service bureau.) But if you do decide to go into large-scale DWF publishing, including multi-sheet DWF files, use the Publish dialog box, as shown in the following steps:

1. **Choose File⇨Publish.**

   The Publish dialog box appears (refer to Figure 15-5). The dialog box lists all tabs (model and paper space layouts) of the current drawing for plotting. The Publish dialog box refers to each tab as a *sheet*.

Figure 15-5:
Hot off the presses: AutoCAD's Publish dialog box.

2. **Click the buttons below the sheet list to preview any sheet, add sheets from other drawings, remove sheets from the to-be-plotted list, or rearrange the plotting order.**

   With the additional buttons, you can save and recall lists of sheets. See Step 4 for more information.

3. **After you specify the sheets that you want to plot, specify whether you want to plot them to an actual plotter or plot (PLT) file (not available in AutoCAD LT) or to a DWF file.**

   You can select a specific plotter configuration for each sheet by choosing a Page Setup in the sheet list. See Chapter 13 for more information about page setups.

4. **Click the Publish Options button to display a dialog box containing additional settings.**

   Most of these options are of concern only if you're creating DWF files. The one exception is Default Output Directory, which also applies to creating plot (PLT) files.

5. **If you anticipate having to publish the same group of drawings again, click the Save Sheet List button to save the current drawings and settings list.**

6. **Click the Publish button to start the process.**

Don't confuse the PUBLISH command (File⇨Publish) with the PUBLISHTOWEB command (File⇨Publish to Web). The PUBLISH command creates sets of DWF files, plot files, or actual plots. The PUBLISHTOWEB Wizard creates a Web page containing images of your drawings. The results of this wizard won't put any Web designers or programmers out of work, but you can use it to create primitive Web page paste-ups of your drawings. See "PUBLISHTOWEB command" in the AutoCAD online help system if you'd like to give it a whirl.

Hand-y objects

No Web file format would be complete without hyperlinks, and DWF has those, too. You can attach a hyperlink to any drawing object in AutoCAD, not just to a text string. As you pass the crosshairs over an object with a hyperlink, the cursor changes from the ordinary pointer to a globe and two links of a chain (as in "World Wide Web" and "link," not "world-wide chain gang"). Right-click the object and select the Hyperlink option from the menu, which opens your browser and navigates to the URL that's attached to the object. If you create a DWF file that includes objects with hyperlinks, Autodesk DWF Viewer displays them in the DWF file so that you can click to navigate to them.

Hyperlinks on objects are a clever trick, but they're of limited practical value in most DWG and DWF files:

- ✔ The drawing images are so small that it's difficult to distinguish the hyperlink on one object from the hyperlink on another object.

- ✔ Most people aren't used to associating hyperlinks with individual lines and other objects. The interface is likely to leave them perplexed.

If you'd like to experiment with hyperlinks on objects, look up "HYPERLINK command, about" in the online help system.

Autodesk DWF Viewer

After you create DWF files, whether with ePlot or PUBLISH, you or the recipient of your DWF files can use Autodesk DWF Viewer to view and print them. Autodesk DWF Viewer, shown in Figure 15-3 earlier in this chapter, is a free viewer from Autodesk. If you send DWFs to people without AutoCAD, they can download the current DWF Viewer version from Autodesk's Web page, www.autodesk.com.

When you install AutoCAD 2008, the setup program, by default, installs Autodesk DWF Viewer as well. Choose Start⇨All Programs⇨Autodesk⇨ Autodesk DWF Viewer or simply double-click a DWF file in Windows Explorer to launch the viewer.

The Drawing Protection Racket

Whether you're sending DWG or DWF files, you may be concerned about their misuse (that is, by the wrong people or for the wrong purposes), abuse (for example, modification without your consent), or reuse (on other projects or by other people without due compensation to you).AutoCAD has two features for securing your drawings when you send them to others:

✔ **Password protection** enables you to lock a DWG or DWF file so that only those who type the password that you've specified can open, insert, or xref it (not available in AutoCAD LT).

Add password protection to drawings only when you really need it:

• If you forget the password, then *you* no longer will be able to open the drawing. Neither AutoCAD nor Autodesk has any magical way to extract the password or unlock the drawing.

• After you password-protect a drawing, others can't insert the drawing as a block or attach it as an xref.

If you're using a password, you probably should do it on a *copy* of the drawing that you send; keep an *unprotected* version for yourself.

✔ A **digital signature** is a high-tech way to add an electronic marker to a DWG file that verifies that someone approved the drawing. You must first get an account with a digital certificate provider, who serves to authenticate you and your computer. Of course, for this feature to be useful, you need to send drawings to someone who wants to receive digitally authenticated drawings from you (or vice versa) and who has the technological savvy to deal with digital certificates. For more information, see "digital signatures, learning more about" in the AutoCAD online help system.

To activate either of these options for the current drawing, choose File⇨Save As to display the Save Drawing As dialog box; then choose Tools⇨Security Options to display the Security Options dialog box before you save the file. If you want to add a digital signature and you have a digital ID from a certificate provider, enter your information on the Digital Signature tab of the Security Options dialog box. If you want to add a password to the current drawing, just type it in the text field on the Password tab of the Security Options dialog box.

After you password-protect and save a DWG file, anyone who tries to open, insert, or xref it will see a dialog box similar to the one shown in Figure 15-6.

Figure 15-6:
Password,
please.

To password-protect a DWF file, use the PUBLISH command and click the Publish Options button in the Publish dialog box.

Although electronic security features such as the ones described in this section can be useful as part of a strategy to protect your work from misuse, they're not a substitute for communicating clearly, preferably in the form of written contracts, what constitutes appropriate use of drawings that you send to or receive from others.

Part V
The Part of Tens

The 5th Wave   By Rich Tennant

"I've used several drafting programs, but this seems to be the best one for designing quilt patterns."

In this part . . .

*T*ens sounds a lot like *tense,* and *tense* is how AutoCAD may make you feel sometimes. *Tens* also may remind you of the metric system, and if you're not used to it, that may also make you feel tense. But never fear — help is on the way! A Top Ten List is a good way to quickly spot the best — or the worst — of almost anything, AutoCAD included. This Part of Tens features lists that help you keep your drawings healthy and trade drawings with other people and programs.

Chapter 16

Ten Ways to Do No Harm

· ·

*H*ippocrates, that ancient Greek fella, is famous for many things, not least of which is the Hippocratic oath sworn by doctors. It may be just a pleasant myth that the Hippocratic oath begins, "First, do no harm," but that doesn't mean there's a prescription to go out and intentionally *do* harm. Most doctors actually do try not to cause their patients harm, and (you were probably wondering where this was going) this is not a bad approach to take when you edit existing drawings with AutoCAD, whether you or someone else originally created the drawings. You can accidentally undo, in minutes, days or weeks of work done by yourself and others. (Of course, you also can *intentionally* undo, in minutes, days or weeks of work done by yourself and others, but I can't give much advice to stop you if you want to do that!)

Follow these guidelines to avoid doing harm to the hard work of others and to your own productive potential.

Be Precise

Throughout this book, I remind you that using precision techniques such as snap, object snaps, and typed coordinates is a fundamental part of good CAD practice. Don't try to use AutoCAD like an illustration program, in which you eyeball locations and distances. Use one of the many AutoCAD precision techniques *every* time you specify a point or distance.

Control Properties by Layer

As I describe in Chapter 5, AutoCAD gives you two different ways of controlling object properties such as color, linetype, and lineweight: by layer and by object. Unless you have a *really* good reason to assign properties by object — such as instructions from your company's CAD manager or the client for whom you're creating the drawing — use the by-layer method: Assign colors, linetypes, and lineweights to layers, and let objects inherit their properties from the layer on which they reside. Don't assign explicit color, linetype, or lineweight to objects.

Know Your Drawing Scale (Factor)

Chapter 4 describes the importance of choosing an appropriate drawing scale factor when you set up a drawing. Knowing the drawing scale *factor* (which is always going to be intimately linked to the drawing *scale*) of any drawing you're working on is important whether you or someone else sets it up. I introduce you to annotative objects in Chapter 10. If you're using annotative text, dimensions, and so on, you may no longer need to do those onerous drawing scale *factor* calculations, but you will need to be aware of the ultimate plotted drawing *scale* so you can correctly assign the appropriate annotation scales to the objects.

Know Your Space

Understand the difference between model space and paper space (described in Chapter 2), and know which space the different parts of the drawing you're looking at reside in. Above all, make sure that you draw objects in the appropriate space. When you're viewing a paper space layout, keep an eye on the status bar's MODEL/PAPER button so that you know which space the crosshairs are currently in. (Chapter 4 describes how to keep your model and paper space bearings.) When you plot, ensure that you've selected the right tab — either the Model tab or one of the paper space layout tabs.

Explode with Care

The EXPLODE command makes it easy to explode polylines (Chapter 6), dimensions (Chapter 11), hatches (Chapter 12), and block inserts (Chapter 14) into their constituent objects. The only problem is that someone probably grouped those objects together for a reason. So until you understand that reason and know why it no longer applies, don't play with that firecracker.

Don't Cram Your Geometry

It's okay to cram for a geometry test, but don't cram geometry, dimensions, text, or anything (and everything) else into your drawings. You might be tempted to put a lot of stuff into every square inch of your drawing, using AutoCAD's flexible panning and zooming capabilities to really work over all the available space. If you give in to this temptation, however, you'll discover that editing is more difficult and adding more information may be impossible! In addition, the result will probably be harder to read. Instead of cramming stuff onto the sheet, use white (empty) space to surround areas of dense geometry. Put details on separate sheets. Attach a page of notes instead of putting a ton of text onto your drawing. Managing a reasonable number of drawings with less on each one is easier than having two or three densely packed sheets crammed with every bit of geometry and annotation needed for the project.

Freeze Instead of Erase

It's common to start with an existing drawing from another discipline when you want to add, say, an electrical system to a floor plan. But if you remove the landscaping around a building because you don't need it for the wiring, you may cause a great deal of rework when the landscaping information is needed again. And what if the person who did the landscaping work has, in the meantime, decided to leaf? (Sorry . . . .) Unless you know that objects are no longer needed, use the AutoCAD Freeze or Off layer setting to make objects on those layers invisible without obliterating them. These settings are in the Layer Properties Manager dialog box, as described in Chapter 5.

Use CAD Standards

Become knowledgeable about CAD standards in your industry and company, and take advantage of any standardized resources and approaches that are available to you. By following standards consistently, you can apply your creativity, expertise, and energy to the interesting parts of the job at hand, not to arguing about which hatching patterns to use. And if you find that things are a mess in your company because no one else pays much attention to industry standards, well, knowing those standards makes you very employable as well.

Save Drawings Frequently

As with all computer documents that you work on, get in the habit of saving your current AutoCAD drawing frequently. Instead of figuring out an appropriate time interval ("Does saving every 20 minutes include my coffee break?"), ask yourself this simple question: "How much work am I prepared to lose?" Hitting the Save button at the end of every significant procedure makes much more sense to me than waiting for the clock to tell you when to save.

Each time you save, AutoCAD writes the current state of the drawing to the *drawingname*.DWG file after renaming the previously saved version *drawingname*.BAK. Thus, you can always recover the next-to-last saved version of your drawing by renaming *drawingname*.BAK to *somethingelse*.DWG and opening it in AutoCAD.

AutoCAD also includes an automatic drawing save feature. It's useful as a secondary backup save, but you shouldn't rely on it exclusively. AutoCAD creates automatic save files with inscrutable names like Drawing1_1_1_1478.SV$ and puts them in the folder specified by the Automatic Save File Location setting on the File tab of the Options dialog box. Save your drawing and save yourself the pain of lost work and the hassle of trying to locate the right automatic save file. If you find yourself in the unfortunate position of needing an automatic save file, move the SV$ files from the automatic save folder to another folder. Rename the files from SV$ to DWG, open them in AutoCAD, and look for the one that corresponds to the drawing you're trying to recover. Note that AutoCAD deletes the SV$ file after you close the drawing, so it's usually useful only after a software or computer crash. You may also never see an SV$ file if you save frequently; each time you explicitly save your drawing by clicking Save or pressing Ctrl+S, the autosave timer is reset to 0.

Back Up Drawings Regularly

Backing up your data is prudent advice for any important work that you do on a computer, but it's doubly prudent for CAD drawings. A set of CAD drawings is a lot harder and more time consuming to re-create than most other computer documents (unless you've just written the sequel to *War and Peace,* that is). Unless you're willing to lose more than a day's worth of work, develop a plan of daily backups onto DVD, CD, an external hard drive, or another high-capacity medium.

Don't be lulled into complacency by the increasing reliability of hard disks. Although hard disk failure is increasingly rare, it still happens, and if it happens to you *sans backup,* you'll quickly understand the full force of the phrase *catastrophic failure*. Also, backups aren't just protection against disk failure. Most of the time, backups help you recover from *pilot error* — accidentally erasing a file, messing up a drawing with ill-advised editing, and so on. Even if you're conscientious and never make mistakes, there's a good chance that someone else in your office who has access to your DWG files hasn't quite achieved your exalted level of perfection. Protect your work and minimize recriminations with regular backups.

Chapter 17

Ten Ways to Swap Drawing Data with Other People and Programs

● ●

*A*t various times, you probably need to transfer information from one kind of document to another. You may even have taken the CAD plunge because you want to import AutoCAD drawing data into your word processing or other documents. If so, this chapter is for you. It covers exchanging AutoCAD drawing data with other programs — what works, what doesn't, and how to do it. I also tell you when to something may not be worth spending too much time on.

This chapter frequently mentions vector and raster graphics file formats. Here's a brief description of what those techie terms mean:

- ✔ A *vector* format stores graphics as collections of geometrical objects (such as lines, polygons, and text). Vector graphics are good for high geometrical precision and for stretching or squeezing images to different sizes. These two characteristics make vector formats good for CAD.

- ✔ A *raster* format stores graphics as a series of dots, or *pixels.* Raster graphics are good for depicting photographic detail and lots of colors. However, you can't squeeze or stretch raster images like you can vector images — if you shrink them too much, you lose pixels, and if you expand them too much, you stop seeing objects and start seeing gigantic pixels — even if you're not pixelated.

Exchanging AutoCAD drawing data with other programs sometimes works great the first time you try it. Sometimes you have to try a bunch of techniques or exchange formats to get all the data to transfer in an acceptable way. Occasionally, no practical exchange method exists for preserving formatting or other properties that are important to you. Where your exchange efforts fall in this range of possibilities depends on the kind of drawings you make, the other programs you work with, and the output devices or formats that you use. I provide recommendations in this chapter, but be prepared to experiment.

Table 17-1 lists exchange formats between common programs and AutoCAD.

Table 17-1	Swapping between AutoCAD and Other Programs
Swap	**Recommended Formats**
AutoCAD to AutoCAD LT	DWG
AutoCAD 2008 to AutoCAD R14	DWG
AutoCAD 2008 to AutoCAD R12	R12/LT2 DXF
AutoCAD to another CAD program	DXF or DWG
AutoCAD to humans who don't have AutoCAD	PDF or DWF
AutoCAD to Word	WMF
Word text to AutoCAD	RTF or TXT
AutoCAD to paint program	BMP
Paint program to AutoCAD	BMP or other raster format (use the AutoCAD IMAGE command; in AutoCAD LT, use Windows Clipboard)
AutoCAD to drawing program	DXF or DWG or WMF
Drawing program to AutoCAD	DXF or DWG or WMF
AutoCAD to the Web	DWF
Excel to AutoCAD	Windows Clipboard, using Paste Special (see Chapter 10)
AutoCAD to Excel	CSV, using AutoCAD TABLEEXPORT command (see Chapter 10 and the online help index)

The remainder of this chapter gives you specific procedures for making most of the exchanges recommended in this table, as well as others.

DWG

DWG, AutoCAD's native file format, is the best format for exchanging drawings with other AutoCAD or AutoCAD LT users. Use the SAVE and SAVEAS commands to create DWG files and the OPEN command to open them.

AutoCAD LT can't *create* every kind of object that AutoCAD can — it can't create raster attachments and most 3D objects, for example — but it can successfully *read* and *save* DWG files that contain these objects.

Round-trip DWG fare

The most demanding — and elusive — kind of data exchange is called *round-trip transfer.* *Round trip* means that you create and save a file in one program, edit and save it in another program, and then edit and save it in the first program again. A perfect round trip is one in which all the data survives and the users of both programs can happily edit whatever they want to. Unfortunately, the perfect round trip, like the perfect vacation, rarely happens, and sometimes your luggage gets lost along the way.

In CAD, round-trip transfer becomes an issue when two people want to work on the same drawings with different CAD programs. AutoCAD and AutoCAD LT have excellent round-trip compatibility, as I explain in Chapter 1. Expect a bumpier road if you're exchanging drawings with users of other CAD programs. Perform some test transfers before you assume that your drawings can get from here to there and back again unscathed.

AutoCAD 2008 can save DWG files that can be opened in versions all the way back to Release 14, which was released back in 1997. If you need to go farther back than R14 (does your coworker sport a mullet and bell-bottoms?), there's still the R12 DXF format. (See the "DXF" section in this chapter for instructions.)

Autodesk does not document the native AutoCAD DWG file format and recommends that all file exchanges between AutoCAD and other CAD programs take place via DXF files (see the next section). But several companies have reverse-engineered the DWG format, and it's now common for other CAD programs to read and sometimes write DWG files directly, with greater or lesser accuracy. Because the DWG format is complicated, isn't documented, and gets changed every couple of years, no one ever figures it out perfectly. Thus, exchanging DWG files with non-Autodesk programs always involves some compatibility risks. AutoCAD warns you in the command window and displays a Non-Autodesk DWG icon in the status bar if the drawing you open was not created by an Autodesk application. Also, when you send DWG files to other people — whether they use AutoCAD or a different CAD program — you need to make sure that their software can read the DWG file version that you're sending. See Chapter 1 for information about AutoCAD DWG file versions.

When you send DWG files to other people, remember to use the ETRANSMIT command to ensure that you send all the dependent files (fonts, xrefs, and raster images). See Chapter 15 for details.

DXF

DXF (Drawing eXchange Format) is the Autodesk-approved format for exchanging drawing data between different CAD programs. (Some other vector graphics applications, such as drawing and illustration programs, read and write DXF files, too.) DXF is a documented version of the undocumented DWG format. Because DXF more-or-less exactly mimics the DWG file's contents, it's (usually) a faithful representation of AutoCAD drawings.

How well DXF works for exchanging data depends largely on the other program that you're exchanging with. Some CAD and vector graphics programs do a good job of reading and writing DXF files, while others don't. In practice, geometry usually comes through well, but properties, formatting, and other nongeometrical information can be tricky. Test before you commit to a large-scale exchange, and always check the results.

To create DXF files, use the SAVEAS command (File⇨Save As) and choose one of the four DXF versions in the Files of Type drop-down list. To open a DXF file, use the OPEN command (File⇨Open) and choose DXF from the Files of Type drop-down list.

DWF

As Chapter 15 describes, DWF is Autodesk's special "lightweight" drawing format for posting drawings on the Web or sharing them with people who don't have AutoCAD. Those people can use Autodesk's free DWF Viewer program to view and print DWF files. Chapter 15 describes how to create and use DWF files.

PDF

Adobe's PDF (Portable Document Format) is the most popular format for exchanging formatted text documents among users of different computers and operating systems. PDF also does graphics, as you probably know from having viewed PDF brochures on Web sites.

Autodesk has worked hard to make DWF the PDF for CAD drawing exchange, but DWF hasn't caught on in a big way quite yet. When AutoCAD and AutoCAD LT users need to send drawings to people who don't have AutoCAD, many prefer to plot the drawings as PDF files (see Chapter 13). Most potential recipients are familiar with PDF and already have the free Adobe Reader, which they can use to view PDFs, installed on their computers. To view DWFs — for the time being at least — they need to visit Autodesk's Web site and download and install the Autodesk DWF Viewer, an additional piece of viewing software that's only good for viewing DWF files. This shortcoming of DWF may disappear in the next little while, however; Autodesk is developing a new XML-based version of DWF named DWFx, and if you're running Windows Vista, you'll be able to view DWFx files without an additional viewing application.

Each format has its strengths and weaknesses. PDF files tend to be much larger than DWFs, while DWFs tend to include more of the drawing's intelligence. You can attach a DWF as an underlay to your AutoCAD DWG (see Chapter 14), and that's something you can't do with a PDF. Current versions of both formats support layering information, markup, and measuring tools. Both formats are competent and efficient means of sharing drawing data, but there's no question that PDF is more prevalent.

If you're reading this book, you probably already have the software for creating DWF files — AutoCAD or AutoCAD LT. The free Adobe Reader views and prints PDF files but won't create them.

WMF

There are lots of different vector and raster graphics file formats, but Microsoft has been pretty successful at making its WMF and BMP formats the standard for exchanging graphical information in Windows.

WMF (Windows MetaFile) is a vector format, so it does a decent job of representing AutoCAD objects such as lines, arcs, and text.

To create a WMF file showing some or all the objects in a drawing, use the EXPORT command (File⇨Export) and choose Metafile (*.wmf) in the Files of Type drop-down list. After you create a WMF file in AutoCAD, use the other program's file insertion command to place the image in a document.

AutoCAD puts objects in the WMF file with the colors and display lineweights that you see on the AutoCAD screen. To create a WMF file that looks like a *monochrome plot* — that is, with varying lineweights and all objects black — you need to set layer and object properties in AutoCAD so the objects look that way on-screen before you create the WMF file.

You can go the other direction, from a WMF file into AutoCAD, by using the WMFIN command (Insert⇨Windows Metafile). The entire WMF comes in as a block, which can then be exploded and edited. (See Chapter 14 for more on blocks.)

BMP, JPEG, TIFF, and Other Raster Formats

BMP (BitMaP) is the standard Windows raster format. AutoCAD can create BMP files from drawing objects (via the EXPORT command) and place BMP files in drawings (via the IMAGE command, or the Windows Clipboard if you're using AutoCAD LT). When you export AutoCAD drawing objects to a BMP file, all the objects get converted to dots. Turning a line into a bunch of dots isn't a swell idea if you want to change the line again. But it is useful if you need to copy a drawing into a company brochure.

One problem with BMP files is their big file size. Unlike some other raster formats, BMP doesn't offer compression. Because CAD drawings are usually fairly large in area, they can turn into monstrously large BMP files.

Creating a BMP file showing some or all of the objects in a drawing is just like creating a WMF file: Use the EXPORT command (File⇨Export) but choose Bitmap (*.bmp) in the Files of Type drop-down list. (AutoCAD LT users must use the BMPOUT command.) After you create a BMP file in AutoCAD, you use the other program's File⇨Open command to open it or use the graphics file insertion command to place it in an existing document.

If you want to go the other direction and bring a BMP file into an AutoCAD drawing, use the IMAGE command (not in AutoCAD LT), as described in Chapter 14.

Although BMP is a standard Windows format for exchanging raster data, it's certainly not the preferred format of many programs. Other common raster formats include PNG, PCX, JPEG, and TIFF (the latter two appear as JPG and TIF in Windows). Among their other advantages, these formats offer image compression, which can reduce the size of raster files dramatically.

If the program that you're trying to work with works best with other formats or you want to avoid huge BMP files, you have a couple of options:

✔ Create an AutoCAD-friendly format (such as WMF or BMP) and translate it to another graphics format with a translation program such as HiJaak (www.imsisoft.com) or VuePrint (www.hamrick.com).

AutoCAD includes JPGOUT, PNGOUT, and TIFOUT commands for creating JPG, PNG, and TIF files in the same way that you export WMF and BMP files. Type the command name, press Enter, specify a raster filename, and select the objects to be included in the image file. Unlike WMFOUT, these commands use the current drawing area background color as the background color for the image. If you want your image background to be white, make sure that the AutoCAD drawing area color is white when you run the command. (Choose Tools⇨Options⇨Display⇨ Colors to change display colors.)

✔ If you need to convert drawings to a raster format other than BMP or TIF, the second option is to use the AutoCAD Raster File Format plotter driver. This driver enables you to plot to a file with one of nine raster formats, including PCX, JPEG, and TIFF. Before you can use the Raster File Format driver, you must create a new plotter configuration: Choose File⇨Plotter Manager and then run the Add-A-Plotter Wizard. After you create the Raster File Format driver configuration, you use the Plot dialog box as described in Chapter 13 to generate plots to raster files.

To go the other direction, raster image file into an AutoCAD drawing, use the External References palette (image files are not an option in LT), as described in Chapter 14.

Windows Clipboard

If you need to transfer lots of WMF or BMP figures, you can do it a bit more quickly with the Windows Clipboard, which bypasses the creation of WMF and BMP files on disk. Instead, Windows uses your computer's memory to transfer the data. Choose Edit⇨Copy in the program from which you want to copy the data; then choose Edit⇨Paste Special in the program into which you want to paste it. In the Paste Special dialog box, choose Picture to paste the image in WMF format or Bitmap to paste it in BMP format.

AutoCAD (but not AutoCAD LT) has a set of image manipulation commands. You can clip images, turn their borders off and on, and generally treat them like regular AutoCAD objects. However, these image commands work only if you use the IMAGE command or the External References palette to load the raster image. If you paste from the Windows Clipboard, the image comes into AutoCAD as an OLE object (see the next section), not as an image object, and the additional image commands do not work on OLE objects.

OLE

Microsoft Windows includes a data transfer feature, Object Linking and Embedding, or OLE. (In case you're wondering, that's *oh-LAY* pronounced like the Spanish cheer, not like the Cockney way of saying *hole.*) Microsoft touts OLE as an all-purpose solution to the challenge of exchanging formatted data between any two Windows programs.

Should you shout, "OLE!"?

Unfortunately, OLE is afflicted with several practical problems:

✔ OLE documents can slow performance — a lot. If you plan to use OLE, you should have a fast computer with lots of memory — or lots of time on your hands.

✔ Supporting OLE well is a difficult programming job, and many applications, including AutoCAD, suffer from OLE design limitations and bugs. (For example, when you link or embed a word processing document, only the first page appears in AutoCAD.)

✔ In versions of AutoCAD prior to AutoCAD 2005, plotted OLE output often underwent creative but undesirable transformations. If you exchange drawings with users of earlier versions, what they see on the screen and plot may not match what you created.

AutoCAD 2005 and later versions include a bevy of OLE improvements, which address some of the limitations:

✔ You can control text size more easily via the MSOLESCALE system variable and OLESCALE command.

✔ Editing of OLE objects with commands such as MOVE and COPY is more consistent with editing of native AutoCAD objects.

✔ You can control the quality of plotted OLE objects with a setting on the Plot and Publish tab of the Options dialog box.

Even with the recent OLE improvements, you should consider carefully and test extensively before embedding or linking documents into drawings. If you want to play it safe, use the alternative methods described in this chapter and save OLE for your next trip to Spain.

If you want to share data between two OLE-aware programs (and most Windows applications are OLE-aware), creating an embedded or linked document shouldn't be much more complicated than cut and paste. At least, that's the theory.

Here's how it works. In OLE lingo, the program that you're taking the data from is the *source*. The program that receives the data is called the *container*. For example, if you want to place some word processing text from Microsoft Word into an AutoCAD drawing, Word is the source, and AutoCAD is the container.

In Word, you select the text that you want to put in the AutoCAD drawing and choose Edit➪Copy to copy it to the Windows Clipboard. Then you switch to AutoCAD and choose Edit➪Paste Special. The Paste Special choice displays a dialog box containing the choices Paste and Paste Link. The Paste option creates a copy of the object from the source document and *embeds* the copied object into the container document. The Paste Link option *links* the new object in the container document to its source document so any changes to the source document are automatically reflected in the container document. In other words, if you link word processing text to an AutoCAD drawing, changes that you make later in the Word document get updated in the AutoCAD drawing automatically. If you embed the same text object in an AutoCAD drawing, changes that you later make to the text in Word aren't reflected in the AutoCAD drawing. Of course, AutoCAD has to be able to find the linked document, so if you're sending your DWG out to someone, don't forget to include the DOC as well!

That's how it's *supposed* to work. In practice, the container application sometimes doesn't display or print all the linked or embedded data correctly. See the "Should you shout, 'OLE!'?" sidebar for details.

Screen Capture

If your goal is to show the entire AutoCAD program window, not just the drawing contained in it, create a *screen capture.* Most of the figures in this book are screen captures. You might use similar figures to put together a training manual or to show your mom all the cool software you use.

Windows 2000 and XP include a no-frills screen capture capability that is okay for an occasional screen capture. It works like this:

1. **Capture the whole screen or active window with one of these steps:**

   • Press the Print Screen key to capture the entire Windows screen, including the desktop and taskbar.

   • Hold down the Alt key and press the Print Screen key to capture just the active program window (for example, AutoCAD).

   It looks like nothing happened, but Windows copied a bitmap image of the active window or the entire screen to the Windows Clipboard.

   Image captures in Windows 2000 and XP may be no-frills, but Windows Vista users have access to a slick new utensil called the Snipping Tool. You can capture specific parts of your screen — even menus — but you should read *Windows Vista Timesaving Techniques For Dummies,* by Woody Leonhard (Wiley), for more information about that.

2. **Paste the bitmap image into another program. You have two options:**

   • Paste into a paint program (such as the Paint program in Windows). Use that program to save a raster image as a BMP file format.

   • Paste the bitmap image directly into a document (such as a Word document or an AutoCAD drawing) without creating another file.

If you do lots of captures, a screen capture utility program makes the job faster and gives you more options. You can control the area of the screen that gets captured, save to different raster file formats with different monochrome, grayscale, and color options, and print screen captures. Two good screen capture utility programs are FullShot by Inbit, Inc. (www.inbit.com) and SnagIt by TechSmith Corporation (www.techsmith.com).

When you create screen captures, pay attention to resolution and colors:

✔ High screen resolutions (for example, above 1280 x 1024) can make your captures unreadable when they get compressed onto an 8½-x-11-inch sheet of paper and printed on a low-resolution printer. The screen captures in this book were taken at 1024 x 768 resolution,

✔ Some colors don't print well in monochrome, and a black AutoCAD drawing area is overwhelmingly dark. Because the screen captures in this book are printed in monochrome, I used a white AutoCAD drawing area and dark colors — mostly black — for all the objects in the drawing.

TXT and RTF

TXT (Text, also called ASCII for American Standard Code for Information Interchange) is the simplest format for storing letters and numbers. TXT files store only basic text, without such formatting as boldface or special paragraph characteristics. RTF (Rich Text Format) is a format developed by Microsoft for exchanging word processing documents (text plus formatting).

Pasting text from a word processor brings it into your drawing in exactly the form it appeared in the word processor document. So far, so good. However, what you've just pasted is another one of those troublesome OLE objects — you can't edit it in AutoCAD's Multiline Text Editor because it's not AutoCAD text. The solution is to save the word-processed text in Rich Text Format (RTF); then start AutoCAD's MTEXT command, right-click inside the In-Place Text Editor window, and choose Import Text. Find the RTF file and click OK. The word-processed text is now AutoCAD text. When you import an RTF file, AutoCAD even brings along most of the text formatting and alignment. Chapter 10 covers MTEXT's In-Place Text Editor window.

Because no rational person would use AutoCAD as a word processor, AutoCAD doesn't provide any special tools for exporting text. If you need to, you can select AutoCAD text, copy it to the Windows Clipboard, and then paste it into another program.

Index

• *C* •

• F •

• G •

• H •